Engineering for Peace and Diplomacy

Engineering for Peace and Diplomacy

Bernard Amadei

JENNY STANFORD
PUBLISHING

Published by

Jenny Stanford Publishing Pte. Ltd.
Level 34, Centennial Tower
3 Temasek Avenue
Singapore 039190

Email: editorial@jennystanford.com
Web: www.jennystanford.com

British Library Cataloguing-in-Publication Data
A catalogue record for this book is available from the British Library.

Engineering for Peace and Diplomacy
Copyright © 2025 Jenny Stanford Publishing Pte. Ltd.

ISBN 978-981-5129-75-5 (Hardcover)
ISBN 978-1-003-65168-0 (eBook)

Contents

Preface

Peace is a revolutionary proposition. Needed is not only a peace culture but also a peace structure.

—Galtung, 1996

Engineers are probably the single most indispensable group needed for maintaining and expanding the world's economic well-being and its standard of living.

—Weingardt, 1998

The engineer of the future applies scientific analysis and holistic synthesis to develop sustainable solutions that integrate social, environmental, cultural, and economic systems.

—Earth Systems Engineering Workshop, Boulder, CO, 2001

Progress is impossible without change, and those who cannot change their minds cannot change anything.

—George Bernard Shaw

The primary content of this book was written during the turbulent years of 2023 and 2024, a period marked by escalating global conflicts that overshadowed humanitarian ethical concerns. The lack of a worldwide response to these conflicts has highlighted a growing widespread indifference to human suffering. The silence of influential groups in economics, media, academia, politics, religion, and engineering education is particularly notable. However, it is not too late for these organizations to rethink how they can genuinely promote the peace and progress they profess to support. For instance, imagine the impact of prioritizing a peace-driven industrial complex over a current military-focused one. Although this shift may be gradual, it requires decision-makers and educators to embrace a new perspective and be prepared to advocate for change despite the challenges that may arise. The engineering profession must participate and provide leadership in that transformation.

The engineering profession is not typically linked to peace-building or diplomacy, nor is it commonly recognized by the public as contributing to the greater good. This book challenges these perceptions, aiming to raise awareness and encourage discussion on the crucial role that engineers play in promoting peace and supporting diplomacy across various societal contexts. It posits that both peace and diplomacy can indeed be engineered.

The role of engineers and scientists in peace and diplomacy is not new, and many examples at different scales illustrate this dynamic. An example of international cooperation in history is the Apollo-Soyuz event on June 17, 1975, when an astronaut and cosmonaut greeted each other in space despite the Cold War.

Despite geopolitical disagreements, examples of scientific and technical cooperation abound globally. They include, for instance, the United Nations Sustainable Development Goals (SDGs), the International Panel on Climate Change (IPCC), the International Panel on Information Environment (IPIE), the Conseil Européen pour la Recherche nucléaire (CERN), Synchrotron-light for Experimental Science and Applications in the Middle East (SESAME), and the Arctic Council. At the regional and local levels, science and engineering have improved the prosperity of communities and addressed transboundary issues with various degrees of development and security. All these examples show that engineers and scientists provide more than technical solutions; they 'make a world of difference' (NAE, 2008). As we progress through the 21st century, scientists and engineers are required to participate locally and globally in humanitarian work, sustainable development, peacebuilding, peacemaking, peacekeeping, and diplomatic efforts.

How should engineers in the 21st century be trained to address the challenges and risks of a vulnerable, uncertain, complex, and ambiguous (VUCA) world where crises threaten societal well-being? In my book *Engineering for Sustainable Human Development* (Amadei, 2014), published approximately 10 years ago, and other publications, I expressed concern about the inadequacy of engineering education in addressing the global problems faced by our planet, particularly in developing communities. At the time, I concluded that engineering students lacked the necessary attitudes, skills, and knowledge to address the issues faced by humanity within the next 20 years. Unfortunately, as I retired in 2024, this remains true today, and in my opinion, the situation has worsened. The global issues facing our planet have become more convergent and severe, and the engineering profession has been slow to adapt to the changes necessary to address them. The world is constantly changing, and it is challenging for the engineering profession to meet its demands.

This narrow-mindedness is predominantly found in today's engineering education, where students are still taught to develop solutions for a world mostly disconnected from reality. In essence, the complex problems of the 21st century cannot be resolved using tools and solutions developed by traditional institutions offering outdated 19th- and 20th-century educational platforms. For the most part, conventional engineering education is of limited relevance to societal problems in the 21st century and does not align with the expectations of students and professionals. A new perspective is required in engineering education and practice to contribute to human development, security, conflict resolution, and diplomacy. As discussed in this book, engineers involved in peace and diplomacy must be informed globally and educated accordingly. Hence, substantial changes to traditional engineering education are necessary to make it more adaptable and aligned with current and future societal needs. Echoing Max Planck (1950), a new scientific idea usually wins approval not by persuading its critics directly but rather by the effect of time as the original skeptics grow old and pass away, and a new generation familiar with the new idea emerges. This phenomenon is not exclusive to science; it also occurs in engineering, especially in engineering academia.

There is no shortage of research highlighting the value of peace and diplomacy in human development and security. Reports from NGOs, INGOs, CSOs, governments, and academic institutions on these topics are abundant, particularly around the time of UN General Assembly meetings in the fall. However, unlike the scientific community, the engineering field has seldom been invited to contribute to such discussions. When engineers are consulted, their insights are often disregarded by professional bureaucrats and academics, who focus more on enhancing their resumes or advancing their political influence. As a result, more time is spent discussing issues rather than proposing solutions, implementing concrete action plans, and ensuring their completion.

What does engineering have to do with peacebuilding and diplomacy? As outlined in my recent book on the peace-sustainability–climate security nexus (Amadei, 2023), it is challenging to envision (i) a sustainable community that is not peaceful and climate-secured, (ii) a peaceful community that has not endorsed sustainable practices and does not support climate adaptation and mitigation, and (iii) a climate-secured community that has not endorsed sustainable practices and is geopolitically unstable. The future of the planet and its inhabitants depends on the contribution of globally engaged engineers who possess attitudes, skills, knowledge, and experience in planning, designing, managing, and operating interventions that lead to prosperous, stable, and peaceful communities worldwide (Amadei, 2014). Their solutions need to be (i) sound from a technical point of view; (ii) equitable and adaptable to the cultural, economic, and social context in which they work; and (iii) developed for the right reasons. If one of these attributes is absent, the solutions must be reconsidered.

Since its inception in the late 1980s, sustainable development has involved more than just providing technical solutions. It is an integrated approach and a growing way of thinking that balances technology, society, and five key elements: people, planet, prosperity, partnerships, and peace, also known as the 5Ps of Agenda 2030 by the United Nations. To operate successfully across the 5Ps in specific contexts and sizes, globally engaged engineers must enhance their core technical skills with the ability to work in interdisciplinary teams, consider environmental and social impact assessments, and communicate and negotiate with various stakeholders. The engineering profession must also recognize its indispensable contribution to peace and diplomacy by participating in projects of varying scales and contexts.

This book explores the value proposition of engineering contributions to peacebuilding, the role of the engineering profession in diplomatic efforts, and the importance of developing programs such as peace engineering and engineering diplomacy to provide engineers with the attitudes, hard and soft skills, knowledge, and experience necessary to operate in the ever-changing world of the 21st century. Lessons can be learned from how science and diplomacy contribute to each other. What is equivalent to engineering? How should engineering interventions contribute to peacebuilding and diplomatic efforts? How do peacebuilding and diplomatic efforts contribute to engineering projects?

The connection between science and engineering, on the one hand, and diplomacy, on the other hand, has become increasingly significant as international relations between countries have become more complex, and scientific research and engineering projects have become more global. Many developmental interventions are transboundary, and water, waste, air, and renewable forms of energy do not share borders. Unfortunately, negative dynamics, such as conflicts, corruption, pollution, biodiversity loss, and population movement, cut across geographical boundaries and do not match the political boundaries that mark the governing areas of countries and regions. Climate change makes these complicated problems more difficult.

Over the years, scientific and engineering solutions have demonstrated the ability to produce positive outcomes through new knowledge, successful interventions, and initiatives that have benefited both people and the environment. However, progress has often been accompanied by the unintended harmful consequences of scientific and technical decisions. As we strive to promote human development and security in the 21st-century world through current engineering solutions, we must learn from the past to avoid repeating mistakes and ensure that our actions do not create problems for the future. There is an urgent need for science and engineering to engage with the ethical, legal, economic, social, and environmental issues surrounding the world.

To address our planet's issues, science, technology, and engineering professionals must adopt a new perspective beyond relying solely on technology to solve problems. Instead, they must focus on creating innovative technologies and solutions while avoiding using mental models that perpetuate materialism, consumerism, and beliefs in unlimited (despite degenerative) growth. By changing mental models and mindsets that shape structures and behaviors, leverage points can be created to address these issues and contribute to genuine social change.

Another aspect of engineering education that is often ignored and needs to be re-evaluated is the need for lifelong learning (K-Gray education instead of K-12), which is now more critical than ever. The rationale is that today's engineering graduates will likely make decisions in a world 20–30 years from now, which will be vastly different from what we know now. Their future jobs do not yet exist, and the tools and technologies they will use have not yet been invented. Engineers must have 21st-century knowledge and skills to operate in this rapidly changing world. Consequently, engineers must demonstrate exceptional adaptability and versatility to meet the demands of the complex and ever-changing world of the future. These attributes require the adoption of convergent or transdisciplinary approaches that transcend disciplines and fields of knowledge to address the interconnected challenges arising from the interaction between technical, societal, and environmental systems. How do we convey the value propositions of lifelong learning in engineering education?

In my publications over the past decade, I have maintained that policymakers and practitioners involved in human development and security must consider a transformative approach to decision-making that considers both the inner and outer dimensions of being human. After 40 years of teaching, I can conclude that the inner human dimension of engineering is not a priority in engineering education. Why? It is regarded as lacking value in engineering because of its immeasurable nature. Until institutions examine their inner points of view, decision-makers cannot develop better mental models and mindsets, build internal capacity, or recalibrate their moral compasses. Failure to do so will result in humanity becoming an obstacle to progress, and peace will remain a theoretical concept.

It is encouraging to note a recent submission to the Club of Rome, *Earth for All: A Survival Guide for Humanity* (Bristow et al., 2024). It underscores the importance of recognizing the internal factors of decision-making to overcome "barriers to collective action and structural transformation." This insight echoes Dr. Gus Speth's statement about the essential perspectives of decision-makers and mental frameworks when approaching complex environmental challenges (Speth, 2019).

> I used to think that the top environmental problems were biodiversity loss, ecosystem collapse, and climate change...
> I thought that with 30 years of good science, we could address

those problems. But I was wrong. The top environmental problems are selfishness, greed, and apathy. And to deal with those, we need a spiritual and cultural transformation—and we scientists [and engineers] don't know how to do that.

What is involved in this transformation? How can it be integrated into the education and training of decision-makers in science, engineering, and technology in the 21st century? How can engineers better understand their roles in benefiting society? This book seeks to spark discussions on these subjects, aiming for a more globally involved engineering profession. Whether engineering is practiced locally or globally, global engagement is essential.

My latest book examined the connection between peace, sustainability, and climate security (Amadei, 2023). The association between these topics and the interplay of engineering, peacebuilding, and diplomacy discussed in this book shares many commonalities. Both books have similar formats and cover akin issues, advocating for a systemic rather than a deterministic approach to complex problems. A systems approach requires decision-makers to implement actions and set policies using a systems mindset, think systemically, and use systems tools.

My interest in peacebuilding and science diplomacy started when I was invited to attend meetings co-sponsored by the US National Academy of Engineering and the US Institute of Peace as early as 2013. It grew during my service as a Science Envoy to Pakistan and Nepal (2013–2015) and was furthered by Dr. Joseph Hughes introducing me to peace engineering in 2016.

Finally, I am relatively new to systems sciences and even newer in peace studies and conflict management. Many times, during my 70 years of existence, I have faced challenges due to my enthusiasm. I ask experienced peers in these fields to forgive the errors in this book and share their feedback. I am grateful for their support and for being introduced to this exciting perspective later in my career.

Bernard Amadei
Lafayette, CO
March 2025

References

Amadei, B. (2014). *Engineering for Sustainable Human Development: A Guide to Successful Small-Scale Development Projects.* ASCE Press.

Amadei, B. (2023). *Navigating the Complexity Across the Peace-Sustainability-Climate Security Nexus.* ISBN 9781032563381. Routledge.

Bristow, J., Bell, R., Wamsler, C., Björkman, T., Tickell, P., Kim, J., and Scharmer, O. (2024). *The system within: Addressing the inner dimensions of sustainability and systems change.* The Club of Rome. Earth4All: deep-dive paper 17. https://www.clubofrome.org/publication/earth4all-bristow-bell/

Earth Systems Engineering Workshop (2001). Unpublished report (B. Amadei, ed.). University of Colorado, Boulder, CO.

Galtung, J. (1996). *Peace by Peaceful Means: Peace and Conflict, Development and Civilization.* International Peace Research Institute, Oslo; Sage Publications, Inc.

National Academy of Engineering (2008). *Changing the Conversation: Messages for Improving Public Understanding of Engineering.* Washington, DC: The National Academies Press. https://doi.org/10.17226/12187.

Planck, M. K. (1950). *Scientific Autobiography and Other Papers.* New York: Philosophical Library.

Shaw, B. (n.d.) George Bernard Shaw: 'Progress is impossible without change, and those who cannot change their minds cannot change anything.' — The Socratic Method (Socratic-method.com)

Speth, G. (2019). https://earthcharter.org/podcasts/gus-speth/

Weingardt, R. (1998). *Forks in the Road.* Palamar, Denver, CO.

Acknowledgments

I want to thank Jenny Stanford Publishing Pte Ltd. for allowing me to publish my work. I would also like to thank Dr. Joseph Hughes for reviewing the first draft of this book. I thank my children, Elizabeth Ann and Alexander, for their support, patience, and love.

I gained insights and benefited from conversations with colleagues interested in peace engineering and science diplomacy over the past 10 years. They include in alphabetic order: A. Brown; B. Cahan; F. Carrero-Martinez; W. Colglazier; C. Darve; H. Edema-Reynolds; S. Himelfarb; J. Hughes; R. Jordan; D. Koechner; M. Leckhoff; D. Lehrer; P. Leroux-Martin; C. Lipchin; N. Levine; N. Meshkati; M. Nelson; J. Niemela; M. Olson; M. Quihuis; R. Rhoads Allen; J. Tangora; T. Vaughan; J. Zack; and many others.

Chapter 1

Introduction

A sustainable world must be peaceful or it will not be. Engineers in the twenty-first century must be more than providers of technical solutions; they must also contribute to peace, diplomatic efforts, and the public good. A new mindset in engineering education and practice is needed to provide engineers with the attitudes, hard and soft skills, knowledge, and experience necessary to work in the complex and challenging contexts of human development and security in their lifetime. This introductory chapter presents a broad perspective on how engineering, peacebuilding, and diplomacy interact and contribute to human development and security in community-based projects and the need for a locally and globally engaged engineering profession.

A world divided by wealth and poverty, health and sickness, food, and hunger cannot long remain a stable [and peaceful] place for civilization to thrive (NAE, 2008).

Engineers are responsible not only for the safety, technical, and economic performance of their activities, but they also have responsibilities to use resources sustainably; minimize the environmental impact of projects, wastes, and emissions; and use their influence to ensure that their work brings [peace and] social benefits which are equitably distributed (Martin et al., 2005).

Engineering for Peace and Diplomacy
Bernard Amadei
Copyright © 2025 Jenny Stanford Publishing Pte. Ltd.
ISBN 978-981-5129-75-5 (Hardcover), 978-1-003-65168-0 (eBook)
www.jennystanford.com

1.1 Background

Over the past 200 years, engineering has played a crucial role in serving humanity and the public good. Multiple inventions have increased health, comfort, transportation, telecommunications, etc., and have created previously unthinkable productivity levels. The 20 great achievements of engineering that contributed to society during the 20th century emphasized by the US National Academy of Engineering 20 years ago (Constable et al., 2003) testify to the importance of engineering in society and are still relevant today.[1] During the last century, economic development and quality of life have been built on a complex and highly productive set of technological, industrial, and municipal systems and structures that engineers have planned, designed, built, operated, and maintained. Engineers have also played an active role in rebuilding societies following conflicts and disasters and stabilizing conflict-affected and conflict-sensitive communities. In short, engineers 'make a world of difference' (NAE, 2008).

Let us cut to the chase and start with a simple question: Has the engineering profession contributed to a more peaceful world? The answer to this question is unclear and depends on the person being asked. On the one hand, we cannot deny that progress in medicine, health, water, sanitation and hygiene, energy, agriculture, telecommunication, transportation, etc., has resulted in better livelihoods for many people. An increase in life expectancy at birth worldwide from an average of approximately 45.5 in 1950 to 73.3 in 2024 is one of the many positive indicators of the contribution of scientific, engineering, and healthcare professionals to humankind (Macrotrends, n.d.). Engineering has significantly contributed to peace through infrastructure development, access to essential services, conflict prevention, community engagement, technological innovation, education and training, community resilience, and community engagement. Engineering also contributes to diplomacy in several ways, including technical and environmental diplomacy.

---

[1]Greatest Engineering Achievements of the Twentieth Century (greatachievements. org)

Conversely, we must acknowledge that scientific and engineering achievements have not always been problem-free and equitable. First, they come at a cost and often contribute to the unplanned and undesirable long-term effects of technology on natural and human systems. Science and engineering have contributed to ethically unacceptable human development and insecurity in several instances. Second, they have primarily benefited populations in developed countries and, to a lesser extent, people in low- and middle-income countries (LMIC) for whom the quality of life and life expectancy are still low and who live in unhealthy, degrading, inequitable, and unsustainable conditions. As Polak (2008) noted, much effort has been made to create products and services solely for the wealthiest 10% of the world's population. A design revolution must occur to cater to the remaining 90%. This revolution has barely started.

Measures of this inequality have been well documented in all MDG and SDG reports since 1990. In 2023, the average life expectancy at birth across Africa was 61 years for men and 65 years for women, with higher and lower numbers in specific countries.[2] Disparities in life expectancy and livelihood are also present in wealthy countries because of inequitable availability and access to resources and infrastructure based on race, gender, and so on. These disparities were evident during the COVID-19 pandemic. For many disadvantaged communities worldwide, living at the end of the day remains a full-time job. They have been ignored in development books and have no voice in decision-making (Narayan et al., 1999). Design for the other 90% (Polak, 2008) and peace (Smith, 2022) are more than taglines. They are about people, the planet, partnerships, prosperity, and peace, also known as the five Ps of sustainable development of the United Nations Agenda 2030 (UNSDG, 2022).

Engineering is all around us, yet it is taken for granted and not always understood by most people (Wulf, 2000). A possible explanation is that the engineering profession has not advertised itself well to the public compared to other occupations. Consequently, the public does not always understand what engineers do and their contributions (NAE, 2008, 2010). Therefore,

[2]https://www.statista.com/statistics/274511/life-expectancy-in-africa/

society appears to have a limited view that engineers are problem-solving individuals who create technical designs for specific services and products. Improving the understanding of engineering has become a critical endeavor (DiscoverE, 2023).

Several definitions of engineering have been suggested in the literature. They generally relate to applying scientific knowledge for practical uses and in technology planning, design, implementation, operation, and maintenance. The public often sees engineering as having something to do with technology, engines, structures, materials, and processes and rarely as human development and security.

A broader perspective views engineering as a social activity, not apart from society (Vincenti, 1991). As emphasized in this book and many of my publications over the past 10 years, the engineering profession must be seen as serving society. Engineers may use technology; however, providing technical solutions is not the ultimate goal. They have an ethical and professional obligation to develop and apply solutions to meet the basic needs of *all* humans, ensure the resilience of the critical infrastructure on which populations depend, and contribute to initiatives that benefit human development and security, from local community development to global initiatives such as the United Nations Sustainable Development Goals. If these needs are met, it may be possible to envision a world where all humans have fulfilling and prosperous lives and live with dignity and peace while respecting the environmental systems they rely on.

Meeting this vision of human development and security in which engineering, peacebuilding, and diplomacy unfold will not be easy and will take many years to achieve. This constraint is in part because, as best summarized by Tooley (2021), we live in a "volatile, uncertain, complex, and ambiguous" (VUCA) world characterized by "predictable unpredictability" (*The Economist*, 2021). In an unpredictable world,

- *Volatility* refers to changes becoming more unpredictable and dramatic and occurring quicker and more often. However, their causes and effects are difficult to determine.
- *Uncertainty* deals with the difficulty of anticipating and predicting events, including those based on experience.

- *Complexity* deals with nontrivial self-organization, adaptation, feedback mechanisms, emergence, and difficulties related to different events.
- *Ambiguity* is no longer about one-size-fits-all solutions and dualistic decision-making. Paradoxes and contradictions are norms. Learning from mistakes is critical.

The United States Army War College introduced the VUCA concept in the late 1980s and the 1990s to describe the world's unstable, complex, and rapidly changing political and economic landscape. This concept is even more relevant in defining today's rapidly changing world and represents the operating landscape of the engineering profession in the foreseeable future (Kamp, 2016). It is at play in different contexts and scales, from local to global.

There is enough evidence that the VUCA world is here to stay and that humanity will continue to face significant development challenges in the rest of the 21st century. These challenges involve complex socioeconomic, environmental, cultural, and geopolitical issues. Short of being exhaustive, they include (i) climate change and security risks; (ii) rapid urbanization; (iii) population growth, migration, and human resettlement; (iv) water, energy, food, and land resource security; (v) access to education, shelter, healthcare, ICT, and employment; (vi) environmental damage and biodiversity loss; (vii) natural and human-induced risks and emergencies; (viii) peacebuilding and violent conflict prevention and recovery; (ix) social equality and inclusive growth; and (x) national and global security. These issues have many common characteristics that make them difficult to address.

1. They unfold into context-specific (e.g., urban vs. rural, cultural, geopolitical) and scale-specific (i.e., local, regional, and global) landscapes.
2. They are interconnected and influenced by socioeconomic, political, environmental, regulatory, and technological issues that may transcend national boundaries and require successful regional and international transboundary collaborations.

3. They are systemic and involve shared interconnected systems and subsystems (social, economic, cultural, ecological, and technical) with often ill-defined, messy, adaptive, and constantly changing components, partly owing to feedback mechanisms and complex causal chains.
4. They affect humanity's most vulnerable sections, many of whom are limited to no voice or representation and have limited capacity and resilience to adapt and cope with crises and adverse events.
5. They must be addressed in a multi-solving, intelligent, systemic, equitable, and compassionate manner for the benefit of all rather than in a compartmentalized manner driven by fear and for the use of a few.

Alone or combined, many of these issues are prone to creating planetary risks and instability if not addressed individually or collectively. According to recent global risk reports of the World Economic Forum (WEF, 2023, 2024), risks can be divided into five interconnected categories: economic, environmental, geopolitical, societal, and technological. The top 10 risks by order of severity over the long term (i.e., 10 years) include: "extreme weather events; critical changes to earth systems; biodiversity loss and ecosystem collapse; natural resources shortage; misinformation and disinformation; adverse outcomes of AI technologies; involuntary migration; cyber insecurity; societal polarization; and pollution."

A question arises as to how to proactively address these risks now and in the future, rather than reactively, by emphasizing (i) environmental protection and nature-based solutions, (ii) conflict resolution, (iii) economic and political stability, and (iv) climate change awareness, adaptation, and mitigation. Another question arises regarding how engineers can be trained to develop radical solutions to address these risks and their connections and work in partnership with policymakers in the future.

Addressing the issues in a VUCA world has been more difficult, as many of the issues seem to be growing faster than the solutions (Schumacher, 1973). Another component is the rapid worldwide spread of disinformation and misinformation, also called "infodemic" (Rothkopf, 2003; Zarocostas, 2020; Eysenbach,

2020; NASEM, 2023), and associated social polarization. As Howard (2020) and Himelfarb and Howard (2021) noted, manipulating information has many negative socioeconomic ramifications and geopolitical consequences, especially for marginalized groups. As pointed out by these authors, we are "in danger of becoming incapable of dealing with existential threats, such as climate change and pandemics," or even a down-to-earth community livelihood. A recent survey by Pew Research involving 24,525 people from 19 countries with advanced economies showed that online misinformation and climate change ranked the highest as significant threats, with 70% for misinformation and 75% for climate change (Thompson, 2022). Other identified threats included cyberattacks from different countries (67%), the global economy (61%), and the spread of infectious diseases (61%). Misinformation and disinformation can threaten human development and security (UN, 2023), create conflicts, and affect other risks, as emphasized by the WEF (2023, 2024). Countering infodemics are being addressed by the recently created International Panel on the Information Environment (IPIE, www.ipie.info).

Another remark about the abovementioned issues is that although they involve different science, technology, and engineering (STE) fields, they cannot be addressed by implementing scientific, technical, and engineering band-aids alone. Wolfe and Smith (2021) remarked that potential solutions to world issues "are also deeply intertwined with psychological, cultural, economic, and political factors that operate mainly at the level of individuals, communities, and societies." According to these authors, the leverage points to address global issues are not just about creating more technological gadgets but rather reside deep in the mental models of society among the "social-psychological factors that shape human thought, preferences, and behaviors." At stake are the mental models that perpetuate (i) the interests of materialism, consumerism, and abundance; (ii) the illusion of infinite growth and consumption; and (iii) the belief in technical optimism, where all societal problems demand a technical solution. As the systems literature emphasizes, such mental models and beliefs form structures that create behavior patterns that result in various issues. Unfortunately, most engineers and scientists are not trained or aware of integrating such factors into their decision-making, as they have been trained to focus on addressing technical development.

Do today's engineering [and science] graduates, educators, and practitioners have technical and non-technical skills and tools to address the global challenges of the VUCA world that our planet and humans face and will confront within the next 20 years and beyond? The answer to this question is categorically no. One reason for this is that current educational methods are primarily shaped by our societal worldview, which is reminiscent of the scientific understanding of the 19th century (Palmer and Zajonc, 2010). The question arises regarding how engineers must be trained to operate in the 21st-century VUCA world and account for the technical and non-technical dimensions of the abovementioned challenges. This book calls this type of engineering *globally engaged engineering* (GEE). This is because 21st-century engineers need a 21st-century curriculum in 21st-century structured educational institutions, not a 20th-century curriculum in 19th-century structured institutions, as Grasso and Burkins (2010) pointed out.

Today's engineering students and recent graduates must be made aware of their formative years that, while embarking on their lifelong professional journey, they must be conscious of a rapidly changing world with changing social needs (Kamp, 2016). They must equip themselves with skills, knowledge, experience, and resources; possess the right attitude; and arm themselves with various multi-solving tools to deal with the complexity of local and global issues for which there are no best solutions, only good enough.

Engineers must recognize that in the future, which may be 20 to 30 years away or even sooner, they will be globally engaged, occupy management and leadership positions in various working settings and tasks, face more intricate challenges than those encountered today, and require tools that are yet to be developed as well as knowledge that rapidly becomes outdated (Kamp, 2016). Therefore, it is crucial for engineers to continuously embrace lifelong learning, critical thinking, flexibility, and adaptability, as these skills are essential for their professional growth and development.

Engineers must also realize that the aforementioned challenges cannot be addressed using only the traditional reductionistic and deterministic tools used in science and engineering over the past century. This approach assumes that every problem requires a technical solution, which, if not satisfactory, requires another technical solution until it is fixed. However, most societal issues require multidisciplinary and systemic approaches. Engineers in the 21st century must be system thinkers.

As emphasized by the author in several of his publications over the past 10 years and as a general theme in this book, the engineering profession must embrace a new mission statement for the twenty-first century:

> To contribute to building a more sustainable, stable, equitable, and peaceful world and promote a culture of peace that benefits the global economy and the world's population more than the current culture of war.

Whether they work locally or globally, engineers are called to become globally engaged changemakers, social entrepreneurs, facilitators of sustainable development, peacemakers, Track 1.5 or 2 diplomats, and citizen diplomats. This new mission statement requires engineers to become local and global thinkers and doers and to be aware of (i) their professional and personal ethical responsibilities, (ii) their role in society as citizen engineers, and (iii) the intended and unintended consequences of their decisions on the design, planning, management, and operation of projects in different socioeconomic, cultural, and political situations. This new mission statement requires engineers to be educated to change the world for the better (Kamp, 2020).

Endorsing a new mission statement represents a challenge for the engineering profession because it implies revisiting traditional engineering education and training to be more in line with the challenges of the VUCA world, accepting lifelong learning, and considering the delivery of projects that are (i) right for people and the environment, (ii) rightly done from a technical point of view, and (iii) developed for the right reasons. At the same time, there is a unique opportunity for the engineering profession to demonstrate the benefits of engineering to the world and, as a result, to promote it to younger generations.

This book examines the role of the engineering profession in human development and security, and its contribution to peacebuilding and diplomacy in the 21st-century world. What is the responsibility of engineers in partnership with other disciplines to contribute to peacebuilding and diplomatic efforts at scales ranging from local to global? How do engineers contribute to the culture of peace spearheaded by UNESCO (1994) and reinforced by United Nations Resolution 53/243 (UNGA, 1999)? How does the triple nexus between engineering, peacebuilding, and diplomacy contribute to human development and security in different contexts and scales? How do we educate globally engaged engineers on the attitudes, skills, and knowledge necessary to address the global challenges of the 21st century? This book does not intend to answer all these questions, but rather to create awareness and an open question-and-answer forum on the role of engineers as peacemakers and diplomats.

1.2 Human Development and Security

Maurice Strong, secretary general of the 1992 Rio Summit (UNCED, 1992), emphasized that it is essential for the engineering profession to play a leading role in achieving sustainable development. This statement reflects the importance of engineering in human development and security, from community-based projects to regional and global programs. It was recognized at the 1992 United Nations Conference on Environment and Development (the Rio Summit) and the publication of Agenda 21 (UNCED, 1992), which served as a blueprint for action in all aspects of human activities. The Rio Summit emphasized the crucial role that science and technology play in determining future societies and the planet's condition. It also acknowledged the vital role of society in shaping technological and economic decisions. Finally, it was noted that humanity's ability to affect planetary change and its challenges through technology is increasing faster than its ability to manage and understand the non-technical consequences of such problems and their solutions. In general, some of these consequences can be detrimental to life.

The Rio Summit's focus on human development originated from the Brundtland Commission in 1987 and the 1990 UNDP Human Development Report. The report notes that human development is about "creating an environment in which people can develop their full potential and lead productive, creative lives according to their needs and interests" (UNDP/HDR, 1990). It is also about providing people with skills and resources to address their basic human needs (e.g., food, health, safe shelter, access to services, and resources) as preconditions for subsequent economic growth, poverty reduction, aid delivery, debt reduction, individual empowerment, community participation, small-scale technology, and local capacity building. Human development generally expands people's choices, opportunities, and freedom through equity, empowerment, and sustainability (UNDP/HDR, 2010).

Following Agenda 21, the 1994 UN Development Report (UNDP/ HDR, 1994) extended the concept of human development to include a broader perspective on *human security* (United Nations Trust Fund for Human Security, n.d.). Closely related and complementary, but not identical to human development or national security, human security is people-centered and focuses on addressing human vulnerability at all developmental levels. As Gomez and Gasper (2013) noted, human security is about "understanding the particular *threats* experienced by particular groups of people, as well as the participation of those people in the analysis process." Among all possible threats are "proactive crises, violent conflicts, natural disasters, persistent poverty, epidemics, and economic downturns" (UN Trust Fund for Human Security, n.d.). These threats can be related to adverse events at different scales, climate change, and mis-/disinformation.

Under UN resolution 66/290 (UNGA, 2012), human security calls for "people-centered, comprehensive, context-specific, and prevention-oriented responses that strengthen the protection and empowerment of all people" and contribute to freedom from fear, want, and indignity. Human security requires a "citizen-oriented state, an active social society, and a robust private business sector" (Schirch, 2013). Seven types of security were introduced in the UNDP/HDR (1994) report: economic, food, health, environmental, personal, community, and political. Other forms of security can be added, as listed in Table 1.1. It should be noted that human

Table 1.1 Different interrelated aspects of human security, including the seven types (economic, food, health, environmental, personal, community, and political) mentioned in the UNDP/HDR (1994) report

Categories of Human Security	Description
Economic	Ensured basic income and employment and access to a social safety net.
Food	Food security occurs when "... all people at all times have physical, social and economic access to sufficient, safe and nutritious food to meet their dietary needs and food preferences for an active, healthy life" (FAO, 1996).
Health	Access to safe water, living in a secure environment, access to health services, access to safe and affordable family planning and essential support during pregnancy and delivery, prevention of HIV/AIDS and other diseases, and having the basic knowledge to live a healthy life.
Environmental	Prevention of water and air pollution, deforestation, irrigated land conservation, and natural hazards such as droughts, floods, cyclones, earthquakes, etc. Development of nature-based solutions.
Personal	Protection of people from physical violence, whether from the state or external states, from violent individuals and sub-state actors, domestic abuse, or predatory adults.
Community	Conservation of traditional cultures, languages, and commonly held values. It also includes abolishing ethnic discrimination, preventing conflicts, and protecting indigenous people.
Political	Protection of human rights and well-being of all people. It also protects people from state repression, such as freedom of the press, speech, and voting. Political security also covers abolishing political detention, imprisonment, systematic ill-treatment, and disappearance.
State	State security refers to the measures, institutions, and activities undertaken by a government to protect the state's integrity, stability, and interests. It involves safeguarding the nation from internal and external threats, maintaining law and order, and ensuring the well-being of its citizens.
Climate	Climate security relates security to risks induced, directly or indirectly, by changes in climate patterns.
Livelihood	Adequate and sustainable access to income and other resources enables households to meet basic needs (Frankenberger, 1996). This security includes sufficient access to food, potable water, health facilities, educational opportunities, housing, and time for community participation and social integration (CARE, 2002).

Categories of Human Security	Description
Infrastructure	Protection of infrastructure and especially critical infrastructure, i.e., systems and assets whose disruption (destruction and incapacitation) "would have a debilitating effect on security, national economic security, national public health or safety, or any combination thereof" (CISA, n.d.). Critical sectors include chemical, communication, commercial, manufacturing, dams, defense, emergency, energy, financial, food and agriculture, government facilities, healthcare and public health, IT, nuclear reactors, materials and waste, transportation, water, and wastewater (CISA).
Energy	Energy security is "… the uninterrupted availability of energy sources at an affordable price" (IEA, n.d.).
Water	Water security guarantees "… the capacity of a population to safeguard sustainable access to adequate quantities of acceptable quality water for sustaining livelihoods, human well-being, and socioeconomic development, for ensuring protection against water-borne pollution and water-related disasters, and for preserving ecosystems in a climate of peace and political stability" (UNU-INWEH, 2013).
Land Tenure	"People's ability to control and manage land, use it, dispose of its produce and engage in transactions, including transfers" (IFAD, 2015).
Land and Soil	"The maintenance and improvement of the world's soil resources so that they continue to provide food, fiber, and freshwater, make major contributions to energy and climate sustainability, and help maintain biodiversity and the overall protection of ecosystem goods and services" (Koch et al., 2013).
Information	Security to risks induced directly and indirectly by misinformation and disinformation.

development and security encompass many of these types of security, which are interdependent, contextual, scale-specific, and rely on the contributions of the engineering profession. Human security and ecological security (biodiversity, ecosystem services, and natural resources) are deeply interconnected, as the health and stability of ecosystems directly impact human well-being and vice versa.

Multiple global crises have impacted aspects of human development and security and threatened the well-being of humanity at different scales during the first two decades of the 21st century. These include the continuously worsening global food and energy crises since 2007 (von Grebmer et al., 2012;

Allouche et al., 2015), the economic crisis of 2008 and its subsequent recession, the growing incidence of violent conflicts in fragile states (OECD, 2018), the global COVID pandemic and unrest of 2020–2021, the Ukrainian-Russian war starting in 2022, the Gaza-Israel war starting in 2023, and the ongoing security risks related to climate change (IPCC, 2023; National Intelligence Council, 2021; The World Bank, 2023). Other humanitarian crises include those in Sudan, South Sudan, Myanmar, Haiti, the West African Sahel, the Horn of Africa, DRC, Syria, Venezuela, and Afghanistan (The New Humanitarian, 2024).

These crises have exacerbated the fragility, multiple vulnerabilities, and flow of various systems (socioeconomic, political, technical, and environmental) involved in addressing planetary challenges on different scales, from local to global. They also revealed numerous forms of injustice, inequity, and inequality (i.e., social, ecological, racial, economic, and gender), negatively impacting peace worldwide (IEP, 2020a, b). Finally, the UN estimates that "in 2024, nearly 300 million people worldwide will need humanitarian assistance and protection due to conflicts, climate emergencies, and other drivers" (OCHA, 2023).

The complexity and interdependencies of the crises mentioned above, combined with poor decision-making at different levels (political, societal, and managerial), democratic structures under attack, misinformation (Howard, 2020), the never-ending pursuit of profit growth, limited institutional capacity to handle crises, and low levels of individual and community resilience (i.e., high vulnerability), especially in disadvantaged areas, have created confusion, uncertainty, and insecurity, and consequently, inaction regarding the future of humanity (Jacobs, 2016). Even before the COVID outbreak, "more than 6 in 7 people worldwide perceived feeling moderately or very insecure" (UNDP, 2022). This number has increased ever since and has been fed by increased loneliness, especially in America, during and after the COVID-19 pandemic (Weissbourd et al., 2021).

The crises mentioned above have also jeopardized the overarching goal of building a more sustainable, stable, peaceful, and equitable world in which all humans have the potential to live with dignity and peace. This vision, central to the Sustainable Development Goals (SDGs) under the Agenda 2030 framework, was established by the United Nations in 2015. Consisting of 17 goals and 169 targets, it represents a comprehensive worldwide action plan involving five critical and interrelated sustainability aspects: people, planet, prosperity, peace, and partnerships (UN, 2015).

The COVID-19 pandemic has forced the international community to readjust the timeline of Agenda 2030 (Lu, 2020; Sumner et al., 2020; UNDP, 2021) while paying particular attention to equitable progress across different world economies. This recommendation was echoed by the authors of the 2021/2022 United Nations Development Report, who reported a nearly universal decline in Human Development Index scores back to their 2016 levels (UNDP/HDR, 2022). The 2023 sustainability development report (Sachs et al., 2023) concluded that "at the midpoint of the 2030 Agenda, all of the SDGs are seriously off track." Ponzio (2023) noted that "only 15 percent of the sustainable development goals targets are on track to be reached by 2030." The Agenda 2030 framework is further affected by climate change and misinformation, representing existential threats to human development and peace.

1.3   Human Development and Peace

Peace is closely related to human development and security. Any decline in human development has had consequences for peace. As emphasized in Agenda 2030, "sustainable development cannot be realized without peace and security, and peace and security will be at risk without sustainable development" (UNESCAP, 2018). The importance of the so-called sustainability–peace nexus has been acknowledged in the literature (Sharifi et al., 2021; Amadei, 2023) since the publication of *An Agenda for Peace* by the United Nations (Boutros-Ghali, 1992). This document defines the concepts of preventive diplomacy, peacemaking, peacekeeping, and peacebuilding.

Among the Sustainable Development Goals, SDG 16 (Peace, Justice, and Strong Institutions) captures the linkage between peace and sustainable development and consists of 12 targets.[3] It is to "promote peaceful and inclusive societies for sustainable development, provide access to justice for all, and build effective,

---

[3] Goal 16: Peace, justice and strong institutions – The Global Goals

accountable, and inclusive institutions at all levels" (SDSN, 2020). Meeting SDG 16 is about developing the right relationships, a concept contained in principle 16f of The Earth Charter (1987), where peace is defined as

> The wholeness created by the right relationships with oneself, other persons, other cultures, other life, Earth, and the larger whole of which all are a part.

Peace also appears in the SDG, crosscutting gender equality issues, governance, health, inequalities, security, support of vulnerable states, and sustainable cities. The SDGs community has recognized that not effectively addressing peace may jeopardize all other SDGs (Virji et al., 2019). Unfortunately, as of 2023, SDG 16 is the least successful of all SDGs, with some targets that are off-track and some even regressing (UNDP, 2023; TAP Network, 2023).

Although peace is intimately linked to development in general (Milante and Oxhorn, 2009; Dews, 2013), it is essential to note that not all forms of peace contribute positively to socioeconomic development and vice versa. Likewise, socioeconomic development can positively or negatively impact peace, depending on the type of development being implemented. It can have positive consequences or create unintended issues (Bush, 1998). This dynamic is further discussed in Chapter 2.

Peace brings personal, environmental, and economic security and creates an environment conducive to developing desirable socioeconomic partnerships (IEP, 2021). The relationship between peace and conflict is complex as conflict can take different forms, ranging between (i) peaceful manifestations, (ii) low-intensity violence, (iii) high-intensity violence, and (iv) armed conflicts (Lemos, 2018). According to Galtung (1964, 1990), peace is not merely the lack of war and direct or organized aggression, termed *negative peace*. It also involves creating and sustaining conditions and values (harmony, unity, well-being, security, and respect) conducive to prosperity, known as *positive peace*. According to Galtung (1996), "peace is the context for conflicts to unfold [and transform] nonviolently and creatively" and is a "revolutionary proposition."

When violent, conflicts can be destructive or expensive. As noted by Collier et al. (2003), the relationship between war, violent conflicts, and development is as follows:

Where development succeeds, countries become progressively safer from violent conflict, making subsequent development easier. Where development fails, countries are at a high risk of becoming caught in a conflict trap in which war wrecks the economy and increases the risk of future war.

In 2022, violent conflict was estimated at $16.5 trillion or $2,117 per year per person worldwide (IEP, 2022). As noted by Hayden (2018), "The World Bank estimates that loss of productivity, failure of state institutions, capital flight, and increased military spending reduces average income at the end of civil wars by 15 percent less than they would have been otherwise, driving people into extreme poverty and deprivation." Intra-state conflicts have dominated inter-state disputes since WWII, especially in developing countries (e.g., Yemen, Soudan, Syria, and the Sahel). Forcibly displaced populations are associated with violent conflicts. In September 2023, the Office of the United Nations High Commissioner for Refugees (UNHCR, 2024) announced that "The number of people displaced due to war, persecution, violence, and human rights violations worldwide probably exceeded 114 million" (Africa News, 2023; The New Humanitarian, 2024). Also associated with war is irreversible damage to society and the environment, as in Ukraine (Conflict and Environment Observatory, 2024) and Gaza (UNEP, 2024; Zwijnenburg and Hall, 2023).

The multiple effects of climate change jeopardize human development and peace. The nexus between peace, sustainability, and climate change is substantial. As noted by Amadei (2023), it is challenging to envision (i) a sustainable community that is unstable and climate-secured; (ii) a peaceful community that has not endorsed practices that sustain livelihoods and the environment and does not support climate security practices; and (iii) a climate-secured community that has not endorsed sustainable practices and is geopolitically unstable.

The dynamics between peace, sustainability, and climate security have mainly been acknowledged in environmental peacebuilding, which relates to the role of natural resource management in conflict prevention, mitigation, resolution, and recovery to build resilience in communities affected by conflict.[4]

---

[4]https://www.environmentalpeacebuilding.org/

In addition to having the goal of stopping violence against nature and humans, it is based on the "assumption that the biophysical environment's inherent characteristics can act as incentives for cooperation and peace, rather than violence and competition" (Dresse et al., 2019). Environmental peacebuilding recognizes that environmental change combined with the mismanagement of natural resources and climate change increases the risk of conflict, especially "in places already fractured by socioeconomic inequality, ethnic divisions, or ideological instability" (Brown and Nicolucci-Altman, 2022). Rapaport (2024) reviews several examples of relationship between environmental security, conflict, and peace with a focus on the Israeli–Palestinian conflict since 1948. According to the International Committee of the Red Cross (ICRC, 2020), 14 of the 25 countries considered most vulnerable to environmental degradation and climate change are currently experiencing conflict and violence.

1.4 Engineering and Peace

Engineers are not often directly seen as contributing to peace, even though engineering has contributed to designing, building, operating, and maintaining the technological, industrial, and municipal systems and structures needed to improve the quality of life worldwide. Engineers have also actively contributed to the reconstruction and stabilization of conflict- and disaster-affected communities. Engineering can play different roles in peace studies and conflict management and contribute to peace efforts in several ways.

- Engineers contribute to *peacebuilding* by addressing fundamental root causes and drivers of potentially violent social conflicts, reducing barriers to peaceful outcomes, ensuring human security, addressing development issues (e.g., water, energy, food, transportation, telecom, and health), and building resilient infrastructure and capacity so that conflicts related to adverse events (natural and human-created) are less likely to unfold or relapse.

- Engineers contribute to *peacemaking* by collaborating with negotiating and mediating units on stabilization, bringing together different parties to agree and collaborate on joint solutions (technical and non-technical), especially in transboundary or conflict-prone areas.
- Engineers contribute to *peacekeeping* by restoring essential community services and capacity, contributing to reconstruction efforts, and being responsible for the sustainable functioning of infrastructure as communities recover from conflict while benefitting from peacekeeping operations over a defined period.

Peacebuilding, peacemaking, and peacekeeping efforts support human development and security. They generally interact before, during, and after conflicts and disasters, and their boundaries are not always well-defined. For convenience, the at-large definition of peacebuilding proposed by the USIP (Snodderly, 2018) is used in this book with the understanding that depending on the context, it might be necessary to focus on a specific effort.

Originally conceived in the context of post-conflict recovery efforts to promote reconciliation and reconstruction, *peacebuilding* has more recently taken on a broader meaning. It may include providing humanitarian relief, protecting human rights, ensuring security, establishing nonviolent modes of resolving conflicts, fostering reconciliation, providing trauma-healing services, repatriating refugees and resettling internally displaced people, supporting broad-based education, and aiding in economic reconstruction. As such, it also includes conflict prevention in the sense of preventing the recurrence of violence, conflict management, and post-conflict recovery. In a larger sense, peacebuilding involves a transformation toward more manageable, peaceful relationships and governance structures–the long-term process of addressing root causes and effects, reconciling differences, normalizing relations, and building institutions that can manage conflict without resolving to violence.

Another at-large and more succinct definition of peacebuilding proposed by Moriarty-Lempke et al. (2022) is as follows:

An umbrella term that encapsulates efforts aimed at directly addressing the dynamics of a conflict. This includes efforts to prevent, manage, mitigate, de-escalate, or reconcile after a conflict.

Another way to look at peacebuilding is as a process focusing on changing individuals, relationships, cultural patterns, and structures away from harm and toward human security. The process unfolds at four levels: personal, relational, cultural, and structural (Schirch, 2013).

As this book discusses, even though engineering has provided systems and structures to improve the quality of life worldwide, it has not always brought about peaceful solutions and well-being. Despite the positive aspects of twentieth-century engineering achievements, the engineering profession has also had unplanned or undesirable effects on natural and human systems in the developed and developing worlds. Although technically sound, many engineering projects related to natural resource development have resulted in air, water, and land pollution, thereby affecting the depreciation and collapse of human populations and ecosystems. These projects have also resulted in population displacement and inequalities within and between countries. Projects that ignore the socioeconomic and political impacts of engineering decisions and issues related to ethics, social justice, and equity are sources of political conflict and violence worldwide (Muscat, 2014; Riley, 2008; Armstrong et al., 2014; Bowen, 2014; Leyden and Lucena, 2017). The focus on economic growth and consumption has also impacted socio-ecological systems owing to unaccounted externalities (Raworth, 2018).

Engineering has resulted in more harm than good in certain situations, particularly when technologies are being developed for military purposes (Vesilind, 2010). The war-industrial complex has benefited from ongoing conflicts since WWI and perpetuates a "forever war" mentality. The global annual military expenditure in 2023 was estimated to have reached an all-time high of $2,440 billion (Le Guardian, 2024; Tian et al., 2024), or approximately $77,300 per second annually. The defense industry supports university R&D programs that recruit engineers, perpetuating their participation in war-industry activities (Olivier, 2022). As noted by Vesilind (2010), the current state of affairs in engineering schools appears to favor military engineering. While defense is necessary for a nation's security, it is essential to acknowledge that the world would be better if a significant portion of military expenditure were directed toward sustainable development and peacebuilding. It remains unclear whether military engineering is categorically constructive or destructive.

In summary, there are many cases in which the engineering profession has exacerbated conflict rather than promoting peace and has not lived up to its code of ethics. Engineers often find themselves in a moral predicament when faced with such situations and may need to go against their principles and ethical values (Vesilind, 2010; Kamp, 2016). Integrating peace education into the engineering curriculum can help overcome this challenge. According to Jenkins (2019), peace education is defined as

> education both about and for peace. It is an academic field of inquiry, and the practice(s) of teaching and learning, oriented toward and for the elimination of all forms of violence, and the establishment of a culture of peace. Peace education has its origins in responses to evolving social, political, and ecological crises and concerns of violence and injustice.

This book introduces peace engineering, which supports peacebuilding by enhancing social, economic, and political stability. Vesilind (2005, 2010) defines peace engineering as "The proactive use of engineering skills to promote a peaceful and just existence for all," a noble cause. Peace engineering is an interdisciplinary field that applies engineering principles and technology to promote peace, resolve conflicts, and address the underlying causes of violence.

1.5   Engineering and Diplomacy

In conflict management and peace studies, peacebuilding, peacemaking, and peacekeeping are intimately related to diplomacy, narrowly defined as "the fundamental means by which foreign policy is implemented" (Snoderly, 2018). Diplomacy focuses on negotiations, mediation, and international cooperation to resolve conflicts and promote peace. Peacebuilding, peacemaking, and peacekeeping create conditions for diplomacy and vice versa.

Diplomacy, defense, and development are interconnected pillars in the three Ds of "national policy decisions regarding investment, security, economic development, the environment, and engagement" (Mr. Y, 2011). A balance between these three Ds is necessary but insufficient for sustainable peace. These three pillars benefit from investments in science, technology, and engineering (Reynolds, 2013; Deghan and Colglazier, 2012; Colglazier and Lyons, 2014).

Engineers are involved in defense and development projects. Their role in diplomacy and foreign policy is less evident in the global open and ever-changing world of the 21st century. The concept of engineering diplomacy has been advanced in the literature (Meshkati, 2012) as a field that is to the engineering profession what the existing area of science diplomacy is to science. Science diplomacy is an umbrella term often used to describe how science can serve as a vehicle for creating transboundary and cross-disciplinary partnerships through scientific collaboration and how diplomacy can facilitate scientific collaboration.

According to Van Langenhove (2016), science diplomacy can be understood as (i) science in diplomacy (e.g., scientific research addressing global issues in support of policies), (ii) science for diplomacy (e.g., scientists and policymakers' joint advocacy and advising in-between states), and (iii) diplomacy for science (e.g., policies facilitating scientific collaboration). Numerous publications on policy have highlighted the connections between science, technology, engineering, and diplomacy (NRC, 1999, 2014, 2015; NASEM, 2017).

In this book, engineering diplomacy is understood as a vehicle for integrating engineering in and for diplomacy (Amadei, 2016). It can take different forms, such as "supporting education and research capacity, exchanging faculty and students, and 'building bridges' via partnerships to implement engineering and technology-related projects" (Meshkati, 2012). Engineers play a critical role in and for diplomacy by providing specialized knowledge, aiding infrastructure development, supporting environmental diplomacy, offering technical support and training, being involved in conflict resolution, and promoting science and technology diplomacy. Their expertise is crucial for addressing intricate global challenges and fostering cooperation among nations, ultimately leading to peace, stability, and strong diplomatic ties worldwide.

Engineering can intersect diplomacy in various ways (OpenAI, 2023), such as

- *Technical Diplomacy*: Collaboration on engineering projects between nations, such as joint ventures in space exploration or the construction of international infrastructure, can lead to the development of diplomatic relations. For example, infrastructure connecting neighboring countries can symbolize cooperation and strengthen ties between nations.

- *Environmental Diplomacy*: Engineering is crucial for solving global challenges such as climate change. International accords and negotiations require regular engineering strategies to decrease greenhouse gas emissions and to adjust to environmental changes.

- *Arms Control and Disarmament*: Engineering expertise is critical for ensuring compliance with arms control treaties and disarmament agreements, promoting transparency, and building trust among nations.

Engineers and diplomats must work together to effectively address the intersection between technical issues and international diplomacy. Like science diplomacy, engineering diplomacy can be interpreted as a Track 1.5 or 2 form of diplomacy that complements the more traditional Track 1 official government diplomacy related to the policymaking world of diplomats and officials. Scientists and engineers can gain insights into diplomacy, while diplomats can similarly draw upon scientific and engineering expertise to overcome apprehension towards science within diplomatic circles.

Several examples of science and engineering diplomacy initiatives are discussed herein. However, one of these stands out for me. On June 17, 1975, the American Apollo and Soviet Soyuz spacecraft docked in space for the first time (Garan, 2015) (Fig. 1.1). An astronaut and cosmonaut shook hands in space despite the Cold War on Earth.

That 'Apollo-Soyuz moment' is an excellent example of science and engineering for or in diplomacy, showcasing that collaboration of goodwill and peace is possible through science, technology, and engineering innovation despite geopolitical disagreements. Policies facilitating scientific and technical cooperation (diplomacy for science) also contributed to the project's success. A more recent example of collaboration in space diplomacy over the past two decades is the International Space Station (ISS), a platform for scientific exploration in low earth orbit involving multiple countries. Other international public and private space initiatives are being considered for exploring the Moon, Mars, and beyond.

Figure 1.1 The 1975 Apollo-Soyuz Moment. 1:25 scale model of the ASTP mission lasted from July 15–24, 1975 (Photo Credit: B. Amadei).

Other international science-policy nexus initiatives suggested by Van Langenhove (2016) include the Intergovernmental Panel on Climate Change (IPCC) and the United Nations Sustainable Development Goals. Another example is the recently created IPIE (https://www.ipie.info), which addresses misinformation and disinformation. These three initiatives transcend national boundaries and involve intergovernmental (transnational and regional) bodies.

At the regional level, an excellent example of a science diplomacy initiative is the International Center for Integrated Mountain Development (http://www.icimod.org/), which is based in Nepal and involves collaborative scientific work on climate change and natural hazard mitigation, affecting human development and security in eight countries in the Hindukush-Himalayan region. These countries face similar issues, particularly regarding the effects of climate change on glacier melting, wildlife migration, and forest fires. In the Middle East, since 1996, the Arava Institute for Environmental Studies (https://arava.org/) has brought together Israelis, Palestinians, Jordanians, and other international students and educators on its Negev campus. Its Center for Applied Environmental Diplomacy promotes cross-border environmental and humanitarian cooperation amid political conflict. The Arctic Council (https://arctic-council.org/) facilitates collaboration and discourse among Arctic nations, indigenous peoples, and overall Arctic inhabitants, focusing on common concerns.

At the European level, science diplomacy initiatives include the EU Science Diplomacy Alliance (https://www.science-diplomacy.eu/), a hub for scientific cooperation. Another example is CERN (https://home.cern/), based in Switzerland and involving physicists from 23 member states. Additionally, SESAME (https://www.sesame.org.jo) is a physics research center in Jordan. It includes member countries such as Bahrain, Cyprus, Egypt, Iran, Israel, Jordan, Pakistan, Palestine, and Turkey. SESAME's spirit of scientific collaboration makes it significant despite some member countries having strained diplomatic relationships, such as Iran and Israel, which have not had direct diplomatic ties since 1979. The World Academy of Science (TWAS), based in Trieste, Italy, involves scientists and engineers from 100 countries, with strong participation from developing countries. It supports science diplomatic efforts toward "sustainable prosperity through research, education, policy, and diplomacy" (https://twas.org). In the United States, the American Association for the Advancement of Science (AAAS) Center for Science Diplomacy (https://www.aaas.org/programs/center-science-diplomacy) "aims to build bridges between communities, societies, and nations through closer interactions between science and diplomacy and elevate the role of science in foreign policy to address national and global challenges." Finally, the importance of science and engineering diplomacy has been recognized in science summits at UN General Assembly meetings since 2021.

One can add many projects for which science and engineering are critical in addressing transboundary, in-country, and local community issues. It is noteworthy that where people share similar problems (e.g., limited resources) despite geopolitical stressors, science and engineering diplomacy represents a common ground and constructive way in which people join forces and develop mutual understanding and solutions, promote social cohesion, and create more inclusive societies (e.g., Kashmir, Israel, and Jordan). Water and sanitation are resources that can bring people together or create conflict. When properly managed in a sustainable and equitable manner, water and sanitation can be a source of peace and prosperity (UN, 2024).

An excellent example of cross-border cooperation and geopolitical diplomacy from 2004 to 2016 is the Kaesong industrial complex along the border between North and South Korea (Ahn and Yi, 2021). At one point, the complex employed 54,000 North Korean workers and involved 124 companies from various industries, including clothing and textiles, car parts, and semiconductors (BBC, 2016). The closure of the industrial complex occurred in 2016 in response to North Korea's nuclear and missile tests.

1.6 The Engineering–Peacebuilding– Diplomacy Nexus

This book explores the triple nexus between engineering, peacebuilding, and diplomacy and how it unfolds in human development and security. The term nexus implies the consideration of multiple sectors and their dynamic interactions. They also influence and depend on each other. Nexus thinking is systems thinking, which is discussed further in Chapters 5 and 6.

1.6.1 Triangular Representation

Figure 1.2 shows a triangular representation of the interactions and feedback mechanisms between the three nexus sectors. These interactions occur in an environment or landscape, such as a community, and involve multiple socioeconomic, environmental, political, and cultural factors. The success of engineering, peacebuilding, and diplomatic efforts depends on the dynamics of the environment, which in turn depends on how the three sectors change and interact over time. Peace and diplomacy can be engineered to affect decision-making in engineering.

It is not always clear what drives the first of the three nexus sectors, as there is often weak and contradictory evidence in their causal interaction chains. This interaction may or may not hinder human development and security, depending on the available capacity. It can follow multiple pathways, take various forms, and change over time. For instance, although peacebuilding efforts may be present, diplomatic agreements from negotiation to implementation may or may not sufficiently contribute to successful engineering efforts. Likewise, diplomatic efforts may be in place, but poor engineering interventions and a lack of peacebuilding efforts may jeopardize any agreement. Finally, engineering efforts may induce conflict if not thoughtfully planned and implemented or without agreement between parties. The bottom line indicates multiple ways for the nexus to unfold; trade-offs and synergies must be considered on a case-by-case basis.

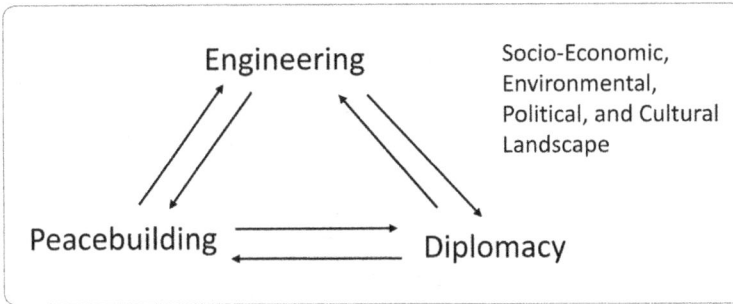

Figure 1.2 Feedback dynamics among engineering, peacebuilding, and diplomacy.

1.6.2   Cross-Impact Matrix Representation

Another representation of nexus dynamics is presented in Table 1.2. In this cross-impact matrix representation, each row represents the direct influence (impact) of each nexus sector (diagonal term) on the other two sectors. Similarly, each column represents the direct dependence of each sector (diagonal term) on the other two sectors. Table 1.2 shows how the three nexus sectors positively (enabling) influence each other. If the statements in Table 1.2 are reversed, they can also show how the three nexus sectors can negatively (constraining) affect each other.

If required, each level of influence can be defined qualitatively as high, medium, or low, or using semi-quantitative measures ranging from 1 to 3 for positive (enabling) impact, -1 to -3 for negative (constraining) influence, and 0 for neutral. Metrics

Table 1.2 Cross-impact representation of positive (enabling) influence in the engineering–peacebuilding–diplomacy nexus

Engineering (E)		
	- Provides access to services (e.g., water, energy, food, transportation, telecom, healthcare, etc.) contributing to better livelihood security - Repairs and builds resilient infrastructure and capacity so that conflicts related to adverse events are less likely to unfold or relapse - Restores essential community services and capacity, contributing to reconstruction efforts and community stability - Contributes to conflict prevention with infrastructure and urban planning, promoting inclusivity and reducing inequalities - Helps build trust and ensure projects meet populations' specific needs and aspirations - Provides training and education for capacity building and resilience - Coordinates building and repair efforts among groups of stakeholders - Identifies and manages risks associated with unintended consequences of projects - Builds resilience into infrastructure and flexibility and adaptability of programs to changing conditions - Designs and implements systems for delivering humanitarian aid, including clean water, shelter, and medical facilities, which are essential for peace and stability - Develops warning systems and communication networks to help prevent conflicts from escalating	- Brings people together around common issues - Promotes collaboration with negotiating and mediating units on stabilization - Brings together different parties to agree and collaborate on joint solutions (technical and non-technical), especially in transboundary or conflict-prone areas - Identifies and addresses some root causes and drivers of social conflicts - Reduces barriers to peaceful outcomes - Ensures human security - Considers possible negative consequences of projects that could create conflict - Provides unique expertise and technical assistance in analyzing the nature and causes of conflicts - Creates collaboration around transboundary issues such as environmental issues, climate change mitigation, adaptation, and negotiate and implement resource management - Helps negotiate agreements between nations - Helps in mediation or advising, helping parties find joint ground solutions - Contributes to negotiation around technical issues and resource management - Promotes collaboration and innovation between countries in R&D - Helps negotiate and develop collaborative agreements when developing international standards and regulations

	Peacebuilding (P)	Provides stability and security foundation for sustainable development
- Provides more reliable planning and design of infrastructure and long-term operation and maintenance - Supports more equitable access to resources - Contributes to more institutional stability, capacity, and resilience, which are necessary for project durability	- Facilitates collaborative work - Builds bridges via partnerships to implement engineering and technology-related projects - Creates conditions for engineering projects to take place sustainably	- Promotes more resilient, prosperous, inclusive, tolerant, healthier societies with diversity and integrity - Creates a safer and more secure socioeconomic environment for stable governance, longer-term productivity and investment, and the management and allocation of resources at different scales - Ensures long-term diplomatic gains - Provides activities to sustain peace and prevent the occurrence of violence - Strengthens diplomatic relations between nations
	- Creates conditions for peacebuilding to occur - Facilitates transboundary exchanges and shared resource management - Assists in post-conflict rehabilitation and reconciliation - Helps find common ground - Diplomatic channels help negotiate peace agreements, which can lead to peacebuilding initiatives - Diplomatic efforts can result in garnering international support for reconstruction activities - Provides diplomatic negotiations for effective implementation and peacebuilding efforts - Lays the groundwork for peacebuilding activities - Negotiations and mediation bring conflicting parties to the table and facilitate peaceful settlements - Addresses the root causes of conflicts and finds diplomatic solutions to prevent future conflicts - Encourages cooperation between countries, organizations, and stakeholders to support peacebuilding initiatives	Diplomacy (D)

must be defined for each level of influence, either qualitatively or semi-quantitatively. For instance, what does a positive or negative medium impact of engineering on peacebuilding and diplomacy look like, and how does it differ from a high or low impact? As discussed in this book, answers to these questions depend significantly on context and scale and cannot be generalized.

The interdependency demonstrated in Table 1.2 can be utilized to evaluate the direct impact of intervening in one sector of the nexus on the other two sectors, identify where leverage is most effectively applied within the nexus, and identify the center of gravity in the community where influence on different systems is dominant. For instance, do peacebuilding interventions significantly influence engineering and diplomacy? Do diplomatic interventions have a more substantial impact, or is it an engineering intervention?

In addition to the six direct (binary) influences and dependencies, indirect connections may exist among all three nexus sectors. There are six possible tertiary interactions among the three sectors. An example is the E-P-D interaction: engineering affects peacebuilding by developing infrastructure and technology, and peacebuilding contributes to diplomacy by supporting conflict-affected and conflict-sensitive landscapes or promoting economic stability. Nexus interactions worth exploring include (i) E-D-P and E-P-D when starting with engineering, (ii) P-E-D and P-D-E when starting with peace, and (iii) D-P-E and D-E-P when starting with diplomacy. Note that more complex interactions can emerge from tertiary interactions owing to the multiple feedback mechanisms shown in Fig. 1.2.

1.6.3   A Tripod Representation

Another possible representation of the nexus is that of a three-legged tripod, as illustrated in Fig. 1.3. The tripod's overall stability, which represents human development and security in a specific environment, depends on the stability and strength of each leg (peacebuilding, engineering, and diplomacy) and all three legs simultaneously (integrated nexus approach). The tripod representation can help illustrate how human development and security would be compromised if at least one of its three nexus sectors was weaker than the others. For example, not prioritizing one sector of the nexus can affect the others. For example, inadequate diplomatic efforts can lead to poor partnerships and conflicts in engineering projects.

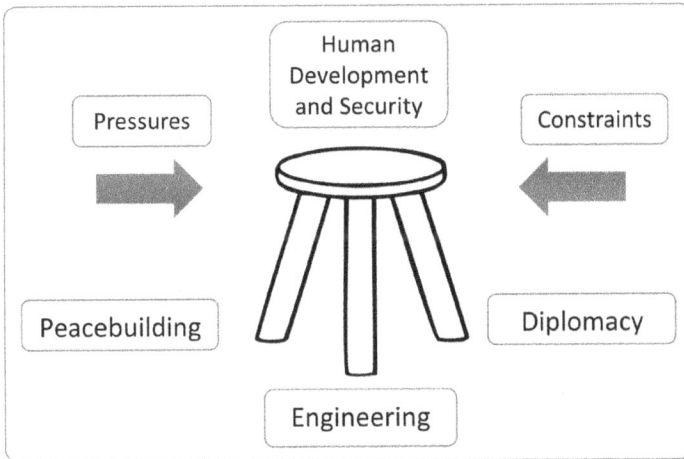

Figure 1.3 A tripod representation of the engineering–peacebuilding–diplomacy nexus.

Furthermore, the stability of a tripod depends on its interaction with the surrounding landscape or environment. This environment creates stressors and constraints (internal or external, soft or hard) on the tripod's existence and stability; too much pressure can even topple the tripod. By analogy, human development and security may be at risk owing to socioeconomic, geopolitical, and environmental stressors and constraints (limiters). Stressors and constraints can act synergistically and even exacerbate conflict, unsuccessful delivery of engineering projects, and a breakdown in negotiations.

Figure 1.3 also shows that interventions selected to address issues across the nexus—whether technical or non-technical and specific to each sector—need to (i) encompass the multiple dimensions of the nexus, (ii) consider the environment in which the nexus unfolds, and (iii) be synchronized across the nexus. Solving one issue associated with one sector of the nexus can positively or negatively affect one or two sectors. This dynamic is due to the dependence and influence properties listed in Table 1.2. For instance, incomplete diplomatic efforts may influence the success of community projects (intentionally or unintentionally) and resume community conflicts.

As discussed further in this book, a challenge in addressing the nexus and any nexus, in general, is how deeply one disaggregates the domains and subdomains of each nexus sector and determines the most appropriate attributes. Another challenge is to qualitatively or quantitatively identify how each sector influences the other two sectors. The challenge is to balance capturing the linkages sufficiently (qualitatively or quantitatively) and being sufficiently comprehensive without falling into paralysis in the analysis. Simply put, there are no specific recipes for finding a balance short of gaining experience through multiple efforts.

1.7 Book Content

The book highlights the engineering–peacebuilding–diplomacy interconnection and the need to educate engineers who can navigate this nexus in an environment of a specific context and scale. Can past and current educational models effectively prepare engineers to become globally engaged and contribute to peace and diplomacy? If not, what should be developed? What should be the body of knowledge of engineers to address 21st-century issues? Engineering educational institutions must reflect today's world, not the world of the 1850–1950 or 1950–1990 eras.

Chapter 2 examines the three quantum leaps in the interactions between engineering and society. In essence, the complex problems of the 21st century cannot be resolved using the tools and solutions developed in the 20th century or by institutions established in the 19th century. A new perspective is required in engineering education and practice to contribute to human development, security, conflict resolution, and diplomacy. Engineers involved in peace and diplomacy must be informed globally and educated accordingly. Substantial changes to traditional engineering education are necessary to make it more adaptable and aligned with current and future societal needs.

Chapter 3 examines the principles of conflict and peace, focusing on various aspects that engineers involved in diplomacy and peacebuilding must comprehend. This entails conducting assessments of conflict and risk and other human development and security evaluations. This chapter presents a model that outlines the sequence of peacemaking, peacebuilding, and peacekeeping, emphasizing the significance of the timing and strength of peace efforts while recovering following a decrease in peace after a crisis. This chapter explores the concepts of engineering for peace and engineering for diplomacy and the body of knowledge for engineers interested in peacebuilding and diplomatic efforts.

Chapter 4 explores the desirable attributes of the mindset and associated mental models necessary for the engineering profession to promote peace and diplomacy in the 21st century. This mindset recognizes engineers as essential actors in human development and security. Mental models significantly influence the system structure of peacebuilding and diplomatic efforts. These structures, in turn, create behavioral patterns and shape how events (peaceful or conflicting) unfold. Embracing a new mindset can stimulate the development of innovative frameworks that encourage inventive problem-solving, ultimately resulting in substantial transformations that contribute to peacebuilding and diplomatic efforts.

Chapter 5 emphasizes the value proposition of adopting a system-aware practice and mindset when considering engineering interventions for peacebuilding and diplomacy. Engineers must embrace the principles of organized complexity and systems science when addressing intricate issues concerning human development and security. Adopting this new mindset represents the most significant opportunity to transform systems. Globally engaged engineers must be system thinkers.

The modeling of the interplay between engineering, peacebuilding, and diplomacy is discussed in Chapter 6. It stresses the need to use system-aware appraisal methods to gather and analyze data and identify issues in conflict-affected and conflict-sensitive communities before modeling. This chapter reviews the pros and cons of existing soft and hard system modeling techniques and steps. It provides guidelines for modeling how engineering, peacebuilding, and diplomacy efforts interact using the system dynamics causal loop and stock and flow representations. This chapter analyzes critical archetypical structures at play in the engineering–peacebuilding–diplomacy nexus.

Chapter 7 presents a system-based methodology that can help decision-makers deal with complex problems spanning engineering, peacebuilding, and diplomacy. The methodology is based on the premise that there is a storyline describing how the community envisions bridging the gap between its current development, security, and peaceful states and its respective desired states. The methodology consists of 10 stages, from defining the community state to developing, selecting, and implementing systemic intervention scenarios. This approach requires meaningful participation and engagement from both internal and external stakeholder groups in community-based projects.

Chapter 8 explores various case studies utilizing the system dynamics method to delve into complex dynamics within conflict-prone communities. It investigates the interplay between conflict, climate change, and migration. Factors such as resource availability, capacity, existing conditions of peace, and proficiency in managing conflicts significantly affect the resilience of areas at risk of conflict.

Finally, Chapter 9 synthesizes the central themes discussed in this book. It underlines the importance of integrating engineering, peacebuilding, and diplomatic efforts through a combined, evolving, multidisciplinary, and collaborative approach. The chapter underscores the necessity of compiling a collection of case studies to operationalize this new approach and illustrate its benefit in human development and security across various contexts and scopes.

1.8 Concluding Remarks

Traditional engineering education and practice during the 19th and first half of the 20th century focused on technical rationality and provided value-neutral technical solutions to well-defined problems by utilizing a deterministic mindset. Similarly, as the Stone Age did not end because it ran out of stones, the compartmentalized model of engineering education would not stop because we ran out of antiquated engineering programs and educators that espouse an older scientific worldview. As they age, new forms of learning, not schooling, must emerge.

To continue to create a world of differences in the 21st century, engineers must possess the required attitudes, knowledge, hard and soft skills, and lifelong experience to address the challenges of a volatile, uncertain, complex, and ambiguous world. Lifelong learning, referred to as K-Gray learning herein, is critical for tracking changes. A new professional engineering mindset with an integrated perspective is necessary. The success of this new mindset depends significantly on the nature of the mental models used in decision-making and how these models translate into actual interventions. A new mindset requires the engineering profession to embrace change, which can be challenging. Schön (1971) noted that the more radical a change threatens to be, the more energy a social system uses to resist it. Despite these roadblocks, embracing complexity and system sciences is needed to address the increasingly complex and challenging problems faced by civilization as it advances in the 21st century.

References

Africa News. (2023, Oct 26). One hundred fourteen million people displaced by war, violence worldwide | Africanews.

Ahn, S.-J and Yi, S.-K. (2021). Methodological framework for analyzing peace engineering: Focusing on the Kaesong Industrial Complex and North Korean innovators in South Korea. *Technological Forecasting and Social Change*, 163.120464.10.1016/j.techfore.2020.120464.

Allouche, J., Middleton, C., and Gyawali, D. (2015). Technical veil, hidden politics: Interrogating the power linkages behind the nexus. *Water Alternatives*, **8**(1), 610–626.

Amadei, B. (2016). Science diplomacy: From theory to practice. *Multiverse* (Apr. 5).

Amadei, B. (2023). *Navigating the Complexity Across the Peace-Sustainability–Climate Security Nexus.* Boca Raton: Routledge, ISBN 9781032563381.

Armstrong, R., Baille, C., and Cumming-Potvin, W. (2014). *Mining and Communities: Understanding the Context of Engineering Practice.* San Diego, CA: Morgan & Claypool.

BBC (2016). What is the Kaesong Industrial Complex? - BBC News

Blue, E., Levine, M., and Nieusma, D. (2013). *Engineering and War: Militarism, Ethics, Institutions, Alternatives.* San Diego, CA: Morgan & Claypool.

Boutros-Ghali, B. (1992). An agenda for peace: Preventive diplomacy, peacemaking, and peacekeeping. *International Relations*, **11**(3), 201–218. https://doi.org/10.1177/004711789201100302

Bowen, W. R. (2014). *Engineering Ethics: Challenges and Opportunities.* Switzerland: Springer.

Brown, O. and Nicolucci-Altman, G. (2022). The white paper on the future of environmental peacebuilding. Geneva Peacebuilding Platform, International Union for Conservation of Nature, PeaceNexus Foundation, Environmental Law Institute, Environmental Peacebuilding Association. Ecosystem for Peace

Bush, K. (1998). A measure of peace: Peace and conflict impact assessment (PCIA) of development projects in conflict zones. Peacebuilding and Reconstruction Program Initiative, International Development Research Center–Canada. Ottawa and Johannesburg. http://conflictsensitivity.org/wp-content/uploads/2015/05/Measure_of_Peace.pdf.

CARE Household Livelihood Security Assessments (2002). A Toolkit for Practitioners, Prepared for the PHLS Unit by TANGO International Inc., Tucson, Arizona. PNADD652.pdf (usaid.gov)

Colglazier, E. W. and Lyons, E. E. (2015). The United States looks to the global science, technology, and innovation horizon. *Science and Diplomacy*, **3**(3). The United States Looks to the Global Science, Technology, and Innovation Horizon | Science & Diplomacy

Collier, P., Elliott, V. L., Hegre, H., and Hoeff (2003). Breaking the Conflict Trap: Civil War and Development Policy. A World Bank policy research report Washington, DC: World Bank Group. http://documents.worldbank.org/curated/en/908361468779415791/Breaking-the-conflict-trap-civil-war-and-development-policy

Conflict and Environment Observatory (CEOBS) and ZOÏ Network (2024). Assessing Environmental Damage in Ukraine. https://ceobs.org/paper-assessing-environmental-damage-in-ukraine/

Constable, G., et al. (2003). *A Century of Innovation: Twenty Engineering Achievements That Transformed Our Lives.* Washington, DC: Joseph Henry. https://doi.org/10.17226/10726

Cybersecurity and Infrastructure Security Agency (CISA) (n.d.) <u>Critical Infrastructure Sectors | CISA</u>

Dehgan, A. and Colglazier, E. W. (2012). Development science and science diplomacy. *Science and Diplomacy*, **1**(4). <u>http://www.sciencediplomacy. org/perspective/2012/development-science-and-science-diplomacy</u>

Dews, F. (2013, Oct. 17). U.N. Deputy Secretary-General Jan Eliasson: No peace without development, no development without peace. *Brookings*. <u>www.brookings.edu/blog/brookings-now/2013/10/17/un-deputy-secretary-general-jan-eliasson-no-peace-without-development-no-development-without-peace</u>

DiscoverE (2023). Messages matter. Effective messages for reaching tomorrow's innovators. <u>https://discovere.org/resources/messages-matter-executive-summary/</u>

Dresse, A., Fischhendler, I., Nielsen, J. O., and Zikos, D. (2019). Environmental peacebuilding: Towards a theoretical framework. *Cooperation and Conflict*, **54**(1), 99–109.

Eysenbach G. (2020). How to fight an infodemic: The four pillars of infodemic management. *Journal of Medical Internet Research*, **22**(6): e21820. <u>https://doi.org/10.2196/21820</u>

Food and Agriculture Organization of the United Nations (FAO) (1996). *Rome declaration on world food security and world food summit plan of action*. Rome: FAO.

Frankenberger, T. (1996). Measuring household livelihood security: An approach for reducing absolute poverty. *Food Forum 24*. Washington, DC: Food Aid Management.

Galtung, J. (1964). An editorial. *Journal of Peace Research*, **1**(1), 1–4. <u>https://doi.org/10.1177/002234336400100101</u>

Galtung, J. (1990). Cultural violence. *Journal of Peace Research*, **27**(3), 291–305. <u>https://www.jstor.org/stable/423472</u>

Galtung, J. (1996). *Peace by Peaceful Means: Peace and Conflict, Development and Civilization*. International Peace Research Institute, Oslo. London: Sage.

Garan, R. (2015). <u>*The Orbital Perspective: Lessons in Seeing the Big Picture from a Journey of 71 Million Miles*</u>. Oakland, CA: Berrett-Koehler.

Gómez, O. A. and Gasper, D. (2013). Human Security: A thematic guidance note for regional and national human development report teams. UNDP. Human Development Report Office. <u>https://repub.eur.nl/pub/50571/Metis_195152.pdf</u>

Grasso, D. and Burkins, M. B. (eds.) (2010). *Holistic Engineering Education, Beyond Technology*. New York: Springer Verlag.

Hayden, N. K. (2018). Balancing belligerents or feeding the beasts: Transforming conflict traps. University of Maryland Center for International Security Studies. https://api.drum.lib.umd.edu/server/api/core/bitstreams/2e1d6f39-f3ab-4db1-8b5b-0f61d7e38c25/content

Himelfarb, S. and Howard, P. (Oct. 7, 2021). What's stunning about the misinformation trend—and how to fix it. Opinion: What's stunning about the misinformation trend -- and how to fix it - CNN

Howard, P. N. (2020). *Lie Machines: How to Save Democracy from Troll Armies, Deceitful Robots, Junk News Operations, and Political Operatives.* New Haven: Yale University Press.

ICRC (2020). When Rain Turns to Dust: Understanding and Responding to the Combined Impact of Armed Conflicts and the Climate and Environment Crisis on People's lives; 07.2020; PDF (icrc.org)

Intergovernmental Panel on Climate Change (IPCC) (2023). *AR6 Synthesis Report: Climate Change, 2023.* AR6 Synthesis Report: Climate Change 2023 (ipcc.ch)

International Energy Agency (IEA) (n.d.). *What is energy security?* http://www.iea.org/topics/energysecurity/subtopics/whatisenergysecurity/ (Sept. 6, 2016).

International Fund for Agricultural Development (IFAD). 2015. *Land tenure security. Scale up note.* https://www.ifad.org/documents/10180/2606bb19-45dc-45af-8a38-a6bcfbcaec87.

Institute for Economics and Peace (IEP) (2020a). *Global Peace Index 2020: Measuring peace in a complex world.* http://visionofhumanity.org/reports

Institute for Economics and Peace (IEP) (2020b). *COVID-19 and Peace.* http://visionofhumanity.org/reports

Institute for Economics and Peace (IEP) (2021). *Economic value of peace 2021: Measuring the global economic impact of violence and conflict.* http://visionofhumanity.org/resources

Institute for Economics and Peace (IEP) (2022). *Positive Peace Report 2022: Analyzing the factors that build, predict, and sustain peace.* http://visionofhumanity.org/resources

Jacobs, G. (2016, Oct. 26). Integrated approach to peace and human security in the twenty-first century. Integrated Approach to Peace & Human Security in the 21st Century* | Cadmus Journal

Jenkins, T. (2019). Comprehensive peace education. In: M. Peters (eds.) *Encyclopedia of Teacher Education.* Singapore: Springer. https://doi.org/10.1007/978-981-13-1179-6_319-1

Kamp, A. (2016). *Engineering Education in the Rapidly Changing World: Rethinking the Vision for Higher Engineering Education* (2nd revised edition). The Netherlands: TU Delft, Faculty of Aerospace Engineering. https://repository.tudelft.nl/record/uuid:ae3b30e3-5380-4a07-afb5-dafd30b7b433

Kamp, A. (2020). *Navigating the Landscape of Higher Engineering Education: Coping with Decades of Accelerating Change Ahead* (1st edition), ISBN 978-94-6366-242-0

Koch, A., et al. (2013). Soil security: Solving the global soil crisis. *Global Policy*, DOI: 10.1111/1758-5899.12096.

Le Guardian (April 21, 2024). Global defense budget jumps to record high of $2440 bn.

Lemos, C. M. (2018). *Agent-Based Modeling of Social Conflict: From Mechanism to Complex Behavior*. Cham, Switzerland: Springer.

Leydens, J. A. and Lucena, J. C. (2017). *Engineering Justice: Transforming Engineering Education and Practice*. Hoboken, NJ: Wiley-IEEE.

Lu, J. (2020, April 17). What will COVID-19 do to the sustainable development goals? https://www.undispatch.com/what-will-covid-19-do-to-the-sustainable-development-goals/

MacroTrends (n.d.) World Life Expectancy 1950-2024 | MacroTrends

Martin, S., Brannigan, J., and Hall, A. (2005). Sustainability, systems thinking, and professional practice. *Journal of Geography in Higher Education*, **29**(1), 79–89.

Meshkati, N. (2012). Engineering diplomacy: An underutilized tool in foreign policy. *Science & Diplomacy*, **1**(2).

Milante, G., and Oxhorn, P. (2009). *No development without peace*. World Bank Open Knowledge Repository. https://openknowledge.worldbank.org/handle/10986/4582

Moriarty-Lempke, et al. (2022). *Conflict Sensitivity in Land Governance: The Do No Harm Framework and Other Tools for Practitioners of Land Activities*. Cambridge, MA: CDA Collaborative Learning Projects.

Mr. Y. (2011). *A National Strategic Narrative*. Washington, DC: Woodrow Wilson International Center for Scholars.

Muscat, M. J. (2014). Peace and conflict: Engineering responsibilities and opportunities. *Proceedings of the ASEE North-Midwest Section Conference*, Iowa City, IA, 16–17, October.

Narayan, D., et al. (1999). *Can anyone hear us? Voices from 47 countries* (Vol. 1 from Voices of the Poor). Washington, DC: The World Bank. https://documents.worldbank.org/en/publication/documents-reports/docu

mentdetail/131441468779067441/voices-of-the-poor-can-anyone-hear-us

National Academy of Engineering (2002). *Raising Public Awareness of Engineering.* Washington, DC: The National Academies Press. https://doi.org/10.17226/10573

National Academy of Engineering (2008). *Changing the Conversation: Messages for Improving Public Understanding of Engineering.* Washington, DC: The National Academies Press. https://doi.org/10.17226/12187.

National Academies of Sciences, Engineering, and Medicine. (NASEM) (2017). *The Role of Science, Technology, Innovation, and Partnerships IN THE Future of USAID.* Washington, DC: The National Academies Press.

National Academies of Sciences, Engineering, and Medicine (NASEM) (2023). *2023 Nobel Prize Summit: Truth, Trust, and Hope: Proceedings of a Summit.* Washington, DC: The National Academies Press, https://doi.org/10.17226/27247.

National Intelligence Council (NIC) (2021). Climate Change and International Responses Increasing Challenges to the US National Security through 2040. NIE_Climate_Change_and_National_Security.pdf (dni.gov)

National Research Council (NRC) (1999). *The Pervasive Role of Science, Technology, and Health in Foreign Policy: Imperatives for the Department of State.* Washington, DC: The National Academies Press.

National Research Council (NRC) (2014). *Strategic Engagement in Global S&T: Opportunities for Defense Research.* Washington, DC: The National Academies Press.

National Research Council (NRC) (2015). *Diplomacy for the 21st Century. Embedding a Culture of Science and Technology Throughout the Department of State.* Washington, DC: The National Academies Press.

OCHA (2023, December 11). Global Humanitarian Overview 2024. Global Humanitarian Overview 2024 [EN/AR/FR/ES] | OCHA (unocha.org)

Olivier, I. (2022, Aug. 18). US universities are pipelines to the defense industry. What does that say about our morals? U.S. universities are pipelines to the defense industry. What does that say about our morals? | Indigo Olivier | The Guardian

Organization for Economic Cooperation and Development (OECD) (2018). States of fragility: Highlights. OECD Highlights documents web.pdf

Palmer, P. J. and Zajonc, A. (2010). *The Heart of Higher Education: A Call to Renewal.* San Francisco, CA: Jossey-Bass.

Polak, P. (2008). *Out of Poverty: What Works When Traditional Approaches Fail?* San Francisco, CA: Berrett-Koehler.

Ponzio, R. (2023, Sept. 11). Six issues to watch at UNGA 78. Six Issues to Watch at UNGA 78 • Stimson Center.

Rapaport, B. (2024). Climate agreements as a foundation for peace. Mitvim Institute, Israel. https://mitvim.org.il/.

Raworth, K. (2018). *Doughnut Economics: SEVEN Ways to Think Like a 21st-Century Economist.* UK: Random House.

Reynolds, A. (2013). Diplomacy, Development, Defense, and Engineering. *Mechanical Engineering*, **153**(3), 18.

Riley, D. (2008). *Engineering and Social Justice.* San Diego, CA: Morgan & Claypool.

Rothkopf, D. J. (11 May 2003). When the buzz bites back. *The Washington Post*, p. B.01. When the Buzz Bites Back - The Washington Post

Sachs, J. D., Lafortune, G., Fuller, G., and Drumm, E. (2023). *Implementing the SDG Stimulus. Sustainable Development Report 2023*. Dublin University Press.

Schirch, L. (2013). *Conflict Assessment and Peacebuilding Planning: Toward a Participatory Approach to Human Security.* Boulder, CO: Lynne Rienner.

Schön, D. (1971). *Beyond the Stable State: Public and Private Learning in a Changing Society.* London: Maurice Temple Smith.

Schumacher, E. F. (1973). *Small Is Beautiful.* New York, NY: Harper Perennial.

Sharifi, A., Simangan, D., Kaneko, S., *et al.* (2021). The sustainability-peace nexus: Why is it important? *Sustainability Science*, **16**, 1073–1077. https://doi.org/10.1007/s11625-021-00986-z

Smith, C. E. (2022). *Designing Peace: Building a Better Future.* New York: Cooper Hewitt. https://www.cooperhewitt.org/publications/designing-peace-building-a-better-future-now/

Snodderly, D. (ed.) (2018). *Peace Terms. Glossary of Terms for Conflict Management and Peacebuilding* (2nd edition). Washington, DC: US Institute of Peace.

Sumner, A., Hoy, C., and Ortiz-Juarez, E. (2020). Estimates of the impact of COVID-19 on global poverty. United Nations University-WIDER. https://www.wider.unu.edu/publication/estimates-impact-covid-19-global-poverty#

Sustainable Development Solutions Network (SDSN) (2020). *Indicators and a monitoring framework: Launching a data revolution for the sustainable development goals.* https://indicators.report

TAP Network (2023). Halfway-to-2030-Report-Digital.pdf (sdg16now.org)

The Earth Charter (1987). Read the Earth Charter - Earth Charter

The Economist (2021, Dec. 18). The new normal is already here. Get used to it. The era of predictable unpredictability is not going away. The new normal is already here. Get used to it | The Economist

The New Humanitarian (2024, January 8). Why these 10 humanitarian crises deserve your attention now? The New Humanitarian | Why these 10 humanitarian crises demand your attention now

The World Bank (2023). The development, climate, and nature crisis: Solutions to end poverty on a livable planet. CCDR-SynthesisReport2023.pdf

Thompson, S. A. (2022, Aug. 31). Many developed countries view online misinformation as a 'major threat.' *New York Times.* Many Developed Countries View Online Misinformation as 'Major Threat' - The New York Times (nytimes.com)

Tian, N., Lopes da Silva, D., Liang, X., and Scarazzat, L. (2024). Trends in world military expenditures, 2023. Stockholm International Peace Research Institute (SIPRI) https://ipb.org/trends-in-world-military-expenditure-2023/

Tooley, C. (2021, Jan. 18). What systems thinking actually means – and why it matters for innovation today. World Economic Forum. What 'systems thinking' actually means - and why it matters today | World Economic Forum (weforum.org)

United Nations. (UN) (2023). Information integrity on digital platforms. our-common-agenda-policy-brief-information-integrity-en.pdf (un.org)

United Nations. (UN) (2024). *The United Nations World Water Development Report 2024: Water for Prosperity and Peace.* Paris: UNESCO. https://www.unwater.org/publications/un-world-water-development-report-2024

United Nations Trust Fund for Human Security (n.d.). What is security? What is Human Security? – The Human Security Unit

United Nations General Assembly (UNGA) (1999). UN resolution 53/243. *Declaration and Programme of Action on a Culture of Peace.* https://undocs.org/en/A/RES/53/243

United Nations General Assembly (UNGA) (2012). UN resolution 66/290. What is Human Security? – The Human Security Unit.

United Nations (UN) (2015). Transforming our world: The 2030 agenda for sustainable development. https://www.un.org/ga/search/view_doc.asp?symbol=A/RES/70/1&Lang=E

United Nations Conference on Environment and Development (UNCED) (1992). Agenda 21. http://www.un.org/esa/sustdev/documents/agenda21/english/Agenda21.pdf

UNHCR (2024). How climate change impacts refugees and displaced populations. How climate change impacts refugees and displaced communities (unrefugees.org)

United Nations Sustainable Development Goals (UNSDG) (2022). The 5Ps of the SDGs: People, Planet, Prosperity, Peace and Partnership. https://unsdg.un.org/latest/videos/5ps-sdgs-people-planet-prosperity-peace-and-partnership

United Nations University (2013). *Water Security and Global Water Agenda. A UN-Water Analytical Brief.* New York, NY: UNU-INWEH.

United Nations Conference on Environment and Development (UNCED) (1992). Agenda 21. http://www.un.org/esa/sustdev/documents/agenda21/english/Agenda21.pdf.

UNDP Human Development Report (UNDP/HDR) (1990). Concepts and measurement of human development. United Nations Development Programme, New York, NY.

UNDP Human Development Report (UNDP/HDR) (1994). New dimensions of human security. United Nations Development Programme, New York, NY.

UNDP Human Development Report (UNDP/HDR) (2010). The real wealth of nations: Pathways to human development. United Nations Development Programme, New York, NY.

UNDP Human Development Report (UNDP/HDR) (2022). The human development report 2021/2022. Uncertain times, and unsettled lives, shaping our future in a transforming world. Human Development Report 2021/2022 | United Nations Development Programme (undp.org)

U.N. Development Programme (UNDP) (2021). *UNDP Annual Report.* UNDP Annual Report 2021 | United Nations Development Programme

U.N. Development Programme (UNDP) (2022). New threats to human security in the Anthropocene: Demanding greater solidarity. srhs2022pdf.pdf (undp.org)

U.N. Development Programme (UNDP) (2023). Global progress report on Sustainable Development Goal 16 indicators: A wake-up call for action on peace, justice, and inclusion. Global Progress Report on SDG 16 | United Nations Development Programme (undp.org)

U.N. Economic and Social Commission for Asia and the Pacific (UNESCAP) (2018). PB78_The nexus between peace and sustainable development in Asia-Pacific countries with special needs_final.pdf (unescap.org)

U.N. Educational, Scientific, and Cultural Organization (UNESCO) (1994). *The culture of peace program: From national programs to a project of global scope.* http://www.culture-of-peace.info/vita/1994/145EX15.pdf

UN Environmental Programme (UNEP) (2024). Environmental impact of the conflict in Gaza: Preliminary assessment of environmental impacts. Nairobi. edocs.unep.org/20.500.11822/45739

Van Langenhove, L. (2016). *Global Science Diplomacy as a New Tool for Global Governance.* Barcelona, Spain: Federació d'Organitzacions Catalanes Internacionalmente Reconegudes (FOCIR).

Vesilind, P. A. (ed.) (2005). *Peace Engineering: When Personal Values and Engineering Careers Converge.* Woodsville, NH: Lakeshore Press.

Vesilind, P. A. (2010). *Engineering Peace and Justice: The Responsibility of Engineers to Society.* London: Springer.

Vincenti, W. G. (1991). Introduction. In: H. E. Sladovich (ed.), *Engineering as a Social Enterprise.* Washington, DC: The National Academies Press, 1–4.

Virji, H., Sharifi, A., Kaneko, S., et al. (2019) The sustainability–peace nexus in the context of global change. *Sustainability Science*, **14**, 1467–1468. https://doi.org/10.1007/s11625-019-00737-1. Accessed May 1, 2020.

von Grebmer, K., Ringler, C., Rosegrant, M. W., Olofinbiyi, T., et al. (2012). *Global Hunger Index, the Challenge of Hunger: Ensuring Sustainable Food Security Under Land, Water, and Energy Stresses.* Bonn/Washington DC: International Food Policy Research Institute. http://dx.doi.org/10.2499/9780896299429

Weissbourd, R., Batanova, M., Lovison, V., and Torres, E. (2021). Loneliness in America: How the pandemic has deepened an epidemic of loneliness and what we can do about it. Loneliness in America: How the Pandemic Has Deepened an Epidemic of Loneliness — Making Caring Common (harvard.edu)

Wolfe, S. E. and Smith, L. K. M. (2021). *Death becomes us: How our emotions can help avoid climate disaster.* Sarah Elizabeth Wolfe and Lauren Keira Marie Smith – Ernest Becker Foundation.

World Economic Forum (WEF) (2023). The Global Risks Report 2023 (18th edition). https://www3.weforum.org/docs/WEF_Global_Risks_Report_2023.pdf

World Economic Forum (WEF) (2024). The Global Risks Report 2024 (19th edition). https://www3.weforum.org/docs/WEF_The_Global_Risks_Report_2024.pdf

Wulf, Wm. A. (2020). Great achievements and grand challenges. *The Bridge*, **30**(3/4), 5–10.

Zarocostas, J. (2020). How to fight an infodemic. *Lancet*, **395**, 676. https://doi.org/10.1016/S0140-6736(20)30461-X

Zwijnenburg, W. and Hall, N. (2023). Uninhabitable: The reverberating public health and environmental risks from the war in Gaza. https://paxforpeace.nl/wp-content/uploads/sites/2/2023/12/PAX_Report_Gaza_Uninhabitable_FIN.pdf

Chapter 2

Engineering Engagement for a Small Planet

Engineering for peace and diplomacy is deeply intertwined with society. Its impact extends from improving people's daily lives to contributing to international relations and resolving conflict. Engineers involved in peace and diplomacy must be globally engaged and educated accordingly. A new epistemology of lifelong engineering education is urgently needed to address the challenges of the 21st-century world, one that is based on the idea of social responsibility and awareness, systems thinking, engagement, leadership, teamwork, reflective and adaptive practice, and field exposure to problems. Engineers must continuously learn to meet the changing and diverse needs of society. Engineering education that prepares students for global engagement should address these needs.

Our economic and social health depends directly on the health of the engineering endeavor, and the health of engineering depends, in turn, on the support of society (NAE, 1985).

Today, engineering has an unprecedented opportunity to exercise leadership in showing how technology can offer the means to create a better world out of the ashes of collapsing or obsolete political and economic systems (Bugliarello, 1991).

Engineers should accept more responsibility for considering potential unintended consequences of their work and seek to minimize the possibility of their occurrences (Anderson, 2022).

Engineering for Peace and Diplomacy
Bernard Amadei
Copyright © 2025 Jenny Stanford Publishing Pte. Ltd.
ISBN 978-981-5129-75-5 (Hardcover), 978-1-003-65168-0 (eBook)
www.jennystanford.com

2.1 Engineering in Society

The interaction between engineering and society has been debated for the past 150 years. Although it is clear to most of us that engineering and society are deeply interconnected (Table 2.1) and have been so for a long time, this was not always the case. For instance, in the first part of the nineteenth century, the dominant view held that engineering should develop apart from society and that technology was nothing more than applied science and economics. Science historians refer to this approach as internalist or determinist (Hughes, 1991). For some authors, such as Florman (1994), the 'existential pleasure' of engineering is independent of how it affects society as long as sound engineering is carried out.

Table 2.1 Engineering and society are deeply interconnected: Positive impacts (OpenAI, 2024)

Impacts of engineering on society*	– Engineers create service structures and critical infrastructures vital to modern societies.
	– Engineers hold a crucial position in the progress of technology, which has numerous social, cultural, and economic repercussions.
	– Engineering has given rise to numerous technological advancements which have greatly enhanced the quality of life for many individuals.
	– Engineers develop sustainable solutions impacting political policies and societal practices.
	– Engineers play a vital role in ensuring safety by designing systems and structures prioritizing human life protection and contributing to adaptation and mitigation of natural and human-induced adverse events.
Impacts of society on engineering	– The values and norms of society can determine the types of engineering projects that receive financial backing and attention. In cultures where sustainability is highly valued, there is a greater likelihood of investment in eco-friendly technology.
	– The growing awareness of climate change has led to a focus on renewable energy in engineering practices shaped by societal ethics.
	– Engineering sectors tend to grow based on which products or services are in demand, which is determined by the economy.

*See also the Greatest Engineering Achievements of the Twentieth Century (great-achievements.org)

Engineering has played an essential role in society over the ages (Sprague de Camp, 1963). Until the late 18th century, military engineering was predominant, centered on building defensive fortifications and developing offensive weaponry (Vesilind, 2010; Klosky and Klosky, 2013). Civilian branches of engineering began to grow and advance in Europe during the 18th century and continued into the Western world throughout the 19th century. During this period, military engineers were tasked with private projects, leading to increased field advancements. Different engineering fields (civil, mechanical, electrical, industrial, chemical, etc.) define the engineering profession, each with its own values, best practices, and ethics. Engineering in the United States has evolved as a mixture of French military techniques and British civil engineering practices (Vesilind, 2010). The American Society of Civil Engineers (ASCE) was founded in 1852, followed by other professional organizations such as ASME in 1880, ASEE in 1893, AIChE in 1908, NSPE in 1934, IEEE in 1963, AIAA in 1963, etc. One must wait until the 20th century and after WWII to see other fields, such as environmental engineering and broader focused engineering programs (rather than disciplines), including biomedical engineering, earth systems engineering, humanitarian engineering, development engineering, and systems engineering, cutting across different technical and non-technical fields.

Three quantum leaps in the relationship between engineering and society are outlined below. It should be noted that this relationship remains unfolding. The question is how it will develop in a VUCA world context in the 21st century and how to prepare engineers accordingly. Today's graduates are likely to (i) make decisions 20–30 years in a different world from now, (ii) have jobs that do not yet exist, and (iii) use tools and technologies that have not yet been invented (Did You Know 3.0, 2011). Engineers are likely to operate in a world where knowledge becomes rapidly obsolete and is replaced by something new within a few years.

2.1.1 First Quantum Leap

The first quantum leap to change the dynamics between technology and society and shape the engineering profession occurred during the second half of the 19th century and the first half of the 20th century. The period from 1850 to 1950 is often regarded as the Golden Age of Engineering when engineers' importance and contributions to society were unquestioned (Florman, 1976). Technology in the Western world meant material progress and growth at all costs, never-ending technical improvement, and "maximization of profits for owners and stakeholders" (Huesemann and Huesemann, 2011). The thinking behind engineering practice and education at that time was based on *technical rationality*, providing value-neutral technical solutions to well-defined problems, following the deterministic attitude of the nineteenth century (Schön, 1983). Deeply rooted in the deterministic values of the Enlightenment period, this mindset helped define "the proper division of labor between the university and the professions" in the Western world and the "split between research and practice" (ibid.). It also helped to craft the concept of the 'expert' as one who focused on narrowly technical practice. However, these experts were not supposed to include socioeconomic, political, or environmental factors and values in their technical decisions. Therefore, experts are less likely to address these global issues. A good example demonstrating the pitfalls of extreme industrialization expertise in the former Soviet Union can be found in the book titled *The Ghost of the Executed Engineer* (Graham, 1993).

An underlying assumption of technical rationality is to constantly provide technical solutions to societal problems and promote new technologies to replace old problematic technologies. However, new technologies create more problems, such as environmental pollution (Commoner, 1972). This dynamic creates "an illusion of infinite material growth and consumption into the future," which is good for the economy from a business standpoint, not necessarily for people and the environment. As mentioned by Karwat (2019), the key question is as follows:

> Why are engineers and corporations almost always willing to design and build the technologies that cause those problems, sometimes despite knowing about the negative consequences of those technologies?

2.1.2   Second Quantum Leap

The second quantum leap, which changed the dynamics between technology and society, shaped the engineering profession from the 1960s to the 1990s (Wallace, 2005). It was driven by the environmental and sustainability movement born out of the publication of *Silent Spring* (Carson, 1962), *The Limits to Growth* (Meadows et al., 2004), sponsored by the Club of Rome, and *Our Common Future* (WCED, 1987), produced by the Brundtland Commission. The latter defined sustainable development as "development that meets the needs and aspirations of the present without compromising the ability of future generations to meet their own needs." The environmental movement emerged as a response to unrestrained confidence in technology and the belief that the economy and environment were compatible, a mindset that had been prevalent for the past half-century (Chertow, 2000).

Since the 1970s, the environmental and sustainability movement has involved multiple twists and turns. At the turn of the 21st century, Nattrass and Altomare (2001) summarized the evolution of this movement from compliance in the 1970s with multiple regulations to beyond compliance in the 1980s, eco-efficiency in the 1990s, and endorsement of sustainable development in the early 2000s. Industry goals and corporate responses differed in each era. They evolved from being unprepared before the 1970s to reactive in the 1970s, anticipatory in the 1980s, proactive in the 1990s, and more open-minded and holistic in the 2000s. This transition can also be seen from "doing nothing" to "doing what pays," "doing a fair share," and "doing no harm" using the terminology of Raworth (2018).

Over the past 20 years, sustainability has become a part of the daily vocabulary of all sectors of the economy: public, private, academia, and government. When not used as a buzzword, it has been presented as a radical new platform for research, education, technology, and business opportunities in the developed world. Despite this enthusiasm, the sustainability movement has been controversial in some political and economic circles. Today, it is perceived in many ways by various political and economic groups as (i) a buzzword and academic virtual concept, (ii) an environmental luxury for wealthy and established communities in the developed world, and (iii) a threat to rapid economic growth in emerging markets. There are still reservations (primarily political) in some corporate sectors regarding the value proposition of sustainable development, as it is often misperceived as a deterrent to economic growth. The same can be said regarding how political and economic groups perceive peace and climate change (Stoddard et al., 2021).

A benchmark in the evolution of sustainable development was the 1992 United Nations Conference on Environment and Development, also known as the Rio Summit. This conference helped pave the way for many issues that are still of concern today: economic development, climate change, and poverty reduction (Wallace, 2005). A significant outcome of the Rio Summit was the publication of *Agenda 21* (UNCED, 1992), a blueprint for action in all aspects of human activities, consisting of 40 chapters with 120 separate action programs. The Rio Summit exemplifies the critical role of science and technology in shaping future societies and global health. It also emphasizes society's crucial role in shaping technological and economic decisions. Several scientific and engineering committees were established, and conferences and workshops were held to address the recommendations of Agenda 21. Roberts (2002) provides a helpful review of these initiatives.

The Rio Summit and subsequent initiatives such as the Millennium Development Goals (MDGs), the Sustainable Development Goals (SDGs) under *Agenda 2030*, and the 14 Global Grand Engineering Challenges,[1] endorsed by several engineering academies in China, the United Kingdom, and the United States, have created a significant revival and a renewed sense of purpose for the engineering profession, something comparable to the "can-do" attitude that drove the Golden Age of the 1850–1950 and the post–World War II area. The quote by Bugliarello (1991) at the start of this chapter is more relevant today than ever and, if acted upon, could support a new vision and rebranding of what engineers do—an "image of the engineer" that is broader,

---

[1]Grand Challenges – 14 Grand Challenges for Engineering (engineeringchallenges. org)

more global-facing, and potentially more relevant to a younger generation. Such a transformation could also help increase engineering enrolment (Moskal et al., 2008).

Sustainable development is not concerned only with implementing technical fixes. Instead, it is an integrated approach and a new emerging mindset that balances technology and several aspects of society, such as social and cultural well-being, justice, the rule of law, a safe and secure environment, and politically stable democracy at the personal, relational, structural, and cultural levels (Schirch, 2013). Another way to look at sustainable development is to see it as unfolding across five essential interacting elements: people, planet, prosperity, partnerships, and peace. These are sometimes called the 5Ps of sustainable development (Ryan, 2020; UNESCWA, 2021), as shown in Figure 2.1. They are integral components of Agenda 2030. The 5Ps approach is, for example, implicitly included in the definition of sustainability by the American Society of Civil Engineers (ASCE, 2023), where sustainability is seen as "a set of environmental, social, and economic conditions (aka 'The Triple Bottom Line') in which all of society has the capacity and opportunity to maintain and improve its quality of life indefinitely without degrading the quantity, quality, or the availability of environmental, social, and economic resources. Infrastructure shall be planned, designed, constructed, operated, maintained, and decommissioned to address quantifiable and non-quantifiable environmental, social, and economic benefits and costs over its entire lifecycle. Sustainable development is the application of these resources to enhance the safety, welfare, and quality of life for all of society."

Sustainable development raises the question of whether we can develop a mindset and strategies to (i) stay within the limits of our available resources and carrying capacities and (ii) avoid (or minimize) irreversible long-term negative environmental, economic, and social consequences in future production-distribution-consumption models that could impact developed and developing countries alike. According to Wallace (2005), sustainable development represents a formidable challenge for society and offers unique opportunities for scientific and engineering professionals to do well by doing good.

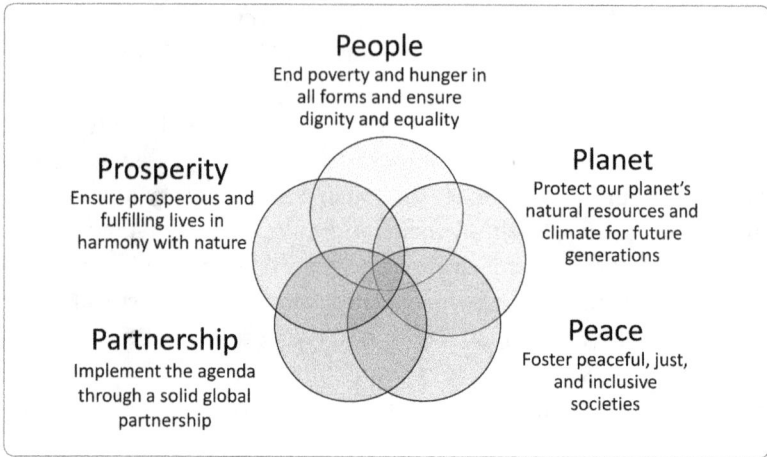

Figure 2.1 Five overlapping components of sustainable development according to Agenda 2030.

Moving toward sustainability will require more or less a complete overhaul of the world's infrastructure, replacing or refurbishing existing systems with new, cleaner, and more efficient processes, systems, and technologies. As such, new world markets for sustainable engineering services are being created as industries and governments begin changing to more sustainable practices.

The question remains whether the human race is ready to transition to a world where "the business of business" is not just about profit but contributes to a thriving world for all (Raworth, 2018).

2.1.3   Third Quantum Leap

At the start of the third decade of the 21st century, a third quantum leap likely to shape the dynamics between technology and society and the engineering profession in the 21st century is emerging. The engineering profession is challenged to address highly complex issues in the VUCA world, as discussed in Chapter 1. Over the next two decades, the global population is estimated to rise to 9 billion, 97 percent of whom will be born in developing regions or states classified as least developed countries (UNDESA, 2015). A peak in the world's population is estimated to occur around 2085, followed by a subsequent rapid decline.

Population growth and worldwide increases in food and energy prices have forced the international community to consider the links between water, energy, and food resources more closely (Dresden Nexus Conference, 2015; Amadei, 2019). By 2050, global food, energy, and water demands will grow by 60 percent, 80 percent, and 55 percent, respectively (Ferroukhi et al., 2015). This growth will occur in the already existing context of uneven resource scarcity, in which the consumption of water, energy, and food resources are interconnected. Water, energy, and food can be the root causes, weapons, or casualties of conflict.

In addition to meeting the demands associated with population growth and providing the necessary infrastructure, other issues affecting human and economic development include increasingly competitive needs for water, energy, and food resources, both within and across various sectors (domestic, industrial, and agricultural), and requests from groups of consumers who may or may not be on different sides of a geopolitical border (The Economist, 2019). If resource allocation is not adequately addressed, compromises in the development, management, and distribution of natural resources across groups and sectors can create unintended negative consequences, risks, uncertainties, and conflicts that could adversely affect large populations, especially those living in poor and marginalized communities.

Climate change is another critical factor for human development and security in the 21st century, as it exacerbates inequity divisions, accelerates poverty in some regions, and creates conflict (The World Bank, 2023; Amadei, 2023). Table 2.2 lists the various effects of climate change on human security as identified by the National Intelligence Council (NIC, 2021).

As noted in the Global Risks reports of the WEF (2023, 2024), climate change–generated risks affect health, ecosystems, infrastructure, the economy, equity, justice, migration, conflict, and so on. These risks will likely "push one-third of humanity out of its most liveable environment… facing extreme heat, food scarcity, and higher death rates" in the 21st century (Lustgarten, 2023). The World Health Organization projects over 250,000 additional deaths each year between 2030 and 2050, attributable to climate change-driven increases in temperature (heat waves), diarrhea, malaria, and malnutrition (crop failure) (WHO, 2021). Climate change could push an additional 100 million people seeking safe havens back into poverty by 2030 (Carter et al., 2018), resulting in population displacement ranging between 143 million (Rigaud et al., 2018) and 1.2 billion (IEP, 2020) by 2050. Displacement may occur in regions threatened by climate change, such as dry areas or low-lying communities that are at risk of coastal-related hazards. Migration to urban areas results in significant challenges regarding food and water security, employment, and economic stability (Wennmann, 2023).

Table 2.2 Multiple effects and impacts of climate change on human security as greenhouse gas emissions and temperature increases (NIC, 2021, p. 2) (in open domain)

Climate Change Effects	Impacts on Human Security
Heat	More intense and frequent heat waves will reduce labor productivity, increase the frequency and intensity of wildfires, undermine human health, and lead to loss of life.
Heavy Precipitation and Flooding	Increased flooding will lead to economic losses, increased calls for humanitarian assistance, and loss of life.
Drought	More frequent, intense, and prolonged droughts will undermine food security in developing countries, cause extreme wildfires, increase political instability, and drive migration.
Sea Level Rise	Rising sea levels will increasingly imperil coastal cities and exacerbate storm surges that damage infrastructure and water systems.
Arctic Ice Melt	The accelerated melting of Arctic ice sheets will affect ocean circulation and salinity, threaten local ecosystems, and increase competition over resources and transit route access.
Tropical Cyclones	More frequent, destructive, and shifting tracks of cyclones will lead to trillions of dollars in economic losses in tropical zones, increase calls for humanitarian assistance, drive population displacement and migration, and lead to loss of life.
Coral Reefs	The disappearance of coral reefs will eliminate an ecosystem that serves 500 million people, impacting economic and food security.
Biodiversity	Loss of species will increase human health risks and threaten food security.

Most deaths and hardships associated with climate change will be experienced in developing countries, those least equipped to manage climate change, and those least responsible for its causes. Engineers are critical for developing mitigating infrastructure, creating awareness, and implementing adaptive and transformative actions for climate-related disaster risk reduction. More specifically, the challenge is to empower resilient communities in different contexts with the capacity to handle climate shocks (e.g., extreme storms, heatwaves, and flooding) and stressors (e.g., droughts, rising sea levels, and rising temperatures). However, climate adaptation finance, planning, and implementation are insufficient to keep up with the accelerating risks and impacts of weather extremes (UNEP, 2023), which is particularly critical in developing countries.

Achieving the United Nations Agenda 2030 and other development goals in the 21st century will be unattainable without the wholehearted involvement of the engineering profession. However, relying solely on the same approaches and knowledge that have contributed to the significant accomplishments of the past century and unforeseen outcomes may be insufficient. Considering our VUCA world's problems, the engineering profession must reassess its mindset and contribute to building a more sustainable, stable, and equitable world by building on its significant achievements in the twentieth century and expanding them to all humans, regardless of their level of development, and not just to a limited number in the developed world. Current engineering solutions promoting human development and security should not exacerbate past weaknesses, nor should they create problems for the future.

The critical question is to identify and address what needs to be done proactively, now and in the immediate future, for all humans to meet their basic needs (i.e., water, sanitation, nutrition, health, safety, meaningful work, etc.) and live with dignity and peace. What role should engineers play in meeting this goal?

2.2 A Technical Wonderland and a Waste World

2.2.1 A Cradle-to-Grave Mindset

The quality of life in many societies is based on a complex and highly productive set of technological, industrial, and municipal systems and structures. Continuing scientific discoveries, the proliferation of knowledge and information, and globalization have resulted in thousands of new products and services, all contributing to previously unthinkable increases in health, comfort, and productivity levels. Moreover, over the past 50 years, these advances have been accomplished more quickly and with surprising ease. With the advent of digital technologies and social media, people, especially those living in the developed world, have been conditioned to expect solutions to new problems to appear almost immediately. All these factors are due in no small way to the contributions of scientists, technicians, and engineers.

Ironically, these technical successes have also contributed to technology's unplanned or undesirable effects on natural and human systems and multiple negative externalities. This dynamic is captured in the $I = PAT$ equation proposed by Ehrlich and Holdren (1971), where I is the environmental impact of human development, P is the human population, A is the consumption per capita (affluence), and T is the environmental impact associated with each unit of consumption related to technology. The product $F = AT$ represents the environmental impact per capita. Chertow (2000) provides a review of the different variants of the $I = PAT$ equation proposed by Ehrlich and Holdren (1971) and Commoner (1972), including a nonlinear variant $I = P(I, F) \times F(P)$.

Technology's unplanned and undesirable effects can potentially create conflicts and affect the 5Ps of sustainable development mentioned above (Fig. 2.1). In many ways, technology has progressed faster than society's ability to adjust to such changes. As Berry (1990) noted, over the past 150 years of the Industrial Revolution, we have witnessed the creation of a technical wonderland alongside a technical wasteland. This dynamic is illustrated in the schematic of Fig. 2.2, which shows a *cradle-to-grave* (take-make-use/consume-waste) production–consumption model that has been the driving force of the Western world (and exported to the rest of the world) throughout the Industrial Revolution.

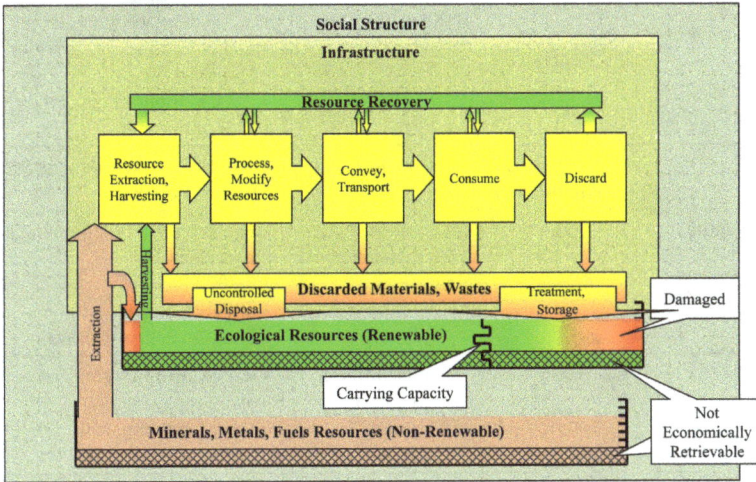

Figure 2.2 Cradle-to-Grave production consumption model: Take-Make-Use/Consume-Waste. Reproduced with permission from Wallace (2005).

The cradle-to-grave model is a linear model of degenerative economic growth. It is resource-intensive, generates considerable waste, and contributes to a significant societal ecological footprint in which essential resources are used faster than they can be replaced or replenished. Waste is absorbed more slowly than is generated and accumulated. The global average human footprint in 2022 was 1.7 planets,[2] far beyond the capacity of the single planet available. This disparity is due to the diverse societal structures that drive the production-consumption model, ranging from country to country. Biocapacity-debtor countries with a footprint more significant than their available biocapacity usually assume that there is an unlimited source of raw non-renewable resources and energy and that technology will continuously develop appropriate solutions (naïve techno-optimism).

---

[2]Ecological Footprint© - Global Footprint Network

Table 2.3 A selected list of events illustrating the unintended harmful consequences of technology and engineering

Events	Year	Causes of problem	Impacts
Kakthovka Dam (Ukraine)	2023	Intentional breaching of the dam spillway	• Loss of power • 52 fatalities • 2,200 displaced people • 1 M with no access to water • Flooding • Drying upper areas of the river • Environmental
DDT	Until 1972, in the US	Irresponsible spraying	• Toxicity to environment and human health
Bhopal, India	1984	Toxic gas leak from a pesticide plant	• Exposure to 500,000 people near a gas leak • 3,787 killed • 558,125 injuries • Long-term health effects
Chernobyl (Ukraine)	1986	The nuclear plant reactor exploded and burned	• Radiation spreading and exposure over large areas • Long-term impact for 20,000 years
Love Canal	1978	Burial of 22,000 tons of hazardous chemical waste	• Long-term exposure to chemical waste • Health issues (leukemia) to 100s of residents
Fukushima	2011	Insufficient cooling of nuclear reactors after shutdown following earthquake and tsunami	• Release of radioactive contaminants in the environment • Displacement of 164,000 residents in the surrounding area • Long-term effects
Oil spills (inland and offshore) Valdez, Nigeria, Liberia, Ecuador, etc.	On-going	Accidental and negligence, illegal activities, human error, natural disasters, aging infrastructure, and weak regulations	• Significant and multifaceted impacts on the environment, wildlife, and human communities
Water contamination in Flint, MI	2014–present	Poor decision-making, failure to implement corrosion control measures, and inadequate government response	• Elevated levels of lead and other contaminants in drinking water • Lead poisoning in many children and outbreaks of Legionnaires' disease resulted in several deaths and illnesses • Socio-economic environmental impact

Events	Year	Causes of problem	Impacts
Rocky Flats, CO	1950s–1980s	Release of radioactive and toxic materials into the environment	• Affecting soil, groundwater, and surrounding areas • Risks to both the environment and public health
Fossil fuel burning	On-going	Negligence driven by human activities and industrial processes	• Impact on the environment, human health, and the global climate
Forever chemicals	On-going	Chemical products that have not been tested persist in the environment for a long time without breaking down naturally	• Widespread environmental contamination caused by accumulation in soil, water, and bodies of animals and humans • Health concerns and risks
Militarism	On-going	Society's prioritization of military power and willingness to use it to achieve political and strategic objectives	• Geo-political, socio-economic, political, and environmental impact • Violence, conflict, destruction, death • Loss of civilian lives, displacement, and human rights violations
Extractive industry, mining, oil and gas extraction, and logging	On-going	Combination of factors related to the industry's operations and resource extraction dynamics	• Socio-economic-environmental-health impact • Climate change and greenhouse emissions • Loss of cultural identity and heritage
Three Gorges Dam China	Date	Flooding of large area	• Displacement and resettlement • Environmental damage
Tacoma Narrows Bridge	1940	Wind effect and flaws in structural design	• Bridge collapse
The Everglades, FL	1910s – 1970s	Draining of swamp to reclaim farming land	• Drying up of swamp areas, loss of wildlife, forest fires
Teton Dam, ID	1976	Dam failure	• 11 dead
Austin Dam, PA	1911	Dam failure	• 78 dead
Malpasset Dam, France	1959	Dam failure	• 423 dead
Vaoint Dam, Italy	1969	Landslide and flooding	• >2,000 dead
St Francis Dam, CA	1928	Dam failure	• 431 dead
Three Miles Island	1979	Mechanical and human errors leading to partial meltdown	• Dangerous radioactive gases were released into the atmosphere
Nuclear explosions (1054 conducted by US)	1945–1992	Uncontrolled radiation. Trinity, Atolls	• Incidences of cancer • Long term contamination

Table 2.3 provides various historical instances (among numerous others) of the unforeseen detrimental impacts of technology and engineering over the past five decades, with some arising from the dynamics illustrated in Fig. 2.2. Additional examples can be found in a study by Muscat et al. (2015).

These undesirable effects on communities worldwide, signs of an uncontrolled growth economy, have been objects of criticism by society, starting with the anti-technology movement of the 1970s in response to issues such as the unrestricted use of DDT (Carson, 1962; Conis, 2017). In her book *Silent Spring*, Carson challenged the notion that DDT and other pesticides are safe for everyday use and questioned the effects of synthetic chemicals on the environment. More comprehensive studies on these effects have been initiated worldwide, examining the impact of chemicals on the environment and the relationship and importance of the environment on global economic growth and development.

Technical decisions with negative consequences have sparked criticism of engineering, particularly those driven by militarism and extractivism. In general, as Karwat (2019) observes, it is essential to acknowledge that.

> The miracles of engineering sit squarely alongside abuse, exploitation, inequity, and degradation in which the pursuits and products of engineering are implicated.

It is reasonable to assert that the impact of all technologies, whether innovative or refined versions of existing ones, is multi-faceted and has both beneficial and detrimental consequences. For example, automobiles and air transport provide both mobility and transportation. They also contribute to urban decay, noise pollution, emissions, particulate matter, urban and rural landscape destruction, human and animal death, dependence on long-distance transportation for goods and services, CO_2 emissions, and the disposal of mined metals, solvents, plastics, and other materials (Karwat et al., 2014). As remarked by Schumacher (1973)

> If that which has been shaped by technology, and continues to be so shaped, looks sick, it might be wise to have a look at the technology itself. If technology is felt to be becoming more and more inhuman, we might do well to consider whether it is possible to have something better—a technology with a human face.

The dual nature of technology is intricately linked to the dual nature of economic development in social structures, as illustrated in Fig. 2.2. Economic growth is essential for improving worldwide economic, social, and political well-being. However, it can also result in negative externalities that harm individuals, communities, and the environment, create geopolitical tensions, and undermine the success of the SDGs (Van Zanten and van Tulder, 2021). Table 2.4 lists the positive and negative impacts of the different sectors of the economy on various activities. Policies are necessary to minimize negative impacts, reduce trade-offs, optimize positive impacts, and create co-benefits. Because engineers play a role in economic development, they need to be aware of the consequences of their decision-making and whether their solutions have positive or negative outcomes. Economic growth is not necessarily conducive to societal well-being.

As no technology is entirely free of negative effects, the challenge is to minimize adverse impacts by being proactive in planning and design rather than simply reacting to unintended consequences after implementation. Many of these consequences can be attributed to human characteristics, such as cognitive dissonance, protective cognition, biases, the bystander effect, incapacitation by slow-moving threats, the power of self-interest, and optimism bias (Abela, 2023).

2.2.2 Guiding Principles

Since the 1970s, there has been growing recognition that to benefit society, engineering projects must follow technical and non-technical guidelines. As early as the 1990s, the US National Academy of Engineering sounded an alarm about the impact of engineering on society in a publication titled *Engineering as a Social Enterprise* (NAE, 1991). According to Hollomon (1991) and Bugliarello (1991), as well as various authors in the fields of Industrial Ecology (Graedel and Allenby, 2009) and Earth Systems Engineering and Science (NAE, 2000; Allenby, 2001; Steffen and Tyson, 2001), the engineering profession must recognize its limitations and re-evaluate its assumptions and guiding principles, some of which are listed below.

Table 2.4 Positive and negative impact of the economy on various activities (adapted from Van Zanten and van Tulder, 2021)

	Positive Impact	Negative Impact
Agriculture, forestry, fishing	• May help end hunger • Sustainable food production • Enhance productivity • Small-scale farmers benefits • Sustainable management of natural resources • Biomass generation	• Excessive water withdrawal • Overuse of pesticides and fertilizers • Water pollution • Biodiversity loss • Overfishing • Deforestation
Mining and quarrying	• Energy provision • Metals for Industry • Stones and cement for infrastructure building	• Degradation of natural habitats • Biodiversity loss • Water and air pollution • Mining waste • GHG production
Manufacturing	• Industrialization • Increased employment and income • Good production	• GHG production • Excessive consumption of water • Water pollution • Substance abuses • Military complex
Electricity, gas stream, and AC supply	• Needed for industrialization • Renewable energies	• GHG emissions from non-renewable sources • Air pollution
Water supply, sewerage, waste management, and remediation activities	• Access to safe and affordable drinking water • Sanitation and hygiene • Waste management	• Inadequate water and distribution systems • Inadequate wastewater management • Pollution
Construction	• Access to housing and urbanization • Infrastructure development	• CHG emission • High consumption of resources • Waste generation • Ecosystems disturbance
Transportation and storage (road, water, air)	• Support industrialization • Mobility	• Leading cause of climate change • Threaten ecosystems (land, river, sea)
Accommodation and food and service activities	• Can contribute to sustainable tourism and access to food	• High water consumption • Municipal waste
Information and communication	• Access to information • Enhance market efficiencies • Promote economic productivity	• CHG emissions from energy consumption

- Many engineering decisions cannot be made independently of the surrounding natural and human systems. Modern engineering systems can significantly affect future social, economic, and environmental systems (e.g., 30–100 years), create collateral damage, generate unplanned suffering for some while benefiting others (Gasper, 2012), and trigger conflict.

- The human capacity to cause planetary change through technology is growing faster than our ability to understand and manage the non-technical consequences of such changes (Leopold, 1992).

- The traditional positivist approach to technology during the 19th century and most of the 20th century has been insufficient to acknowledge that real-world problems often lack technical solutions. This approach has failed to address situations characterized by uncertainty, instability, uniqueness, and value conflicts, resulting in a disconnect between professional knowledge and practical demands (Schön, 1983).

- The quality of engineering decisions in society directly affects the quality of life of humans and natural systems today and in the future.

- All technologies have adverse effects that can backfire. The traditional engineering approach is only a process of devising and implementing a chosen solution among several purely technical options that must be challenged and replaced by one that considers the health of human and environmental systems. The traditional degenerative design associated with the take-make-waste paradigm must be replaced by a generative design that aligns more with Earth's natural processes. A "do no harm" and "do more good" rather than "do less bad" design paradigm, with nature as a model, is required (Raworth, 2018).

- A more comprehensive engineering strategy requires an understanding of the interconnections between engineered and non-engineered systems, including non-technical issues, developing nature-based solutions, and adopting a systematic approach to understanding these associations.

These difficulties involve (i) harmonizing traditional linear engineering models with the complex (nonlinear), open, diverse, dissipative, and adaptive characteristics of natural and human systems; (ii) coping with the unpredictability of the world; (iii) incorporating a logic of failure (Dörner, 1997) and reflective practice (Schön, 1983) into project planning and design; (iv) prioritizing adaptation in projects rather than striving for specification; and (v) settling for satisficing solutions instead of optimizing them (Simon, 1972).

- Preparing engineers to facilitate sustainable development and socio-economic change is one of the most significant challenges the engineering profession faces today. Meeting this challenge may provide a unique opportunity to continue leadership in the engineering profession.

- The compartmentalized 19th-century value-free and technology-focused engineering education model no longer fits society's needs and is out of context with the challenges society faces and out of touch with what students and professionals are demanding and interested in.

- Engineers must recognize their social responsibilities and take significant societal and political leadership positions.

These recommendations are critical because modern engineering interventions can significantly affect social, economic, and environmental systems in the future. The impact of such projects on systems outside their technical boundaries is significant for larger projects. Because the lifespan of infrastructure projects varies significantly (e.g., 30–75 years for bridges, 20–50 years for highways, 30–75 years for coal power stations, 50–100 years for commercial building design, and 50–100 years for housing, railway, and dams), their positive and negative impacts can be long-lasting and require the adoption of policies early on in the design and planning phases to minimize future impact, an issue that is explicitly addressed in the Environmental and Social Framework of the World Bank (2017).

According to Anderson (2022), engineers must continue to uphold guiding principles to address the diverse array of human development and security challenges that we face today. However, it is unfortunate that many of the recommendations mentioned earlier have been gradually adopted by the private and public sectors, which prioritize providing technology, regardless of whether it is harmful, to address human development and security. This approach is fueled by the assumption of infinite material growth and consumption to support political, economic, and social structures. Military engineering is driven by the fear of vulnerability and the need to conserve military advantages (Vesilind, 2010).

Considering all the recommendations, it is essential to conduct a reality check because no matter how advanced and well-planned the technology may be, it will always have harmful effects. The negative consequences of technology's unintended effects and the Cradle-to-Grave model in Fig. 2.2 must be acknowledged by the engineering and scientific community, and vigilance is necessary.

The goal is not to eliminate these negative consequences (that would be utopic) but to minimize them and anticipate them by adopting a cradle-to-cradle model that aligns more with ecosystems' regenerative (or assimilative) capacity. Recalling the $I = PAT$ equation of Ehrlich and Holdren (1971), a place to start is to develop better technology to "reduce the impact associated with each unit of production," T, and to reduce per capita consumption, A (Lepech and Leckie, 2023). As noted by Huesemann and Huesemann (2011), the laws of mass conservation and thermodynamics cannot be bypassed in the development of new technologies and improvements to existing technologies. Figure 2.2 shows that the dynamics of the cradle-to-grave model depend on infrastructure and society. Hence, more change may occur by changing the mindset of society and culture.

The engineering profession should recognize that context and scale affect human development and security. The Western world's solutions may not fit every case and may sometimes be incorrect. Engineers must address the challenges faced by three customer groups. At one end of the spectrum, the challenge for customers in the *developed world* is to consume less and more intelligently while being more efficient and respectful of human and natural systems. Engineers are called on to create innovative and more efficient ways of providing services and replacing the take-make-use/consume-waste cradle-to-grave process, as shown in

Fig. 2.2, with a regenerating and restoring cradle-to-cradle cyclical process to produce, distribute, and consume goods and services with a minimal footprint.

At the other end of the development spectrum, the challenge for customers in the *developing world* is to access the primary resources and skills necessary to meet their daily needs. For some, it is as essential as staying alive until the end of the day. For disadvantaged communities, sustainable development is synonymous with survival. Engineers must develop solutions that are available, accessible, affordable, reliable, and appropriate for people with limited resources. The concept of technology with a human face was promoted by Schumacher (1973) in *Small Is Beautiful*. Exporting the current Western world's dysfunctional production-consumption model of economic growth to millions of people in the developing world would jeopardize their growth by trapping them into a downward spiral of ecological and economic decline with dysfunctional social consequences.

Customers in the burgeoning emerging markets of India, Southeast Asia, South America, etc., fall between the developed and developing world extremes. They are characterized by large populations, purchasing power, and rapid economic growth. In this context, engineers must innovate in developing leapfrogging solutions that do not duplicate the mistakes made by the developed world over the past 150 years. The solutions should focus on creating new development pathways that reduce environmental impact and promote regenerative economic growth. Engineers must also ensure that new economies do not regress to their previous state while dealing with the challenges of the 21st-century world. This dynamic requires that emerging market countries have a chance to do so and are granted the "right to develop." Development requires factors such as equity, rules of law, and democracy. Our planet's future mainly hinges on what newly emerging market consumers and billions of people will follow in subsequent centuries (UNDP/HDR, 2013).

Considering past models of development that have led to the growth of Western economies after WWII, we cannot legitimize the use of the same approach of heavy consumption of resources combined with high waste production (Fig. 2.2) when trying to lift billions of people out of poverty through the development of infrastructure, energy, and market systems that are signatures of a global economy. Instead, an innovative approach to industrialization and consumption is required, resulting in less extraction of non-renewable resources and more significant resource recovery.

Specifically, when it comes to future technological solutions for the entire planet, engineers must recognize that populations cannot afford to perpetuate decisions that (i) substantially deplete natural resources, (ii) eliminate options for the future of natural and human systems, (iii) create inequalities among people and divide them, (iv) escalate costs to prohibitive levels that all cannot afford, and (v) increase the probability of catastrophic future disasters, either natural or technological. We must realize that as the planet grows during the 21st century, it will create unprecedented demands for energy, food, land, water, trans-portation, materials, waste disposal, earthmoving, public healthcare, environmental cleanup, telecommunications, and infra-structure. The involvement of engineers is critical for fulfilling these demands at various scales, ranging from remote small communities to large urban areas (megacities), mainly in the developing world, where fast-growing populations and migration are in effect.

Training engineers in their formative years in ways different from those of the past two centuries is necessary to ensure that they can contribute to peace and diplomacy in the 21st century and beyond. This training should prepare them to be adaptable and versatile in their professional lives, as they can expect frequent changes throughout their careers (NAE, 2012).

2.3   Educating Globally Engaged Engineers

2.3.1   From Schooling to Learning

The above observations have implications for educating engineers to address the local and global planetary challenges of the 21st century and contribute to a more sustainable and peaceful world. Interestingly, traditional silos in engineering education and practice are rigid, monodisciplinary-oriented, and inappropriate for addressing these challenges. Civil, mechanical, and electrical engineering disciplines inherited from the 19th and 20th centuries are firmly grounded today. They are divided into sub-disciplines, each with its own culture, ethics, and best practices. As remarked by Karwat et al. (2014), in this traditional reductionistic approach, engineers (i) "are trained to think ahistorically and act apolitically," (ii) "tend to ignore or dismiss considerations of intangibles like politics, emotions, and other ethical concerns," and (iii) consider facts as more important than values. Furthermore, "engineering coursework is treated as an assembly line to turn students into engineers (and remove defective products along the way)" (Alarcón, 2023). With these attributes, it is not apparent how engineers would embrace and comprehend their role in providing sustainable and peaceful solutions or even stay in engineering for a long time, as younger generations are more socially and environmentally aware and demand more socially relevant and meaningful education.

Unfortunately, the 19th and 20th centuries compartmentalized nature of engineering is still a limiting factor in academia. However, this is not in tune with modern society's needs and the challenges humanity has faced in the past and is still facing today, such as climate change, urbanization, and migration, which cut across many technical and non-technical disciplines in different fields of knowledge (Fig. 2.3).

As Nolan (2011) noted, universities have somehow managed to establish institutions with significant gaps between their brightest minds and the world's most pressing issues. Academia has also failed to recognize that today's global problems cut across disciplinary boundaries and cannot be addressed separately. Furthermore, "they do not respect national boundaries and require [transboundary] cooperation in science and engineering to address them successfully" (Reynolds, 2013).

Using a mathematical vectorial analogy, if traditional education with its separate disciplines and different fields of knowledge on the one hand and real-world problems (e.g., climate change, peace, emergency, refugee issues, Indigenous issues) on the other hand were vectors, their "dot product" would be zero because, as shown in Fig. 2.3, these vectors are perpendicular to each other. One question is how traditional education can better align with real-world issues so that the "dot product" is greater than zero and approaches one.

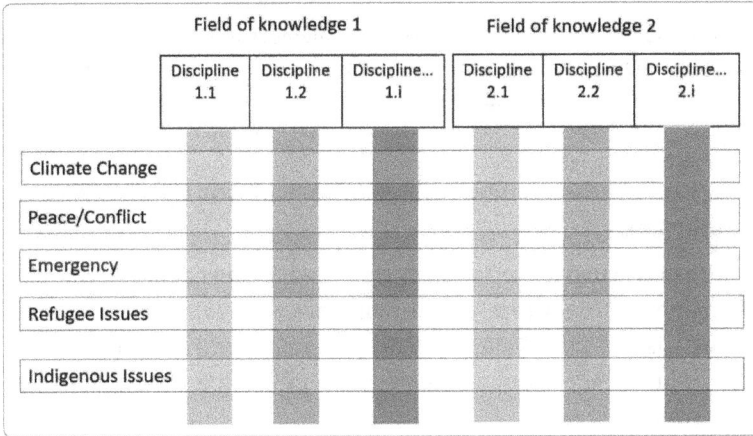

Figure 2.3 Global issues cut across many disciplinary silos and different fields of knowledge.

For engineers to contribute to peace and diplomacy, a new form of engineering education and practice is urgently needed based on awareness of the impact of engineering on society and the environment, social and community engagement, leadership, teamwork, reflective and adaptive practice combined with critical and creative thinking, field exposure to global problems during students' formative years, and professional careers. Lifelong learning is also vital, where education is seen as a "K-Gray continuum from elementary school education into retirement" (Alarcón, 2023) and does not just stop upon graduation. Engineers must exhibit high adaptation and flexibility to address global problems in a dynamic environment where multidisciplinary approaches are the norm. Finally, engineers must be able to manage the formidable challenges associated with the interaction between technical systems and adaptive socio-ecological systems.

One must acknowledge that there is still a disconnect between what is offered in engineering schools, the recommendations of accreditation institutions, and real-world problems. One likely reason for that disconnect is that, as noted by Alarcón (2023), the "hidden curriculum of engineering education is an emphasis on the mindset of 'schooling' as opposed to 'learning' [let alone lifelong learning]." Further,

> The schooling mindset values rote memorization over applied knowledge, grade point average over competency, grading curves over mastery, plug-and-chuck equations over conceptual mapping and understanding, and individualized problem-solving over truly collaborative idea generation and formation. Each of these schooling priorities subverts outlooks that are essential to lifelong learning.

Despite such observations, the need to revisit the education of engineers to address global planetary challenges beyond mere rhetoric is far from being a priority in engineering education and academia, where compartmentalized education and positivism are norms.

Higher education and industry are subject to conflicting demands. On the one hand, there is a need for more specialization (depth) in narrower fields of study to respond to ever-increasing knowledge and complexity. On the other hand, there is a need for more general education (breadth) so that engineers can work in interdisciplinary teams globally. The industry is struggling to find engineers who (i) have both technical and non-technical skills, (ii) account for societal issues, and (iii) are out-of-the-box creative. While universities have much to offer students interested in specialized degrees, the challenge for academia remains in integrating depth and breadth into engineering curricula to prepare engineers to address societal problems. It is unclear where students interested in broader issues, such as peace, climate security, mass migration, or poverty reduction, should enroll on campus without falling into a specialization trap.

2.3.2 Different Engineering Programs

Recently, there has been a growing shift towards unconventional approaches in engineering education and practice that acknowledge the interdisciplinary, multidisciplinary, and transdisciplinary nature of modern challenges. One example is the emergence of biotech and biomedical engineering, which recognizes that various branches of engineering (such as mechanical, chemical, and electrical) significantly affect biology and health. However, this field has not been without opposition from established disciplines, including engineering, biology, and medicine.

Similarly, over the past 20 years, we have seen the inception of humanitarian, development, earth systems, peace, activist, and global engineering programs, among others. Although these programs are not proper disciplinary branches of engineering per se, such as civil and mechanical engineering, they represent emerging mindsets and innovative ways of thinking in the engineering profession while recognizing that solutions to complex problems are holistic, not just technical, and include socioeconomic, cultural, and environmental components. Table 2.5 provides the definitions of some of these programs. They all acknowledge the strong connection between engineering and society and can be regarded as forums for cultivating engineers inclined to address global and local societal issues. The approach of these programs goes beyond disciplinary, multidisciplinary, and interdisciplinary approaches. They can be seen as convergent, which, according to the US National Research Council (NRC, 2014), is a crucial strategy "merging ideas, approaches, and technologies from widely diverse fields of knowledge at a high level of integration for solving complex problems and addressing complex intellectual questions underlying emerging disciplines."

Our intent is not to explore the merits of different engineering programs. One thing for sure is that we must remember that they all have something in common: What engineering stands for in its linkage to society? Engineering involves the application of ingenuity, imagination, and creativity to solve problems that are yet to be partially or entirely resolved. It shares the same roots with genes, ingenious, and ingenieux (in French). In short, engineering is the process of bringing creative scientific solutions into practice for the betterment of humankind.

Table 2.5 Different engineering programs

	Definition	References
Peace engineering	… the proactive use of engineering skills to promote a peaceful and just existence for all.	Vesilin (2005)
	… more about achieving peace, sustainability, and resilience than it is about pure engineering…. It is part of an emerging global movement to transform engineering to save the planet through academic volunteerism and expertise, curriculum tweaks, and transdisciplinary cooperation.	Jordan et al. (2020)
	… a relatively new and interdisciplinary field that aims to apply engineering principles and technology to promote peace, prevent conflicts, and address the root causes of violence and instability in various contexts.	OpenAI (2023)
Development engineering	… responds to the global need for engineers who understand the problems of development and sustainability, can bring to bear on them their engineering knowledge, are motivated by a sense of the future, and can interact with other disciplines, with communities, and with political leaders to design and implement solutions.	Bugliarello (1991)
	… builds 'on techniques from engineering, development economics, behavioral science, and sociology' and designs products and services on behalf of developing countries while addressing market barriers and institutional failures and promoting business models.	Nilsson, Madon and Sastry (2014)
	…a vital field that contributes to improving the well-being of communities and advancing sustainable development goals. Development engineers apply their engineering expertise to tackle complex challenges and create positive impacts on societies around the world.	OpenAI (2023)
Humanitarian engineering	… the application of engineering to improving the well-being of marginalized people and disadvantaged communities, usually in the developing world. Humanitarian engineering typically focuses on programs that are affordable, sustainable, and based on local resources. Projects are generally community-driven and cross-disciplinary, focusing on finding simple solutions to basic needs (such as close access to clean water, adequate heat, shelter, sanitation, and reliable market pathways).	Encyclopedia Brittanica Humanitarian engineering | Definition & Facts | Britannica

	Definition	References
	… educates engineers and scientists to partner with communities seeking to enhance their social, environmental, and economic sustainability.	Colorado School of Mines Humanitarian Engineering. - Humanitarian Engineering (mines.edu)
Activist engineering	… seeks to fundamentally redefine contemporary engineering practice by exposing the political and value-based nature of engineering, applying socio-ecological learning to technological design, imbuing a different sense of responsibility in engineers, and moving the scope of engineering beyond solely technological development.	Karwat et al. (2014)
Globally engaged engineering, Global engineering	… an umbrella term to emphasize a need to educate more competent engineers who can work and collaborate across disciplines, show cultural sensitivity and mobility, and have acquired field experience.	Bourn and Neal (2008), Downey and Beddoes (2011), Graham (2018), Amadei (2014).
Earth systems engineering and science (ESE)	… a multidisciplinary (engineering, science, social science, and governance) solution development process that takes a holistic view of natural and human system interactions. ESE aims to understand complex, nonlinear systems of global importance and develop the tools necessary to implement that understanding.	NAE (2000), Allenby (2001), Steffen and Tyson (2001), Graedel and Allenby (2009)
Engineering for Developing Communities	… educate globally responsible students who can offer sustainable and appropriate technology solutions to the endemic problems of developing communities worldwide, including communities in the US.	Amadei (2014, 2019)

2.3.3 Changing the Mindset

How can traditional engineering education be aligned with real-world problems? Paraphrasing Albert Einstein that current issues cannot be solved with the same level of thinking that created them, a new K-Gray education mindset is required for *globally engaged engineers* (GEEs) to work across disciplines, cultures, and communities. As noted by Kamp (2016),

> The challenge is to design engineering degree programs not as preparation for a career in a particular discipline but rather as the foundation for a lifetime of continuous learning in preparation for their last job.

As Kamp (2016) emphasized, the progress of engineering careers is contingent on the quality, relevance, and efficacy of the education that students obtain. Therefore, it is imperative to change the mindset of engineering education. Table 2.6, in this regard, underscores the salient aspects of what is conventionally emphasized in engineering curricula and the necessity of shifting towards novel modes of thought and learning to maintain relevance and efficacy amidst uncertainty, complexity, ambiguity, volatility, and the intricate nature of the 21st-century world.

Table 2.6 Traditional and forward thinking and learning in engineering education (reproduced with permission from Kamp, 2016, p. 24)

Emphasis remaining on...	Shifting to more...
• Monodisciplinary expert thinking	• Multi- and interdisciplinary systems thinking
• Reductionism	• Integration
• Analysis	• Synthesis
• Abstract learning	• Experiential learning; common sense
• Developing order	• Correlating chaos and resilience
• Techno-scientific base	• Human factor and empathy; business acumen
• Convergent thinking	• Creativity
• Understanding certainty	• Handling ambiguity and failure
• Rational problem solving	• Complex problem solving
• Independence	• Collaboration
• Rounded expert	• Employability and lifelong learning

Implementing this mindset will not come without multiple challenges, as it requires embracing the changes and aspects of the VUCA world. One challenge involves resistance to change, which is sometimes exhibited in conservative, traditional academic, or professional environments. Another challenge is the training of educators. Finally, there are no simple solutions to complex issues in the VUCA world.

Furthermore, achieving a sustainable and peaceful world requires departing from the traditional perspective to a fresh and comprehensive perspective or approach regarding the role of engineering in society (see Table 2.7). Significant progress can only be made through consistent and practical efforts and the development of new tools, techniques, and policies to promote sustainability on a global scale. This new perspective presents a unique opportunity for engineering to lead R&D, contribute to economic growth, and advance human development and security. This perspective emphasizes the importance of engagement and engineers' ethical and professional responsibilities.

Table 2.7 Traditional and new perspectives on how engineers solve VUCA world issues (adapted from Karwat et al., 2014)

Traditional perspective	New perspective
– Quick fixes to solve problems	– Practical and sustainable efforts
– Focus on profits and liability	– Focus on resiliency and sustainability
– Focus on extractive industry and efficient growth	– Focus on modularity, repurpose ability, and sufficiency
– Reliance on large corporations and capitalistic principles	– Reliance on community-scale works, engagement, democracy, and JEDI principles
– The practical approach maximizes net benefits regardless of who gains or does not	– Human issues are a priority; How well are we doing? Who gains or does not gain?
– Apolitical, ahistorical, and value-neutral	– Social, political, and ecological values
– Impersonal	– Relationships with places and people
– Top-down only	– Bottom-up, top-down, and inside-out
– Compartmentalized solutions: The world of experts	– Solutions emerge from the interaction of multiple areas: The world of system thinkers

(Continued)

Table 2.7 (Continued)

Traditional perspective	New perspective
– Infinite material growth and consumption	– Limiting resources and carrying capacity
– A degree is an end	– K-Gray life-long learning
– Knowledge	– Knowledge, skills, and practical experience
– Convergent thinking in the design process	– Divergent thinking in the design process
– Practice is based on solving technical problems using a reductionistic common-and-control approach; reality can only be explained rationally without values	– Praxis is based on critical thinking, reflective action, and moral and ethical guidance upon transforming the world, which is holistic and dynamic, embracing change and engaging
– Deterministic and well-defined problems	– Messy and ill-defined problems
– Optimum solutions	– Good enough solutions
– Technical solutions are the solutions; the world of techno-optimists	– Technical solutions are necessary but not sufficient
– Split between research and practice	– Overlap between research and practice
– Technical rationality	– Technical awareness
– Earth is a limitless source of resources and sinks for waste disposal	– Earth is a finite source of resources and sinks for waste disposal
– Nature is a machine or object with no intrinsic value to be dominated and exploited (e.g., Francis Bacon)	– Nature is sacred, a harmonic web of life; everything needs to be preserved (e.g., native traditions)
– Engineering-based solutions rely on technological innovation and human-engineered systems; the priority is to create financial value	– Nature-based solutions are to use and manage nature or modified environments while giving people, ecosystems, resilience, and biodiversity benefits
– Climate change is a carbon problem only while neglecting other greenhouse gases and their environmental issues and ignoring the social and economic consequences resulting from the multifaceted nature of climate change	– Climate change is profoundly moral and ethical and requires overhauling political, economic, and social structures; a new mental model of interaction between humans and the planet in the socio-economic and political sectors is needed

2.3.4   A Global Perspective of Engineering Education

Given the context in which engineering and society interact and the vision of engineering professionals contributing to a more sustainable, stable, peaceful, and equitable world, the question arises as to what constitutes the body of knowledge (BOK) in the education of globally engaged engineers in the VUCA world. Another way of phrasing this question is in terms of desired outcomes, which, according to ABET,[3] "describe what students are expected to know and be able to do by graduation. These relate to the knowledge, skills, and behaviors the students acquire as they progress through the program."

The need to educate competent engineers to address the complex issues faced by society in the 21st century has been discussed in the literature for at least 20 years (Monat et al., 2022). The question remains as to what it means to become globally competent. Hunter et al. (2006) reviewed several answers to that question and proposed the following definition.

> A globally competent person must be able to identify cultural differences to compete globally, collaborate across cultures, and participate effectively in both social and business settings in other countries.

Traditional engineering methods, primarily based on education in engineering sciences and mathematics and applied to artificially well-defined and closed problems, are no longer adequate for preparing young people to deal with the complex issues faced by society. This approach fails to equip engineers with the attitudes, skills, knowledge, and lifelong experience necessary to address complex geopolitical and economic problems and sustainable development in general.

Readers can find multiple engineering education outcome recommendations in studies by Bugliarello (1991), Bourn and Neal (2008), Downey et al. (2006), Lima and Oakes (2006), Duderstadt (2008), Palmer and Zajonc (2010), Downey and Beddoes (2011), Amadei and Wallace (2009), Amadei (2014), Kamp (2016, 2020), and Beagon et al. (2023), among others. Professional organizations

---

[3]Criteria for Accrediting Engineering Programs, 2022 - 2023 - ABET

such as the American Society of Civil Engineers, World Federation of Engineering Organizations (WFEO), and World Federation of Professional Engineers (FIDIC), as well as accreditation boards such as ABET, the Australian Engineering Accreditation Center, and the UK Engineering Council, have also proposed recommendations.

To better understand the topic and the range of opinions about preparing the engineering profession for the challenges of the 21st century, including engineering education, the reader may want to search the web with keywords such as "global engineering" or "globally engaged education and curriculum." The literature suggests that integrating a global perspective into engineering education is both crucial and overdue. However, there is no consensus on how to achieve this goal.

2.3.5   I-Type, T-Type, and V-Type Education Models

Specific points must be emphasized before discussing the Body of Knowledge (BOK) of globally engaged engineers (GEEs). First, it is crucial to understand that technology cannot address the wide-ranging developmental challenges customers encounter in developed, developing, and emerging nations. The education of competent, globally engaged engineers must extend beyond the dominant engineering mindset of developing technical solutions to problems. Globally engaged engineers must be equipped to consider non-technical factors, such as socioeconomic, cultural, and political issues, that play a significant role in explaining the problems faced by humanity today. In essence, GEEs must be proficient in utilizing technical and non-technical tools in their decision-making processes and be aware of selecting the appropriate tools.

A second remark about globally engaged engineering is that it does not necessarily fit into any specific engineering branch because it is interdisciplinary. No engineering discipline can fully address all the global development challenges mentioned above. In addition, there are no grand solutions to the ill-defined or messy problems of the VUCA world; only step-by-step solutions requiring cross-disciplinary tools. Instead, globally engaged engineering should be seen as an approach (a way of thinking) rather than a discipline that cuts across different engineering silos and uses tools from various technical and non-technical fields to offer solutions to societal challenges. This concept is disruptive to the *orthodoxy* of traditional engineering education, which is accustomed to well-defined domains and hierarchical structures.

A third remark regarding globally engaged engineering is that it refers to different things to different people. For instance, it is possible to envision other types of globally engaged engineering education programs based on the context (cultural, political, environmental, etc.) being addressed and the scale (physical and temporal) at which problems are being considered. For instance, a globally engaged engineering education program interested in the dynamics of an urban environment will have a different body of knowledge from that of a program interested in rural planning or managing slum areas or refugee camps. The same can be said about the BOK of engineering programs that address issues faced by communities in different climatic and geographic regions.

All three remarks mentioned above give the impression that it is difficult to define a common BOK for the education of GEEs and to identify what they should master, their competence, and what they should be exposed to. To a certain extent, this is true because a BOK must be designed to address a wide range of issues, as mentioned previously. At the same time, defining the BOK is not a random process if one sees the education of GEEs as *T-type* or *V-type* education with depth and breadth rather than traditional specialized *I-type* education (Manning and Reinecke, 2016), as shown in Fig. 2.4.

The in-depth part of T-type education deals with the technical tools, rigor, expertise (mastery) expected of engineers in practice, solid proficiency, and practical ability (competence). This depth may include several vertical components (e.g., technical, health, and business). In this case, we will talk about *M-type* or *comb-type* education. On the other hand, the breadth part deals with the various non-technical socioeconomic, policy, ethics, and cultural tools that engineers must be aware of (exposure) to address the global problems mentioned above. These socially relevant tools are primarily taught in non-engineering departments and colleges. In Fig. 2.4, V-type education differs from T-type education in broadening the depth and breadth of lifelong learning over time.

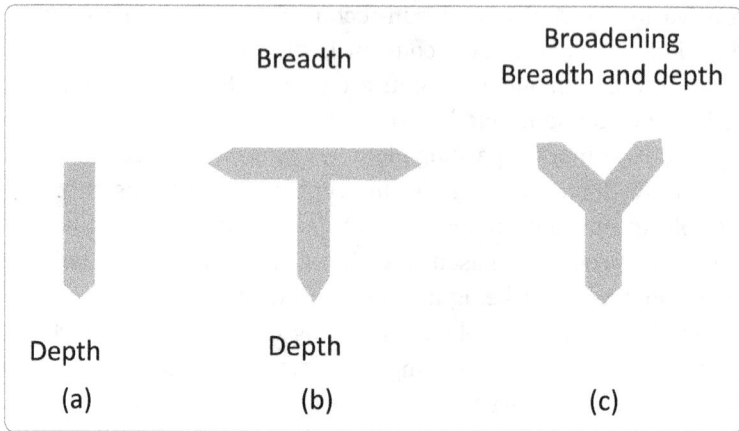

Figure 2.4 Three different types of engineering education: (a) traditional I-Type, (b) T-Type, and (c) V-type lifelong.

It should be noted that the balance between T-type and I-type education continues to be a topic of significant discussion in the engineering profession. In this discussion, the concern is not whether T-type education is better suited than I-type education to address today's global issues; academia usually accepts this. Instead, the matter is the perceived difficulty of integrating all non-technical components of a T-type of education, such as the skills mentioned above, into a four-year (BS) or five-year (BS/MS) curriculum that is already at capacity (Grasso and Burkins, 2009). One way to overcome this obstacle is to use the socio-humanistic (S-H) electives or other electives required in many engineering curricula to integrate the global dimension of T-type education in the form of undergraduate or graduate certificates and minors. Elective tracks related to sustainability, peace, climate security, and various nexuses that complement the core engineering curriculum can be envisioned. Another way would be to integrate social concepts into the technical curriculum, which would require more holistic training of engineering educators.

Engineering education is hesitant to adopt T-type education (let alone V-type) because it is subject to conflicting societal demands. On the one hand, there is a need for more in-depth specialization or I-type education in narrower and more abstract fields of study to keep up with constantly increasing knowledge and complexity. However, there is a need for more general education so that engineers can work effectively in diverse global areas, interdisciplinary teams, and different contexts and scales. The balance between these two types of education remains a significant topic of discussion in engineering. Moreover, engineers must develop lifelong learning skills that complement their depth and breadth of knowledge in the long run (NAE, 2012).

Among the "why," "what," and "how" of a T-type of globally engaged engineering education, the first two are generally better defined. Regardless of the globally engaged engineering emphasis, engineers must have at least acquired the following *core competencies* and attributes:

- Personal and cultural awareness, awareness of the human aspects of engineering, and what it means to be a responsible global citizen
- Awareness of the impact of engineering solutions in different contexts and scales
- Skills (hard and soft) and tools for approaching structured and unstructured issues
- Awareness of the social and environmental components of engineering decision-making and professional and ethical responsibilities
- The ability to think across disciplines and handle technical and non-technical issues necessitates the acquisition of development ethics and the consideration of empathy, justice, equity, diversity, and inclusion
- Project management skills for a wide range of contexts and scales
- Flexibility and resourcefulness in dealing with unfamiliar equipment and approaches
- Critical thinking, analytical thinking, and systems thinking skills
- Familiarization with objective and subjective decision-making methods
- Importance of intrapersonal reflection and interpersonal skills, such as communication, cooperation, and teamwork

- Practical ingenuity, imagination, and creativity
- Active-learning engineering, project-oriented learning, problem-based learning, and service-learning experience in formative years
- Anticipating and estimating consequences in uncertain, complex, and ambiguous settings
- Awareness of the importance of lifelong learning, professional development, and employability
- In addition to providing technical solutions, engineers are also called changemakers, peacemakers, facilitators of sustainable development, and innovative policymakers

These learning outcomes can also be understood in terms of different forms of mobility (UNESCO, 2010), including (i) physical mobility (traveling, studying, and working abroad), (ii) professional mobility (changing jobs during one's career), (iii) social mobility (dealing with different societal stakeholders), (iv) cultural mobility (interacting with different cultures), (v) transdisciplinary mobility (dealing with technical and non-technical issues), (vi) methodological mobility (using different approaches to problems), (vii) technological mobility (using different tools), and (viii) thought mobility (thinking differently in different contexts and on different scales).

As engineers embark on lifelong learning and adapting to change, one must add to the attributes mentioned above the need for self-reflection and awareness of social responsibility. According to Bugliarello (1991), it is about

> upholding the dignity of humankind, avoiding dangerous or uncontrolled side effects and by-products; making provision for consequences when technology fails; avoiding buttressing social systems that perform poorly and should be placed; and participating in formulating the 'why' of technology.

Table 2.8 lists several questions that engineers may want to reflect on the value and social implications of their decision-making in project design, planning, and implementation, according to Karwat (2019). Answering these questions represents much-needed and lifelong introspection.

Table 2.8 List of questions for self-reflective engineers (Karwat, 2019) (used with permission from Springer Nature)

Sphere/Realm	Questions
	Why am I an engineer? For whose benefit do I work? What is the full measure of my moral and social responsibility?
Social and political considerations	• Who is your work for, and what are their values and goals? • How much social and political capital does your employer have? • Who has the most to gain and lose from your work directly? How and why? • How quickly will the marginalized in society benefit from your work? • Who are you leaving out of your consideration, and why?
Environmental and ecological considerations	• How does your work affect local, regional, and larger environments and ecological systems? • What material resources are used in the design, deployment, maintenance, and subsequent decommissioning of the technology or system? • What environmental and ecological concerns are you leaving out of your consideration? Why?
Economic considerations	• How is the economic value (revenue, access to capital, etc.) generated by your engineering work distributed? • Who owns your work's products (intellectual, physical, etc.), and for how long? • Do groups of people have to pay more or less than others to use your technical intervention? Why or why not?
Peace and security considerations	• In what ways does your work reduce the potential for violent conflict, prevent the need for weapons or anything else that can cause mental or physical harm or trauma or death—intentional or otherwise—and increase the ability to promote diplomacy and dialogue to resolve conflict?
Praxis, connections, and feedback	• How are feedback from stakeholders and data from evaluation built into your design and implementation process? • How responsive are the configuration and performance of the technical systems you design to changing social values and needs? • How might emphasizing one set of considerations here enhance or detract from another?
Alternative problem-solving approaches	• What non-technical interventions (business, community building, resource sharing, etc.) might achieve similar outcomes to the ones you might achieve through your technical work? • How do you think existing technologies and materials could be used differently to achieve similar outcomes to your work?
Personal conflicts	• Are you dissatisfied with any of your answers to the above questions? What would you rather the answers be? Why? • Is there anything you do that contradicts your values or those of the people you claim to serve?

The 'how' of T-type engineering education is more challenging than the 'why' and 'what.' Questions remain, for instance, regarding how to (i) expose engineering students to real-world problems through internships, co-op programs, fieldwork, outreach/service-learning activities, and experiential learning to gain real-life experiences; (ii) promote leadership and integrate social responsibility and ethics across the entire curriculum; (iii) encourage students to explore a minor around at least one global issue (e.g., human development, environmental sustainability, resilience, peace, and conflict studies, etc.); (iv) encourage traditional research-oriented and teaching-oriented faculty members to include new concepts on world issues in their work; (v) encourage more women and minority groups in STEM (or STEAM, including the arts and humanities) fields by emphasizing the societal dimension of engineering; and (vi) engage stakeholders from non-academic sectors in curriculum development. Another critical question is determining what represents successful globally engaged engineering education and practice for life (K-Gray lifelong learning).

2.3.6   An Example of a T-type Engineering Program

In 2004, a program called Engineering for Developing Communities (EDC) was created in the Civil, Environmental, and Architectural Engineering (CEAE) Department at the University of Colorado, Boulder (UCB). The program emphasized the global engineering dimension and was later renamed the Mortenson Center in Engineering for Developing Communities (MCEDC) in 2009, following an endowment from the Mortenson Construction Company and the Mortenson family in Minneapolis, MN. The program was based on the belief that all engineers must be exposed to human development issues as part of their education and have a contextual understanding of how technical decisions interact with cultural issues and society in developed and developing countries, thus emphasizing T-type education (Amadei and Sandekian, 2010).

The EDC program consists of three interdependent components: education, research/development, and service/outreach. The relationship between these three components within the context of community development and capacity building has the following objectives.

- *Education*: Create awareness of developing world issues and provide knowledge and tools for engineering professionals in recovery and development.
- *Development research*: Coordinate research, design, and development of holistic solutions for developing communities that account for technical and non-technical issues.
- *Capacity*: Build local community capacity through collaboration with organizations working in developing communities worldwide.

From 2010 to 2018, MCEDC offered a Graduate Certificate in Engineering for Developing Communities. The BOK covers five significant areas: engineering/technology, public health, social entrepreneurship, public policy and governance, and security/vulnerability. Students are trained to use an integrative and participatory framework for development projects in communities in developing countries on real case studies during the academic year and through a 4–6 weeklong in-country practicum during the summer following their coursework. The MCEDC body of knowledge is divided into mastery, competence, and exposure.

- *Mastery* (expertise). Students must demonstrate proficiency in field preparedness, practical experience, systems thinking, integrative and participatory frameworks for development projects, appropriate and sustainable technologies, environmental sustainability, and sustainable development.
- *Competence.* Students must become proficient in public health, teamwork, leadership, cultural sensitivity, and behavior-change communication.
- *Exposure. Students* are encouraged to explore social entrepreneurship, security issues, public policy, and governance, which will help them gain exposure to these critical areas.

The MCEDC graduate certificate consists of four courses taught over 12 months: *Sustainable Community Development I* (fall), *Sustainable Community Development II* (spring), and *a systems course* (spring). A *Sustainable Community Development Field*

Practicum (summer) is also required for students to learn by doing so while immersed in real complex problems. The graduate certificate was integrated into four graduate tracks that offered MS and PhD degrees in civil engineering at CU Boulder. These include environmental engineering, civil systems engineering, building systems, and construction engineering and management. The MCEDC BOK was developed to provide engineering students with the opportunity to provide technical expertise to development agencies or various engineering firms in a manner that recognizes the different technical and non-technical facets of community development that lead to sustainable solutions.

In 2018, the MCEDC was renamed the Mortenson Center in Global Engineering (MCGE), emphasizing the development and validation of applicable methods, technologies, and evidence generation. The original MCEC curriculum was restructured to replace the four required semester-long courses that generally retain a project-level civil and environmental engineering perspective with one-credit, five-week modules. These modules include introductions to global health, development economics, geography, remote sensing, statistical analysis, policy, service delivery, and impact evaluation. A required field practicum still embeds students with global development agencies for at least three months, with some continuing to engage with these agencies for many years.

The MCEDC educational framework was designed to teach students core values and principles necessary to deal with the challenges they are likely to encounter when interacting with communities regarding future development projects in their professional careers. In addition to acquiring much-needed engineering skills, they were taught the following:

- The planning, management, and implementation of projects in communities at different development levels cannot be achieved using the same blueprint approach. Engineers must be able to make decisions in a flexible, learning, and adaptive environment that changes rapidly, is characterized by complexity and uncertainty, and involves community partnerships.

- Doing a project right is necessary but insufficient because it focuses more on project performance. Doing the right project is equally important because it focuses more on whether the project is in balance with the societal, economic, and environmental systems with which it interacts.

- They must abide by a strict *professional code of ethics* about behavior, accountability, quality control, quality assurance, and project delivery, whether in a developed or developing world context.

- They need to be conscious of their *mission, vision, values, approach to development*, and the intervening organization that employs them.

- They must take *responsibility* for educating themselves and acquiring the necessary skills before conducting projects.

- For long-term sustainability, a participatory and integrated approach must be implemented in all projects, particularly in capacity and resiliency building.

- Project *innovation* is driven by users' needs and capacity and not outsiders' needs to introduce new and fancy solutions. This drive often means that the most effective and appropriate solution could be to modify the existing ones at the community level. It also implies that these solutions should not be introduced unless they are relevant and likely to work.

- *Collaboration* between internal and external stakeholders is vital for project development. *Teamwork* in this context includes working with culturally and intellectually diverse groups and continually mentoring future local leaders and changemakers.

- *Interventions* (time and tasks) must be designed to maximize the direct response to community needs and desires while considering the available resources and the project phase.

- Long-term *commitment* to the community is vital for sustained success.

- *Monitoring and evaluation* are needed to assess the progress of a project from the start and to allow students to decide on necessary changes and respond to identified shortcomings.

- An exit strategy and long-term sustainability (benefits) plan must be in place at the start of a project or shortly after that.

The MCEDC curriculum was crafted to guide the education of engineers in the 21st century, who are destined to contribute to global peace and security within a rapidly changing and increasingly complex world.

2.3.7 Engineering for Sustainable Development

The role of the engineering profession in sustainable development is another area that requires globally engaged engineers with T-type or V-type education. Since the 1992 Rio Summit and the publication of Agenda 21, engineering for sustainable development has received considerable attention in engineering education and practice (Roberts, 2002; FIDIC, 2013; Amadei, 2014; Kelly, 2016; Mathebula, 2018; ISI, 2018; UNESCO, 2021; Anderson et al., 2023; Lepech and Leckie, 2023). As reviewed by Beagon et al. (2023), many universities and institutions world-wide offer courses and training in sustainability and sustainable development and how to address the challenges of the SDGs. UNESCO (2017, 2021) has promoted education for sustainable development concerning the SDGs. Organizations such as the International Federation of Engineering Education Societies (IFEES), Engineering Education for Sustainable Development (EESD), and Engineering for One Planet (EOP) have proposed in-depth curriculum guidelines that address engineering education.

2.3.7.1 The Barcelona Declaration

A milestone in engineering education for sustainable development initiatives was the 2004 Barcelona Declaration, which emphasizes the importance of engineering in society and a complex world. The Declaration (ESSD, 2004) stated that "today's engineers must be able to

- Understand how their work interacts with society and the environment, locally and globally, to identify potential challenges, risks, and impacts.

- Understand the contribution of their work in diverse cultural, social, and political contexts and consider these differences.
- Work in multidisciplinary teams to adapt current technologies to the demands imposed by sustainable lifestyles, resource efficiency, pollution prevention, and waste management.
- Apply a holistic and systemic approach to solve problems and move beyond the tradition of breaking reality down into disconnected parts.
- Participate actively in discussing and defining economic, social, and technological policies to help redirect society towards more sustainable development.
- Apply professional knowledge according to deontological principles, universal values, and ethics.
- Listen closely to the demands of citizens and other stakeholders and let them have a say in developing new technologies and infrastructures."

Despite updates through biennial meetings, the core components of the 2004 EESD recommendations for engineers' education have remained unchanged, with the most recent meeting occurring in 2023 in Fort Collins, CO. To achieve the seven learning outcomes outlined above, the Barcelona Declaration also recommends that educational institutions work with the engineering and scientific community to (i) promote an integrated approach to knowledge, attitudes, skills, experience, and values in teaching; (ii) incorporate disciplines of the social sciences and humanities into the engineering curriculum; (iii) promote multidisciplinary teamwork; (iv) stimulate creativity and critical thinking; (v) foster reflection and self-learning; (vi) strengthen systemic thinking using a holistic approach; (vii) train people motivated to participate and make responsible decisions; and (viii) raise awareness of the challenges posed by global issues.

In summary, the Barcelona Declaration acknowledged that attaining sustainable development, enhancing society, and fostering personal growth depends heavily on education. It is recommended that higher education institutions not be restricted to producing disciplinary knowledge and skill development. Instead, they ought to impart the moral and ethical principles that society demands. Finally, the declaration urged aspiring professionals to apply their expertise to address significant social, political, environmental, and scientific or technological concerns.

2.3.7.2 The Engineering for One Planet framework

In 2022, the Lemelson Foundation launched the Engineering for One Planet (EOP)[4] framework to integrate sustainability-focused learning into engineering education. The framework prioritizes the core student outcomes that are essential for engineering curricula and classifies them into three proficiency levels: low (remember and understand), medium (apply and analyze), and high (evaluate and create).

The overarching EOP framework encompasses four categories of learning outcomes: (i) systems thinking as the foundation; (ii) knowledge and understanding (environmental literacy, responsible business, and economy, social responsibility); and (iii) skills, experiences, and behaviors consisting of technical skills (design, material selection, environmental impact assessment) and leadership skills (critical thinking, communication, and teamwork). Each category comprises multiple topic areas with interconnected core learning outcomes (Anderson et al., 2023). The detailed outcome formulation can be found on the EOP website.

The EOP framework was formulated to facilitate instructors' ability to address pivotal inquiries about the four learning outcome categories mentioned above. A key question remains as to what level of proficiency students should acquire to demonstrate their knowledge and skills upon completion of the curriculum.

2.3.7.3 Knowledge, skills, and attitude (KSA)

As noted by Beagon et al. (2023), despite great interest in embedding sustainability and sustainable development in engineering education worldwide, there is "a lack of agreement on which competencies should be prioritized to prepare engineering students to resolve [current and] future sustainability challenges" and to prepare them to address the challenges of the SDGs.

---

[4]EOP_Framework_2023.pdf (engineeringforoneplanet.org)

This conclusion was reached by surveying the perspectives of three stakeholder groups on sustainability: industry, academia, and students.

The literature review by Beagon et al. (2023) on engineers' competency in addressing SDGs led to the identification of 54 competencies regrouped into three significant and interdependent categories:

- Technical competencies include fundamental technical and application skills.
- Nontechnical competencies include people-oriented skills (outward-facing) and ways of thinking (inward-facing).
- Attitude competencies include worldview, character, and ethical orientation.

Engineers must possess skills, attitudes, and knowledge in these three categories to effectively navigate and achieve success in the complex landscape of the 21st century. According to Kumar (2012), these three categories form a triangle of success. Skills include goal setting, time management, reasoning, communication, and interpersonal skills. Attitudes include self-motivation, self-confidence, integrity, honesty, optimism, enthusiasm, cooperation, and commitment. Finally, knowledge consists of basics, theories, information, facts, figures, descriptions, learning, science, etc.

Having taught engineering for the past 40 years and observing the evolution of engineering education, especially after the 1992 Rio Summit, there is no doubt that education is changing despite being slow. However, a gap remains between the knowledge imparted by institutions and the skills, attitudes, and experiences necessary to operate in the VUCA world.

2.4   Engineering Engagement Initiatives

Engaging students in civic engagement, outreach, experiential learning, and service-learning activities represents a unique way to understand the linkages between engineering and society and to acquire knowledge, skills, attitudes, and real-life experiences that are not taught in the classroom. These activities can take several forms. For instance, the Engineering Projects in Community

Service (EPICS) program, initiated in 1995 at Purdue University in Indiana, is an exemplary service-learning program that focuses on the human aspect of engineering. This program aims to engage undergraduate students in designing, constructing, and implementing systems to tackle engineering-related challenges in community services and educational institutions. The projects can last for several years, allowing students to tackle significant tasks with significant impact.

Engagement, that is, learning by doing, is integral to all engineering programs listed in Table 2.5. Without engagement, the curriculum remains an intellectual exercise, which is unfortunately found in many engineering programs worldwide. In the related fields of service learning and social engagement, there has also been a strong push toward integrating changes in engineering education and the overall university mission. In 2005, several universities launched the Talloires Network (Tuffs University, 2013). Convened by Tufts University's president in the United States, the Talloires network consists of an international collection of individuals and institutions devoted to strengthening universities' civic roles and social responsibilities worldwide. It acknowledges that academic institutions are committed to the social good and are not isolated from society. It also believes that (i) there is no dichotomy between civil engagement and excellence, (ii) the university's mandate is to educate and train responsible and dedicated citizens, and (iii) civic engagement should be a priority in research and scholarships.

Since 2000, various extracurricular and volunteer student-driven groups have emerged to address the engineering needs of developing communities worldwide. Examples include the Engineers Without Borders (EWB) International Network consisting of national groups such as EWB-USA, Bridges to Prosperity, Engineers Against Poverty, Engineers for a Sustainable World, Engineers in Action, and Engineering World Health, to name a few. A review of some of these initiatives in accreditation, service learning, hands-on experience, awareness building, and curriculum development can be found in Amadei and Sandekian (2010). These initiatives have had multiple positive effects on society and the engineering profession. They attract talented young individuals who are eager to learn the role of engineering in addressing societal needs, many of whom have become leaders in their fields of interest. These programs also provide multiple benefits by exposing students to real development projects during their formative years. For example, EWB projects:

1. Allow students to experience all engineering aspects, from problem identification to assessment, design, implementation, and monitoring.

2. Allow students to work with professional mentors during their school year, develop good contacts within the industry, and learn by doing.

3. Provide students with direct hands-on engineering educational experience in a new and safe environment.

4. Allow students to work in teams on more significant projects instead of discipline-specific projects.

5. Demonstrate to students that engineering problems can be complex and not always well-defined, can be solved in more ways than one, and often require working effectively with people who think differently and have different cultural backgrounds.

6. Teach students to interact with different cultures and think 'outside the box' with limited tools.

7. Train students to develop awareness of professional ethics and the role that engineering plays in addressing societal needs.

Above all, EWB-type engagement projects provide students with a cultural outlook on both national and international scales, similar to traditional study-abroad programs. Additionally, these projects foster a sense of belonging and engagement through teamwork, allowing students to express their passion and empathy and provide a societal context for engineering work that contributes to peace. They also offer a means for self-reflection, value development, and action on issues that students are passionate about. Furthermore, EWB-type projects facilitate collaboration with other professionals and help students develop their leadership skills, leading to a global perspective and local action. A notable outcome of these projects has been the increased recruitment of women (up to 45%) attracted to engineering because of the social dimension. Finally, the engineering industry endorses and supports EWB-type fieldwork projects. Companies view these activities as a pipeline for recruiting talented engineering leaders exposed to project management before graduation, including teamwork and dealing with complex and poorly defined issues in complex settings.

The seven characteristics of EWB projects mentioned above complement the traditional classroom instruction expected from engineering program accreditation boards. However, engineering engagement has faced several challenges, as experienced by the author over the past 20 years. For instance, one of the challenges of EWB trips is the amount of time students can spend in the field, as most implementation trips occur during academic breaks. Sustainable projects require continuous commitment and planning from one academic year to the next. For this reason, EWB projects require a five-year commitment from volunteers. Short of that, EWB trips would be more like volunteerism.

Another challenge is preparing students to work in diverse cultural and societal settings. As Nolan (2011) highlights, students (especially Americans) often struggle to function in foreign cultures due to their inability to "look beyond facts and figures to uncover meanings and patterns, to learn in unfamiliar surroundings, and to gain entry into the cultural world of others." In the author's experience, this lack of preparedness extends to the faculty members responsible for their education.

Engineering programs typically strongly emphasize technical aspects, which can sometimes overshadow the practical aspects of the field. This is evident from the author's observations of numerous exceptional undergraduate and graduate students who, despite possessing extensive engineering knowledge, struggle with manual work and field projects. Remedial workshops are necessary to bridge the gap between the academic world and reality. These workshops provide students with additional hands-on skills that they do not acquire in the classroom, including language proficiency, cultural awareness, first aid, fundraising, management and leadership skills, conflict analysis, and the ability to analyze risks and develop evacuation and emergency response plans.

Finally, participants in engineering engagement projects must become aware of the actual project dynamics and gain insight into the consequences (intended and unforeseen) of engineering decisions as they interact with various communities, as discussed in Section 2.3.6. Participants must be familiar with the fundamentals of project management (PMI, 2017).

2.5   Concluding Remarks

It is crucial to establish a new narrative for engineering education and practice that prioritizes human development and security and its contributions to peace and diplomacy because traditional narratives are no longer adequate to address contemporary societal challenges. Engineers must have the tools necessary to address today's world and not the world of the last century.

This chapter analyzed the interdependence between engineering and society, underscoring the importance of educating and training globally engaged engineers who can tackle problems of varying sizes and settings in the 21st century, encompassing conflicts. Engineers must be proficient in their respective fields by correctly executing and delivering projects that benefit the environment and community.

The messy and ill-defined nature of the VUCA world issues necessitates engineering education that builds on the one that produced the remarkable technical accomplishments of the 20th century. The focus should be on finding solutions to global problems, avoiding repeated mistakes, and not creating new ones. It requires adopting development ethics, defined as "the examination of ethical and value questions posed by development theory, planning, and practice, to diagnose value conflicts, assess policies, and assess valuations placed on development performance" (Goulet, 1997).

This chapter examined the building blocks of various engineering education frameworks proposed in the literature. However, there is no consensus on what the training of engineers in the 21st century represents. Nor is there mention of educating engineers to address peace and conflict issues at different scales, from local to global. Engineering education should be interpreted as being multiple with (i) core components such as those proposed by the Barcelona Declaration and the Engineering for One Planet framework and (ii) other components that are context- and scale-specific. Peace engineering and engineering diplomacy must be integrated into the engineers' body of knowledge.

Engineering competencies can be summarized into four main categories: technical, social, personal, and strategic. Technical competencies are essential for engineering tasks but are most effective when complemented by social, individual, and strategic competencies. Engineers who possess practical communication skills (social competency), adaptability to changing situations (personal competency), and the ability to make informed decisions that align with project objectives (strategic competency) are likely to excel in their engineering careers. A comprehensive skill set incorporating all these competencies is essential for engineering.

Educational institutions must reevaluate their curricula and consider the global implications of their decisions. It is difficult to envision how institutions that lack a clear sense of purpose can effectively prepare engineers with a comprehensive understanding of themselves and their societal roles. Unfortunately, this situation is prevalent in research universities. Any new educational philosophy must have internal and external dimensions, provide solutions that benefit both people and the environment, foster prosperity, encourage partnerships, and contribute to peace to address the challenges of the 21st century. Ultimately, educational institutions must recognize that human development and security in the 21st century require the humanization of the engineering profession and the understanding that engineering in this context is, above all, about people.

This chapter explored the building blocks of the body of knowledge of engineers in general. The next chapter builds on this body of knowledge and considers additional components required in engineering for peace and diplomacy.

References

Abela, P. (2023, Sept. 10). Seven psychological reasons why we are failing to solve the climate crisis. 7 Psychological Reasons Why We're Failing to Solve the Climate Crisis | Transformative

Alarcón, I. V. (2023). How to build engineers for life. *Issues in Science and Technology*, **40**(1) (Fall 2023): 25–27. https://doi.org/10.58875/DPWD5864

Amadei, B. and Wallace, W. A. (2009). Engineering for humanitarian development: A socio-technical approach, *IEEE Technology and Society Magazine*, **28**(4), 6–1.

Amadei, B. (2014). *Engineering for Sustainable Human Development*. Reston, VA: ASCE Press.

Amadei, B. (2019). *A Systems Approach to Modeling the Water-Energy-Land-Food Nexus* (Vols. I and II), New York: Momentum Press.

Amadei, B. (2023). *Navigating the Complexity Across the Peace-Sustainability-Climate Security Nexus*. Boca Raton: Routledge, ISBN 9781032563381.

Allenby, B. (2001). Earth systems engineering and management. *IEEE Technology and Society Magazine*, **19** (Winter 200/2001), 10–24.

Amadei, B. and Sandekian, R. (2010). A model of integrating humanitarian development into engineering education. *ASCE Journal of Professional Issues in Engineering Education and Practice*, **136**(2), 84–92.

American Society of Civil Engineers (ASCE) (2023). Policy Statement 418 - The role of the Civil Engineer in sustainable development | ASCE

Anderson, C., Cooper, C., and Roberts, D. (eds.) (2023). *Engineering for One Planet Framework: Comprehensive Guide to Teaching Learning Outcomes*. Portland, OR: The Lemelson Foundation, 26 pages.

Anderson, J. L. (2022). Global challenges addressed by engineering and technology. NAE Website - Global Challenges Addressed by Engineering and Technology.

Beagon, U., Kövesi, K., Tabas, B., Nørgaard, B., et al. (2023). Preparing engineering students for the challenges of the SDGs: What competencies are required? *European Journal of Engineering Education*, **48**(1), 1–23. DOI: 10.1080/03043797.2022.2033955

Berry, T. (1990). *The Dream of the Earth*. San Francisco, CA: Sierra Club Books.

Bourn, D. and Neal, I. (2008). *The Global Engineer: Incorporating Global Skills Within UK Higher Education of Engineers*. London, U.K.: Institute of Education. http://engineersagainstpoverty.org/_db/_documents/WEBGlobalEngineer_Linked_Aug_08_Update.pdf

Bugliarello, G. (1991). The social function of engineering: A current assessment. In: H. E. Sladovich, *Engineering as a Social Enterprise*. Washington, DC: The National Academies Press, 73–88.

Carson, R. (1962). *Silent Spring*. Boston, MA: Houghton Mifflin Company.

Carter, R., Elias-Trostmann, K., and Boehm, S. (2018, June 15). Climate change could force 100 million people into poverty by 2030. 4 ways we can step up adaptation. World Resources Institute. https://www. wri.org/insights/climate-change-could-force-100-million-people-poverty-2030-4-ways-we-can-step-adaptation

Chertow, M. R. (2000). The IPAT equation and its variants. *Journal of Industrial Ecology*, **4**(4), 13–29.

Commoner, B. (1972). The environmental cost of economic growth. *Chemistry in Britain*, **8**(2): 52–56 passim. PMID: 5059126.

Conis, E. (2017). Beyond Silent Spring: An Alternate History of DDT | Science History Institute

Did You Know 3.0 (YouTube)? Shift happens. Bing Videos

Dörner, D. (1997). *The Logic of Failure: Recognizing and Avoiding Error in Complex Situations*. New York: Perseus Books.

Downey, G. and Beddoes, K. (eds.) (2011). *What is Global Engineering Education For? The Making of International Educators*. Williston, VT: Morgan & Claypool.

Downey, G. L., Lucena, J. C., Moskal, B. M., Parkhurst, R., et al. (2006). The globally competent engineer: Working effectively with people who define problems differently. *Journal of Engineering Education*, **95**(2), 107–122.

Dresden Nexus Conference (2015). State of the Nexus Approach 2015: Management of Environmental Resources. DNC2015 Conference Report. Dresden, United Nations University Institute for Integrated Management of Material Fluxes and Resources (UNU-FLORES).

Duderstadt, J. J. (2008). *Engineering for a Changing World: A Roadmap to the Future of Engineering Practice, Research, and Education*. Ann Arbor, MI: University of Michigan. http://milproj.ummu.umich.edu/publications/EngFlex%20report/download/EngFlex%20Report.pdf.

Ehrlich, P. and Holdren, J. (1971). Impact of population growth. *Science*, **171**, 1212–1217.

Engineering Education for Sustainable Development (EESD) (2004). The Barcelona declaration. https://www.upc.edu/eesd-observatory/who/declaration-of-barcelona/BCN%20Declaration%20EESD_english.pdf

Federation Internationale des Ingenieurs Conseils (FIDIC) (2013). Project sustainability management; Application Manual. http://fidic.org/

books/project-sustainability-management-applications-manual-2nd-edition-2013>

Ferroukhi, R., Nagpal, D., Lopez-Peña, A., Hodges, T., et al. (2015). Renewable energy in the water, energy, and food nexus. United Arab Emirates: International Renewable Energy Agency (IRENA) Policy Unit. www.irena.org/Publications.

Florman, S. C. (1994). *The Existential Pleasures of Engineering* (2nd edition). New York, NY: St. Martin's Griffin.

Gasper, D. (2012). Development ethics: Why? What? How? A formulation of the field. *Journal of Global Ethics*, **8**(1), 117–135, DOI: 10.1080/17449626.2012.672450

Goulet, D. (1997). Development ethics: A new discipline. *International Journal of Social Economics*, **24**(11), 1160–1171.

Graedel, T. E. H. and Allenby, B. R. (2009). *Industrial Ecology and Sustainable Engineering*. UK: Pearson.

Graham, L. R. (1993). *The Ghost of the Executed Engineer: Technology and the Fall of the Soviet Union*. Cambridge, MA: Harvard University Press.

Grasso, D. and Burkins, M. (eds.) (2009). *Holistic Engineering Education: Beyond Technology*. New York: Springer.

Hollomon, J. H. (1991). Engineering's great challenge: The 1960s. In: *Engineering As a Social Enterprise*. Washington, DC: The National Academies Press, 104–110.

Huesemann, M. and Huesemann, J. (2011). *Techno-Fix: Why Technology Won't Save Us and The Environment*. Gabriola Islands, BC: New Society Publishers.

Hughes, T. P. (1991). From deterministic dynamos to seamless web systems. In: *Engineering as a Social Enterprise*. Washington, DC: The National Academies Press, 7–25.

Hunter, W., White, G. P., and Godbey, G. (2006). What Does It Mean to Be Globally Competent? *Journal of Studies in International Education*, **10**(3), 267–285. https://doi.org/10.1177/1028315306286930

Institute for Economics and Peace (IEP) (2020). *Global Peace Index 2020: Measuring Peace in a Complex World*. http://visionofhumanity.org/reports

Institute for Sustainable Infrastructure (ISI) (2018). *Envision*® *Sustainable Infrastructure Framework Guidance Manual*. https://sustainableinfrastructure.org/wp-content/uploads/EnvisionV3.9.7.2018.pdf

Jordan, R., Amadei, B., et al. (2020). Peace engineering consortium: Outcome of the first global peace engineering conference. *Procedia Computer Science*, 139–144, https://doi.org/10.1016/j.procs.2020.05.021

Kamp, A. (2016). *Engineering Education in the Rapidly Changing World: Rethinking the Vision for Higher Engineering Education* (2nd revised edition). The Netherlands: TU Delft, Faculty of Aerospace Engineering. https://repository.tudelft.nl/record/uuid:ae3b30e3-5380-4a07-afb5-dafd30b7b433

Kamp, A. (2020). *Navigating the Landscape of Higher Engineering Education: Coping with Decades of Accelerating Change Ahead* (1st edition), ISBN: 978-94-6366-242-0

Karwat, D. M. A., Eagle, W. E, Wooldridge, M. S., and Princen, T. E. (2014). Activist engineering: Changing engineering practice by deploying praxis. *Science and Engineering Ethics.*, **21**, 227–239. https://doi.org/10.1007/s11948-014-9525-0

Karwat, D. M. A. (2019). Self-reflection for activist engineering. *Science and Engineering Ethics.*, **26**, 1329–1352. https://doi.org/10.1007/s11948-019-00150-y

Kelly et al. (2016). Engineering education for sustainable development. Microsoft Word - GSDR_Brief_2016_Engineering_education_(un.org)

Klosky, L. and Klosky, W. (2013). Men of action: French influence and the founding of American civil and military engineering. *Construction History*, **28**, 69–87.

Kumar, V. P. (2012). Master the Triangle of Success – Knowledge, Skills, Attitudes – V Pradeep Kumar

Leopold, A. (1992). Engineering and conservation. In: B. Callicott and S. Falder (eds.), *The River of the Mother of God: And Other Essays by Aldo Leopold.* Madison, WI: University of Wisconsin Press.

Lepech, M. D. and Leckie, J. O. (2023). The value of engineering for sustainability. *The Bridge*, Fall.

Lima, M. and Oakes, W. (2006). *Service Learning: Engineering in Your Community.* New York, NY: Oxford University Press.

Lustgarten, A. (2023, June 6). Climate crisis is on track to push one-third of humanity out of its most livable environment. *ProPublica.* Climate Crisis Has Stranded 600 Million Outside Most Livable Environment — ProPublica

Manning, S. and Reinecke, J. (2016). We're failing to solve the world's "wicked problems." Here's a better approach. *The Conversation*, 2 October.

Mathebula (2018). Engineering Education for Sustainable Development: A Capabilities Appr (routledge.com)

Meadows, D. H., Randers, J., and Meadows, D. (2004). *Limits to Growth: The 30-Year Update.* Vermont: Chelsea Green Publishing.

Monat, J. P., Gannon, T. F., and Amissah, M. (2022). The case for systems thinking in undergraduate engineering education. *International Journal of Engineering Pedagogy* (iJEP), **12**(3), 50–88. https://doi. org/10.3991/ijep.v12i3.2503

Moskal, B. M., Skokan, C., Muñoz, D., and Gosink, J. (2008). Humanitarian engineering: Global impacts and sustainability of a curricular effort. *International Journal of Engineering Education,* **24**(10), 162–174.

Muscat, R. J., Bielefeldt, A. R., Riley, D. M., and Bates, R. A. (2015). Peace, conflict and sustainability: Addressing global and ethical issues in engineering education. Paper presented at 2015 ASEE Annual Conference and Exposition, Seattle, Washington. 10.18260/p.24553

National Academy of Engineering (NAE) (1985). *Engineering in Society.* Washington, DC: The National Academies Press.

National Academy of Engineering (NAE) (1991). *Engineering as a Social Enterprise.* Washington, DC: The National Academies Press.

National Academy of Engineering (NAE) (2000). Earth systems engineering exploratory workshop. Unpublished report. Washington, DC.

National Academy of Engineering (NAE) (2003). *Century of Innovation: Twenty Engineering Achievements That Transformed Our Lives.* Washington, DC: The National Academies Press.

National Academy of Engineering (NAE) (2012), *Life-Long Learning Imperatives in Engineering.* Washington, DC: The National Academies Press.

National Intelligence Council (NIC) (2021). Climate Change and International Responses Increasing Challenges to US National Security through 2040. NIE Climate Change and National Security.pdf (dni.gov)

National Research Council. (2014). *Convergence: Facilitating Trans-disciplinary Integration of Life Sciences, Physical Sciences, Engineering, and Beyond.* Washington, DC: The National Academies Press. https:// doi.org/10.17226/18722.

Nattrass, B. and Altomare, M. (1999). *The Natural Step for Business: Wealth, Ecology and the Evolutionary Corporation.* Gabriola Islands, BC: New Society Publishers.

Nilsson, L., Madon, T., and Sastry, S. S. (2014). Toward a new field of development engineering: Linking technology design to the demands of the poor. *Procedia Engineering*, **78**, 3–9.

Nolan, R. (2002). *Development Anthropology: Encounters in the Real World.* Boulder, CO: Westview Press.

Nolan, R. (2011, November 12). What do we know, and what can we do with what we know? Anthropology, international development, and U.S. higher education. Keynote lecture at Collective Motion 2.0, Princeton University.

OpenAI (2023). *ChatGPT* (Feb 13 version) [Large language model]. https://chat.openai.com

OpenAI (2024). *ChatGPT* (May 10 version) [Large language model]. https://chat.openai.com

Palmer, P. J. and Zajonc, A. (2010). *The Heart of Higher Education: A Call to Renewal.* Francisco, CA: Jossey-Bass.

Project Management Institute (PMI) (2017). *A Guide to the Project Management Body of Knowledge* (6th edition).

Raworth, K. (2018). *Doughnut Economics.* Vermont: Chelsea Geen Publishing.

Reynolds, A. (2013, March). Diplomacy, Development, Defense, and Engineering. *Mechanical Engineering*, 18 AQ.

Rigaud, K., et al. (2018). *Groundswell: Preparing for Internal Climate Migration.* Washington, DC: World Bank.

Roberts, D. (2002). *Engineers and Sustainable Development.* Washington, DC: World Federation of Engineering Organizations ComTech Committee.

Ryan, C. (2020). Introduction to the 5Ps. PowerPoint Presentation (unescap.org)

Schirch, L. (2013). *Conflict Assessment and Peacebuilding Planning.* Boulder, CO: Kumarian Press.

Schön, D. A. (1983). *The Reflective Practitioner: How Professionals Think in Action.* London: Routledge.

Schumacher, E. F. (1973). *Small Is Beautiful.* New York, NY: Harper Perennial.

Simon, H. A. (1972). Theories of bounded rationality. In: C. B. McGuire and R. Radner (eds.), *Decisions and Organization.* Amsterdam, The Netherlands: North-Holland Publishing, 161–176.

Sprague de Camp, L. (1963). *The Ancient Engineers.* New York, NY: Ballantine Books.

Steffen W. and Tyson, P. (eds.) (2001). Earth system science: An integrated approach. *Environment*, **43**(8), 21–27.

Stoddard, I., et al. (2021). Three decades of climate mitigation: Why haven't we bent the global emissions curve? *Annual Review of Environment and Resources*, **46**, 653–689.

The Economist (2021, Dec. 18). The new normal is already here. Get used to it. The era of predictable unpredictability is not going away. The new normal is already here. Get used to it | The Economist

The World Bank (2017). The World Bank Environmental and Social Framework. https://thedocs.worldbank.org/en/doc/837721522762 050108-0290022018/original/ESFFramework.pdf

The World Bank (2023). The development, climate, and nature crisis: Solutions to end poverty on a livable planet. CCDR-SynthesisReport 2023.pdf

Tufts University (2013). The Talloires Network. http://talloiresnetwork. tufts.edu/

U. N. Educational, Scientific, and Cultural Organization (UNESCO) (2010). *Engineering: Issues, Challenges, and Opportunities for Development.* Paris: UNESCO Publishing.

U. N. Educational, Scientific, and Cultural Organization (UNESCO) (2017). *Education for Sustainable Development Goals: Learning Objectives.* ISBN 978-92- 3-100209-0. Education for Sustainable Development Goals: Learning Objectives | UNESCO

U. N. Educational, Scientific, and Cultural Organization (UNESCO) (2021). Engineering for sustainable development: delivering on the Sustainable Development Goals | UNESCO

UNDP Human Development Report (UNDP/HDR) (2013). *The rise of the South: Human progress in a diverse world.* United Nations Development Programme, New York, NY. http://www.undp.org/con- tent/dam/undp/library/corporate/HDR/2013GlobalHDR/English/ HDR2013%20Report%20English.pdf.

United Nations Conference on Environment and Development (UNCED) (1992). *Agenda 21.* http://www.un.org/esa/sustdev/documents/ agenda21/english/Agenda21.pdf.

United Nations Economic and Social Commission for Western Asia (UNESCWA). the_5ps_of_the_sustainable_development_goals.pdf (unescwa.org)

United Nations Environmental Programme (UNEP) (2023). Adaptation Finance Gap Update 2023. In: *Adaptation Gap Report 2023:*

Underfinanced. Underprepared. Inadequate investment and planning on climate adaptation leaves the world exposed. Nairobi.

United Nations Department of Economic and Social Affairs (UNDESA) (2015). International decade for actions. Water for Life 2005–2015. http://www.un.org/waterforlifedecade/water_and_energy.shtml

van Zanten, J. A. and van Tulder, R. (2021) Towards nexus-based governance: Defining interactions between economic activities and Sustainable Development Goals (SDGs), *International Journal of Sustainable Development & World Ecology*, **28**(3), 210–226, DOI: 10.1080/13504509.2020.1768452

Vesilind, P. A. (ed.) (2005). *Peace Engineering: When Personal Values And Engineering Careers Converge.* Woodsville, NH: Lakeshore Press.

Vesilind, P. A. (2010). *Engineering, Peace, and Justice: The Responsibility of Engineers to Society.* London: Springer.

Wallace, W. (2005). *Becoming Part of the Solution: The Engineer's Guide to Sustainable Development.* Washington, DC: American Council of Engineering Companies (ACEC).

Wennmann, A. (2023). Pragmatic peacebuilding for climate change adaptation in cities. USIP Press, No. 191. Pragmatic Peacebuilding for Climate Change Adaptation in Cities | United States Institute of Peace (usip.org)

World Commission on Environment and Development (WCED) (1987). *Our Common Future.* Oxford: Oxford University Press.

World Economic Forum (WEF) (2023). The Global Risks Report 2023 (18th edition). https://www3.weforum.org/docs/WEF_Global_Risks_Report_2023.pdf

World Economic Forum (WEF) (2024). The Global Risks Report 2024 (19th edition). https://www3.weforum.org/docs/WEF_The_Global_Risks_Report_2024.pdf

World Health Organization (WHO) (2021). Climate change and health. Climate change and health (who.int)

Chapter 3

Peace, Conflict, and Diplomacy

We may not think of engineers as peacemakers first. However, our well-being relies on the work of engineers who implicitly provide various resources and services that foster peace and community security. Peace can refer to different things for different people. This chapter examines various aspects of peace and conflict that are crucial for engineers to participate effectively in peacebuilding and diplomatic initiatives. Peace and conflict analyses complement other human development and security issues. This chapter offers suggestions for a body of knowledge on peace engineering and engineering diplomacy.

Engineering and technology are empowering practically every aspect of our lives. Diplomacy has been largely absent from this convergence, but opportunities exist for such empowerment as science and diplomacy become increasingly connected (Yortsos, in Druhora, 2017).

The most important result of these [EWB] projects is changing the worldviews of engineering students, who discover that they want to continue using their engineering skills for peace engineering (Vesilind, 2010).

Engineering for Peace and Diplomacy
Bernard Amadei
Copyright © 2025 Jenny Stanford Publishing Pte. Ltd.
ISBN 978-981-5129-75-5 (Hardcover), 978-1-003-65168-0 (eBook)
www.jennystanford.com

3.1 Introduction

Peace is a concept that humans have long contemplated (Stearns, 2014). Although numerous studies have demonstrated the significant benefits of peace for human and economic development, social justice and stability, the promotion of human rights, and overall well-being and peace, like other related community development concepts, such as sustainability and resilience, peace is challenging to comprehend and quantify in diverse contexts and scales.

A formal analysis of the diverse cultural and historical interpretations of peace, including philosophical, political, religious, and legal perspectives, can be found in Dietrich (2012), Dietrich and Pearce (2019), and Stearns (2014). This analysis reveals that peace can be characterized as a state of wholeness, harmony, completeness, well-being (physical and spiritual), and harmonious coexistence. These four emergent human development and security properties are reflected in the etymological definitions of peace in Greek, *Eirene*, and Semitic languages, such as *Shlamah* in Aramaic, *Salaam* in Arabic, and *Shalom* in Hebrew. Additionally, the concept of peace as wholeness is also present in the definition proposed by The Earth Charter (1987), which posits that "peace is the *wholeness* created by right relationships with oneself, other persons, other cultures, other life, Earth, and the larger whole of which all are a part." Gittins and Velasquez-Castellanos (2016) state that there are approximately 35 theories of peace at the university level. This book uses the definitions of peace-related concepts found in *Peace Terms* published by the US Institute of Peace (Snodderly, 2018).

The literature on peace and conflict studies offers numerous contributions to the understanding of various aspects of social conflict and peace. Although peace is commonly viewed as a universal value, it can have different meanings for diverse populations and cultures (Groff, 2008; Cortright, 2008; Dietrich, 2012; Stearns, 2014). Similarly, there are various forms of social conflict, ranging from peaceful demonstrations to armed conflicts (Lemos, 2018), and it is unrealistic to expect a uniform and optimized static state of peace. Instead, it is more practical to acknowledge the existence of 'many [dynamic] peace(s)' (Dietrich and Pearce, 2019), which are contingent upon specific contexts and scales, both physical and temporal. Dietrich (2012) noted that "peace has to be read as a plural" as it is context and scale specific. Moreover, it is essential to recognize that conflict and peace are both temporal and that their dynamics can change over time.

Diamond and McDonald (1996) noted that "peace is not a measurable commodity. It must be seen instead as a potential, a possibility, an ever-changing condition... a direction in which to head, one step at a time." On the one hand, peace can be viewed as a process (i.e., a verb) encompassing various efforts to create an environment conducive to lasting peace, such as peacebuilding, peacemaking, and peacekeeping. On the other hand, peace can also be considered an outcome (i.e., a noun), representing a state that *emerges* from the interaction of multiple socioeconomic, engineering, and environmental systems operating in a constrained landscape of a specific context and scale. These systems constitute a so-called *peace infrastructure*, a concept proposed in the peace studies and conflict management literature (Lederach, 2012; Davis, 2016).

Peace impacts other emerging states, such as community health, well-being, sustainability, and resilience. All of these concepts are dynamic; they change as a community develops. Consequently, there is no such thing as one unified and optimized static state of peace, as there are no single unified and optimized stationary states of well-being, health, sustainability, or resilience. Another characteristic of these states is that it is easier to define them by what they are *not* rather than what they are. This characteristic leaves room for exploring many acceptable or good enough states. The same can be said about health, well-being, sustainability, resilience, and development.

Peace is intimately linked to community development (Dews, 2013), and peace and development can be either cause or effect. For instance, peace can be the cause of development, or development can be the cause of peace. The linkages between peace and development can either be enabling or constraining. Although peace is an underlying prerequisite to development, its benefits depend primarily on the design, implementation, and evaluation of peace resolution and transformation in peacebuilding, peacemaking, and peacekeeping activities (Ricigliano, 2012). For instance, not addressing the root causes and underlying factors of conflict may result in resuming conflict and negatively affecting development in the near future (Ricigliano, ibid). One case in point is the fragility of stability, security, and socio-economic development, which has been mainstream in Somalia since 1991 due to intermittent armed civil conflict (Hayden, 2018). The same can be said about whether aid and development agencies contribute to reducing or fueling violent conflicts (Anderson, 2010).

Likewise, socioeconomic development can inevitably positively or negatively impact society depending on the type of development being implemented (see Table 2.4). It can have positive consequences, create unintended issues, and exacerbate conflicts (Bush, 1998). For instance, a combination of inappropriate decision-making and trade-offs in activities such as the supply and demand of water, energy, and food resources; inadequate associated infrastructure planning and design; poor decisions in resource management and allocation; and poor governance may result in divisions, unrest, conflict, violence, and insecurity. The dynamic of prioritizing urban development over rural development has the potential to create resentment and conflict. In short, not all forms of socioeconomic development lead to long-term peace and vice versa (Brown and Nicolucci-Altman, 2022). Syria is an example in which the government's mismanagement of natural resources, such as water, combined with a drought between 2007 and 2010, led to internal migration from rural to urban areas, unrest, government repression, and external migration to Europe from 2010 to the present (see Chapter 8).

The following questions arise: (i) What represents a state of sustainable peace at the community level in the short and long term? (ii) What peacebuilding, peacemaking, and peacekeeping processes are more likely to build, make, and sustain a state of peace? What changes are necessary to secure sustainable peace?

Another related question is how peace can be measured. Measurement is essential for scientists and engineers because they are taught to believe that it is difficult to manage something if it cannot be measured. If so, a question arises regarding how to measure peace indirectly through indicators and proxies and monitor and evaluate peace over time. The challenge here is how to measure a state that is the outcome of many interacting systems and subsystems (e.g., social, economic, environmental, infrastructure) with various levels of complexity, uncertainty, and adaptability, and subject to multiple constraints (geopolitical, environmental, cultural, etc.). Systems science provides tools to address these challenges.

3.2   Defining Peace

The noble goal of promoting lasting and sustainable peace for all people has been a topic of intense discussion by various governmental and non-governmental organizations since the publication of *An Agenda for Peace* by the United Nations (Boutros-Ghali, 1992). This document helped define preventive diplomacy, peacemaking, peacekeeping, and peacebuilding concepts. Since 1992, multiple papers and policy statements have been published to clarify the nature of peace and its relationship with human development and global security. For example, the United Nations Sustainable Development Goal 16 (Peace, Justice, and Strong Institutions) is to "Promote peaceful and inclusive societies for sustainable development, provide access to justice for all and build effective, accountable and inclusive institutions at all levels" (SDSN, 2020).

The peace and conflict study literature often refers to Johan Galtung's work, which pioneered the concept of *negative peace* and *positive peace* in the early 1960s (Grewal, 2003; Fischer, 2007; Lawler and Williams, 2008; Galtung, 1964, 1990). A helpful analogy Galtung (1990) offers is that negative and positive peace are akin to curative and preventive measures in the health realm. Galtung (1990) added *cultural peace* to both positive and negative peace. Table 3.1 describes the attributes of the three types of peace and provides examples of associated activities, according to Fischer (2007).

Table 3.1 Three aspects of peace and examples of associated activities

Peace sectors	Attributes (Galtung, 1964, 1990)	Activities (Fischer, 2007)
Negative peace	*The absence* of war and direct or organized violence. Something undesirable (personal violence) ceases to exist.	Address the direct factors that reduce direct violence, including ceasefires, disarmament, prevention of terrorism and state terrorism, and nonviolence.
Positive peace	*The presence* and *prevalence* of positive attributes, conditions, and priorities that promote "social and economic justice, environmental integrity, human rights, and development" and contribute to the structural "integration of human society."	Address the indirect factors that may drive violent conflicts, including building a life-sustaining economy at the local, national, and global levels in which everyone's basic needs are met, good governance and participation, self-determination, and human rights.
Cultural peace	Aspects of a culture that serve to justify and legitimize direct [negative] peace and structural [positive] peace.	Promotion of a culture of peace and mutual learning; global communication and dialogues; development of peaceful deep cultures and deep structures; peace education; peace journalism.

Negative peace, positive peace, and cultural peace interact with each other and form, according to Galtung (1990), a "(virtuous) peace triangle" rather than a "(vicious) violence triangle," the latter consisting of the interaction between direct violence (a quick and visible process), indirect or structural violence (a slow and invisible process), and cultural violence (a legitimizing process). As suggested by Galtung, peace should start at "all three corners at the same time, not assuming that basic change in one will automatically lead to changes in the other two." Figure 3.1 represents the peace triangle, including feedback between the three types of peace.

In the peace triangle, one can interpret the area of the triangle as representing the extent of the enabling environment in which peace unfolds "nonviolently and creatively" over time (Galtung, 1996). Equivalently, in the violence triangle, that space represents the constraining environment in which violence unfolds. Outside these triangles are the external conflict-affected and conflict-sensitive landscapes (of a specific context and scale) that influence the three interacting components of peace and violence over time. In this environment, multiple systems and subsystems affect each triangle with constraints and stressors. Likewise, positive, negative, and cultural peace or direct, indirect, and cultural violence affect the performance of these systems.

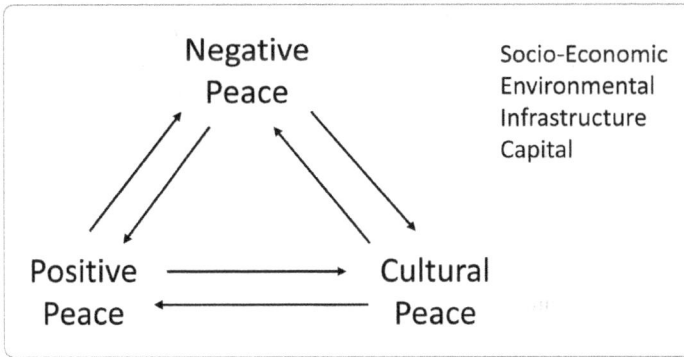

Figure 3.1 Peace begins at all corners of the triangle. The state of peace resides in the triangle (enabling setting) where the three aspects of peace overlap. Outside the triangle is the landscape in which peace unfolds.

Another possible representation of the direct interactions between the three types of peace is presented in Table 3.2. Each row in this cross-impact table represents each type of peace's direct influence (impact) on the other two types. Similarly, each column represents the direct dependence of each type of peace on the other two types.

Six indirect tertiary connections exist among all three types of peace: (i) PP-NP-CP and PP-CP-NP starting with positive peace, (ii) NP-CP-PP and NP-PP-CP starting with negative peace, and (iii) CP-PP-NP and CP-NP-PP starting with cultural peace. An example of PP-NP-CP is that positive peace affects negative peace, which impacts cultural peace. Figure 3.1 shows that many feedback mechanisms can lead to more complicated interactions than tertiary ones.

Table 3.2 Cross-impact interaction matrix showing the influence and dependence for each type of peace on the others

Positive Peace (PP)	By investing in factors that foster positive peace, such as reducing economic disparities, advancing education, and ensuring access to necessities, societies are better equipped to prevent the escalation of violent conflicts.	Addressing underlying inequalities and fostering inclusiveness leads to preserving cultural diversity and promoting harmony within communities, a defining characteristic of positive peace.
Promoting positive peace requires creating an enabling environment where people can engage in productive activities, invest in education and healthcare, and work towards social and economic development without fear of violence.	Negative Peace (NP)	Ensures the conditions for conserving and celebrating cultural diversity and harmony within communities.
Prioritizing and advocating for cultural harmony is more likely to establish the conditions required for preserving and enhancing positive peace, resulting in a more stable and cohesive environment for its members.	Placing a high value on cultural peace and actively promoting it is more likely to foster an environment free from violence and conflict, leading to a more peaceful and stable setting.	Cultural Peace (CP)

It should be noted that the three forms of peace suggested by Galtung, sometimes called *just peace* (Lederach, 2012), are the three forms of *outer peace* usually emphasized in Western culture. As Groff (2008) states, it is also imperative to recognize the significance of fostering inner peace at the individual level as a crucial precondition for a peaceful world. This endeavor draws upon the vast spiritual-religious traditions of Hinduism, Buddhism, and other such practices. Groff (ibid) also considered Gaia peace as peace between humans and their environment, a central tenet of "earth-based religions and cultures." Regardless of culture, inner peace is positively correlated with outer peace and is often seen as where peace builds outward at the individual and institutional levels (Cortright, 2008). The individual can influence the collective, and the collective can also impact the individual (Milligan et al., 2022).

To ensure all aspects of peace at the community level, such as (i) securing water, energy, land, food, housing, health, and other resources by building capacity; (ii) providing access to skills and resources; (iii) holding up the rule of law, promoting good governance, social justice, equality, and economic equity; (iv) creating ways for people to embrace a culture of peace; and (v) fostering inner peace individually, it is essential to use an interdisciplinary integrated method. This approach must manage the various "self-regulating processes" within the community (Fischer, 2007). Policymakers and practitioners involved in peacebuilding must comprehensively understand the community landscape systems contributing to effective peacebuilding. This recommendation requires understanding the current state of peace, being aware of deviations from desired goals, and appreciating the various feedback mechanisms in the regulatory processes necessary to guide the community toward its desired state.

3.3   Measuring Peace

Several institutions have attempted to capture the multidimensional aspects of peace. Since peace is not a direct, measurable commodity and is difficult to conceptualize in different contexts and scales, questions arise about how to (i) measure it *indirectly* through indicators and proxies, and (ii) monitor and evaluate peace over time. The challenge is being able to measure a dynamic state that is the outcome of many interacting systems and subsystems (e.g., social, economic, environmental, infrastructure) with various levels of complexity, uncertainty, and adaptability, and subject to multiple constraints (e.g., geopolitical, environmental, cultural, etc.)

Peace indicators can be classified into various groups: security, social, political, legal, economic, environmental, and physical and mental well-being (Fisher et al., 2000). Within each category, the indicators of conflict differ depending on whether the conflict is hidden, emerging, or explicit and as it progresses from pre-conflict, confrontation, and crisis to post-conflict resolution.

Two indices for measuring peace are presented below: (i) the Fragile State Index proposed by the Fund for Peace and (ii) the positive and negative peace indices proposed by the Institute for Economics and Peace (IEP). Both indices measure peace (i.e., outer peace) in a qualitative or semi-quantitative manner at the *country* level.

To both the Fund for Peace and IEP frameworks, which use top-down measurements, one can add the approach proposed by Everyday Peace Indicators.[1] It relies on directly assessing the conflict issues of communities and what they seek as peaceful solutions. Communities themselves are asked to establish their everyday indicators. This approach is grassroots and bottom-up, with the advantages of being context- and scale-specific and not already using made-up recipes.

3.3.1 The Fragile State Index (FSI)

The Fragile State Index (https://fragilestatesindex.org/) uses 12 indicators to rank annually 179 countries based on the "different pressures [normal and vulnerable] they face that impact their levels of fragility" and their vulnerability to internal conflict and societal deterioration. According to the Fund for Peace (2017), possible examples of emerging state fragility include: "the loss of physical control of its territory or a monopoly on the legitimate use of force; the erosion of legitimate authority to make collective decisions; an inability to provide reasonable public services; or an inability to interact with other states as a full member of the international community."

The FSI is determined annually by combining three data streams: qualitative, quantitative, and expert validation. The indicators are divided into four categories, each with three sub-

---

[1]https://www.everydaypeaceindicators.org

indicators and multiple search questions (Fund for Peace, 2017), as follows:

- *Cohesion indicators*: security apparatus, factionalized elites, and group grievances.
- *Economic indicators*: Economic decline, uneven development, human flight, and brain drain.
- *Political indicators*: State legitimacy, public services, human rights, and rules of law.
- *Social and cross-cutting indicators*: Demographic pressures, refugees, internally displaced people, and external intervention.

3.3.2 The IEP Framework

The Institute for Economics and Peace (IEP) in Sydney, Australia, proposed a more comprehensive measure of positive peace called the Positive Peace Index (PPI). It considers Galtung's positive peace as representing "the attitudes, institutions, and structures that create and sustain peaceful societies" (IEP, 2017). According to the IEP, a country-level optimum positive peace environment is founded on eight interdependent pillars or domains, as shown in Fig. 3.2.

The Positive Peace Index (PPI) is calculated at the country level by evaluating each of the eight domains presented in Fig. 3.2. As shown in Table 3.3, each domain comprises three indicators rated on a scale of one to five. The PPI is determined by taking the weighted average of 24 indicators and is expressed on an inverted scale, with one being the most positive peace and five being the least positive peace.

The indicators in Table 3.3 are the most recent ones proposed by the IEP (2024a). They have been updated since 2018 (IEP, 2018) and are based on the common characteristics of peaceful countries. The 24 indicators are divided into three interdependent domains: "*Attitudes*-related indicators measure social views, tensions, or perceptions; *institutions-related* indicators represent the impact that formal and informal institutions of society exert on peacefulness, social well-being, and the economy;

and *structures-related* indicators assess the underpinning of the socio-economic system, such as poverty and equality, or are the result of aggregate activity, such as GDP. Usually, these are the indicators that measure infrastructure or socio-economic development."

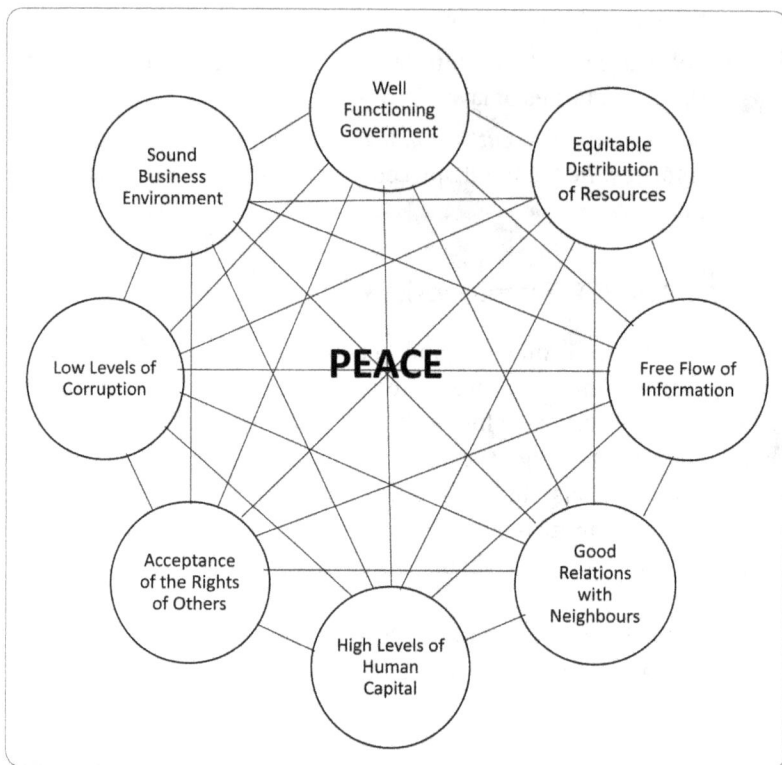

Figure 3.2 According to the IEP (2022), eight pillars (domains) contribute to positive peace. © Institute for Economics and Peace. Positive Peace Report 2022: Analyzing the factors that sustain peace. Sydney, January 2022. Available from: http://visionofhumanity.org/resources.

According to the IEP (2022) and Killelea (2021), countries with the most positive peace tend to exhibit greater resilience, robust and thriving economies, favorable ecological measures, higher levels of well-being and happiness, more robust social cohesion, and greater satisfaction with living standards, based on data analysis from 2009 to 2020.

Table 3.3 Positive peace index pillars, structures, institutions (Inst.), and attitudes indicators (IEP, 2024a). ©Institute for Economics and Peace. *Positive Peace Report 2024: Analyzing the factors that build, predict, and sustain peace.* Available from http://visionofhumanity.org/resources

Positive Peace Pillars	Domain	Indicators	Positive Peace Pillars	Domain	Indicators
Well-Functioning Government	Inst.	Government Openness and Transparency	Free Flow of Information	Structures	Freedom of the Press
	Inst.	Government Effectiveness		Attitudes	Quality of Information
	Inst.	Rule of Law: Estimate		Structures	Telecom Infrastructure (Internet, Mobile, Broadband)
Sound Business Environment	Inst.	Regulatory Quality	Good Relations with Neighbors	Attitudes	Law to Support Equal Treatment of Population Segments
	Inst.	Financial Institution Index		Structures	International Tourism
	Structures	GDP per Capita		Inst.	Freedom to Trade Internationally
Low Levels of Corruption	Inst.	Control of Corruption	Equitable Distribution of Resources	Structures	Inequality-Adjusted Life Expectancy Index
	Attitudes	Factionalized Elites		Inst.	Education and Income Inequality
	Inst.	Public Sector Theft		Attitudes	Equality of Opportunity
High Levels of Human Capital	Structures	Shares of Youth not in Employment, Education, or Training (NEET)	Acceptance of the Rights of Others	Attitudes	Gender Inequality
	Structures	Researchers in R&D		Attitudes	Group Grievance
	Structures	Healthy Life Expectancy (HALE)		Attitudes	Exclusion by Socio-Economic Group

The IEP also proposed a Global Peace Index (GPI) to measure negative peace (i.e., the level of country peacefulness) for the same 163 independent states and territories as the PPI. As shown in Table 3.4, it is calculated as the weighted average of 23 indicators divided into three domains: ongoing domestic and international conflict, societal safety and security, and militarization. Similar to PPI, GPI varies between one (the most negative peace) and five (the least negative peace). Values of country GPIs can be found at http://visionofhumanity.org/indexes/global-peace-index/.

An analysis of the overall PPI and GPI scores at the country level indicated that both indices were highly positively correlated. The IEP (2022) report concluded that, compared to 2008, the current level of peacefulness in the world is lower, as indicated by a 3.2% decrease in the average peacefulness score of countries over the past 14 years. Additionally, there has been an annual decrease in 11 of the last 14 years.

Based on their values in the GPI and PPI, the IEP (2019) categorizes countries into four possible states of peacefulness. They include (i) countries with sustainable peace (high positive and negative peace), (ii) countries with positive peace deficits (low positive peace and high negative peace) that are likely to experience violence in the future, (iii) countries with a positive peace surplus (high positive peace and low negative peace) with the potential to become more peaceful over time, and (iv) countries trapped in violence (low negative and positive peace). Apart from sustainable peace, all other sectors represent several aspects of unsustainable peace (Amadei, 2020). Reychler and Paffenholz (2001) define sustainable peace as a

> A situation characterized by the absence of physical violence; the elimination of unacceptable political, economic, and cultural forms of discrimination; a high level of internal and external legitimacy or support; self-sustainability; and a propensity to enhance the constructive transformation of conflict.

Although not initially proposed by the IEP, a third index, the Cultural Peace Index (CPI), can be introduced to measure cultural peace (Amadei, 2020). Although its indicators are yet to be determined, the CPI could be introduced to range between 1 (the most cultural peace) and 5 (the least cultural peace) for consistency with the PPI and GPI. Amadei (2020) argued that a 3D peace vector with PPI, GPI, and CPI components can be introduced to represent the evolution of the state of peace at the country level.

Table 3.4 Global Peace Index groups and indicators (IEP, 2024b). © Institute for Economics and Peace. *Global Peace Index 2024. Measuring peace in a complex world*. Available from: http://visionofhumanity.org/resources

Negative Peace Groups	Indicators
Ongoing domestic and international conflict	• Number and duration of internal conflicts • Number of deaths from external organized conflict • Number of deaths from internal organized conflict • Number, duration, and role in external conflicts • Intensity of organized internal conflict • Relations with neighboring countries
Militarization	• Military expenditure as a percentage of GDP • Number of armed services personnel per 100,000 people • Volume of transfers of major conventional weapons as recipient (imports) per 100,000 people • Volume of transfers of major conventional weapons as supplier (exports) per 100,000 people • Financial contribution to UN peacekeeping missions • Nuclear and heavy weapons capabilities
Societal safety and security	• Level of perceived criminality in society • Number of refugees and internally displaced people as a percentage of the population • Political instability • Political Terror Scale • Impact of terrorism • Number of homicides per 100,000 people • Level of violent crime • Violent demonstrations • Number of jailed populations per 100,000 people • Number of internal security officers and police per 100,000 people • Ease of access to small arms and light weapons

The IEP's proposed framework, which has been in place since 2017, acknowledges the multidimensional and multidisciplinary nature of peace at the macro (country) level. It recognizes that the various elements that contribute to peace are interconnected and that a systemic approach is more effective than assuming that the components operate independently in creating peaceful communities (IEP, 2024c).

3.4   A Systems Definition of Peace

Regarding the peace–sustainability–climate security nexus (Amadei, 2023), a systems approach is more effective than a deterministic one in recognizing the state of stability or dynamic equilibrium that characterizes peace. It acknowledges that peace arises in landscapes with multiple interrelated and interwoven systems (social, economic, financial, technical, and environmental) and a hierarchy of embedded subsystems involving various flexible actors. Such a landscape represents a space of possibilities, or an environment (stable or in conflict) influenced by different factors and barriers (e.g., political, ethical, security, economic, and socio-cultural). Peace is a part of the landscape system and cannot be separated from it.

With this in mind, it is appropriate to consider a systems-based definition of peace if one is interested in exploring how peace interacts with other aspects of human development and security through a systemic lens. As suggested by Amadei (2020), peace can be defined as an *emerging organizing principle* and

> An enabling, violent-free state of dynamic equilibrium emerging from the right relationships among different populations and their interactions with the various systems in the landscape upon which they depend.

This definition of peace builds on that of sustainability presented by Ben-Eli (2018), which is defined as "a dynamic equilibrium in the processes of interaction between a population and the carrying capacity of an environment such that the population develops to express its full potential without adversely and irreversibly affecting the carrying capacity of the environment upon which it depends."

The two definitions of peace and sustainability capture the peace–sustainability nexus well (Sharifi et al., 2021) and acknowledge that "sustainable development cannot be realized without peace and security, and peace and security will be at risk without sustainable development" (UNESCAP, 2018). As noted by Ricigliano (2012), a peaceful society requires sustainable levels of human development, which correspond to how well people's basic needs are met, as well as healthy processes of change, referring to individual or group abilities to deal with issues, opportunities, and challenges in ways that improve, or at least do not compromise, their ability to meet basic needs in the future.

The above definition of peace captures the wholeness and right relationship aspects of peace suggested by The Earth Charter (1987) and the Greek and Semitic languages' definitions of peace mentioned earlier in this chapter. The National Peace Academy (n.d.) outlines five interrelated and codependent realms of peace and right relationships, which span the personal (with oneself), social (with other individuals), political (within and among various groups, institutions, communities, etc.), institutional (within and among organizations, governments, etc.), and ecological (with the natural environment) dimensions.

The definitions of peace used here and of sustainability of Ben-Eli lend themselves well to using a systems approach to capture their coherence. As discussed for the peace–sustainability–climate security nexus (Amadei, 2023), a systems approach helps decision-makers and practitioners to:

- Sense how well parts of a community landscape work together and form structures and patterns through feedback mechanisms.
- Identify and address conflicts and barriers to peace and development.
- Acknowledges the relationships between landscape components from multiple perspectives.
- Look at community events as part of the behavioral patterns created by internal structures resulting from patterns and modes of thought.
- Understand the dynamic, adaptable, unpredictable, and changing nature of community life, including the effects of time and delay (information and materials).

- Recognize how a small community event can influence others and the associated consequences of such interactions.
- Identify leverage points in the community landscape.
- Explore the importance of trade-offs and synergies across systems and subsystems.

These conditions can contribute to a safe and secure environment, rule of law, stable governance, sustainable economy, and social well-being. They represent end states of stabilization through reconstruction and peacekeeping in conflict-affected or sensitive environments to prevent violent conflicts (USIP/NAE, 2009).

Adopting a systems perspective of the peace–sustainability nexus entails recognizing and embracing its inherent complexity, involving dynamic and interconnected processes. This approach acknowledges that there are no universal solutions to the challenges posed by peace and sustainability, as each context is unique and requires tailored strategies.

A systems approach to any nexus involving peace comes with its share of challenges, which are addressed in more detail in Chapters 5 and 6. The first challenge is determining the interaction threads of the nexus once a specific project has been selected and characterized. Another challenge is experimenting with different integrated solutions and intervention scenarios and exploring the most promising regarding reduced trade-offs and increased synergies in each context and at a specific scale.

3.5 Peace and Conflict

3.5.1 The Conflict Spectrum

This book considers peace as an emerging state of wholeness, harmony, tranquility, and well-being. Positive elements include justice, equality, inclusion, diversity, social harmony, and economic and political stability. Human development and security depend on these factors.

Peace is not merely an absence of conflict. Indeed, overt conflicts such as wars, armed conflicts, or violent disputes are not involved. In this sense, peace can be viewed as the absence of physical or verbal violence. Simultaneously, non-destructive conflict can positively influence change, uncover hidden problems, and promote growth and constructive transformation (Fisher et al., 2020). Peace and conflict influence each other in a mutually responsive environment: (i) conflict can obstruct peace, and (ii) efforts in peacebuilding, peacemaking, and peacekeeping can avert and settle conflicts alongside diplomatic measures, such as conflict resolution, negotiation, and sustaining long-term relationships.

Among the many definitions of conflict available in the literature, the following (Rasmussen, 1997 in GPPAC, 2017) was selected:

> Conflict is an escalated competition at any system level between groups whose aim is to gain an advantage in the area of power, resources, interests, and needs, and at least one of the groups believes that this dimension of the relationship is mutually incompatible.

Another more straightforward way of looking at conflict is to see it as a situation in which two or more parties have opposing interests, incompatible goals, or values, and are engaged in some form of struggle or disagreement. As summarized in Table 3.5, and drawing from the research by Fisher et al. (2000), which builds on Mitchell's (1981) findings, there are various causes of conflict. Each type requires a different approach and goal tailored to address the causes of conflict.

According to Lemos (2018), conflicts appear in diverse forms, from non-violent protests to varying levels of violence and full-scale armed confrontations. The level of human development and security and how societal needs are met control one's position on that spectrum. Collier et al. (2003) noted that countries gradually become more secure from violent conflicts when successful development facilitates further socioeconomic development. Conversely, countries that experience development failures are at significant risk of becoming embroiled in a conflict trap, where war causes considerable damage to society and the economy and increases the likelihood of future conflicts.

Table 3.5 A summary of different causes of conflict and corresponding responding goals and approaches (adapted from Fisher et al., 2000, p. 8)

Causes of conflict	Goals/Approach
Community Relations: Persistent division, suspicion, and hate among different groups within a community	– Enhancing dialogue and comprehension between opposing groups – Encouraging broader tolerance and acceptance of diversity within the community
Principled Negotiation: Conflicting parties adopting mutually exclusive stances and a 'zero-sum' perspective on the conflict	– To help disputing parties distinguish between personal differences and the actual issues, enabling them to negotiate according to their interests rather than entrenched stances – To promote agreements that provide mutual benefits for all involved
Human Needs: Unfulfilled physical, psychological, and social needs are often the source of significant conflict	– To help conflicting parties pinpoint and convey their unfulfilled needs and develop options for addressing them – To support parties in creating agreements catering to the fundamental human needs of all involved
Identity: Threatened identity often stems from unresolved past trauma and loss	– To provide workshops and discussions for conflicting sides to recognize the threats and fears they have, fostering empathy and reconciliation among them – To collaboratively achieve agreements that acknowledge the fundamental identity needs of all parties involved
Intercultural Miscommunication: A mismatch between varying cultural communication styles	– To broaden the understanding of each other's culture among conflicting parties. – To diminish the negative stereotypes they hold about one another – To improve effective communication across cultures
Conflict Transformation: Disparities and unfairness manifested through divergent social, cultural, and economic systems	– To alter structures and frameworks that lead to inequality and injustice, including economic redistribution – To enhance long-term relationships and attitudes among conflicting parties – To establish processes and systems that advance empowerment, justice, peace, forgiveness, reconciliation, and recognition

Conflicts can occur in multiple contexts and at different scales. They are non-linear and consist of repeated cycles of non-violence and violence. When conducting a conflict analysis, it is essential to be aware of the diverse types of conflict unfolding, the levels of societal deprivation, and the nature of the conflict-affected and conflict-sensitive environment. It is equally important to assess the conflict stage, whether in pre-conflict, confrontation, crisis, outcome, or post-conflict situations (Fisher et al., 2000). Each stage has its own signature, characterized by specific activities, tension, and violence levels.

The main emphasis in this book is on social conflict, which can be understood as the "confrontation of social powers" (Lemos, 2018), which can range from power over (hard power) to power with others or power to (soft power) change (Fisher et al., 2020). These power dynamics can unfold within society from individuals to institutions, groups, associations, etc. Lemos (2018) cited Collins's (1975) work on the general characteristics of social conflict in historical and geopolitical contexts: (i) potential conflicts are caused by inequities in the distribution of scarce socioeconomic, cultural, and power resources and often involve differences in social identity, social structures, and societal norms and issues such as inequalities, unequal human rights, lack of access to essential services, disparities, and differences in social identity, among others; (ii) potential conflicts become actual conflicts when opposing groups are mobilized; (iii) conflicts create subsequent conflicts; and (iv) the intensity of conflict decreases when mobilized resources are used. Lemos (2018) also referred to Gurr (1968), who examined the influence of psychological factors on violence in social conflicts. Among these factors is the polarization, relative deprivation, and dehumanization of some members of society, which translates to frustration and aggression.

Social conflicts can often be sparked by various other types of conflicts, such as environmental, political, economic, and cultural conflicts. For instance, environmental conflicts can arise as disputes related to ecological degradation and the overuse of natural resources, leading to the scarcity and unequal distribution of these resources (BenDor and Scheffran, 2019). The OECD (2005) observed that water availability and allocation can cause friction (or even minor violence) but are not usually a significant cause of violent conflicts. Water can, however, be a trigger, weapon, or casualty of conflict (Pacific Institute, 2024).

Environmental and water-related conflicts "frequently overlap with other types of conflicts on gender, class, territory, or identity" (Scheidel et al., 2020). Adverse events, such as war and climate change, also contribute to environmental damage, such as the war in Ukraine (Conflict and Environment Observatory, 2024) and Gaza (UNEP, 2024; Zwijnenburg and Hall, 2023).

3.5.2 Conflict Assessment, Analysis, and Mapping

In conflict-prone areas, the purpose of conflict assessment and analysis is to delve into the underlying "causes, actors, and dynamics of conflict" (GPPAC, 2017), map the conflict, determine appropriate interventions for each conflict phase, and encourage peacebuilding efforts. From Galtung's perspective (1996), it is essential to understand that conscious and subconscious factors shape conflict. Behavior is invariably a conscious element of conflict. However, in Galtung's view, while attitudes, feelings, and values are fully conscious in direct conflicts, they remain hidden or latent and part of the collectively held civilization subconscious in structural or indirect conflicts. As noted by Galtung (1996, p. 213), different civilizations hold different opinions (some pathological) about what constitutes reality regarding nature, self, society, the world, time, transperson, and episteme.

Conflict assessment and analysis differ from those centered on development or environmental factors. However, they complement each other by revealing the interconnectedness of these dynamics, as peace and development are deeply intertwined. The primary objective of conflict mapping is to develop a *baseline map* that outlines the various factors driving and mitigating conflict within a conflict-affected and conflict-sensitive environment. This map should encompass the conflict stages, timeline, driving forces, dynamics, and key actors or stakeholders (including connectors and dividers) involved. After a thorough analysis, intervention scenarios must be chosen, implemented, monitored, and evaluated to address the conflict effectively.

Table 3.6 A non-exhaustive list of questions in conflict assessment (adapted from Herbert, 2017; Fisher et al., 2000, 2020; and Schirch, 2013)

What	What is the context and scale of the conflict?
	What is the nature of the conflict?
	What are the stages and patterns of the conflict?
	What drives and mitigates the conflict?
	What are the physical and temporal boundaries of the conflict?
	What was the impact of past conflicts on livelihoods and human security?
	What is the history of conflict?
	What political, socio-economic, and environmental institutions and structures have shaped conflict?
	What divides people? What are their motivations?
	What are conflicting parties' attitudes, interests, needs, positions, feelings, values, and behaviors?
	What are the context, systems, and structure experienced by conflicting parties?
	What are the structural and proximate causes of conflict?
	What factors of the conflict profile, actors, causes, and dynamics reinforce or undermine each other?
	What resolution is possible in the shorter and longer terms?
	What are the mutual interests that unite people?
	What role do power, culture, identity, gender, and rights have in the dynamics of the conflict?
Why	Why is there conflict in the first place?
	Why are stakeholders acting the way they do?
Who	Who is involved in the conflict and could resolve the conflict?
	Who are the primary and non-main actors and stakeholders?
	Who could be considered conflict spoilers?
	Who exercises leadership and how?
	Who is related to whom?
	Who are the leading and non-main parties in the conflict?
When	When did the conflict start?
	Is there a definite conflict timeline?
	When was the last conflict (history of conflict)?
	Are there historical patterns or cycles of conflict?
	When can the conflict be expected to change for the better or worse?
Where	Where is the conflict occurring?
How	How did past conflicts express themselves, and how were they resolved?
	How do parties share conflict challenges?
	How do conflicting and cooperating parties interact?
	How were things when so-called normal?

Detailed guidelines and tools for participatory conflict analysis and mapping are available in Fisher et al. (2000, 2020), Schirch (2013), CDA (2016), GPPAC (2017), and GSDRC (Herbert, 2017). A conflict evaluation must determine the what, who, where, when, and how of the conflict (Table 3.6). These questions address the profile, actors, causes, and dynamics that influence or reduce conflict (PCIA, 2013; Schirch, 2013; Herbert, 2017). To answer these questions, data such as those shown in Table 3.7 need to be gathered after the context, scale, and boundaries of the conflict-affected and conflict-sensitive landscape have been defined.

In addition to the list of data mentioned in Table 3.7, there is also a need to collect data that are more specific to the type of conflict. A good example is determining data related to the dynamics of self-determination conflicts (Conciliation Resources, 2011). Dresse et al. (2019) recommend gathering information about the building blocks of environmental peacebuilding efforts (starting conditions, mechanisms, and anticipated results) along three pathways (technical, restorative, and sustainable development).

Another factor to consider is the stage of conflict that the environment is in and the severity of the conflict. For example, the *Global Partnership for the Prevention of Armed Conflict* (GPPAC, 2017) uses different datasets for conflict phases (Table 3.8).

Table 3.7 A non-exhaustive list of input data for conflict analysis (adapted from GPPAC, 2017, p. 27)

Categories of Data	Description
Positive factors for peace/resolution/ transformation (political, economic, social, technical, legal, environmental)	• Factors that bring people together • Elements that can be strengthened or built upon in peace work • Prominent individuals or groups, traditional institutions, mechanisms for conflict resolution
Negative factors producing conflict/ tension/barriers to peace (political, economic, social, technical, legal, environmental)	• Key factors of conflict • Factors that push people apart • Factors that contribute to migration • Patterns of violence and dehumanization

Categories of Data	Description
Key actors/stakeholder analysis	• Roles, means of power/influence, interests, needs, values, positions, willingness to negotiate, etc. • Actors for peace and actors that contribute to conflict
Long-term structural issues and short-term operational issues/ triggers	• Latent conflicts, emergent, already manifest but not yet violent, violent conflicts
Effects of conflict on different people/groups	• Differences across groups, genders, ages, and geographic areas • Cohesion and coherence between migrants and host communities
Elements that contribute to conflict	• Historical, economic, social/relational, political, security, justice/human rights, and environmental factors
Specific questions	• What changes are needed? • Immediate and long-term threat analysis (current, past, forthcoming, potentially violent) • Orientation to specific groups, such as women, youth, minority groups, religious leaders, businesspeople, etc. • Examining various layers/levels of conflict (local to province/state to national to regional, etc.) • Issues of particular interest (land issues, environmental, ethnicity, religious tensions, youth, gender, etc.) • Existing peace efforts: who is doing what? What have been the results (positive and negative)? Are there significant gaps, issues not addressed, groups not involved, etc.?

Assessing conflict is vital for the success of development and security initiatives, with the goal of creating a thorough assessment that manages data effectively. As Schirch (2013) remarked

All conflict assessment processes face time and resource con-straints. But, skimping on conflict assessment wastes time and resources. Analysis paralysis is less dangerous than action without assessment.

Table 3.8 Lines of inquiry for different phases of conflict (adapted from GPPAC 2017, p. 30)

Conflict Phases	Data
Early Intervention for Conflict Prevention	• What are the more profound, long-term structural and cultural causes of conflict? • What issues, if left unaddressed, could lead to violent conflict? • What policies or groups are attempting to address these issues? How? To what effect?
Emerging Crises/Urgent Conflict Prevention	• What immediate issues or events could trigger widespread political violence? • What are the warning signs for these issues or any other identified triggers? What forces are attempting to manage these issues? • Is there an increase in violence against women or any other silent warning signs?
Period of Open Violence	• What are the underlying causes of conflict? Why did these factors lead to violence? Were any unsuccessful efforts made to avoid descent to war? • How has the conflict shifted during the period of violence? Have new issues emerged? • What efforts are being made to stop fighting? Are official negotiations planned or underway? If so, are there barriers to progress? What support is being provided for the negotiation process, and with what success? What issues are on/off the table? • Are there opportunities for Track 2/unofficial dialogue or negotiation? Is anyone doing this already, and if so, to what effect? What other initiatives would support a movement towards peace?
Cyclical Violence or Low-Intensity Conflict	• What are the underlying causes of cyclical violence? Why do these issues emerge when they do, and what allows for relative calm during other periods? Does violence target specific members of society more often than others? • Who is doing what to address the underlying causes and immediate triggers? To what effect? • What can prevent the recurrent cycles of violence regarding short-term and long-term strategies?

Conflict Phases	Data
Post-Violence/ Post-War/ Post-Peace Agreement	• What were the underlying causes of the war/violence? How did these factors change during the war? What new factors emerged?
	• Which causes identified (if any) were addressed in any peace agreement? What is the critical "unfinished business," or what are the persistent issues that, if unaddressed, could threaten a relapse into violence?
	• In post-conflict peacebuilding funding and programming, what drivers of conflict are being addressed and how? Are these efforts successful or effective? What issues are being ignored or actively avoided?
	• What is the strategy for recovery? To what extent is it necessary—and are people willing—to address issues of trauma from war or violence? Is there a need for some form of transitional justice or other forms of healing? Are their cultural factors, perceptions, or gender roles that hinder people's ability to address issues of recovery and healing?

3.5.3 Conflict and Risks

The emergence of conflicts can pose significant risks in conflict-prone environments that require effective management. Moreover, various forms of risk can lead to disputes. The question arises regarding where conflicts may occur in the global network of risks discussed in Section 1.1 and where short- and long-term interventions should be implemented. Risks represent the possibility that an undesired outcome or the absence of a desired outcome disrupts something (e.g., a project or society) (Smith and Merritt, 2002). In human development and security, risks may originate from multiple reasons, such as decision-making, policies, and uncontrollable factors associated with one or several adverse events:

- Everyday events (e.g., lack of water and sanitation, poor shelter, living conditions, livelihood, illness, economy, etc.)
- Extreme events (e.g., floods, volcanoes, earthquakes, landslides, wildfires, hurricanes, etc.)
- Small- or periodic medium-scale events, including drought (periodic or chronic), soil degradation, deforestation, epidemics, health risks, and hazards.

- Conflict, war, or the breakdown of governments causes disastrous consequences at the local and global levels.

Risk analysis complements conflict analysis and involves identifying and managing potential uncertainties and hazards, in this case, conflict. According to Smith and Merritt (2002), risk analysis consists of several steps: (i) identification of risks and impacts; (ii) analysis of risks (drivers, probabilities, and loss) and risk-heat maps; (iii) ranking of risks (risks to be managed first); (iv) resolving risks (avoidance, transfer, redundancy, mitigation such as prevention, contingency, and reserves); and (iv) monitoring of risks (status and closing of risks, new risks). Integrating insights from conflict and risk analyses enables a more comprehensive management and decision-making approach when dealing with conflicts.

Figure 3.3 shows a risk management framework using the cascading risk model proposed by Smith and Merritt (2002). A risk event defined as "conflict" has multiple consequences and impacts, which take time to manifest. All three have their own drivers and likelihoods. Suppose that the magnitude of the total loss associated with conflict, L_t, can be determined, and the probabilities of the occurrence of the risk event, consequences, and impact are estimated. In this case, the expected loss L_e can be calculated as the product of L_t and the probabilities of occurrence of the risk event, consequences, and impact.

A challenge in Fig. 3.3 is identifying and ranking the drivers and mapping all consequences and their respective impacts for a specific context and scale. All drivers depend on the type of conflict assessed and analyzed. In turn, drivers dictate the most appropriate types of peacebuilding efforts. Are there issues with wealth, military matters, power, markets, beliefs, the economy, etc.? Another challenge is quantitatively estimating the value of the total loss, which can be expressed in financial/economic terms, time, loss of lives, infrastructure, etc. Another option is to qualitatively describe the total loss, such as high, medium, low, or semi-quantitative, using a scale ranging from 1 to 10 for importance. Finally, a detailed description must be provided for each loss level.

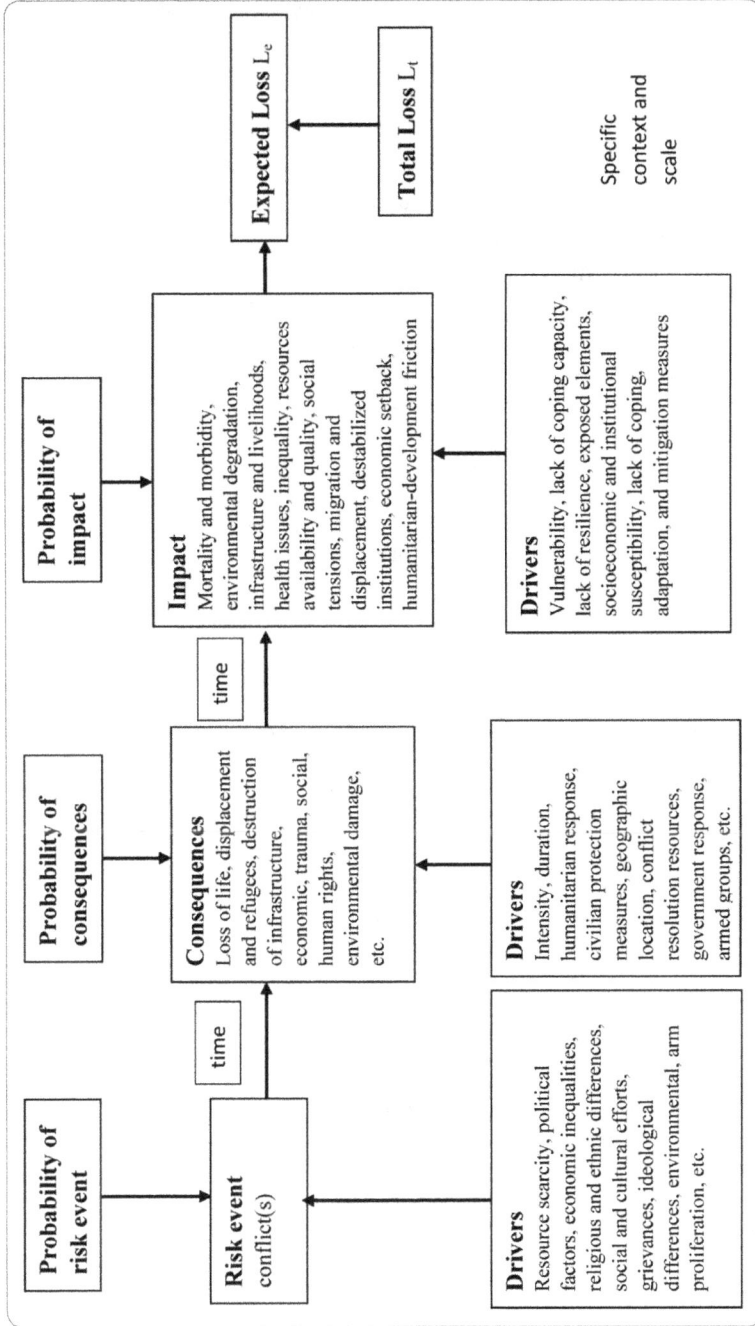

Figure 3.3 Cascading risk representation of a risk management framework showing the consequences and impact of conflict.

3.6 Peacemaking, Peacekeeping, and Peacebuilding

Peacemaking, peacekeeping, and peacebuilding refer to three distinct ways of addressing, resolving, and preventing conflicts, respectively (Table 3.9). Although it is widely accepted that peacemaking comes first, this sequence is not always straightforward. It can vary based on conflict characteristics, setting, and extent. Consequently, as discussed in Chapter 1, a broad definition of peacebuilding is frequently used (Snodderly, 2018).

Table 3.9 Components of peacemaking, peacekeeping, and peacebuilding (OpenAI, 2024)

Peacemaking	• Refers to the diplomatic efforts and negotiations undertaken to resolve a conflict and reach a ceasefire or peace agreement. Political and military needs might be necessary.
	• Involves mediation, negotiation, and often the involvement of third-party mediators, such as diplomats or international organizations.
	• Typically, this occurs during an ongoing conflict when the parties seek a resolution.
Peacekeeping	• Involves the deployment of international peacekeeping forces to maintain peace and security in regions or countries that have experienced conflict.
	• Aims to monitor ceasefire agreements, separate conflicting parties, and create a secure environment for humanitarian efforts and the implementation of peace agreements.
	• Typically follows a peacemaking agreement and is meant to support its implementation. Using force might be necessary.
Peacebuilding	• A long-term process that aims to address the root causes of conflicts and establish the conditions for sustainable peace.
	• Involves activities such as promoting good governance, economic development, social justice, and reconciliation among conflicting parties.
	• Typically, occurs following the resolution of a conflict or during the post-conflict period.

Peacebuilding generally involves transforming relationships and institutions and operates on various premises regarding conflict (Abu-Nimer, 2009).

- Conflict is an inherent process that can drive positive outcomes when peacemakers incorporate beneficial components, techniques, and strategies into their work.
- Peacebuilding strategies that do not involve violence are more effective than those that do.
- Changing the dynamics of conflict is both possible and beneficial.
- Cooperation and willingness to see different perspectives can help resolve differences.
- The effective resolution of conflict issues hinges on communication, collaboration, viewpoint shifts, and the openness to leave one's stance to empathize with others.
- Sustainable relationships are formed when parties in conflict address their past problems, recognize current differences, and agree to work toward fostering collaboration and connections.
- Resolving conflicts necessitates systemic transformation and spans social, economic, cultural, and political dimensions.

Figure 3.4 shows a possible mental model of the peacebuilding, peacemaking, and peacekeeping sequence. In this mental model, the peace state, represented by P_o, initially prevails; however, it eventually deteriorates over time due to a range of factors, such as a diminished focus on peacebuilding, complacency, reduced resources, climate change, and political decisions. At a pivotal moment t_c, a crisis, such as conflict or disaster, emerges, causing a sharp decline in the peace state. If left unaddressed, this decline continues over time.

Peacemaking and peacebuilding efforts start at time t_{int}. Figure 3.4 shows the importance of the rate of these efforts (slope of the dashed line) in determining when the final desired state of peace P_d is reached. A higher rate leads to a shorter time t_d. Similarly, initiating peacemaking and peacebuilding efforts as soon as possible after a crisis (a smaller t_{int}) leads to a faster recovery time, t_d. Waiting for too long can lead to an extended recovery period, and there is a possibility that a low level of peace may not result in reaching a desirable and peaceful state over a reasonable time. Peacemaking and peacebuilding efforts could also begin before the crisis by building and strengthening capacities well in advance.

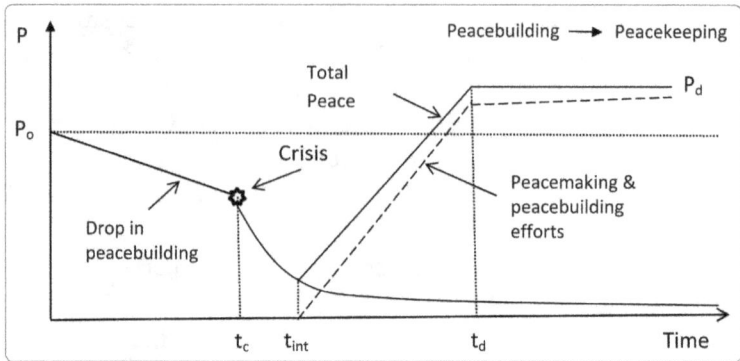

Figure 3.4. A possible mental model of the peacebuilding, peacemaking, and peacekeeping sequence following a crisis. The dashed line represents peacemaking and peacebuilding efforts.

It is essential to acknowledge that the lines depicted in Fig. 3.4 are theoretical. In practical applications, there may be fluctuations in peacemaking, peacebuilding, and peacekeeping processes following a crisis. Another crisis can even be created. Illustrative numerical examples of the dynamics of Fig. 3.4 are presented in Chapter 8.

To fully comprehend the dynamics depicted in Fig. 3.4, estimating the current state of human development and security associated with the initial state denoted by P_o is essential. At the community level, a thorough evaluation or assessment of the community's state is required to establish a *baseline profile* that can be used to determine the overall state of the community, its typical patterns of behavior and capacity, and the structural components that contribute to its state of peace, sustainability, well-being, and overall livelihood wholeness (see Section 6.1).

3.7 Peace Engineering

As discussed in Sections 1.4 and 2.2, engineers can contribute to peace through peacebuilding, peacemaking, and peacekeeping efforts. They can sometimes create unintended consequences that may lead to conflicts. Peace engineering, or engineering for peace, stands at the crossroads between what engineers are expected to do (i.e., develop solutions), conflict management, and peace studies. It was initially proposed by Vesilind (2005) as "the proactive use of engineering skills to promote a peaceful and just existence for all." Another more recent definition was proposed by Jordan et al. (2020), where peace engineering is "the intentional application of science, technology, and innovation (STI) principles for trans-disciplinary systemic-level thinking to build and support conditions for peace." Finally, OpenAI (2023) provides a more comprehensive definition of peace engineering as

> a relatively new and interdisciplinary field that aims to apply engineering principles and technology to promote peace, prevent conflicts, and address the root causes of violence and instability in various contexts. It involves collaboration between engineers, social scientists, policymakers, and other stakeholders to develop innovative solutions for peace and stability.

Peace engineering is not a traditional engineering field; instead, it is an *emerging field* in which engineering principles and practices are applied to create intervention strategies for working in and on conflicts, resolving conflicts, fostering peace, promoting and upholding human rights and social justice, and enhancing diplomatic efforts. Peace engineering is at the intersection of several fields. It utilizes engineering principles, conflict resolution strategies, and peacebuilding approaches. Its impacts include preventing conflicts, engaging stakeholders, mitigating risks, building resilience, advocating policies, providing education, offering humanitarian assistance, and promoting sustainable development to foster peace and stability in the complex and rapidly changing environments of the VUCA world. Peace engineering is a multidisciplinary and collaborative field that involves engineers, peacebuilders, policymakers, researchers, and community members. Peace engineering also encourages engineers to think critically, creatively, and ethically about the problems they are trying to solve and their proposed solutions. Peace engineering concerns what engineers do and how they do so.

As a type of globally engaged engineering, a question arises regarding the appropriate body of knowledge (BOK) for engineers interested in building and supporting conditions for peace. How should engineers be trained to develop sound nature-based solutions for people and the environment and to create prosperity and partnerships through collaborative work? How can engineers be best equipped with the attitudes, skills, knowledge, attitudes, and lifelong experience necessary to work at the crossroads between the technical and non-technical components of conflict and peace through collaboration with social scientists, policymakers, and other stakeholders? How should they handle challenges such as political obstacles and cultural sensitivity? Understanding conflict and the dynamics among the engineering–peacebuilding–diplomacy nexus sectors outlined in Table 1.2 is critical to peace engineering.

It is interesting to note that peace education and understanding of conflict are rarely addressed in the engineering BOK, even though conflict is a part of engineering work and manifests itself among project stakeholders and in the landscape in which projects unfold. Peace education offers multiple benefits.

- It is conducive to enhanced collaboration and teamwork among engineers, which can result in more creative and efficient outcomes.
- It aids engineers in devising technically robust, socially ethical, and sustainable solutions.
- It offers engineers an avenue to support global peace and stability by creating technologies and infrastructure that foster equality, diminish conflict, and enhance the welfare of communities worldwide.

Incorporating the tenets of peace education within the engineering field can transform it into a discipline that is more focused on humanity and holistic development, potentially resulting in a more peaceful and fair world. Engineers must be peace-sensitive.

Compared to the many educational and training programs on conflict analysis and resolution available worldwide, to our knowledge, only two academic programs in the United States have started to examine the BOK in the emerging field of peace engineering. The University of St. Thomas in Minneapolis (MN) has a Peace Engineering Program[2] "designed for engineering students interested in becoming responsible critics of contemporary

---

[2]www.stthomas.edu/engineering/undergraduate/minor/peaceengineeringprogram.

societies and effective agents for positive social transformations." Students work toward (i) a BS degree in engineering; (ii) a minor in justice and peace studies with courses on justice, peace, and social conflict; and (iii) an engineering design clinic incorporating technical skills and peace studies components.

Another educational initiative on peace engineering was launched in 2016 at Drexel University in Philadelphia. It offers undergraduate classes and a Master of Science degree in Peace Engineering. The program resulted from collaboration between multiple disciplines (e.g., engineering, arts and sciences, health, law, and business) across the Drexel campus. It was initially developed in collaboration with the PeaceTech Lab in Washington, DC, USA. Through classwork, fieldwork, and internships, students enrolled in the Drexel Peace Engineering program are expected to acquire competencies in different aspects of conflict management, peace, and conflict studies; develop new system-based and project management skills related to peacebuilding; and appraise multiple socioeconomic-political dimensions of conflicts. Graduate students are expected to explore an engineering area of emphasis further. Table 3.10 lists the components of the Drexel Peace Engineering Curriculum that is still under development.

Although peace engineering programs are currently lacking in engineering schools and colleges, there is increasing interest in developing such programs. For example, the University of New Mexico (https://peaceengineering.unm.edu/) and George Mason University (https://cec.gmu.edu/program/peace-engineering) are creating undergraduate and graduate peace engineering programs and are already offering courses.

Considering the previously provided definitions of peace engineering, the Body of Knowledge (BOK) of peace engineering must encompass a comprehensive understanding of engineering principles, including systems thinking. In addition to the pre-requisites for globally focused engineering education and engineers involved in development work discussed in Chapter 2 (e.g., the Barcelona framework, EOP framework, and accreditation boards), the BOK must also encompass an understanding of the underlying causes of conflict, the diverse forms of conflict, the risks associated with conflict, the conflict-affected and conflict-

Table 3.10 Basic components of the Peace Engineering Curriculum at Drexel University[3]

Courses	Description
Systems engineering for peacebuilding	Application of systems thinking and systems tools in the context of peacebuilding. Introduction to systems engineering and system dynamics.
Introduction to peacebuilding for engineers	Introduction to the concepts and skills practiced in international peacebuilding and conflict transformation.
Conflict management for engineers	Introduction to the concepts and skills needed to use technology expertise in serving conflict-affected and conflict-sensitive communities. Introduction to the theory and practice of conflict analysis, strategic peacebuilding, and negotiation.
Peacebuilding skills	Intercultural communication and facilitation in the context of peacebuilding.
Peace engineering experiential learning	Direct experience working and conducting field-based research in peacebuilding.
Peace engineering seminars	Introduction to peacebuilding cases and understanding how engineering approaches can be applied to peace-building.

sensitive environment, and the development of solutions that address both technical and non-technical issues, including those that intersect with society, culture, economics, and politics. More specifically, engineers contributing to peacebuilding efforts must have the following attitudes, skills, knowledge, and experience to work on:

- Various parts of the peacebuilding, peacemaking, and peacekeeping continuum.
- Conflict resolution strategies and technologies to mediate disputes and prevent escalation.
- Peacebuilding technology platforms and early warning systems for conflict detection and prevention.
- Projects and technologies to improve the capacity, resilience, and standard of living in conflict-affected and conflict-

---

[3]http://catalog.drexel.edu/coursedescriptions/quarter/grad/peng

sensitive environments by addressing issues such as access to clean water, energy, and healthcare and promoting the 5Ps of sustainable development.

- Measures to foster communication, unity, and confidence building among disputing entities.
- Developing and integrating solutions intersecting humanitarian aid, development, and peace.
- Training and educating communities and local decision-makers in conflict-prone regions to resolve conflicts and promote sustainable development.

These activities are challenging in both the short and long terms. They require acquiring resources and dealing with multiple political obstacles and cultural sensitivities that are likely to be physically and temporally scale- and context-specific.

3.8   Engineering Diplomacy

3.8.1   Multiple Tracks

As shown in Table 1.2, the relationships among engineering, peacebuilding, and diplomacy are multifaceted and interconnected. Engineering is vital in peacebuilding and diplomacy because it contributes to infrastructure development, humanitarian aid, and conflict prevention. On the other hand, diplomacy promotes peace through negotiations, mediation, and international cooperation to resolve conflicts. Collaboration between engineers and diplomats has a strong value proposition in potential conflict and past, current, and post-conflict settings. Engineering diplomacy is also critical when addressing global challenges and the SDGs (Meshkati, 2012, 2022; SWE, 2023).

Diplomacy can occur in multiple forms (Mamchii, 2023) or in tracks that engage various participants. Track 1 is traditional diplomacy, which is that of diplomats and government representatives. Science and engineering diplomacy can be seen as Track 1.5 or Track 2 'backchannel' diplomacy, which, according to the USIP (Staats et al., 2019), can be defined as follows:

Track 1.5 dialogues are conversations that include a mix of government officials—who participate in an unofficial capacity—and non-governmental experts, all sitting around the same table. On the other hand, Track 2 diplomacy brings together unofficial representatives on both sides with no government participation. Neither track 1.5 nor track 2 discussions carry the official weight of traditional diplomacy [track 1], as they are not government-to-government meetings. They offer a private, open environment for individuals to build trust, hold conversations that their official counterparts sometimes cannot or will not, and discuss solutions.

Staats et al. (2019) highlight that Tracks 1.5 and 2 should be considered as complementary to Track 1, such as bilateral and multilateral diplomacy, rather than as substitutes.

Science and engineering diplomacy can also be integrated into the more complex multitrack diplomacy framework proposed by Diamond and McDonald (1996). It comprises nine tracks of peacebuilding practices: Track 1 (government), Track 2 (professional conflict resolution), Track 3 (business), Track 4 (private citizen), Track 5 (research, training, and education), Track 6 (peace activism), Track 7 (religion), Track 8 (funding), and an overlapping Track 9 (media and public opinion). Tracks 2–9 are considered sub-components of Tracks 1.5 and 2.

A new track, Track 10, "Engineering and peacemaking through science, technology, and innovation," can be added to the nine tracks. It refers to the community of scientists, technologists, and engineers who provide science, technology, and solutions to understand the interaction between people and their environment before, during, and after a conflict.

Regarding the relationship between engineering and diplomacy, we consider engineering in and for diplomacy. Table 3.11 lists various roles the engineering profession can play in these contexts.

Engineering in diplomacy occurs when engineering activities address issues in support of policies. Engineering enables diplomacy to tackle intricate global issues, encourages collaboration among countries, and supports sustainable development and peacekeeping initiatives. Engineers play a significant role in the diplomatic sphere by utilizing their technical proficiency, ultimately impacting decisions and molding international relations. Examples of engineering in diplomacy include the Marshall Plan to rebuild Europe after WW II; the Panama Canal, the International Space Station; the 2015 Climate Paris Agreement; the Nuclear Nonproliferation Treaty; the International Space Treaty; International Standard Organizations; Humanitarian engineering projects; cybersecurity cooperation, and Global Health Initiatives (OpenAI, 2024).

Engineering for diplomacy is when engineers and policymakers jointly advocate and advise states and provide tools for diplomacy. This involves applying engineering skills and knowledge to tackle global challenges, fostering cooperation between nations, and supporting sustainable development and peacekeeping efforts worldwide. Engineers are essential for shaping international relations and encouraging collaboration between countries by leveraging their technical proficiency and problem-solving abilities. Examples of engineering for diplomacy initiatives include CERN, SESAME; The Aswan High Dam and the Suez Canal Expansion in Egypt; The Channel Tunnel between France and the UK; the International Space Station (ISS); The Inter-Korean Industrial Complex (Kaesong Industrial Region); Transboundary Water Management Projects; International Telecommunications Infrastructure; Renewable Energy Partnerships; Global Disaster Response Teams (disaster diplomacy).

Diplomacy in engineering occurs when diplomacy affects engineering activities, such as when policies facilitate engineering. Diplomacy is critical for facilitating international engineering cooperation, promoting collaboration, and addressing global challenges. Examples of diplomacy in science and engineering include International Research Collaboration platforms such as CERN and SESAME, the Iran Nuclear Deal (Joint Comprehensive Plan of Action - JCPOA), the International Collaboration in Space Exploration, International Technology Transfer Bilateral Trade Agreements; the Sustainable Development Goals (SDGs); Technology Export Controls: and Humanitarian-Related Activities (e.g., health and disaster diplomacy). Table 3.12 lists various roles of diplomacy in engineering.

Table 3.11 Engineering roles in and for diplomacy (OpenAI, 2024)

Roles	Description
Technical advising	Engineers provide insights into complex technical issues and help policymakers make informed decisions in infrastructure development, energy policy, and environmental sustainability.
Infrastructure development	Engineers are crucial in diplomacy related to large-scale infrastructure projects that involve multiple countries. They design and manage projects such as transportation networks, energy facilities, and telecommunications systems that can promote economic cooperation and regional stability.
Environmental diplomacy	Environmental engineers and experts can contribute to international efforts to address climate change and ecological challenges. They provide technical knowledge and sustainable solutions in diplomatic negotiations and agreements.
Technical assistance and capacity building for crisis response	Engineers are vital during international crises, including natural disasters, humanitarian emergencies, and conflict zones. They can assist in providing technical solutions, coordinating relief efforts, and rebuilding infrastructure in collaboration with international organizations and governments.
Science and technology diplomacy	Engineers and scientists engage in science diplomacy by fostering international collaboration in research and development. This can lead to shared technological advancements, innovation, and the promotion of peaceful relations among nations.
Peacekeeping missions	Engineers can be part of peacekeeping missions in conflict zones. They contribute to post-conflict reconstruction efforts, demining operations, and rebuilding essential infrastructure to establish peace and stability.
International Standards and Regulations	Engineers may participate in developing international standards and regulations related to various industries. Their expertise ensures consistency and cooperation among nations, particularly in trade, technology, and safety.
Economic diplomacy	Engineers can support economic diplomacy by facilitating international trade and business partnerships. They play a role in negotiations involving technical standards, quality control, and supply chain management, which are crucial for global commerce.
Cybersecurity	Engineers specializing in cybersecurity can participate in international diplomatic efforts. They address cyber threats and negotiate agreements on cyber norms, regulations, and cooperation to enhance global cybersecurity.

Table 3.12 Role of diplomacy in engineering (OpenAI, 2024)

Role	Description
Negotiations and collaboration	Diplomacy skills, such as effective communication and negotiation, are crucial for fostering cooperation and resolving team conflicts.
International projects	Engineers may need to navigate diplomatic channels, address regulatory issues, and build relationships with foreign counterparts to ensure project success.
Cross-cultural negotiations	Diplomacy skills are vital for understanding and respecting cultural differences, promoting effective communication, and avoiding misunderstandings.
Environmental and regulatory compliances	Diplomatic skills can help engage with regulatory authorities, address compliance issues, and mitigate environmental concerns.
Project stakeholder engagements	Diplomacy is essential when dealing with various project stakeholders, including government agencies, local communities, environmental organizations, and businesses. Engineers must navigate competing interests and build consensus to move projects forward.
Conflict resolution	Engineering projects can encounter conflicts related to technical disagreements, budget constraints, or stakeholder interests. Diplomatic skills, such as mediation and negotiation, are valuable in resolving these conflicts and maintaining project progress.
Policy and advocacy	Engineers may engage in policy discussions about their field, advocating for regulations or standards aligning with engineering best practices. Diplomacy is essential when communicating with policymakers and stakeholders to influence policy decisions.
International relations	Engineers in specialized technical fields, such as nuclear energy or aerospace, may be involved in international relations and negotiations regarding technology transfer, arms control, or trade agreements.
Ethical issues	Engineers face ethical dilemmas in their work, such as ensuring the safety of products or addressing social and environmental impacts. Diplomatic skills can be helpful in ethical decision-making and addressing moral concerns with stakeholders.
International project management	Diplomacy is crucial when managing international engineering projects, as it involves coordinating activities across borders, addressing legal and cultural differences, and ensuring project success while maintaining good diplomatic relations.

3.8.2 Citizen Diplomacy

It may not always take the ideal theoretical form expected of diplomats and bureaucrats who populate the halls of foreign ministries and embassies worldwide. As mentioned above, science and engineering diplomacy can be associated with collaborative projects that generate international news. Examples include the Apollo-Soyuz moment on June 17, 1975, when the American Apollo and Soviet Soyuz spacecraft docked in space for the first time (Garan, 2015), and the ISS station. Despite geopolitical disagreements, they are excellent examples of science and engineering diplomacy, showing that goodwill and peace are possible through science, technology, and engineering collaborations.

Science and engineering diplomacy can also unfold at the grassroots level through educational collaboration, such as study abroad and outreach programs, the Viberti iPodia program[4] at the University of Southern California, and the Global Learning and Observations to Benefit the Environment (GLOBE) program[5] based in the US. It can also take the form of fieldwork involving students and professionals from various fields of science and engineering. These forms of diplomacy can be regarded as *citizen* or public diplomacy. This entails the involvement of individuals who are not necessarily government officials in fostering international understanding and cooperation through various activities and initiatives. This form of diplomacy promotes goodwill and peaceful relations by creating connections between people from various countries and cultures.

Examples of citizen diplomacy initiatives include EPICS, Engineers Without Borders (EWB-USA), and the EWB-international network. These programs were designed to involve student engineers and professionals in the development of community projects. They give participants a local, national, and international cultural experience. In addition, the projects provide them with a sense of belonging and engagement through teamwork, a way of expressing passion and empathy, and a societal context for their engineering work. It also allows them to reflect on themselves,

[4]https://ipodia.usc.edu/
[5]https://www.globe.gov/

develop values, act on things they are passionate about, become good listeners, work with other professions, and ultimately 'think globally and act locally.'

The author's concept of citizen diplomacy originated from observing or facilitating conversations between individuals from diverse backgrounds, cultures, and fields of expertise. Most of the time, people had never met or assumed that they had nothing in common before they met or were told that they would dislike each other. For example, in 2010, the author hosted a meeting in Cyprus that brought about 40 participants from engineers without border groups from the USA, Israel, Palestine, Egypt, Jordan, Lebanon, and Greece. The goal was to develop a collaborative platform and initiatives in the Eastern Mediterranean region around water, energy, and food issues and ultimately create a peace engineering-driven initiative in that region. The participants worked together for four days to develop joint engineering initiatives. Of course, most of the initiatives did not materialize due to the participants' geopolitical constraints upon returning to their respective countries. A follow-up meeting was held in 2011 to reinforce the decisions made in 2010.

Although the two Cyprus meetings never made it into inter-national news, several positive outcomes have emerged. First and foremost, priceless life-long friendships were created among the participants. Second, joint projects on water and energy issues were considered and planned. Third, and more importantly, the two meetings showed that peace is possible when engineers and scientists from various countries collaborate on critical issues despite geopolitical or other constraints. Finally, the two conferences represented another form of the 'Apollo-Soyuz moment' in their lives.

There are many other examples of citizen diplomacy programs in which individuals, rather than just governments, can significantly promote international understanding and cooperation. Examples include the *Fulbright* program in the US, which supports people-to-people exchange, academic research and teaching engagement, peace and experience, and long-term friendships. Another example of a citizen diplomacy program is the *Erasmus* program, which promotes international student mobility and academic exchange among European countries.

Finally, multiple governments and organizations offer fellowships in science and engineering diplomacy for researchers and scholars, such as the UNITAR Global Diplomacy Initiative fellowship program; the UN General Assembly President's Fellowship Program HOPE; the National Science Policy Network; the Jefferson Science Fellowships; the U. S. Department of State (DoS) Embassy Science Fellows (ESF) program; and the AAAS, IEEE, IIASA Science Diplomacy Fellowship, among others.

3.8.3   BOK of Engineering Diplomacy

The above are examples of many possible citizen-driven initiatives involving engineering and peace. They show that engineering diplomacy is alive and well. At the same time, it is still not commonly accepted by the public and media that engineers are involved in peace work or diplomacy. The engineering community must scale up and advertise different engineering diplomacy initiatives to overcome this limitation and become standard practice. Thus, a community of practices related to peace and engineering diplomacy is necessary. It is a powerful platform for recruiting young people to various fields of science and engineering. This community of practice is required to develop a body of knowledge to train scientists, technologists, and engineers on the fundamentals of diplomacy and how to train diplomats to integrate science, technology, and engineering into their daily decision-making. The peace and engineering diplomacy platform is a springboard for innovation, business development, and job creation.

How do engineers acquire and apply the skills necessary for diplomacy in their professional work? Although there is no established or universally accepted corpus of knowledge in engineering diplomacy, it embraces various areas of expertise and abilities. In addition to the T-type engineering education discussed in Chapter 2, the knowledge, skills, and attitudes required for engineering diplomacy are listed in Table 3.13. As peace and diplomacy are interrelated, the BOK of engineering diplomacy overlaps with that of Peace Engineering.

Table 3.13 Areas of expertise and abilities in engineering for diplomacy (OpenAI, 2024)

Areas of abilities	Description
International Relations and Diplomacy	Understanding the principles and practices of diplomacy and international relations, including knowledge of diplomatic protocols, negotiation strategies, and international institutions.
Policy and Governance	Knowledge of policy analysis, government structures, and decision-making processes at the national and international levels. Understand how engineering and technology policy is formulated and implemented.
Cross-Cultural Communication	Effective communication across cultures, sensitivity to cultural norms, languages, and practices, and the ability to bridge cultural differences.
Global Engineering Challenges	Familiarity with global engineering challenges and issues, such as infrastructure development, energy sustainability, water resources management, and disaster resilience. Understanding the technical aspects of these challenges and their international implications.
Ethics and Moral Values	Knowledge of engineering ethics and responsible engineering practices in addressing possible dilemmas. Promoting and supporting moral values.
International Law and Regulations	Familiarity with international legal frameworks related to engineering and technology, including treaties and agreements. Navigating legal aspects of international cooperation.
Innovation and Technology Transfer	Understanding the innovation process, intellectual property rights, and technology transfer mechanisms.
Environmental and Sustainability Knowledge	Significance of environmental issues in international diplomacy, knowledge of environmental engineering, and sustainability principles.
Data and Information Management	Managing and utilizing data and information effectively. Access and analyze technical data and information to inform diplomatic negotiations.
Interdisciplinary Thinking	Addressing complex, interdisciplinary problems and being able to integrate knowledge from various engineering fields.

(Continued)

Table 3.13 (*Continued*)

Areas of abilities	Description
Science and Technology Diplomacy	Familiarity with the principles of science and technology diplomacy and the role of engineering in advancing diplomatic objectives.
International Project Management	Skills in project management, including planning, execution, and monitoring of international engineering projects.
Conflict Resolution and Mediation	Skills in conflict resolution and mediation in resolving disputes related to engineering and technology.
Networking and Relationship Building	Building and maintaining relationships with engineers, policymakers, and diplomats from different countries.

A literature review shows that science and engineering diplomacy is not mainstream in academia, and few institutions provide coursework or accredited degrees as minor or major. The Viberti Engineering School at the University of South California includes engineering diplomacy as part of a minor in engineering innovation for global challenges (Druhora, 2017).

3.9   Concluding Remarks

Peace is a state that emerges from the interaction of many systems and subsystems involved in human development and security. There are no direct ways to measure peace, and indicators and proxies are necessary. A complete description of the state of peace requires an understanding of all the factors that contribute to it and how they interact. Therefore, a systematic approach is required. Engineers who work on peace and diplomatic initiatives must have a broad perspective on peace and incorporate technical and non-technical factors into their decision-making processes. Adopting a systems approach to peace requires decision-makers, practitioners, and policymakers to possess a systems mindset, cultivate systemic thinking habits, and be proficient in utilizing systems tools, as discussed in the next chapter.

This chapter delved into the concepts of peace engineering and engineering diplomacy, a novel perspective accentuating the significance of engineering in peacebuilding, peacekeeping, peacemaking, and diplomatic efforts. Engineers focused on global peace must possess a T- or V-type education. They must develop a compassionate and inquisitive mindset to understand conflict origins and its various types and create resolutions that tackle technical and societal facets entwined with culture, economy, and politics. Engineering and diplomacy are crucial for promoting peace and stability worldwide. Engineering plays a vital role in infrastructure development, humanitarian aid, and conflict prevention, whereas diplomacy promotes peace through negotiations, mediation, and international cooperation to resolve conflicts. Collaboration between engineers and diplomats has a significant value proposition in pre-, conflict, and post-conflict settings.

The world is yearning for numerous forms of Tracks 1.5 and 2 and citizen diplomacy. One can only hope that in the years to come, international engineering and scientific communities will realize how critical science, engineering, and technology will make the world a better place while contributing to initiatives such as the UN Sustainable Development Goals and other global initiatives (IPCC, IPIE, CERN, and SESAME). Scientists and engineers must know that they are more than providers of scientific and technical knowledge and solutions. They can also be entrepreneurs, peacemakers, and facilitators of sustainable human development. Improving the world for everyone is not just a choice for scientific and engineering professionals but a responsibility. Diplomacy serves as a guide for achieving this goal.

References

Abu-Nimer, M. (2009). Chapter 1: Toward the theory and practice of positive approaches to peacebuilding. In: Sampson, et al. (eds.), *Positive Approaches to Peacebuilding.* Chagrin Falls, OH: The Taos Institute Publications.

Amadei, B. (2020). Revisiting positive peace using systems tools. *Journal of Technology, Forecasting and Social Change.* https://doi.org/10.1016/j.techfore.2020.120149

Amadei, B. (2023). *Navigating the Complexity Across the Peace–Sustainability–Climate Security Nexus.* Boca Raton: Routledge. ISBN 9781032563381

Anderson, M. B. (2010). *Do No Harm: How Aid Can Support Peace or War.* Boulder, CO: Lynne Rienner.

Ben-Eli, M. (2018) Sustainability: Definition and five core principles. A systems perspective. *Sustainability Science*, **13**, 1337–1343, https://doi.org/10.1007/s11625-018-0564-3

Boutros-Ghali, B. (1992). An agenda for peace: Preventive diplomacy, peacemaking, and peacekeeping. *International Relations*, **1**(3), 201–218. https://doi.org/10.1177/004711789201100302

Brown, O. and Nicolucci-Altman, G. (2022). The white paper on the future of environmental peacebuilding. Geneva Peacebuilding Platform, International Union for Conservation of Nature, Peace Nexus Foundation, Environmental Law Institute, Environmental Peacebuilding Association. Ecosystem for Peace

Bush, K. (1998). *A Measure of Peace: Peace and Conflict Impact Assessment (PCIA) of Development Projects in Conflict Zones.* Ottawa: International Development Research Centre, Working Paper 1.

Collaborative for Development Action (CDA) (2016). *Designing Strategic Initiatives to Impact Conflict Systems: Systems Approaches to Peacebuilding. A Resource Manual.* Cambridge, MA: CDA Collaborative Learning Projects. https://www.cdacollaborative.org/wp-content/uploads/2016/12/Designing-Strategic-Initiatives-to-Impact-Conflict-Systems-Systems-Approaches-to-Peacebuilding-Final.pdf#:~:text=This%20manual%20focuses%20on%20systems%20approaches%20to%20conflict%20analysis%20and

Collins, R. (1975). *Conflict Sociology: Toward An Explanatory Science.* New York: Academic Press.

Collier, P., Elliott, V. L., Hegre, H., Hoeffler, A., et al. (2003). *Breaking the Conflict Trap: Civil War and Development Policy.* Oxford: Oxford University Press. http://hdl.handle.net/10986/13938

Conciliation Resources (2011). Mediating self-determination conflicts. Sasakawa Foundation. https://www.c-r.org/learning-hub/mediating-self-determination-conflicts

Conflict and Environment Observatory (January 2024). Ukraine conflict environmental briefing: Nature - CEOBS

Cortright, D. (2008). *Peace: A History of Movements and Ideas.* Cambridge, MA: Cambridge University Press.

Davis, Q. (2016). Building infrastructure for peace: The role of liaison offices in Myanmar's peace process. A Center for Peace and Conflict Studies Learning Paper. Australian Government.

Dews, F. (Oct. 17, 2013). UN Deputy Secretary-General Jan Eliasson: No peace without development, no development without peace. *Brookings*. www.brookings.edu/blog/brookings-now/2013/10/17/un-deputy-secretary-general-jan-eliasson-no-peace-without-development-no-development-without-peace

Diamond, L. and McDonald, J. (1996). *Multi-track Diplomacy: A Systems Approach to Peace* (3rd edition). Boulder, CO: Kumarian Press.

Dietrich, W. (2012). *Interpretations of Peace in History and Culture.* London: Palgrave Macmillan.

Dietrich, W. and Pearce, J. (2019). Many violences, many peaces. *Peacebuilding* **7**(3), 1–15. https://doi.org/10.1080/21647259.2019.1632056

Dresse, A., Fischhendler, I., Nielsen, J. O., and Zikos, D. (2019). Environmental peacebuilding: Towards a theoretical framework. *Cooperation and Conflict,* **54**(1), 99–109.

Druhora, D. (2017). Students turn to engineering diplomacy to solve 21st-century grand challenges. https://viterbischool.usc.edu/news/2017/02/training-21st-century-diplomacy/

Fischer, D. (2007). Chapter 13: Peace as a self-regulating process. In: C. Webel and J. Galtung (eds.) *Handbook of Peace and Conflict Studies.* Oxon: Routledge.

Fisher, S., et al. (2000). *Working with Conflict: Skills and Strategies for Action.* New York: Zed Books.

Fisher, S., Matovic, V., Walker, B. A., and Mathews, D. (ed.) (2020). *Working with Conflict 2: Skills and Strategies for Action.* New York: Zed Books.

Fund for Peace (2017). Fragile states index methodology. https://fragilestatesindex.org/wp-content/uploads/2017/05/FSI-Methodology.pdf

Galtung, J. (1964). An editorial. *Journal of Peace Research,* **1**(1), 1–4. https://doi.org/10.1177/002234336400100101

Galtung, J. (1990). Cultural violence. *Journal of Peace Research,* **27**(3), 291–305. https://www.jstor.org/stable/423472

Galtung, J. (1996). *Peace by Peaceful Means: Peace and Conflict, Development and Civilization.* International Peace Research Institute, Oslo. Thousand Oaks, CA: Sage.

Garan, R. (2015). *The Orbital Perspective: Lessons in Seeing the Big Picture from a Journey of 71 Million Miles.* Oakland, CA: Berrett-Koehler.

Gittins, P. and Velasquez-Castellanos, I. O. (2016). *Peace and Conflict in Bolivia.* La Paz, Bolivia: Konrad Adenauer Stiftung.

Global Partnership for the Prevention of Armed Conflicts (GPPAC) (2017). *Conflict analysis framework: Field guidelines and procedures.* Conflict Analysis Framework: Field Guidelines and Procedures | GPPAC

Grewal, B. J. (2003). *Johan Galtung: Positive and negative peace.* School of Social Science, Auckland University of Technology, Auckland.

Groff, L. (2008). Contributions of different cultural-religious traditions to different aspects of peace: Leading to a holistic, integrative view of peace for the twenty-first-century independent world. *FUTUREtakes,* **7**(1). v7n1_article8.pdf (futuretakes.org)

Gurr, T. (1968). Psychological factors in civil violence. *World Politics,* **20**(2), 245–278. https://doi.org/10.2307/2009798

Guy, S. (2023). An expanding global stage makes way for engineering diplomacy, *Society of Women's Engineers (SWE),* **69**(5). An Expanding Global Stage Makes Way for Engineering Diplomacy - Society of Women Engineers - Magazine (swe.org)

Hayden, N. K. (2018). *Balancing belligerents or feeding the beasts: Transforming conflict traps.* CISSIM Policy Brief, University of Maryland Center for International Security Studies. Hayden CISSM Policy Brief Feb2018_Rev8 (umd.edu)

Herbert, S. (2017). *Conflict Analysis: Topic Guides* GSDRC, University of Birmingham, International Development Department. Conflict Analysis: Topic Guide (gsdrc.org)

Institute for Economics and Peace (IEP) (2017). *Positive peace report 2017: Tracking peace transitions through a systems thinking approach.* http://visionofhumanity.org/reports

Institute for Economics and Peace (IEP) (2018). *Positive Peace Report 2018: Analyzing the factors that sustain peace. Measuring peace in a complex world.* http://visionofhumanity.org/reports

Institute for Economics and Peace (IEP) (2019). *Global Peace Index 2019: Measuring peace in a complex world.* http://visionofhumanity.org/reports

Institute for Economics and Peace (IEP) (2022). *Positive Peace Report 2022: Analyzing the factors that build, predict, and sustain peace.* http://visionofhumanity.org/resources

Institute for Economics and Peace (IEP) (2024a). *Positive Peace Report 2024: Analyzing the factors that build, predict, and sustain peace.* http://visionofhumanity.org/resources

Institute for Economics and Peace (IEP) (2024b). *Global Peace Index 2024. Measuring peace in a complex world.* http://visionofhumanity.org/reports

Institute for Economics and Peace (IEP) (2024c). Halo, Positive Peace, and Systems Thinking 2024: Advancing a systems-based approach to understanding and building peace, Sydney, March 2024. http://visionofhumanity.org/reports

Jordan, R., Amadei, B., et al. (2020). Peace engineering consortium: Outcome of the first global peace engineering conference. *Procedia Computer Science*, **172**, 139–144, https://doi.org/10.1016/j.procs.2020.05.021

Killelea, S. (2021). *Peace in the Age of Chaos: The Best Solution for a Sustainable Future.* Melbourne: Hardie Grant Books.

Lawler, P. and Williams, P. D. (ed.) (2008). Peace studies. In: *Security Studies: An Introduction.* New York: Routledge.

Lederach, J. P. (2012). The origins and evolutions of infrastructures for peace: A personal reflection. *Journal of Peacebuilding & Development*, **7**(3), 8–13. https://www.jstor.org/stable/48603417

Lemos, C. M. (2018). *Agent-Based Modeling of Social Conflict: From Mechanism to Complex Behavior.* Switzerland: Springer International Publishing AG

Mamchii, O. (2023). Types of Diplomacy and Diplomatic Practice in the 21st Century. https://bestdiplomats.org/types-of-diplomacy/

Meshkati, N. (2012) Engineering diplomacy: An underutilized tool in foreign policy, *Science & Diplomacy*, **1**(2). http://www.sciencediplomacy.org/perspective/2012/engineering-diplomacy.

Meshkati, N. (2022). Engineering Diplomacy is Necessary to Tackle Global Grand Challenges. https://doi.org/10.1126/scidip.adf8094

Milligan, K., Zerda, J., and Kania, J. (2022). The relational work of systems change. *Stanford Social Innovation Review.* https://doi.org/10.48558/MDBH-DA38

Mitchell, C. (1981). *The Structure of International Conflict.* London: MacMillan.

National Peace Academy (n.d.) National Peace Academy's program framework: A conceptual framework for peace education and peacebuilding programs. https://nationalpeaceacademy.us/about-us/5-spheres-of-peace

OpenAI (2024). *ChatGPT* (June 1 version) [Large language model]. https://chat.openai.com

OpenAI (2023). ChatGPT (Feb. 10 version) [Large language model]. https://chat.openai.com

Organization for Economic Cooperation and Development (OECD) (2005). Water and violent conflicts. *Issues Brief.* 92767-water-violent-conflict_EN.pdf

Pacific Institute (2024). *Water Conflict Chronology.* Oakland, CA: Pacific Institute. https://www.worldwater.org/water-conflict/. Accessed: 3 Sept. 2024.

PCIA (2013). *Peace and Conflict Impact Assessment Handbook* (4th version). https://reliefweb.int/organization/peacebuilding-centre

Reychler, L. and Paffenholz, T. (ed.) (2001). *Peace-Building: A Field Guide.* Boulder, CO: Lynne Rienner.

Ricigliano, R. (2012). *Making Peace Last: A Toolbox for Sustainable Peacebuilding.* Boulder, CO: Paradigm Publishers.

Scheidel, A., Bene, D., Liu, J., Navas, G., et al. (2020). Environmental conflicts and defenders: A global overview. *Global Environmental Change,* **63**(102104), ISSN 0959-3780, https://doi.org/10.1016/j.gloenvcha.2020.102104

Schirch, L. (2013). *Conflict Assessment and Peacebuilding Planning.* Boulder, CO: Kumarian Press.

Sharifi, A., Simangan, D., Lee, C. Y., Reyes, S. R., et al. (2021). Climate-induced stressors to peace: A review of recent literature. *Environmental Research Letters,* **16,** 073006. doi: 10.1088/1748-9326/abfc08.

Smith, P. G., and Merritt, G. M. (2002). *Proactive Risk Management.* New York: Productivity Press.

Snodderly, D. (ed.) (2018). *Peace Terms. Glossary of Terms for Conflict Management and Peacebuilding* (2nd edition). Washington, DC: U. S. Institute of Peace.

Staats, J., Walsh, J. and Tucci, R. (2019). A primer for multitrack diplomacy: How does it work? A primer for multitrack diplomacy: How does it work? | United States Institute of Peace (usip.org)

Stearns, P. N. (2014). *Peace in World History.* New York: Routledge.

Sustainable Development Solutions Network (SDSN) (2020). *Indicators and a monitoring framework: Launching a data revolution for the sustainable development goals.* https://indicators.report

The Earth Charter (1987). Read the Earth Charter - Earth Charter

UN Economic and Social Commission for Asia and the Pacific (UNESCAP) (2018). PB78_The nexus between peace and sustainable development in Asia-Pacific countries with special needs_final.pdf (unescap.org)

UN Environment Programme (UNEP) (2024). Environmental impact of the conflict in Gaza: Preliminary assessment of environmental impacts. Nairobi. edocs.unep.org/20.500.11822/45739

United States Institute of Peace (USIP)/NAE. (2009). *Guiding Principles for Stabilization and Reconstruction.* Washington, DC: United States Institute of Peace Press. http://www.usip.org/sites/default/files/resources/guiding_principles_full.pdf.

Vesilind, P. A. (2005) (ed.). *Peace Engineering: When Personal Values and Engineering Careers Converge.* Woodsville, NH: Lakeshore Press.

Vesilind, P. A. (2010). *Engineering, Peace, and Justice.* London: Springer.

Zwijnenburg, W. and Hall, N. (2023). Uninhabitable: The reverberating public health and environmental risks from the war in Gaza. https://paxforpeace.nl/wp-content/uploads/sites/2/2023/12/PAX_Report_Gaza_Uninhabitable_FIN.pdf

Chapter 4

A New Decision-Making Narrative

Addressing the complexities of human development, security, peacebuilding, and diplomacy in the contemporary world necessitates adopting a fresh perspective and corresponding mindset when making critical decisions. A new narrative is essential for globally engaged engineers to navigate the peacebuilding and diplomatic challenges of the 21st century. The success of this approach depends on the nature of the mental models used by decision-makers and the inner and outer dimensions of decision-making when translating these mental models into practice. Mental models significantly influence the system structures of peacebuilding and diplomatic efforts. These structures, in turn, create behavioral patterns and shape how events (peaceful or conflicting) unfold.

> The future may arrive long before we have begun to change (Kamp, 2016).

> The only constant in the universe is change (Heraclitus).

> Everywhere we look, we see complexity. In everything we do, we participate in complexity (Theise, 2023).

> Thus, the task is not so much to see what no one yet has seen, but to think what nobody yet has thought about that which everybody sees (A. Schopenhauer).

Engineering for Peace and Diplomacy
Bernard Amadei
Copyright © 2025 Jenny Stanford Publishing Pte. Ltd.
ISBN 978-981-5129-75-5 (Hardcover), 978-1-003-65168-0 (eBook)
www.jennystanford.com

4.1 Shifting Mindsets

4.1.1 Navigating Change

As we have seen in the previous two chapters, the engineering profession requires globally engaged engineers to tackle the problems of the 21st-century world. These engineers need to be trained and acquire the attitude, skills, knowledge, and lifelong experience necessary to promote and support conditions for peace and contribute to positive changes at scales ranging from people to society and distinct levels from the project to the overall policy or oversight level. This chapter explores the desirable components of the new mindset (i.e., attitudes, beliefs, and perceptions) or perspective necessary for globally engaged engineers and decision-makers to navigate the complexities of human development, security, peacebuilding, and diplomacy in the 21st-century world. They must navigate ambiguous and complex situations, innovate quickly, take risks, and be willing to learn and improve through lifelong learning. They must also be able to reflect on the values and social implications of their decision-making in project planning, design, and implementation (see Table 2.7).

The process of shifting from an old mindset to a new one can be likened to navigating two S-shaped curves, as illustrated in Fig. 4.1, which extends from the current or old limiting approach (e.g., a compartmentalized way of thinking) to a new expansive approach (e.g., an integrated perspective). The new approach builds on past innovations and lessons learned and gradually supplements the old way of thinking, which declines in effectiveness over time. However, this old mindset may remain somewhat relevant and should not be disregarded.

The success of a new mindset depends on the mental models and tools used in decision-making and how these models are converted into action. Sterman (2000) defined mental models as cognitive and virtual representations of the actual world that modelers and decision-makers use to describe and explain (i) the causes and consequences of an issue, (ii) the structure and relationships believed to be responsible for some observed behavioral patterns associated with the issue, and (iii) possible circular feedback mechanisms (circular causation) at play within one issue or across multiple issues. Mental models guide perception, behavior, and decision-making.

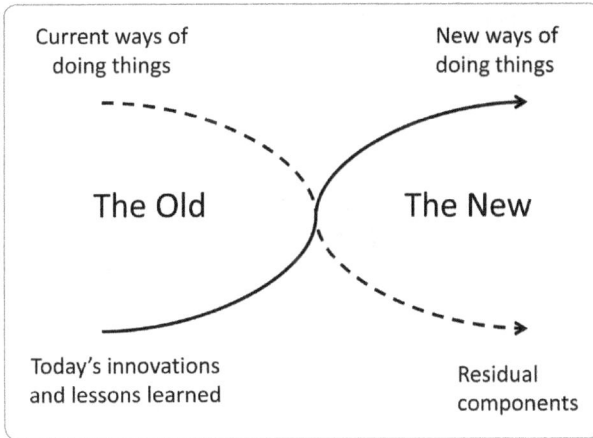

Figure 4.1 Riding the old and new S-shaped curves of change.

Changing the mindset of institutions and decision-making processes is not simple. It necessitates a gradual approach, wherein the value proposition must be delineated, comprehended, experimented with, executed, and appraised before it is embraced by many stakeholders and decision-makers, ultimately becoming a widely accepted norm. Furthermore, adopting a fresh mindset is initially difficult because it entails behavioral modifications and embraces novel mental frameworks. This transformation typically requires time and may prove challenging for traditional stakeholders, policymakers, and practitioners engaged in human development and security.

With that in mind, creating a more sustainable, peaceful, and equitable world where all humans live with dignity and peace must be done in an intelligent, systemic, fair, and compassionate mindset where normal is seen "as a plural." It requires departing from the twentieth century's dominant mindset and the 21st century's first two decades, characterized by compartmentalization, fear, greed, individualism, apathy, and for the benefit of a few.

4.1.2 The Iceberg Model

A common metaphor used in literature to illustrate how mental models and structural and behavioral patterns influence events is that of an iceberg floating in seawater (Sweeney and Meadows, 2010). The iceberg metaphor conveys that a limited portion of an event's information or reality is visible on the surface. A significantly more significant and typically critical part remains concealed beneath the surface. The iceberg metaphor is a visualization tool that encourages decision-makers to consider what lies beneath apparent problems when evaluating situations or making choices. What are the causes of the problems?

Figure 4.2 represents the iceberg model, including the visible portion above the waterline and the underlying factors contributing to the issues. The visible portion represents outward manifestations of problems such as conflicts, climate change effects, biodiversity loss, population displacement, and poverty. Decision-makers often focus on these events and try to find quick solutions without considering the underlying causes, patterns, trends, and cognitive frameworks that contribute to these occurrences. For example, this occurs when Western development agencies use fast fixes and interventions to address low- and middle-income community issues.

This purely *reactive* unipolar approach often results in recurrence. For example, conflicts often relapse when their causes are not fully addressed. A study by the Peace Research Institute Oslo (Jarland et al., 2020) found that half of all conflicts resurface, 35% of conflict pairs recur at least once, unresolved grievances often fuel recurring conflicts around similar issues, and new armed actors frequently emerge in these situations. Coleman (2011) states that 5% of difficult conflicts are self-perpetuating, resist mediation, and worsen over time.

A more effective decision-making approach involves examining various levels of issues, from observable events to their underlying causes. In conflict-affected community settings, current conflicts are represented by the tip of the iceberg, as shown in Fig. 4.2. Below the surface, the second tier identifies patterns that detail how conflict events unfold and what has occurred in the community over time, including the history of conflict, livelihoods, and current events. These patterns may include recurring issues, such as exclusion, domination, competition, collaboration on shared efforts, the impact of climate change (drought and flooding), and economic insecurity. Some of these recurring patterns may be indicative of archetypal system behaviors, as identified by Kim and Anderson (2007), Benson and Marlin (2017), and Griffith University (2022).

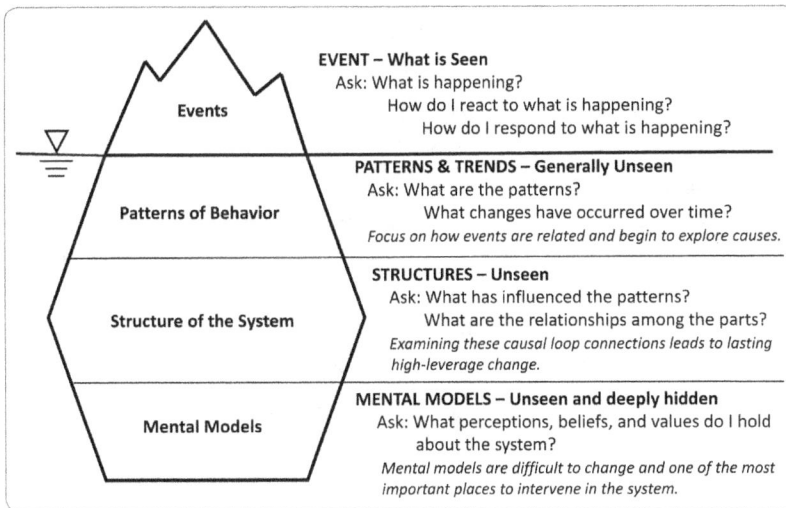

EVENT – What is Seen
Ask: What is happening?
How do I react to what is happening?
How do I respond to what is happening?

PATTERNS & TRENDS – Generally Unseen
Ask: What are the patterns?
What changes have occurred over time?
Focus on how events are related and begin to explore causes.

STRUCTURES – Unseen
Ask: What has influenced the patterns?
What are the relationships among the parts?
Examining these causal loop connections leads to lasting high-leverage change.

MENTAL MODELS – Unseen and deeply hidden
Ask: What perceptions, beliefs, and values do I hold about the system?
Mental models are difficult to change and one of the most important places to intervene in the system.

Events
Patterns of Behavior
Structure of the System
Mental Models

Figure 4.2 The iceberg model. *Source*: © 2020 Waters Center for Systems Thinking, WatersCenterST.org. Reproduced by permission.

Farther below the iceberg in Fig. 4.2, the second-to-last tier considers the systemic tangible structures that influence conflict patterns. These structures may include various community systems and subsystems (i.e., social, economic, cultural, ecological, and infrastructure) at play as issues unfold. These may consist of governance institutions, the built environment, structures that provide a secure environment, legal frameworks, and structures that provide social and cultural well-being. In addition, a detailed analysis of these structures may reveal how different systems are organized and can be modified, how information flows, and how embedded subsystems influence each other and contribute to peace or conflict.

At the base of the iceberg lies the lowest tier, which encompasses mental frameworks and models that underpin structural and behavioral performance. According to Wolfe and Smith (2021), the socio-psychological traits that shape human behavior are also present at this level. These include apathy, intolerance, fear, dogmatism, violence, power, ego, greed, corruption, hatred, denial, consumption, ignorance, exclusion, politics, competition, and jealousy. This level houses intangible elements, such as dominant community preferences, moral values, habits, biases, priorities, culture, religious beliefs, loyalties, policies, and procedures, which represent the inward dimensions of human development, security, peace, and conflict issues, as well as how problems are addressed and reality is perceived.

According to Meadows (1997), the lowest tier of the iceberg is where interventions are the most effective, and *leverage* resides; small changes can lead to significant effects across all aspects of the system. Leverage in community development is everywhere but needs to be identified for specific scales and tailored to contexts. According to Meadows (1999), the leverage category with the most substantial influence resides in the big picture of envisioning system changes by considering new paradigms and mental models to change the system, and it has the flexibility to change paradigms as needed. Another place of leverage resides in how systems are structured and how information flows across their components. They are in the second to last tier of Fig. 4.2. In turn, system structures create behavior patterns (the third tier in Fig. 4.2) and dictate how events unfold.

The mental models and structure in the lower two tiers of Fig. 4.2 are critical leverage entry points when selecting peacebuilding and diplomatic interventions. It should be noted that leverage concerns why, what, who, where, when, and how interventions must occur when addressing human development and security issues. For instance, a crisis may be an opportunity for intervention and change, such as not rebuilding vulnerability or increasing community resilience after natural hazards.

From the bottom to the top of the iceberg model in Fig. 4.2, the four tiers form a *system storyline* that connects mental models, structural and behavioral patterns, and events at the scale and context of interest. The storyline must feature dynamic hypotheses explaining who, what, why, when, where, and how community development, security, and conflict interact (see Table 3.6). Combining each issue's mental model and dynamic hypotheses creates a *reference model* (Rouwette and Vennix, 2015). A visual representation of the reference model is sometimes referred to as a *behavior-over-time* graph (Benson and Marlin, 2017) or a *reference behavior pattern* (Ritchie-Dunham and Rabbino, 2001). Figure 3.4 is an example of a behavior-over-time graph showing the variation in the peace sector before, during, and after a crisis and the importance of the timing and intensity of peacebuilding and peacemaking efforts to recover from the situation.

The storyline is the backbone of the peace and diplomacy inter- vention methodology described in Chapter 7. It helps decision- makers map, identify, and rank problems; find forms of leverage; develop strategies; implement holistic solutions and interventions; and propose coherent governance and policies in the short and long term.

4.1.3   Reverse Analysis

Addressing human development and security challenges necessitates the identification of the underlying cognitive frameworks and structures that underpin observable behavior patterns, such as those in conflict-affected and conflict-sensitive environments. This inference can be made using *reverse analysis*, considering the storyline inherent in the iceberg model depicted in Fig. 4.2. Given that the structure of a system determines its behavior (Meadows, 2008), the underlying premise of this *inductive method* is that by identifying the mental models and structures of the system, potential areas of intervention in, for instance, a conflict-affected and conflict-sensitive environment can be identified and targeted, ultimately enabling the selection and implementation of inter- ventions that will lead to a desired outcome. After the interventions, the environment could display a new behavior pattern that is more aligned with the desired results.

However, the primary obstacle in conducting reverse analysis of complex systems is the absence of well-defined methodologies, let alone a method that can guarantee definite, effective, conclusive, and successful outcomes. Furthermore, there are no singular solutions for the reverse analysis of complex nonlinear problems because diverse mental models and structures can give rise to similar behavior patterns and trends. Nevertheless, discerning a system's structure from its behavior does not necessarily involve a haphazard approach that relies solely on intuition and experience. Various system-based tools have been introduced in recent years to analyze complex systems and understand their behavior, which will be discussed later in this chapter. In addition to systems tools, archetypes can help identify the relationships between observed events and their underlying factors. Archetypes are *generic structures* (Senge, 1994) that may emerge in social systems and create recurring shared behavior patterns. They will be discussed further in Chapter 6.

4.1.4   Mental Filters

The traditional approach to addressing human development and security issues in a specific landscape often ignores what is below the iceberg's surface. It focuses on the external manifestation of problems by providing quick remedial solutions that ignore the issues of 'what, why, who, where, when, and how. Unfortunately, shallow and compulsive answers to complex problems often result in short-term solutions with significant unintended consequences. This dynamic is particularly critical when decisions are made with pathological forms of human thought, preferences, behaviors, and values (e.g., selfishness, greed, and apathy). More recently, bad-faith information has permeated the structures of society and affected decision-making. These mental filters affect all layers of the iceberg model by corrupting the mental models, changing the community fabric and structure, creating dysfunctional community behavior patterns and trends, and ultimately creating harmful and unintended consequences for people and their environment. They may also derail the selection, implementation, and performance of the intervention scenarios.

One of the main difficulties is convincing decision-makers to consider mental models first and not just to react and respond to events, that is, to evaluate the system storyline inherent in the iceberg model in Fig. 4.2 and to embrace the creative/transformative and adaptive/proactive aspects of decision-making that reside below the iceberg tip. This recommendation opposes traditional conservative decision-makers, who favor more straightforward and simplistic explanations of reality than more complex ones because of their limited understanding, perceptions, perspectives, beliefs, emotions, and expertise (Dörner, 1997). As remarked by Mencken (n.d.), "For every complex problem, there is an answer that is clear, simple, and wrong."

This divergence can result in disagreements and conflicts between decision-makers, negatively impacting planning, execution, and long-term interventions in conflict-affected and conflict-sensitive environments. Undertaking a change in perspective can be daunting, as it necessitates modifying one's behavior and gradually embracing new mental constructs. The inherent reluctance to embrace change can be ascribed to the constraints of bounded rationality (Simon, 1972; Jones, 1999; Callebaut, 2007; Schön, 1971). When confronted with such issues, humans often activate mental filters, resort to pathological behavioral patterns, and dismiss or trivialize challenges.

With the system storyline and mental filters in mind, the question arises as to what mindset, principles, and attributes the engineering profession should uphold while participating in human development, security, peacebuilding, and diplomatic efforts. Below, I suggest some possible components (among many others) of this new mindset, among many possible others. All of them share similar characteristics. First, they reside in the three bottom tiers of the iceberg model, as shown in Fig. 4.2. Second, they acknowledge Albert Einstein's recommendation that current issues cannot be solved with the same level of thinking that has created them. We can add "with the same level of leadership and compassion (if any)" that created them. Finally, the new mindset components must be creatively and respectfully disruptive to business as usual.

4.2 Embracing and Practicing Change

Addressing 21st-century global challenges calls for a new story in which the engineering profession is actively involved. There are many ways engineers can be agents of positive change in addressing these challenges and can contribute to peacebuilding and diplomatic efforts. As engineers address the challenges of the 21st-century world, they must be aware of their functional dynamics and how they unfold in different socio-economic-political-cultural contexts, scales, and across systems. They must also be mindful of their decision-making's inner and outer dimensions.

4.2.1 Recognizing Externalities

As discussed in Chapter 2, engineering is deeply connected to society. Hence, when implementing solutions, engineers must be aware of the socioeconomic landscapes and priorities that drive the challenges in the 21st century. For example, landscapes with economies built on growth alone, measured in terms of GDP, cannot be protected from economic and environmental hazards and conflicts. The concept that economic growth and policies that stimulate growth are good for the environment is a fallacy (Raworth, 2018).

Undoubtedly, economic development is essential for improving the well-being of communities worldwide. However, it can also result in negative externalities (Table 2.4) that harm individuals, communities, and the environment and create geopolitical tensions and conflicts. Engineers often contribute to these externalities.

Table 4.1 lists some positive and negative impacts of economic development externalities on the people, planet, prosperity, peace, and partnership (5Ps) aspects of Agenda 2030 of the United Nations. Policies are necessary to minimize negative externalities, optimize positive externalities, reduce trade-offs, and create co-benefits and synergies.

Decision-makers must also be aware of society's preferences. As noted by Tanabe (2020), a crucial question is what should take precedence—society or the economy, public health or profit, or the well-being of citizens in terms of their physiological, psychological,

Table 4.1 Positive and negative economic development externalities (OpenAI, 2024)

The 5Ps	Positive externalities	Negative externalities
People	Economic development may result in more job opportunities, higher earnings, greater accessibility to education and healthcare, and an overall improvement in the quality of life.	The well-being of people can be negatively impacted by various external factors, such as health risks associated with pollution, displacement of communities, and unequal distribution of benefits, which exacerbates inequality.
Planet	The adoption of cleaner technologies, the allocation of resources towards renewable energy, and the implementation of conservation measures contribute to reducing pollution and preserving natural resources.	The adverse consequences, such as environmental degradation, habitat destruction, resource consumption, and pollution, harm ecosystems and accelerate climate change's effects.
Prosperity	Economic growth can result in greater prosperity by generating employment opportunities, stimulating economic expansion, and enhancing living standards. These advantages have a favorable impact on both individuals and communities.	Economic growth without proper regulation can cause overuse of resources, financial crises, and economic instability, resulting in adverse consequences that hinder prosperity.
Partnerships	Collaboration among government entities, corporations, civil society, and international organizations is vital for economic growth. By working together, these entities can exchange effective strategies, transfer knowledge, and pool resources, resulting in mutually beneficial outcomes that further development.	The absence of cooperation and coordination can lead to unfavorable consequences, including transnational environmental degradation, trade conflicts, and regulatory disparities that hinder sustainable development initiatives.
Peace	Economic development can promote peace by enhancing living standards, alleviating poverty, and tackling social and economic disparities, which can be catalysts for conflict.	Improper management of economic development may result in disputes related to resources, land, and opportunities, leading to negative consequences for peace and stability and generating harmful externalities.

intellectual, and spiritual needs, as opposed to the interests of the wealthy elite? Another question concerns the role of members of society in fostering healthy development and security. The values behind these recommendations differ from those in traditional human development and security, where citizens remain passive actors subject to policies that maximize economic benefits [for a solid capitalist elite] while sparingly pursuing humankind's social, cultural, and spiritual development or maturation (Tanabe, 2020). These recommendations highlight the importance of self-awareness, engagement, and development ethics in engineering practice (Gasper, 2012).

4.2.2   Collaboration and Transdisciplinary Work

In the 21st century, global challenges have become multifaceted and interconnected, necessitating collaboration and cooperation across diverse fields of study. Although technology is essential, it is insufficient to address these challenges. To develop comprehensive solutions, globally engaged engineers must adopt a transdisciplinary approach that encompasses both technical and non-technical sectors. To implement this approach, collaborators must establish a shared narrative, show empathy, be open to creative solutions, think in an integrated manner, and be willing to learn from one another. As suggested by Kania and Kramer (2013), this requires following a *collective impact approach* by selecting a common agenda, sharing data collection and measurement methods, engaging in reinforcing activities, maintaining continuous communication, and practicing effective management.

The necessity of collaboration cannot be overstated sufficiently, considering the long-standing practice of addressing human development and security concerns through reductionist methods. These approaches typically involve experts devising discrete, logical, and independent solutions to problems in a fragmented manner. Unfortunately, this compartmentalized and stagnant approach is limited in scope, as it fails to recognize the interrelatedness and interdependence of issues and the common root causes that, when addressed collectively, could lead to more comprehensive and practical solutions.

Promoting collaboration and fostering socioeconomic partnerships are critical for preventing global instability in the vein of crises in the first two decades of the 21st century. As Moritz (2020) posited, achieving this imperative requires concurrently addressing both immediate enhancements to the present challenges and long-term planning across five key areas: (i) *repairing* what is currently the most damaged, (ii) *rethinking* change without going back to how things were (i.e., without rebuilding the vulnerability of business-as-usual), (iii) *reconfiguring* change so that it can happen, (iv) *restarting* change, and (v) *reporting* how change progresses with the ability for course correction through monitoring and evaluation. Critical thinking, reflective practice, using innovative development tools, and re-evaluating priorities are crucial in all five areas, and are essential for implementing human development and security praxis that are both effective and sustainable (Karwat et al., 2014; Mahon et al., 2020). Additionally, building capacity and resilience at multiple levels, including individual, household, community, country, region, and global scales, are paramount. Capacity development must be conducted in a comprehensive and integrated manner to ensure success.

4.2.3   Creative and Innovative Solutions

Engineers have the potential to significantly positively impact society by conducting research and developing creative and innovative (i.e., ingenious) solutions to tackle the global challenges of the 21st century. Engineers can promote peace and address pressing human development and security issues by creating innovative technologies, materials, processes, or systems that are more sustainable, efficient, resilient, and beneficial to all. However, creative and innovative solutions are not just technical. According to Kamp (2016) and based on the work of Taylor and Gantz (1969), creative behavior should be seen holistically as consisting of five levels based on the type of output expected from them.

- *Expressive spontaneity* refers to improvisation and innovation that delves into imagination.
- *Technological creativity* refers to the practice of producing something that is valuable to others.

- *Inventive ingenuity* involves the generation of inventions and discoveries. They are based on a fresh perspective of reality or the creation of novel connections between existing elements.
- *Innovative creativity* is based on intuition and empathy. The objective is to discover methods or strategies that enable the reception of new viewpoints or the integration of objects or concepts into society.
- *Emergent originality* encompasses exceptional transcendental innovations that are unparalleled by their impact. It is characterized by the creation of novel paradigms, principles, or frameworks that have the potential to revolutionize society as a whole.

Although technical creativity is expected of engineers, it is not sufficient. Other types of creativity are necessary for developing integrated solutions to address the global challenges of the 21st century. Sadly, these are often neglected in conventional undergraduate engineering education, where schooling is more important than learning, and analytical (left-brain) convergent thinking rather than holistic divergent (whole-brain) thinking prevails.

Creative solutions are context- and scale-specific and promote community empowerment and the right relationships. In all cases, they must align with the five pillars of Agenda 2030: human welfare, environmental conservation, prosperity, partnerships, and peace (UNESCWA, 2021). In community development, these solutions must enable communities to cope with the challenges posed by conflict, unsustainable practices, and climate change by fostering resilience and capacity building. Such nature-based solutions must positively contribute to the well-being of individuals and the environment while promoting prosperity and security (UNEA, 2022).

Creative solutions must also be inclusive and benefit all segments of the global population rather than just the wealthiest. Unfortunately, scientific and technical advancements have favored individuals residing in developed nations (about 10% of the world's customers) and, to a lesser extent, those living in low- and middle-income countries, who continue to grapple with poor quality of life and low life expectancy. These individuals often inhabit unhealthy, degrading, and unsustainable environments characterized by inequality. Polak (2008) noted that "a revolution in design is needed to reach the other 90%."

The Design for the other 90% revolution has multiple components that the engineering profession must know. First, its solutions must avoid unintended social, psychological, and environmental consequences as well as the negative externalities associated with science, technology, and engineering, as discussed in Chapter 2. Second, the solutions must be appropriate to those who benefit from them, a concept promoted by E. F. Schumacher (1973) in his book *Small is Beautiful*. According to that author, appropriate (initially called intermediate) technology is "technology with a human face," standing between the sophisticated high technologies in the developed world and indigenous ones. According to Hazeltine and Bull (1999), appropriate technology has unique characteristics.

- It is small-scale, energy-efficient, environmentally sound, labor-intensive, and community-controlled.
- It is simple enough to be maintained by people using it.
- It matches both the user and the need in complexity and scale.
- It provides goods, services, and jobs that are unavailable elsewhere.
- It fosters self-reliance, responsibility, cooperation, and frugality.

According to *Practical Action* (2013), other characteristics of appropriate technology include the following:

- It uses local skills and materials, that is, native capabilities.
- It paves the way for a better future for all.
- It is affordable.
- It helps both men and women earn a living.
- It meets people's needs.

Appropriate technology is more than merely a catalog of technical gadgets. Instead, it incorporates a symbiotic relationship between technology, those who use and benefit from it, and the environment in which human–technology interaction occurs. It has hardware components (tools, materials, and equipment) and software components (knowledge, skills, attitude, and behavior). Finally, and often not recognized by those in the Western world, appropriate technology is an integral component of sustainable community development, whether used in developed or developing world projects (Amadei, 2014). Another aspect of appropriate technology that results from the above characteristics is that it is a perfect entry point into *social entrepreneurship* by providing suitable and affordable solutions for most of the world's population rather than promoting expensive and potentially harmful tech-nologies. That concept is an integral component of *Jugaad Innovation* (Radjou et al., 2012), where "Jugaad is a colloquial Hindi word that roughly translates as 'an innovative fix; an improvised solution born from ingenuity and cleverness."

It is important to note that Schumacher's vision of appropriate technology and that of many others, mainly in the NGO world, is still not mainstream in academia and engineering practice today. Despite a clear need at the international level, small-scale technology has been less attractive to the Western engineering industry. They have been inadequately marketed and are sometimes blocked to prevent competition from expensive solutions. This practice is based on the misconception that small-scale technology delivers only small profits, whereas large-scale complex technologies command higher compensation for higher profits. Small-scale technology often does not find its way into conventional engineering curricula. Throughout their four-year studies, many US engineering students lack exposure to appropriate forms of technology, also called frugal, disruptive, or reverse innovation.

Nevertheless, organizations have recognized the potential gains of embracing creative and innovative design principles for the other 90%, especially when integrated with social entrepreneurship and business strategies. In the United States, notable instances include MIT's D-Lab (https://d-lab.mit.edu/), the Design for Extreme Affordability program (https://extreme.stanford.edu/) at Stanford University, and the Frugal Innovation Hub (https://www.scu.edu/engineering/labs--research/labs/frugal-innovation-hub/) at Santa Clara University. In addition, valuable contributions to this culture of innovation come from private and non-profit research entities, such as Design that Matters (https://www.designthatmatters.org/) in Boston, MA, and IDEO (https://www.ideo.com/) in California, which both prioritize human-centered design. These examples are just a few among the many groups that have acknowledged the importance of social innovation and design in meeting the necessities of hundreds of millions by delivering affordable solutions that do not sacrifice quality.

Finally, creative and innovative solutions do not always need to be new. Much can be learned from indigenous cultures, their wisdom, and traditional knowledge, leading to remarkable outcomes when combined with more recent scientific innovations. After all, many indigenous cultures have had the opportunity to develop solutions closer to the five Ps mentioned in this book over time. For example, the seven-generation approach (an Iroquois principle), a holistic, long-term approach across seven generations, is oriented toward people, the environment, and peace. It also focuses on prosperity and partnership, not greed and not the mindless exploitation of natural resources.

The Global Landscape Forum (https://www.globallandscapes-forum.org/), the world's largest knowledge-led platform for sustainable and inclusive landscapes, documents many examples of renewed indigenous technologies with significant impacts. As reviewed by Evans (2021), some examples include (i) the creation of seed banks in New Zealand; (ii) using controlled firebreak burning practices early in the dry seasons to maintain biodiversity and keep humans safe in Australia; (iii) new methods of crop rotation to revive degraded land in Thailand; (iv) intercropping of corn, beans, and squash using traditional Iroquois practices in the US; (v) the revival of traditional farming techniques to retain water in soils in Burkina Faso; (vi) restoring ancient Inca canals in Peru, where enough water is stored during the dry seasons; and (vii) using a non-linear conception of time more in tune with seasons and natural rather than human cycles. Other native technologies are well documented on the Global Landscape Forum website, which documents the mitigating nature of such technologies in restoring landscapes following the impact of climate change. According to The World Bank (2003), indigenous people care for 80% of the Earth's biodiversity. What would it take for globally engaged engineers to learn from native cultures and natural laws?

4.2.4 Design and Technology for Peace

A critical aspect of the design for the other 90% is how it must contribute to peacebuilding and do no harm. Although engineering encompasses more than merely utilizing technology to address societal problems, engineers must consider the role of technology in fostering a culture of peace rather than a culture of conflict when addressing issues related to human development and security. As detailed in the book *Designing Peace* (Smith, 2022), incorporating peace into the creative design process is crucial. It explores how design can (i) support humane forms of peace and security, (ii) address the root causes of conflict, (iii) engage in creative confrontation, (iv) embrace truth and dignity in the search for peace and justice, and (v) facilitate the transition from instability to peace.

Designing Peace provides multiple illustrative examples of science and art, demonstrating how design contributes to peacebuilding on different scales. It also illustrates how stimulating the right and left brains (or the whole brain) for creativity by combining science, engineering, and the arts supports human forms of peace and security (Murphy, 2022). Finally, it emphasizes intuition and imagination, learning-by-doing, and the need for immersion in real complex problems.

What is technology for peace? Often referred to as *PeaceTech,* low- and high-tech solutions can serve various purposes. They can contribute to the well-being of communities worldwide, support non-proliferation regimes and institutions, maintain a strategic deterrent to conflict, reduce the impact of conflict on non-combatants, and design resilient infrastructure and communities (Armenta, 2019). The Global PeaceTech (GPT) Hub in Lucerne, Switzerland (Davletov et al., 2022) (https://www.globalpeacetech.org/) defines PeaceTech as

A new term that broadly refers to any type of technology that can be used to support peacebuilding, peacemaking, peacekeeping, and peace enforcement efforts. It includes everything from simple communication technologies, such as radios and social media, to more complex systems, like satellite imagery and early warning systems, which can be used to satisfy different definitions of peace, from positive to negative at a writ little to writ large level to support different ways to achieving peace.

The GPT Hub has five primary objectives: (i) serving as a transnational hub for research and policy debate on technology for peace, linking knowledge and expertise in the public, private, and academic sectors; (ii) mapping existing PeaceTech initiatives related to transformations in conflict prevention, peacebuilding, and global diplomacy; (iii) developing new conceptual tools and methods to study PeaceTech, investigating regulatory frameworks, and identifying the main actors and technological developments that can affect the outcome of global peace development; (iv) Leading the European and global political and academic debate on technology for peace through high-level scholarly contributions and high-level policy dialogues; and (v) nurturing and training young talents, leaders, and change-makers in global peace technology, capable of driving policy innovation and political change across borders. The GPT Hub also acknowledges that

Most instances of PeaceTech are 'dual-use,' meaning that while these technologies have the potential to make a positive impact in the world, there is a risk that they could be misused and create harm. Hence, it is important to map PeaceTech to understand better how it is used and where the potential risks and benefits emerge.

The significance of technology in furthering peace-related activities has also been recognized over the past 10 years by the PeaceTech laboratory (www.peacetechlab.org) in Washington, DC, and the Peace Innovation Lab (https://peaceinnovation.stanford.edu) at Stanford University in California. PeaceTech Direct (2020) has also highlighted how digital technologies intersect with peacebuilding efforts.

From 2015 to its dissolution in 2023, the PeaceTech Lab (PTL) focused on the function of technology, media, and data in the prevention, diffusion, and recovery of violent conflicts. Through case studies, PTL has demonstrated how technology can transform data into action to detect hate speech, prevent election violence, and predict the worldwide social and economic disruptions caused by violent conflicts. The PTL also led in-country training of the next generation of peacebuilders through the *PeaceTech Exchanges* program, where peacebuilders in conflict zones are empowered to develop low-cost, easy-to-use technology. In addition, the organization developed an 'accelerator' platform to support entrepreneurs and startups interested in creating technologies to predict and avoid violent conflicts, mitigate and diffuse existing conflicts, and aid in recovery from conflicts.

The Peace Innovation Lab (PIL) has emphasized the significance of mediating technologies in fostering positive peace (Guadagno et al., 2018; Quihuis et al., 2015). Technologies such as sensors, satellites, communication, and computation facilitate positive engagement between individuals from diverse backgrounds. Furthermore, these technologies extend to diverse types of community infrastructure that provide shared services, such as water, energy, food, transportation, and communication.

PIL has substantially contributed to technology-enhanced peace measurements. By collecting peace data, PIL revealed the potential of mediating technologies to uncover hidden positive social interactions in hostile environments. Furthermore, PIL's research underscores the economic value proposition of peace through entrepreneurial activities. Overall, PIL's work emphasizes the potential of mediating technologies to promote positive peace and highlights their importance in quantifying the economic value of peace.

According to GPT, PTL, and PIL, there are numerous prospects for R&D, innovation, business expansion, and entrepreneurial pursuits in technology-driven peace across borders. Given that approximately eight billion customers (as of 2024) prefer peace to conflict, the PeaceTech sector has a promising outlook. However, the challenge is to establish a global, sustainable ecosystem that supports innovation and entrepreneurship (both commercial and social) while safeguarding innovators on a worldwide scale and fostering an environment that encourages prosperity by promoting peace.

4.2.5   First- and Second-Order Solutions

Creative engineering solutions are not all born equal. Globally engaged engineers must be aware that, depending on their formulation, solutions can result in first- and second-order changes (Watzlawick et al., 1974), which can be positive or negative. First-order change solutions address issues without modifying the systems that create them. In contrast, second-order change solutions fundamentally alter the system by adopting a new approach or mentality or redefining the system's capability. In the iceberg metaphor in Fig. 4.2, a first-order change is likely to affect the events represented by the tip of the iceberg. In contrast, second-order change solutions address what lies beneath the water level: changes in mental models, structure, and behavior patterns. According to Meadows (1997), second-order change can be considered a "change of change."

Both first- and second-order thinking are required to address complex issues. Let us now examine a case related to peacebuilding. In a particular community, inhabitants must choose between safeguarding natural resources, which they have been entrusted with and benefitted from for a considerable period, and rapid economic growth. A first-order approach would be to view conservation and development as antagonistic and prioritize economic growth, which could result in conflict and division between existing groups and, possibly, the infringement of human rights. On the other hand, a second-order and more beneficial solution would be to draft and implement an action plan that fosters human prosperity while preserving natural resources and a reasonable level of external collaborative economic development. In other words, second-order change presents a mutually beneficial situation for environmental protection and economic growth. This perspective aligns with the recommendation made by The Nature Conservancy (2018), which states that "ensuring a sustainable future depends on our ability to achieve both flourishing human communities and abundant and healthy natural ecosystems."

As a second example, Killelea (2021, p. 97) highlights the benefits of employing an integrated approach to address conflicts arising from competition over natural resources and environmental concerns among nomadic herders and farmers in northern Kenya. Killela explains that sustainable solutions established by farmers, villagers, and the government led to an ecosystem that considers the future of the environment, endangered species, herders, and farmers. However, maintaining and expanding these solutions over time remains a challenge.

The conflict between pastoralists and commercial agricultural farmers has been a significant source of discourse worldwide. Pastoralists do not always follow the same patterns of herding from year to year as they adapt to and take advantage of changing conditions, thus creating uncertainty for farmers. Scoones and contributors (2023) cite several examples of this dynamic in India, Tibet, China, Sardinia, Italy, Tunisia, Ethiopia, and northern Kenya. The variability of pastoralist groups requires agreement and relationships between pastoralists and farmers. All of these activities can be regarded as second-order approaches to prevent conflicts. Monitoring and visually representing pastoralists' movements and activities can reinforce second-order solutions.

A third example involves a community facing difficulties in obtaining crucial resources, such as water, energy, food, and shelter, due to stressful natural occurrences such as climate change. A first-order solution would be for outsiders, such as government agencies or NGOs, to provide immediate aid to the community and address its immediate needs: to drill more wells. A second-order solution entails collaborating with the community to develop a proactive and integrated strategic plan of development that addresses their current situation, encourages participation in identifying vulnerabilities and building resilience, and establishes a sustainable plan for capacity building for five to fifteen years in water resource management. An example of this dynamic was documented by the *International Crops Research Institute for the Semi-Arid Tropics* (ICRISAT) in Hyderabad (Wani et al., 2003) regarding an Indian village. The integrated nature of the abovementioned interventions provided sufficient year-round water for humans, cattle, and agriculture in the town.

The interventions also raised the water table by several meters. They resulted in tangible outcomes, such as economic growth, no instances of farmers' suicide in the village, and encouraging the youth to stay in the community—the opposite of what was happening in neighboring towns. This example demonstrates that second-order thinking can create scalable, tangible success stories and has positive effects. Several additional examples of well-planned systemic interventions leading to second-order changes in communities can be found in a study by Taylor et al. (2012).

Finally, an illustrative example of a first-order solution is a community fostering a culture of external dependence in response to natural disasters (e.g., earthquakes, wildfires, hurricanes, and floods). Conversely, a second-order solution involves promoting a culture of resilience at the community level by implementing adaptation and mitigation measures that all community members embrace. An example of such an initiative related to natural hazards is the Resilient City Program of the San Francisco Bay Area Planning and Urban Research Association (SPUR, 2011). This citizen-driven initiative outlines how the San Francisco Bay Area responds to earthquakes and other adverse events. The author participated in a study funded by the US National Research Council (2012), which examined several communities across the US that had faced or could face crises. This study aimed to determine if the US was a resilient country (it is not) when dealing with crises. Among the case studies, two communities in Louisiana and Mississippi, hit by Hurricane Katrina in 2004, had different recovery models, even though they experienced the same event. A Vietnamese community in Mississippi used higher-level cooperative and adaptive solutions to rebuild itself quickly. However, an African American community in Louisiana, located 100 km away, remained stuck in a dependent state.

4.2.6   Positively Deviant Solutions

Creative solutions do not always need to come from outside the community. Regardless of the level of community development, there are instances where specific individuals, households, institutions, and groups within a community find innovative and practical solutions to problems despite having access to the same resources and facing similar challenges. These individuals or groups achieve better outcomes than their peers by positively deviating from norms.

This concept, called *Positive Deviance* (Pascale et al., 2010) or strength-based approach (Winterford et al., 2023), acknowledges that ingenuity, talent, and creativity exist locally and are easier to scale than reinvent the wheel. Paraphrasing Schumacher (1973), it is about discovering what people do and collaborating to improve it. It is empowerment rather than telling others.

Much can be learned from native and non-native cultures regarding engineering, peacebuilding, and diplomacy. Engineers involved in human development and security and participating in peacebuilding and diplomatic efforts must recognize instances where positive deviance can be used to design, plan, and implement solutions. What existing solutions are working? What are the existing assets and strengths? How can the solutions be used to achieve change and achieve preferred futures? How can the solutions, strengths, and assets be scaled up through capacity building?

In the peacebuilding sector, restorative justice is one of the positive deviant solutions used to address conflicts in different contexts. *Restorative justice* is an approach to conflict resolution that focuses on repairing the harm caused by wrongdoing and restoring the relationships between the involved parties (victims, offender, and community) rather than punishing the offender, as in *retributive justice*. Who was harmed? What needs to be done to repair the harm? Who is responsible for this repair? Restorative justice can involve various methods, such as dialogue, conferencing, or circles, that allow victims, offenders, and other community stakeholders to communicate, express their feelings, understand each other's perspectives, and agree on a fair and satisfactory outcome. Restorative justice can help heal the wounds of violence, foster empathy and forgiveness, promote social cohesion, and prevent future conflicts. Some examples of restorative justice initiatives include the Truth and Reconciliation Commission in South Africa (Stanley, 2001), Gacaca courts in Rwanda (Nyseth Brehm et al., 2014; Herath, 2018), and Aboriginal sentencing circles in Canada (Green, 1998).

One of the challenges of positive deviance in diplomacy is to identify and support local actors who have the potential to change the status quo and create opportunities for dialogue and cooperation. These actors may be individuals, groups, or organizations that positively influence their communities, possess unique insights or skills, and are willing to take risks for peace. They may be hidden, marginalized, or unrecognized by mainstream society or the international community. Positive deviance in diplomacy requires finding and engaging these actors, learning from their experiences and strategies, and facilitating their participation in peace processes. Some examples of positive deviant actors in diplomacy are the women's peace movements in Liberia and Northern Ireland (Gbowee, 2019), religious leaders who mediated the end of the civil war in Mozambique (Berkley Center, 2013), and grassroots activists who initiated the Arab Spring (Çakmak, 2017). At the local level, positive deviance may take the form of negotiation among leaders, such as how chieftains or tribal leaders solve the conflict between farmers and herders, which is a challenging issue in many regions of the Middle East and Sub-Saharan Africa.

Positive deviance in engineering involves creative solutions and unconventional problem-solving techniques that lead to better-than-average outcomes in projects or processes. Examples may include recycled materials used in infrastructure, innovative water and energy harvesting methods, biomimicry-inspired solutions, etc. Positive deviance in engineering may consist of learning local and indigenous practices regarding water, energy, land, and food management that have worked for a long time but could be improved using modern solutions. This dynamic is illustrated in Hart and London (2005) and Korten (2006). Much can also be learned from nature.

4.2.7 Education and Advocacy

As we saw in Chapter 2, engineers must be globally engaged. By global engagement, we mean addressing all issues with an integrated approach (rather than a reductionistic one), whether the projects are local or global. It is about the ongoing education of engineers who serve humanity and have the required attitude, skills, and knowledge to tackle various challenges, from the local to the global, at the intersection of peace, sustainability, and climate security, and for different contexts and scales. They must be aware of (i) their professional and personal ethical responsibilities, (ii) their role in society as citizens, and (iii) the intended and unintended consequences of their decisions when implementing solutions for different socioeconomic, cultural, and political situations. We saw in Chapter 2 that to educate engineers in the 21st century, we need to focus on learning, not schooling, activating both sides of the brain, fostering intuition and creativity, hands-on learning, and lifelong learning.

The BOK of engineers involved in peacebuilding and diplomatic efforts discussed in Chapter 3 strongly emphasizes engineers' acquisition of the fundamentals of conflict resolution and diplomacy. These topics have not traditionally been taught in engineering schools. How do engineers make decisions in conflict-affected and conflict-sensitive environments and transboundary geopolitical settings? What data and information do they need to collect and analyze? How do they interact with policymakers? How do they make decisions in settings (e.g., refugee and rapid response situations) requiring immediate response compared to those requiring more reflection time and different rounds of planning, design, and implementation levels? Resolving conflicts and developing rapid-response solutions require attention in the engineering profession.

4.2.8 Adopting and Implementing Solutions

Once solutions are developed, engineers must ensure their adoption and implementation on a large scale and be participatory. This scaling may involve working with governments, businesses, and communities to integrate new solutions and practices into existing systems. Engineers can educate the public and policymakers about the importance of addressing challenges and the role of engineering in finding solutions. This approach could involve advocacy efforts, public outreach, or educational initiatives.

The new mindset requires the interaction and participation of multiple stakeholders in peacebuilding and diplomatic efforts from the local to the global level. Stakeholders can generally be arranged into three groups: (i) local stakeholders (e.g., community members) who contribute to bottom-up solutions; (ii) governmental institution stakeholders who provide top-down solutions; and (iii) outsiders (e.g., NGOs, donors, and private sector organizations) who contribute to outside-in solutions. The effectiveness of these three groups of stakeholder dynamics depends on many factors, such as (i) willingness to participate in dialogue and decision-making, (ii) the capacity to make meaningful contributions, and (iii) having time for dialogue and decision-making. Another aspect is to avoid the dominance of one decision-making group. This dynamic is crucial when decisions are shaped by external actors (e.g., multilateral agencies, bilateral in-country agencies, NGOs, and the private sector) who may have special interests and use a top-down informative, contractual, and consultative approach with limited input from bottom-up beneficiaries.

4.2.9 The Three Rs of Project Delivery

Addressing the global challenges of the VUCA world mentioned at the beginning of Chapter 1 and keeping in mind the dynamics of the interactions between engineering, peacebuilding, and diplomacy listed in Table 1.2, engineering solutions must "balance technological innovation, economic competitiveness, environmental protection, and social flourishing" (Kamp, 2016). These characteristics resonate with the 5Ps of sustainability discussed in Chapter 2.

Engineers must ensure that, in the short and long terms, solutions to the problems they are facing (i) are the *right ones* with minimum adverse effects on social and ecological systems; (ii) are *rightly done* (i.e., technically sound) for the beneficiaries in the context and at the scale being considered; and (iii) are selected for the *right reasons*. All three characteristics must be considered in consultation and collaboration with project recipients and stakeholders. The first and third characteristics can result from creative thinking and the second from critical thinking.

Table 4.2 provides a more detailed description of the attributes of each component of the 3Rs mindset. It represents the three connected legs of a tripod, representing a project subject to constraints (socioeconomic, cultural, political, and environmental) and pressure. Any missing or weak leg may compromise the entire project's success and lead to unintended consequences.

Table 4.2 The 3Rs mindset (adapted from Karwat et al., 2014)

3Rs	Description
Right solutions	– Suitable for the people (social justice)
	– Good for the environment (ecological stewardship)
	– Nature-based solutions
	– Create partnerships and prosperity and not division
	– Develop solutions that are contextual and scale-appropriate
	– Undertake initiatives and create solutions advocating for promoting and supporting underlying principles such as human rights, social justice, environmental sustainability, and cultural diversity (JEDI)
Rightly done solutions	– Sound from a traditional design, planning, and intervention point of view
	– Sound engineering
	– Reliable and encouraging participation, operations and maintenance
	– Instrumentation included and monitoring and evaluation
	– Innovative and adaptive technologies that support humanitarian aid, disaster recovery, and peacekeeping and peacebuilding operations
	– Enhance communications collaboration and trust among stakeholders
Right reasons solutions	– Does the problem require an engineering intervention?
	– Is there a need to improve technical solutions continuously?
	– Big or small solutions?
	– Appropriateness, affordability, longevity, scalability
	– Must improve living standards
	– Must reduce conflict

The three Rs represent the components of what Karwat et al. (2014) called *orthopraxis*, a correct engineering practice used by what these authors called "activist engineers" who are legitimately and deeply concerned about socioecological welfare. This practice requires engineers to be trained holistically or in an integrated manner, where the emphasis is not just on delivering technical solutions. By embracing a 3Rs mindset, engineers are forced to step out of the specialized left-brain technical box and consider other factors that would benefit from or be affected by technological solutions.

Finally, project delivery is not static. Hence, engineers must be adaptable and continue to innovate and improve existing solutions. Ongoing research, monitoring, and evaluation are required to ensure that the solutions remain adequate and relevant to the 3Rs.

4.2.10   Right Relationships with Life

Engineering for peace and diplomacy must recognize that solutions to challenges are not just about humans. The new mindset includes a need for humanity to adopt forms of proper relationships (i.e., planetary stewardship), reciprocity, and solidarity with all life forms on Earth, as captured in the planet component of the 5Ps of sustainable development. Much can be learned by exposing engineers to worldwide native and indigenous traditions (Cajete, 2020) and Eastern traditions (e.g., Taoism, Buddhism, Hinduism, Confucianism), emphasizing interconnectedness and strengthening the whole person's inner dimension concurrently with socio-economic development and respect for each other.

Taking lessons from nature instead of solely learning about it can pave the way for promoting sustainable human progress and safety. It also presents an avenue for investigating remedies for managing disasters and climate-related risks (UNDRR and UNU-EHS, 2023). As emphasized in biomimicry (Benyus, 2002), nature has designed and developed solutions for millions of years and is ripe for practical applications (https://asknature.org/innovations/). The Biomimicry Institute has identified 10 common patterns of nature that could inspire innovative solutions for human development and security and be part of the knowledge base of engineers. They include:

- Nature uses only the energy it requires and relies on freely available energy.
- Nature recycles all materials.
- Nature is resilient to disturbances.
- Nature tends to optimize rather than maximize.
- Nature provides mutual benefits.
- Nature uses chemistry and materials that are safe for living beings.

- Nature builds using abundant resources, incorporating rare resources only sparingly.
- Nature is locally attuned and responsive.
- Nature uses shape to determine its functionality.

These characteristics of nature must be compared with those of technology. As remarked by Schumacher (1973)

> Technology recognizes no self-limiting principle — in terms, for instance, of size, speed, or violence. It therefore does not possess the virtues of being self-balancing, self-adjusting, and self-cleansing. In the subtle system of nature, technology, and in particular, the super-technology of the modern world, acts like a foreign body, and there are now numerous signs of rejection.

According to the National Peace Academy (n.d.), right relationships and peace go hand in hand and manifest at five different but synergistic levels: (i) *personal,* with an emphasis on developing proper relationships with ourselves; (ii) *social,* with relationships with others; (iii) *political,* where relationships are established within and between groups of people, communities, and organizations; (iv) *institutional,* with emphasis on relationships within and between all types of organizations, government(s), businesses, systems of organizations and civil society structures; and (v) *ecological,* where relationships are established "with Earth and its ecosystems of which we are a part and on which our survival and quality of life depend." What are the right relationships taught in Western forms of education?

4.2.11 Inner and Outer Dimensions of Decision-Making

Since 1990, discussions on human development and security have focused on meeting concrete goals, such as the 17 SDGs, with a primary concern for fulfilling the basic physiological and safety needs highlighted by Maslow (1943). However, there has been little focus on the mindset, principles, and mental frameworks required to achieve those needs. For example, what Agenda 2030 misses is "the ethical framework to guide decisions, practices, and actions in implementing the SDGs" (Khayesi, 2021). Questions arise as to (i) whose ethics of development affects whom, (ii) "whose definition and measurement of development [beyond economic indicators] should be considered in programs designed to support the SDGs" (Khayesi, 2021), and (iii) who is accountable at different levels of decision-making. Addressing the ethical dimension of human development and security with proper development ethics practices (Gasper, 2012) and answering these questions is critical if the SDGs need to become mainstream and the world does not revert to past practices. All these questions highlight the importance of factoring in the inner dimension of decision-makers in human development and security.

The significance of the inner human dimension in achieving sustainable development has gained attention over the last decade. For instance, it was highlighted in a report submitted to the Club of Rome titled *Earth for All: A Survival Guide for Humanity* (Bristow et al., 2024). This report underscores the necessity of considering the inner dimension of decision-making as critical leverage to overcome "barriers to collective action and structural transformation." In that report, the inner dimension refers to

> The domain of cognition, emotion, consciousness, and culture; a complex interplay between individual subjective experience, un-conscious processes and neurophysiology, interpersonal relation-ships, collective beliefs, and social constructs. It is contrasted by the material 'outer' world of landscapes and objects, but neither realm is truly separate or distinct, and both exist in dynamic inter-dependence, continuously influencing and informing one another.

Integrating the inner dimensions of decision-makers in engi-neering, peacebuilding, and diplomatic outer efforts involves bal-ancing internal and external work, recognizing the mind–body–soul nexus, committing not to harm, respecting dignity and auton-omy, acting trustfully and honestly, considering the links between introspection and extrospection, and using mindfulness practices. A quote from Meister Eckhart (Meister Eckhart and Parke, 2010) is pertinent here:

> The outer work can never be minor when the inner work is a major one, and the outer work can never be major or good when the inner work is minor and without value.

Therefore, any external intervention related to human development and security must also consider revisiting the inner work of the institutions and the dominant values of their decision-makers. With this in mind, one can question the quality of our Western society's inner work, institutions, and decision-makers based on how such groups (including ourselves) have managed planetary challenges over the past 200 years and are likely to handle current and future ones in the so-called Anthropocene, an unofficial epoch of Earth's history, where human activities are closely inseparable from Earth's climate and ecosystems. Not only has Western society contributed to irreparable damage to Earth's ecosystems, but it has also manipulated the inner dimensions of society to justify that damage through misinformation and disinformation (Bristow et al., 2024).

The importance of combining inner development (inner work) with outer work and the necessary shift in values and leadership capacities to address the global challenges of the 21st century (outer work) has also been emphasized in the new *Inner Development Goals* (IDGs) framework launched in 2021 in Sweden (https://innerdevelopmentgoals.org/). The "inner development for outer change" (inner to outer work) mission is based on the five dimensions of being, thinking, relating, collaborating, and acting. These five dimensions involve 23 skills and qualities of inner human growth and development, as shown in Table 4.3.

Integrating values and inner work in sustainable development decision-making has also been emphasized as part of the sustainability competencies frameworks proposed by GreenComp,[1] the RSA,[2] the Inner Green Deal (https://innergreendeal.com/), and the Mindful Society Global Institute (https://www.mindfulinstitute.org/).

In summary, can we envision a change in mindset from the Anthropocene to the Symbiocene, where humans work with and in nature (Crist, 2019) and value the intrinsic value, beauty, and even the Soul of creation, elements, plants, and animals? This mindset would differ from the current ones of scarcity, materialism, conflict, and the belief that development is only for a fraction of humanity. Can we expect a better way for humans to treat each

---

[1] The GreenComp Framework | Digital Version | Education for Climate (europa.eu)
[2] Capabilities for life - Design for Life - The RSA - RSA

other? If not, why not? What holds humanity back? In recent human history, what Abraham Lincoln called "the better angels of our nature" (Wikipedia, 2024) or the best of humanity have always surfaced and dominated when faced with crises (Reckford, 2019), though not without challenges. Where are these better angels in the engineering profession? Short of educating what I would call "warrior-sage decision-makers" who make peace with themselves and are mindful of their decision process, it is challenging to envision adequate and practical solutions to ongoing planetary issues.

Table 4.3 The five dimensions and 23 inner development goal framework skills (https://innerdevelopmentgoals.org/framework/) (Open source)

Being Relationship to self	Thinking Cognitive skills	Relating Caring for others and the world	Collaborating Social skills	Acting Enabling change
Inner compass	Critical thinking	Appreciation	Communication skills	Courage
Integrity and authenticity	Complexity awareness	Connectedness	Co-creation skills	Creativity
Openness and learning mindset	Perspective skills	Humility	Inclusive mindset and intercultural competence	Optimism
Self-awareness	Sense-making	Empathy and compassion	Trust	Perseverance
Presence	Long-term orientation and visioning		Mobilization skills	

4.3 Concluding Remarks

Paraphrasing Albert Einstein, current issues cannot be solved with the same level of thinking that created them. One can add that they cannot be solved with the same lack of leadership and compassion that has made them. This chapter explored suggestions for a new mindset for globally engaged engineers to address 21st-century issues. New forms of leadership and compassion-in-action must accompany this new mindset; the latter is rarely mentioned in engineering education. Developing a new mindset is a prerequisite for adopting a systemic perspective on peace-building and diplomacy, as discussed in the next chapter.

Interestingly, there has been growing interest in recognizing the role of inner values and qualities in addressing sustainable development over the last decade. Integrating this component in engineering education and practice and the interaction between engineering, peacebuilding, and diplomacy remains challenging.

References

Amadei, B. (2014). *Engineering for Sustainable Human Development.* Reston, VA: ASCE Press.

Benson, T. and Marlin, S. (2017). *The Habit-forming Guide to Becoming a Systems Thinker.* Pittsburg, PA: Systems Thinking Group.

Benyus, J. (2002). *Biomimicry: Innovation Inspired by Nature* (2nd edition). New York: Harper Perennial.

Berkley Center for Religion, Peace, and World Affairs (2013). Mozambique: Religious Peacebuilders Broker End to Civil War. https://berkleycenter. georgetown.edu/publications/mozambique-religious-peacebuilders-broker-end-to-civil-war

Bristow, J., Bell, R., Wamsler, C., Björkman, T., et al. (2024). The system within: Addressing the inner dimensions of sustainability and systems change. The Club of Rome. Earth4All: deep-dive paper 17. https://www.clubofrome.org/publication/earth4all-bristow-bell/

Çakmak, C. (ed.) (2017). *The Arab Spring, Civil Society, and Innovative Activism.* London: Palgrave Macmillan.

Cajete, G. (2020). *Native Science: Natural Laws of Interdependence.* Santa Fe, New Mexico: Clear Light.

Callebaut, W. (2007). Herbert Simon's silent revolution. *Biological Theory*, **2**(1), 76–86.

Coleman, P. T. (2011). *The Five Percent: Finding Solutions to Seemingly Impossible Conflicts.* New York, NY: Public Affairs.

Crist, E. (2019). *Abundant Earth: Toward An Ecological Civilization.* Chicago, IL: The University of Chicago Press.

Davletov, B., et al. (2022). PeaceTech topic map. A research base for an emerging field. University of Lucerne, GOVLAB.

Dörner, D. (1997). *The Logic of Failure: Recognizing and Avoiding Error in Complex Situations*. New York: Perseus Books.

Evans, M. (2021). 7 Indigenous technologies changing landscapes. https://www.resilience.org/stories/2021-03-08/7-indigenous-technologies-changing-landscapes/

Gasper, D. (2012). Development ethics: Why? What? How? A formulation of the field. *Journal of Global Ethics*, **8**(1), 117–135. https://doi.org/10.1080/17449626.2012.672450

Gbowee, L. (2019). When women stand together as one: The power of women's grassroots peace movements. *Journal of International Affairs*, **72**(2), 13–18. https://www.jstor.org/stable/26760829

Green, R. G. (1998). *Justice in Aboriginal Communities: Sentencing Alternatives.* Purich Publishing, Canada.

Griffith University (2022). Everyday patterns for shifting systems. Everyday patterns for shifting systems (griffith.edu.au)

Guadagno, R. E., Nelson, M., and Lock Lee, L. (2018). Peace data standard: A practical and theoretical framework for using technology to examine intergroup interactions. *Frontiers in Psychology*, **9**, Article 734.

Hart, S. and London, T. (2005). Developing native capability: What multinational corporations can learn from the base of the pyramid. *Stanford Social Innovation Review.* https://ssir.org/articles/entry/developing_native_capability#

Hazeltine, B. and Bull, C. (1999). *Appropriate Technology: Tools, Choices, and Implications*. San Diego, CA: Academic Press.

Herath, D. (2018, May 31). Post-conflict reconstruction and reconciliation in Rwanda and Sri Lanka, *Accord,* https://www.accord.org.za/conflict-trends/post-conflict-reconstruction-and-reconciliation-in-rwanda-and-sri-lanka

Jarland, J., et al. (2020). How should we understand patterns of recurring conflict? *Conflicts Trends 03*. Oslo: Peace Research Institute.

Jones, B. D. (1999). Bounded rationality. *Annual Review of Political Science.*, **2**, 297–321.

Kamp, A. (2016). *Engineering Education in the Rapidly Changing World: Rethinking the Vision for Higher Engineering Education* (2nd revised edition). The Netherlands: TU Delft, Faculty of Aerospace Engineering.

Kania, J. and Kramer, M. (2011). Collective Impact. *Stanford Social Innovation Review*, **9**(1), 36–41. https://doi.org/10.48558/5900-KN19

Karwat, D. M. A., Eagle, W. E, Wooldridge, M. S., and Princen, T. E. (2014). Activist engineering: Changing engineering practice by deploying praxis. *Science and Engineering Ethics*, **21**, 227–239. https://doi.org/10.1007/s11948-014-9525-0

Khayesi, M. (2021). What is the ethical reflection of the sustainable development goals? *Sustainability and Climate Change*, **14** (3). https://doi.org/10.1089/scc.2020.0073

Killelea, S. (2021). *Peace in the Age of Chaos: The Best Solution for a Sustainable Future*. Melbourne: Hardie Grant Books.

Kim, D. H. and Anderson, V. (2007). *System Archetype Basics: From Story to Structure*. Waltham, MA: Pegasus Communications.

Korten, D. (2006). *The Great Turning: From Empire to Earth Community*. San Francisco, CA: Berrett-Koehler.

Mahon, K., Heikkinen, H. L., Huttunen, R., Boyle, T., and Sjølie, E. (2020). What is educational praxis? In: K. Mahon, C. Edwards-Groves, S. Francisco, M. Kaukko, S. Kemmis, K. Petrie (eds.), *Pedagogy, Education, and Praxis in Critical Times*. Singapore: Springer. https://doi.org/10.1007/978-981-15-6926-5_2

Maslow, A. H. (1943) A theory of human motivation. *Psychological Review*, **50**(4), 370–396. https://psycnet.apa.org/doi/10.1037/h0054346

Meadows, D. H. (1997). Places to intervene in a system in increasing order of effectiveness. *Whole Earth*, Winter, 78–84.

Meadows, D. (1999). Leverage points. Places to intervene in a system. The Sustainability Institute. http://www.donellameadows.org/wp-content/userfiles/Leverage_Points.pdf

Meadows, D. (2008). *Thinking in Systems*. Vermont: Chelsea Green Publishing.

Meister Eckhart, J. and Parke, S. (2010). *Conversation with Meister Eckhart*. White Crow Books.

Mencken, H. L. (n.d.) For every complex problem there is an... (brainyquote.com)

Moritz, R. E. (2020, July 17). To reinvent the future, we must all work together. We can create the future we want – if we all work together | World Economic Forum (weforum.org)

Murphy, M. (2022). An architecture of peace. In: C. H. Smith (ed.), *Designing Peace: Building a Better Future*. New York: Cooper Hewitt.

National Peace Academy (n.d.). *A conceptual framework for peace education and peacebuilding programs.* https://nationalpeaceacademy.us/images/files/ProgramFramework1.pdf

National Research Council (NRC) (2012). *Disaster Resilience: A National Imperative.* Washington, DC: The National Academies Press.

Nyseth Brehm, H., Uggen, C., and Gasanabo, J.-D. (2014). Genocide, Justice, and Rwanda's Gacaca Courts. *Journal of Contemporary Criminal Justice*, **30**(3), 333–352. https://doi.rg/10.1177/1043986214536660

OpenAI (2024). ChatGPT (August 10 version) [Large language model]. https://chat.openai.com

Pascale, R., Sternin, J., and Sternin, M. (2010). *The Power of Positive Deviance: How Unlikely Innovators Solve the World's Toughest Problems.* Cambridge, MA: Harvard University Press.

Peace Tech Direct (2020). Digital pathways for peace: Insights and lessons from a global online consultation. Executive summary. https://www.peacedirect.org/wp-content/uploads/2020/08/PD-LVP-Tech-Report-Summary-v3.pdf

Polak, P. (2008). *Out of Poverty: What Works When Traditional Approaches Fail?* San Francisco, CA: Berrett-Koehler.

Practical Action (Oct. 15, 2013). What is appropriate technology. http://practicalaction.org/media/view/20259

Raworth, K. (2018) *Doughnut Economics.* Vermont: Chelsea Geen Publishing.

Quihuis, M., Nelson, M., and Guttieri, K. (2015). Peace technology: Scope, scale, and cautions. *Building Peace*, **5**, 14–16.

Radjou, N., Prabhu, J., and Ahuja, S. (2012). *Jugaad Innovation.* San Francisco, CA: Jossey-Bass.

Reckford, J. (2019). *Our Better Angels: Seven Simple Virtues That Will Change Your Life and the World.* New York: St. Martin's Essentials.

Ritchie-Dunham, J. L. and Rabbino, H. T. (2001). *Managing with Clarity: Identifying, Aligning, and Leveraging Strategic Resources.* New York: John Wiley.

Rouwette, E., and Vennix, J. A. M. (2015). Group model building. *Encyclopedia of Complexity and Systems Science.* DOI: 10.1007/978-3-642-27737-5_264-3.

San Francisco Planning and Urban Research Association (SPUR) (2011). *Resilient city: Ideas and actions for a better city.* San Francisco, CA. http://www.spur.org/policy/the-resilient-city.

Schön, D. (1973). *Beyond the Stable State: Public and Private Learning in a Changing Society.* Harmondsworth: Penguin.

Schumacher, E. F. (1973). *Small Is beautiful.* New York, NY: Harper Perennial.

Scoones, I. (ed.) and contributors (2023). *Pastoralism, Uncertainty, and Development.* Rugby, Warwickshire, UK: Practical Action Publishing. www.practicalactionpublishing.com

Senge, P. (1994). *The Fifth Discipline: The Art & Practice of the Learning Organization.* New York City: Doubleday.

Simon, H. A. (1972). Theories of bounded rationality. In: C. B. McGuire and R. Radner (eds.), *Decisions and Organization.* Amsterdam, The Netherlands: North-Holland Publishing, 161–176.

Smith, C. E. (2022). Designing Peace: Building a Better Future. New York: Cooper Hewitt https://www.cooperhewitt.org/publications/design-ing-peace-building-a-better-future-now/

Stanley, E. (2001). Evaluating the truth and reconciliation commission. *Journal of Modern African Studies,* **39**(3), 525–554.

Sterman, J. (2000). *Business Dynamics: Systems Thinking and Modeling for a Complex World.* Irvine, CA: McGraw Hill.

Sweeney, L. B. and Meadows, D. (2010). *The Systems Thinking Playbook.* Vermont: Chelsea Green Publishing.

Tanabe, J. (2020). Exploring a post-COVID-19 sustainable peace model social ethics society. *Journal of Applied Philosophy,* Article 4, 73–103. ses-journal.com/wp-content/uploads/2020/07/Article-4_Tanabe_SESJuly2020.pdf

Taylor, I. A. and Gantz, B. S. (1969). A transactional approach to creativity and its implications for education. Value dilemmas in the assessment and development of creative leaders. American Association for the Advancement of Science, Washington, DC Paper presented at American Association for the Advancement of Science Meeting, Boston, December, 1969.

Taylor, D. C., Taylor, C. E., and Taylor, J. O. (2012). *Empowerment on an Unstable Planet: From Seeds of Human Energy to a Scale of Global Change.* New York, NY: Oxford University Press.

The Nature Conservancy (Oct. 13, 2018). The science of sustainability. Can a unified path for development and conservation lead to a better future? A Sustainable Future: Two Paths to 2050 (nature.org)

The World Bank (2003). *Implementation of Operational Directive 4.20 on Indigenous Peoples: An Independent Desk Review* (English). Sector or

Thematic Evaluation. Washington, DC: World Bank Group. http:// documents.worldbank.org/curated/en/570331468761746572/ Implementation-of-Operational-Directive-4-20-on-Indigenous- Peoples-an-independent-desk-review

Theise, N. (2023). *Notes on Complexity: A Scientific Theory of Connection, Consciousness, And Being.* New York: Speigel and Grau.

United Nations Environment Assembly. (UNEA) (2022) Resolution 5/5: Nature-based solutions for supporting sustainable development.

United Nations Economic and Social Commission for Western Asia (UNESCWA). the_5ps_of_the_sustainable_development_goals.pdf (unescwa.org)

UNDRR and UNU-EHS (2023). Nature-based Solutions for Comprehensive Disaster and Climate Risk Management, United Nations Office for Disaster Risk Reduction. https://www.undrr.org/publication/ nature-based-solutions-comprehensive-disaster-and-climate-risk- management

Wani, S. P., et al. (2003). Farmer participatory integrated watershed management: Adarsha watershed, Kothapally, India: An innovative and upscalable approach. *International Crops Research Institute for the Semi-Arid Tropics* (ICRISAT), Patancheru, India.

Watzlawick, P., Weakland, J. H., and Fisch, R. (1974). *Change: Principles of Problem Formation and Problem Resolution* (Reprint edition, April 25, 2011). New York: W. W. Norton.

Wikipedia (2024). https://en.wikipedia.org/wiki/Abraham_Lincoln%27s_ first_inaugural_address

Winterford, K., Rhodes, D., and Dureau, C. (2023). *Reframing Aid. A Strengths- based Approach for International Development.* Rugby, Warwickshire, UK: Practical Action Publishing.

Wolfe, S. E. and Smith, L. K. (2021). *Death becomes Us: How our emotions can help avoid climate disaster.* Sarah Elizabeth Wolfe and Lauren Keira Marie Smith – Ernest Becker Foundation

Chapter 5

Embracing a Systems-Aware Practice

This chapter explores another component of the new mindset that globally engaged engineers must adopt: a systems-aware practice to address the dynamics of conflict-affected or conflict-sensitive community landscapes and challenges. Such practices can lead to constructive and innovative outcomes in peacebuilding and diplomatic efforts. Globally engaged engineers must understand systems, become system thinkers, promote systemic change, and make integrated decisions that depart from traditional compartmentalized approaches. This chapter presents the limitations of the traditional reductionist approach to address 21st-century challenges and advocates for an alternative complexity-based, multi-solving system approach. Globally engaged engineers must acquire a systemic perspective on human development and security and its contributions to peace and diplomacy.

5.1   Introduction

Engineers who work on human development and security and engage in peacebuilding and diplomatic efforts must understand that community landscapes, where conflict might occur, involve many systems (social, economic, infrastructure, ecological, etc.) that are always interrelated and cannot be separated. Peace and

Engineering for Peace and Diplomacy
Bernard Amadei
Copyright © 2025 Jenny Stanford Publishing Pte. Ltd.
ISBN 978-981-5129-75-5 (Hardcover), 978-1-003-65168-0 (eBook)
www.jennystanford.com

conflict and the success of diplomatic efforts emerge from the interaction of these systems, behavioral patterns, structures, and mental models.

Hence, adopting a systems-aware practice (i.e., understanding systems, becoming a systems thinker, promoting systemic change, and making decisions across systems) is vital for addressing the dynamics of conflict-affected and conflict-sensitive community landscapes. Figure 5.1 shows multiple interactions between peace-building, engineering, and diplomacy with different community systems. First, it captures the horizontal interaction of these three sectors with the vertical system silos. These three sectors interact to form a nexus. Second, the nexus may interact with other nexuses, such as the water–energy–land–food nexus, the water–energy–food–ecosystem nexus, the food–healthcare–nutrition nexus, the climate– fragility–peacebuilding nexus, the environment– fragility–peace nexus, and the peace–sustainability–climate security nexus. Other context-specific nexus types can also be considered.

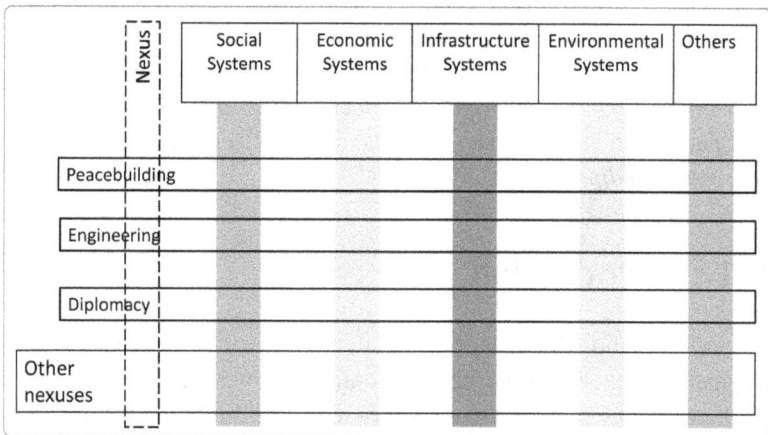

Figure 5.1 A systems perspective versus a silo approach to the peace-building–engineering–diplomacy nexus.

This chapter underlines the importance of engineers adopting a systems-aware practice that complements their traditional linear and reductionistic approaches. It involves collaboration and transdisciplinary interaction with stakeholders with various roles and backgrounds, such as practitioners, policymakers, peacebuilders, researchers, community members, and changemakers. A systems view also requires globally engaged engineers to deal with volatility, uncertainty, complexity, and ambiguity in various situations and levels.

5.2 From Reductionistic to Systems Practice

5.2.1 A Tunnel Vision

A systems practice is a much-needed supplement to traditional reductionistic practice. Since the seventeenth and eighteenth centuries of the Enlightenment, Western science has been dominated by a default reductionistic view of reality that views the universe as a highly stable mechanism consisting of fixed parts, comprises physical phenomena, and is governed by universal laws (i.e., physical determinism). This mechanistic view of reality originated from the work of Descartes. It was further reinforced by other scientists and Western philosophers of the Enlightenment (e.g., Newton, Bacon, Kant, etc.) and has been the driving force of the Industrial Revolution.

Descartes enunciated four basic mechanistic rules to evaluate reality in *Discourse on the Method* (1637). Among them, one rule, "Divide each of the difficulties under examination into as many parts as possible and as might be necessary for its adequate solution," stands out. This rule led Western culture to view reality as consisting of parts and disciplines that were assumed to be independent and addressed in isolation.

This mechanistic mindset is responsible for how today's institutions (social, educational, economic, etc.) are organized into disciplines, sectors, specializations, parts, etc., and hierarchically run on the power of instruction. It is also responsible for how humanity sees humans as separate from each other and nature as a machine to be controlled. Finally, it relies on the opinions of experts who do not necessarily collaborate and follow a rational decision-making model. As noted by BenDor and Scheffran (2019; based on the remarks of Shmueli et al., 2008), these experts "work in isolation, define problems, collect and select the information they deem to be objective (scientific), build technical models pointing the way toward problem explanations, and after that, unilaterally develop optimal solutions for use by formal decision-makers." This so-called 'barbarism of specialization' approach (Ortega y Gasset, 1994) and "false security of linear, disciplinary, and reductionistic ways of thinking and working" (Woodhill and Milicant, 2023) has been dominant in dealing with human development and security issues. It was also prevalent in how engineering projects were approached from 1850 to 1950, as discussed in Chapter 2, and how most engineers have been educated up to this day.

Another limiting aspect of the reductionistic approach is its command-and-control approach to how problems, in general, should be addressed. First, to be considered, the issues must be "well-rounded, clearly defined, relatively simple, and generally linear with respect to cause and effect" (Harford, 2012) and quantifiable. Second, problems must have solutions expected to be "direct, appropriate, feasible, and effective over most relevant spatial and temporal scales" (Holling and Meffe, 1995). Third, solutions must not evolve or adapt over time (Harford, 2012). Finally, the solutions must be predictable and optimal (best). Simply put, such expectations are impossible in the uncertain and unfamiliar settings of the VUCA world.

Combined with a belief in positivism, which asserts that reality can only be explained rationally and is devoid of choice, values, and consciousness, reductionism has been used to address issues in a world that does not resemble reality. Its narrow focus can capture only a small fraction of the complex and interconnected nature of reality. An example of this narrow focus is how the issue of climate change is addressed, primarily by focusing on carbon emissions. This so-called 'carbon tunnel vision' with a net-zero goal distracts from addressing other crucial and interdependent development issues such as pollution, human rights abuses, biodiversity loss, poverty, inequality, resource scarcity, health, resources insecurity, ecosystem degradation, and externalities that are influenced by or impact carbon emissions (Konietsko, 2022). A multidisciplinary and systemic approach is necessary to fully address climate change (Achakulvisut et al., 2022).

5.2.2 Stepping Out of the Deterministic Box

Since the 1920s, especially after WWII, there has been a strong realization that Descartes's reductionism cannot explain real-world organized complexity and wholeness. Some scientists and decision-makers have recognized the limitations of the deterministic view of the universe in addressing planetary issues despite its dominance over the past 400 years (Lent, 2017). They dared to open the door and step out of the academic reductionist box, as shown in Fig. 5.2. Others are less comfortable with change and perpetuate an illusionary view of the world.

Figure 5.2 Opening the door of the reductionist box in academia. From reductionism to real-world complexity and wholeness. Source: Image credit Virpi Oinonen: http://www.businessillustrator.com/ (reproduced by permission).

The traditional method of thinking in science and engineering, which is reductionistic and deterministic, is not inherently flawed. However, it is essential to recognize that this is not always the case. This approach has proven helpful for handling simple and complicated systems. For example, applying Newton's three laws and the law of universal gravitation was instrumental in sending people to the Moon and back multiple times. Advancements in science, engineering, and technology have also been greatly facilitated by reductionistic thinking, including the development of modern transportation and telecommunication systems and multiple medical breakthroughs.

However, reductionistic thinking is inadequate to address the complex human development and security issues and risks mentioned in Section 1.1 at the start of this book. The complex problems in a VUCA world are mostly ill-defined, messy, intertwined, and sometimes called "wicked" (Rittel and Weber, 1973). As initially defined by Churchman (1967), these issues belong to "a class of social system problems which are ill-formulated, where the information is confusing, where there are many clients and decision-makers with conflicting values, and where the ramifications in the whole system are thoroughly confusing." The term "mess" suggested initially by Ackoff (1981) describes the management of such problems.

The words 'messy' or 'ill-defined' have also been proposed in the literature as synonymous with wicked problems; both are used throughout this book. Such issues can be interpreted as 'malignant,' 'vicious,' 'tricky,' or 'aggressive.' Paraphrasing Rittel and Weber (1973), messy and ill-defined problems have unique characteristics, unlike "tamed" problems.

- They exhibit complex interlocking patterns of dysfunction.
- They are challenging to formulate and can be defined differently depending on the context and physical and temporal scales.
- They are characterized by organized complexity.
- They have no stopping rules and no true or false answers.
- They are challenging to evaluate.
- They create unique and unintended consequences.
- They are irreversible, and attempting to correct unintended consequences may create more disruptions.
- Multiple solutions require compromises (trade-offs) between numerous objectives.
- They require caution, flexibility, and adaptability when selecting the most appropriate solutions if they can be found.
- They are unique and cannot be regrouped into classes with similar characteristics or solutions.
- They are intended to be discovered in unique ways.
- They can be the cause or effect of other ill-defined or messy problems.
- They emerge from the interactions between multiple systems and subsystems.

It is important to note that many problems encountered in conflict-affected and conflict-sensitive environments exhibit these characteristics.

Ill-defined and messy issues must be handled using advanced analytical methods borrowed from various branches of systems science and the scientific study of complexity (Waldrop, 1992; Laszlo, 2001; Mitleton-Kelly, 2003). Addressing these issues requires adopting a *system practice* that encompasses new thinking habits, tools, and integrated decision-making methods. Table 5.1 lists questions for decision-makers to decide whether such a practice is better suited to address their challenges or use more traditional reductionistic and deterministic approaches.

The value proposition of using a systems practice is especially relevant when addressing *nexus problems* that cannot be resolved using a compartmentalized approach. By definition, nexus issues involve the interaction of several linked sectors, such as engineering, peacebuilding, and diplomacy, as considered in this book (Table 1.2). Other nexus types that have been addressed using systems thinking include the water–energy, water–energy–food, and water–energy–land–food nexus (Amadei, 2019); the water–energy–food–ecosystem nexus (EcoFuture, n.d.); the peace, sustainability, and climate security nexus (Amadei, 2023); the humanitarian aid–development–climate change nexus; and the food–healthcare–nutrition nexus (SPRING, 2015). Several publications have explored the nexus among the 17 United Nations SDGs (Scharlemann et al., 2020; Haskins, 2021; ICSU, 2015; Schmidt-Traub, 2015; Nilsson et al., 2016, 2017; Zhang et al., 2016; Randers et al., 2019; Pedercini et al., 2020; van Zanten and van Tudler, 2021).

Unlike the traditional reductionist approach to addressing sectors in isolation (i.e., as decoupled), nexus thinking requires decision-makers to adopt an integrated perspective that considers the characteristics of each nexus component, their connectedness, the attributes of their linkages, their common purpose, and possible constraints and barriers. They also need to acquire systems habits. In short, nexus thinking is systems thinking. A challenge in using a nexus approach resides in collecting data on each sector and their interactions.

Table 5.1 Choosing between traditional practice (left column) and system practice (right column). *Source:* The Omidyar Group (2017) under Attribution-Share Alike 4.0. International

How complex is your challenge? Use this chart to reflect on the complexity of your challenge. A systems practice may be a good match if you lean toward the right on these complexity spectrums.

The problem is well understood. We know what causes it, and there is solid evidence that our proposed actions will have the intended effects.	What is the nature of the challenge?	We are not sure we fully understand the problem, let alone the solution.
There is a high consensus among stakeholders and experts about what to do.	How are people engaging with the challenge?	There is a significant diversity of opinion and even conflict among stakeholders and experts about what to do.
The problem is relatively self-contained and not intertwined with its broader environment, which is stable and predictable (political, social, and economic).	What is the nature of the environment?	Many diverse and dynamic interconnections exist between the problem and the broader environment, which is unstable and dynamic (political, social, and economic).
It is a short-term goal.	What is the nature of your intended goal?	To make a sustained change at a broad scale.
I can probably use other approaches to develop a solid strategy.	Add it all up. Which side do you lean toward?	Systems practice could be beneficial for helping your team grapple with this messy problem.

Unfortunately, although systems practice has been recognized as better suited to addressing complex problems since the 1920s, progress in using such a practice has been slow. It has been met with reservations in science and engineering from many opponents, pragmatists, and supporters. In engineering education, for instance, multiple reservations about adopting a systems practice have been proposed. According to Monat et al. (2022), the reasons include: (i) administrators and instructors do not grasp its benefits; (ii) instructors do not fully grasp its methodology and tools; (iii) it is seen as an alternative to traditional, proven engineering methods rather than a supplement; and (iv) engineering programs are packed and cannot include extra courses.

Although there was some initial hesitation, the early 2000s saw renewed interest in using a systems perspective to tackle complex global issues, as evidenced by various books on systems. This trend will likely gain momentum in the coming decades as the problems of the VUCA world demand a new approach and cannot be solved in a reductionist manner alone.

5.2.3 A Transdisciplinary Approach

As outlined in Chapter 3, peace can be viewed as either a state or a culture characterized by stability or as a dynamic equilibrium emerging from multiple systems' interactions within a contextual and scale-based landscape. The same can be said about sustainability, health, and climate security. For example, consider a conflict-affected and conflict-sensitive community landscape. In this case, peace emerges from a holarchy of interdependent and interconnected systems (social, economic, financial, technical, and environmental) and their nested subsystems involving various adaptive actors. Systems, subsystems, and their components interact and cannot be treated in isolation (Laszlo, 2001). Conflict-affected and conflict-sensitive landscapes serve as spaces of possibilities or environments that are either stable or not and are subject to various enabling and constraining factors and barriers (political, ethical, security, economic, and sociocultural factors).

Disciplinary - Within one academic discipline - Disciplinary goal setting - No cooperation with other disciplines - Development of new disciplinary knowledge and theory	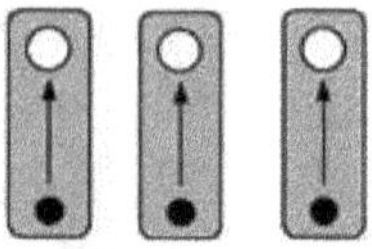
Multidisciplinary - Multiple disciplines - Multiple disciplinary goal setting under one thematic umbrella - Loose cooperation of disciplines for exchange of knowledge - Disciplinary theory development	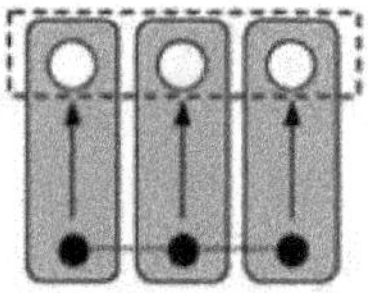
Interdisciplinary - Crosses disciplinary boundaries - Common goal setting - Integration of disciplines - Development of integrated knowledge and theory	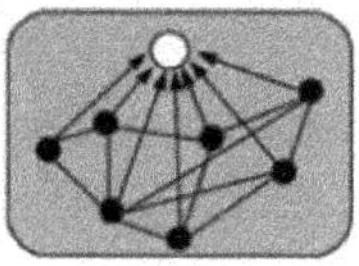
Transdisciplinary - Crosses disciplinary and scientific/academic boundaries - Common goal-setting - Integration of disciplines and nonacademic participants - Development of integrated knowledge and theory among science and society	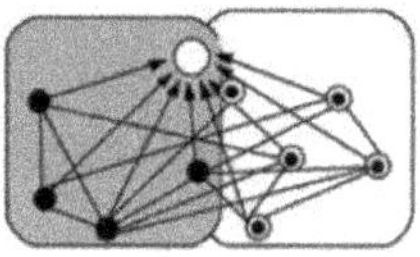
- Discipline ● - Non-academic participants ◉ - Goal of a research project ○ - Movement towards goal → - Cooperation and integration —	- Thematic umbrella - Academic knowledge body - Non-academic knowledge body

Figure 5.3 Disciplinary, multidisciplinary, interdisciplinary, and transdisciplinary approaches to reaching goals that involve academic and non-academic participation (after Tress et al., 2005). Reproduced with permission from Springer Nature.

Hence, adopting a systems approach encompassing new thinking habits, tools, and integrated decision-making methods is vital for addressing human development and security issues to support peace and diplomacy. The practice recognizes the need to approach complex problems not in a *single disciplinary* way but instead in a *multidisciplinary* manner (i.e., several disciplines look at the same issue through their lens, and their findings supplement each other) or an integrated *interdisciplinary* approach (i.e., crossing disciplinary boundaries with findings integration). Finally, a more integrated approach is *transdisciplinary*, encompassing different sectors and technical and non-technical fields (Tress et al., 2005; NRC, 2014; Morton et al., 2015; Utrecht University, n.d.). Figure 5.3 illustrates the characteristics of each approach.

The transdisciplinary approach best acknowledges and embraces the intricacies of systems when addressing issues related to human development, security, peacebuilding, and diplomacy. Viewing complexity as a chance for positive change and applying systems thinking, tools, and collaborative elements can result in creative and effective solutions (Leadbeater and Winhall, 2020). These solutions must also take into "consideration a variety of other key factors, such as gender, trauma, justice, culture, and the environment" (Schirch, 2013).

5.3 Fundamental Principles of Systems

This section presents a concise summary of the fundamental principles of systems, particularly as they relate to the role of globally engaged engineers in addressing human development and security concerns, which contributes to peacebuilding and diplomatic initiatives in conflict-affected and conflict-sensitive landscapes. As a must in their body of knowledge, engineers interested in peace engineering and engineering diplomacy should recognize different types of systems and archetypes, make appropriate decisions, and acquire system habits. They should also be familiar with different system modeling tools, including their pros and cons. Readers interested in learning more about systems and associated terminology may want to explore systems science and complexity science literature.

Since 2010, there has been growing interest in incorporating systems thinking and tools into conflict analysis and management (Jones, 2015; CDA, 2016; Coleman et al., 2007; USAID, 2011a,b; Ricigliano, 2011, 2012; Schirch, 2013; NAE/USIP, 2013; Usenik and Turnsek, 2016; BenDor and Schreffan, 2019; among others). These tools help (i) understand the outcomes of conflict assessments, (ii) anticipate how conflicts might change, (iii) find areas where actions can be taken to resolve the conflict, and (iv) suggest efficient actions that foster peace and stability. A common observation regarding using systems tools to analyze conflicts is their predominantly qualitative nature. As Kasman et al. (2023) highlighted, integrating systems science into peacebuilding is still in its nascent stage of development. Nonetheless, valuable insights can be gleaned from decision-making processes in the scientific and engineering fields, which frequently employ qualitative and quantitative systems approaches. This presents an opportunity to adapt effective practices in these contexts for peacebuilding.

Systems can generally be described as collections of inter-connected components connected by the exchange of energy, matter, and information (Meadows, 2008). Systems comprise linked components or units that form an integrated whole (Von Bertalanffy, 1973) and have boundaries (physical and temporal). The pursuit of objectives is often guided by a shared goal among the various components of a system, although some elements may possess conflicting objectives. This concept can be viewed as unification and differentiation. In other words, as many systems thinkers have stated, nothing exists in isolation, and everything is interconnected in systems.

One of the defining features of systems is that they are governed by many rules that operate at both the component and system levels, as well as by how they engage with their surroundings. Moreover, individuals who interact with these systems and researchers who analyze them become integral parts of them, with both the observers and the observed becoming interconnected. A good example is how exogenous stakeholders in a project (e.g., humanitarian aid, development, and peacekeeping agencies) may become endogenous to the project over time (Hayden, 2018). For example, UN field workers brought cholera to Haiti, which killed thousands of people in 2016. Another one concerns the UN High Commission of Refugees (UNHCR)'s humanitarian aid efforts during Bosnia's 1992–1995 war (Cutts, 1999), where well-intentioned humanitarian diplomacy occasionally supported the regimes that caused civilian misery.

Engineers must know the different types of systems involved in development, peacebuilding, and diplomacy and how to manage them. According to Snowden and Boone (2007), systems can be divided into four groups: simple, complicated, complex, and chaotic (Table 5.2). As observed by Patton (2011), these systems differ in (i) the "degree of certainty" with which problems can be solved and (ii) "the degree of agreement" on how to solve such problems. Different contexts require different approaches to systems and situational recognition by decision-makers (Gell-Mann, 1996; Patton, 2011; Britt, 2013; Glouberman and Zimmerman, 2002). As noted by Snowden and Boone (2007), selecting an appropriate approach when assessing a system and making decisions on how to intervene in that system depends significantly on whether the system is ordered (i.e., simple or complicated) or unordered (i.e., complex or chaotic).

Table 5.2 Four types of systems with different practices and response modes, according to the Cynefin framework of Snowden and Boone (2007)

	Ordered		Unordered	
Types	Simple	Complicated	Complex	Chaotic
What do we know?	We know the knowns.	We know the unknowns.	We don't know the unknowns.	Too turbulent to know anything
Practice	Best	Good	Emergent	Novel
Response	Sense **Categorize** Respond	Sense **Analyze** Respond	**Probe** Sense Respond	**Act** Sense Respond

It is essential to intervene appropriately in any system context and consider the temporal and physical scales and associated boundaries within which the system or its components function. For example, different interventions are needed in a community's rapid response, recovery, and development phases following conflict or adverse events. Likewise, Leroux-Martin and O'Connor (2017) noted that different system types can coexist in conflict-affected and conflict-sensitive environments and require different interventions. A country can be complex, but certain parts may experience chaos and violence because of localized conflicts. The challenge is to prioritize (e.g., triage) the modes of intervention with existing resources. Certain modes of intervention may be better at a specific scale (physical and temporal) than others.

Complex systems are the most challenging among all the system types listed in Table 5.2. They possess many unique characteristics that are difficult to comprehend, model, or manage.

- The whole transcends the characteristics of its components.
- Nonlinearity, feedback structures, emergence, dynamic behavior, adaptation, unpredictability, and uncertainty are typical.
- Unexpected events are frequent.
- Through synergy, behavioral patterns can develop.
- Their behavior depends significantly on the dependencies of their components. Removing a particular element can disrupt the behavior of the entire system.
- Phase transitions may lead to the emergence of system properties and reciprocal causality.
- Although best practices cannot be established, practical, relevant, and meaningful practices are still possible.
- Only good enough (i.e., satisficing) and not optimal solutions are possible (Simon, 1972).

Complex systems include living systems, the Earth's climate, the human body, the stock market, healthcare systems, enterprise network systems, communities, and neighborhoods in villages, cities, and megacities. They are more a rule than an exception in human development and security and dominate peacebuilding and diplomatic efforts. The scientific study of complex systems is sometimes referred to as complexity science (Waldrop, 1992; Mitchell, 2009). It incorporates various approaches and lines of research.

Natural and human living systems belong to a distinct group of complex systems that merit special attention, as they are frequently encountered in conflict-affected and conflict-sensitive environments. These *complex adaptive systems* rarely maintain their original form and continuously evolve as they progress towards new states of normalcy (Miller and Page, 2007; Waldrop, 1992). In addition to the characteristics of the complex systems mentioned above, they exhibit self-organization, self-stabilization, self-correction, self-maintenance, reciprocal causality, and adaptation through evolutionary and co-evolutionary changes in their structure, behavior patterns, and interaction rules (Mitleton-Kelly, 2003). Although not always present simultaneously, some of these traits may be more prevalent in specific contexts. In contrast, others can be closely related and potentially interact in disruptive ways in certain situations. It is impossible to expect constant development, security, and peace in complex adaptive systems. Hence, sustainable development, peacebuilding, peace-making, and peacekeeping are dynamic and cannot create a permanent state; they are ongoing.

Viewing human systems as complex adaptive entities, they can be likened to evolving organisms that exhibit a certain level of sentience. These organisms depend on their environment and affect it through many feedback loops. This dynamic is prevalent in how humanitarian response can negatively damage the environment and how a degraded climate affects humanitarian response (Hoffman and Henly-Shepard, 2023, on behalf of Sphere).

When unpredictability is amplified, overly complex systems become *more chaotic*. Such systems are characterized by severe turbulence; small objects can have enormous consequences, and bifurcation leading to rapid change is possible (Lorenz, 1972; Briggs and Peat, 1999; Sweeney, 2001). Countries that experience intra- and inter-conflicts and disasters exhibit chaotic behavior. If possible, chaotic systems require immediate action, sensing, and response to re-establish a reasonable sense of order; thus, they can be handled as complex systems. Peacebuilding, peacemaking, peacekeeping, and diplomatic efforts can facilitate these activities.

Complexity is often seen as a roadblock for decision-making in conflict-affected and conflict-sensitive landscapes. There is a perception that greater complexity signifies that the systems in the landscape have a more significant number of subsystems to manage and synchronize. Consequently, more potential points of failure are possible, and increased energy and resources are required for information acquisition and processing (Kauffman and Kauffman, 2021). Conversely, a key advantage of complex systems is their ability to handle more information than simple or complicated systems, predict environmental changes more accurately, and quickly learn and adapt. These characteristics enable complex systems to respond more effectively to changing conditions (Kauffman and Kauffman, ibid.). As best summarized by Westley et al. (2007), decision-makers must make "a fundamental [and intentional] shift in perception—from complexity as an obstacle, to complexity as an opportunity" and be constantly and thoroughly aware of that value proposition.

5.4   Systems Thinking

5.4.1   Value Proposition

At the core of the systems-aware practice is systems thinking. It is vital in any systemic approach to peacebuilding and diplomacy. Several definitions of systems thinking have been proposed in the literature and reviewed by Arnold and Wade (2015). According to Sterman (2006), systems thinking is "an iterative learning process in which we replace a reductionist, narrow, short-term, static view of the world with a holistic, broad, long-term, dynamic view, reinventing our policies and institutions accordingly." Systems thinking may also be regarded as a form of divergent thinking that encourages creativity and innovation, in contrast to more traditional convergent thinking (Rieken et al., 2019). Arnold and Wade (2015) see systems thinking as a "system of thinking about systems" and as

> A set of synergistic skills used to improve the capability of identifying and understanding systems, predicting their behaviors, and devising modifications to them in order to produce desired effects. These skills work together as a system.

The value proposition of systems thinking in addressing complex and messy problems has been demonstrated in various ways in the literature. First, as a vantage point, it provides a distinct perspective and collection of abilities to view and understand systems holistically as wholes rather than as collections of parts. Systems thinking acknowledges that, as a whole, a system is greater than the sum of its parts and has different forms of behavior from each component in isolation.

Second, systems thinking can be viewed as a discipline necessary for organizations to grow and learn. Senge (1994) referred to this as the fifth discipline. The other four include acquiring personal mastery, creating mental models, building a shared vision, and team learning.

Table 5.3 A summary of systems thinking and associated skills, according to Richmond (1997). Conflict-related examples have also been added

Types of System Thinking	Description
Dynamic thinking instead of static equilibrium thinking.	Accounting for how situations change and develop patterns over time. Conflict dynamics change over time.
System-as-cause thinking instead of system-as-effect thinking.	Finding causes for a problem or issue residing within the system instead of being driven by external forces. Conflict emerges from inner community dynamics. Outer components may also affect conflict.
Forest thinking instead of tree-by-tree thinking.	Looking at trends within a system instead of focusing on specific system parts (which could result in analysis paralysis). Conflict can unfold at different interdependent scales.
Operational thinking instead of factor thinking.	Exploring how behavior is generated through the systems structure and its components. See the storyline in the iceberg model of Fig. 4.2.
Loop thinking instead of linear thinking.	Considering causal loops within a system and a circular instead of linear one-way causality between cause and effect. Repeated peacebuilding, peacemaking, and peacekeeping cycles are possible due to conflict reemergence.
Quantitative and scientific thinking.	Developing models of problems consisting of quantifiable components, which can be tested to see whether they match what is being observed in the real world and, if needed, require correction. Models are dynamic and may need to be updated as conflict evolves.

Third, systems thinking gives decision-makers unique skills to address complex problems, particularly in conflict-affected and conflict-sensitive environments. These skills are listed in Table 5.3. Richmond (2004) later added the skills of nonlinear thinking (i.e., no proportional relationship between cause and effect) and empathic thinking (e.g., sharing and understanding).

Fourth, systems thinking can be viewed as a middle ground between critical and creative thinking (Vaughan, 2013). *Critical thinking* is required to ensure that issues are correctly addressed from a technical perspective (one of the three Rs in Table 4.2). It is analytic, focused, objective, linear, and left-brain-dominant. Simultaneously, *creative thinking* is necessary to address the uncertainty of the problems and ensure that they are suitable for beneficiaries and their environment (the other two Rs in Table 4.2). It is generative, subjective, associative, and right-brain-dominant. Critical and creative thinking support each other and constantly interact with human development and security. According to Vaughan (2013), "the output of critical thinking is the answers to the questions 'Why?' and 'How?' [in the system]. This output then feeds into creative thinking to produce a range of options [and intervention scenarios], which generates new questions and further refines the options available until a preferred course of action [for a system] is reached." Creative thinking can, in turn, affect critical thinking.

Finally, and more specifically to peacebuilding and diplomatic efforts in conflict-affected and conflict-sensitive environments, systems thinking allows decision-makers to:

- Account for the complexity, nonlinearities, and feedback between conflict causes and effects.
- Map, analyze, and model conflict situations in a more integrated manner using an evidence-based approach.
- Sense conflict dynamics and storyline-related structures, behavior patterns, and events.
- Gain insight into the different dimensions and attractors of conflict.
- Identify and address conflicts and barriers to peace and development.
- PinPoint key leverage areas where small changes can have a significant impact.
- Understand the dynamic, adaptive, and unpredictable nature of different intervention scenarios.
- Analyze how a small event can affect peace and development.

- Undertake adaptable and flexible decision-making while simultaneously addressing the challenges of trade-offs and synergies.
- Observe the inter- and multi-connectedness of concepts, facts, and ideas that can result in new learning, discoveries, and innovations.

All the aspects of systems thinking mentioned above have been demonstrated in diverse fields of study, from global to local. For example, system thinking has been used to explore and predict global planetary and country-level changes in frameworks and integrated assessment models such as World3, World3-03 (Meadows et al., 2004), TARGETS (Rotmans and deVries, 1997), and the International Futures platform (Hughes and Hillebrand, 2006).

The benefits of systems thinking have also been demonstrated by addressing a wide range of complex issues at the local scale. These include peace and conflict (USIP, 2013; USAID, 2011a,b); healthcare (De Savigny and Adam, 2009; Adam, 2014; Peters, 2014); the water cycle and management; water, sanitation, and hygiene (Huston and Moriarty, 2018; Adanke et al., 2019); food and nutrition (Hammond and Dube, 2012; SPRING, 2015); and critical infrastructure. The International Council on Systems Engineering has published several reports emphasizing the value proposition of systems engineering in its 2035 vision to address global societal challenges (INCOSE, 2021).

5.4.2 Remarks and Limitations

Notably, systems thinking is an alternative to deterministic thinking. It is just a way of thinking that recognizes the complexity and interrelated nature of the world. It does not stand alone and must be integrated into a methodology, framework, and practice (see Chapter 7) that guides decision-makers when (i) mapping, identifying, and ranking complex problems; (ii) developing strategies; (iii) selecting and implementing holistic solutions and interventions; and (iv) proposing coherent governance and policies in the short and long term. Systems thinking must be supplemented with appropriate modeling tools, as discussed in Chapter 6.

Table 5.4 Conventional and systems perspectives. *Source*: CDA (2016), used with permission from the CDA Collaborative

A Conventional Perspective	A Systems Perspective
The world is full of problems. Adopt a problem-solving approach and fix them.	The world is full of systems. Adopt a learning approach. Understanding informs action.
Problems should be broken down into parts. Each part should be addressed individually.	Issues exist within complex contexts. Change requires understanding this interconnectedness.
Following a series of pre-determined actions, executed in order, solves problems.	Influencing complex systems requires careful planning and adaptive action: monitor the system for its feedback (response) and adjust actions accordingly. Support positive change developing in the system.
Work is assessed based on its intentions. Unintended consequences are no one's fault, and we cannot anticipate them.	Work is assessed based on its effects. Decision-makers are responsible for all results, including unintended consequences, which they should and can anticipate and mitigate.
Events and issues should be monitored and addressed as they arise.	Underlying social structures and dynamics produce discrete events. Change requires addressing underlying issues that drive events.
Outsiders can affect but are not part of the problems being addressed.	If one interacts with a system, one becomes a part of it.
With the proper understanding, outsiders are just as capable of creating change as insiders.	Insiders intuitively understand social systems in ways few outsiders can master.
Work that targets specific constituencies can have an impact beyond those constituencies.	Impacts are essential at both individual and socio-political levels of change and with key and more people.

The transition from reductionist to systemic thinking is complex. It requires cultivating new decision-making habits and viewing the world through a different lens, as explored in the following section. However, using a systems approach to tackle global problems offers benefits over traditional methods. Table 5.4 compares the attributes of both perspectives. The conventional reductionist approach applies to predictable and straightforward situations and uses various *objective* tools to break the issues into smaller parts in conflict-affected and conflict-sensitive environments.

5.5   Habits of Systems Thinkers

Resolving conflicts and other social issues using systems thinking requires the "thinker" to adopt habits different from those more familiar with traditional reductionist thinking. Seelos (2020) remarked, "Without changing the mindset and adopting new habits, using the term 'system' is pointless in terms of explanatory power or intervention design." Habits forge the mental model section of the iceberg representation, as shown in Fig. 4.2. The development of these habits requires time and exposure to complex environments.

Based in Pittsburgh, Pennsylvania, the Waters Foundation (2016) (now the Waters Center for Systems Thinking, WCST) proposed a series of habits they deemed necessary for decision-makers to adopt when faced with systems. They are listed in Table 5.5, with illustrative examples dealing with peacebuilding and diplomacy. Exemplary case studies are found in Appendix A. These habits represent thinking strategies (visual, listening, speaking, and kinesthetic) that decision-makers might want to follow to address complex problems at the community level and across the engineering–peacebuilding–diplomacy nexus. Some of these habits also depend on one another. Underlying these habits is the need for good communication, cooperation, and thinking outside the box.

Table 5.5 Habits of systems thinkers and linkages, and illustrative examples of applications. *Note:* The left and center columns are adapted from Benson and Marlin (2017). *Source:* © 2020 Waters Center for Systems Thinking, WatersCenterST.org, used by permission

Habits and Description	Description	Peacebuilding and diplomacy examples
1. Seek to understand the big picture.	A systems thinker focuses on the forest and the details of any single tree.	– Peace at the local level depends on what's happening globally and vice versa. – Transboundary issues at the regional scale (e.g., the Arctic, Middle East) are common. – Selected interventions create desirable and undesirable patterns of change at different scales (e.g., household, community, and regional).
2. Change perspectives to increase understanding. Related to Habit # 5	A systems thinker increases understanding by changing the way they view aspects of the system.	– Stakeholders may have different opinions about peace. – Participatory dialogue is needed to find a common diplomatic ground. – Each intervention's what, why, who, where, when, and how changes from looking at the big picture to examining specific details.
3. Consider how mental models affect current reality and the future. Related to Habits # 14 and 5	A systems thinker knows how beliefs and attitudes influence a systems behavior.	– Mental models are at the bottom of the iceberg in Fig. 4.2. Conflict may result from belief systems that are no longer valid. Mental models can change. – Different mental models lead to distinctive intervention methods. Structure, behavior, events. – Mental models create reference frames on how to see reality. They are time and physical characteristics.
4. Observe how elements within systems change over time, generating patterns and trends.	A systems thinker sees change over time as the "dynamics" of a system.	– What story has led to the current situation, and how has it evolved? – How have events and their effects affected communities? – How has conflict constrained economic growth over time? – Learning from past events will help us to do better in the future. – The behavior patterns of complex and adaptive systems change over time due to changes in their internal structure and external effects.

Habits and Description	Description	Peacebuilding and diplomacy examples
		– A value proposition for monitoring and evaluating peacebuilding, peacemaking, and peacekeeping interventions.
		– Linear growth vs. exponential growth.
		– See Table 3.6 of the what, why, who, when, where, and how in conflict assessment.
5. Surfaces and test assumptions.	A systems thinker actively tests theories and assumptions, perhaps with others, to improve performance.	– Monitor and evaluate implementations, identify and manage risks, and make changes accordingly.
		– Assumptions behind interventions must be re-evaluated regularly to see if they are still relevant to explain current dynamics.
Related to Habits # 3 and 4		– Avoid making decisions based on assumptions and belief systems that are no longer valid and relevant.
6. Recognize that a systems structure generates its behavior.	A systems thinker focuses on system structure and avoids blaming when things go wrong.	– Peace is an emerging property from the interaction of multiple systems.
		– Peace is entangled with other community characteristics.
		– Decisions to address issues in a system need to be made by first considering the structure and feedback that generate the problems rather than being reactive to these issues.
Related to Habit # 8		– Avoid applying Band-Aids to address apparent issues and behavior patterns immediately.
		– Systems create cultures, and cultures develop systems.
7. Identify the circular nature of complex cause-and-effect relationships	A systems thinker sees the interdependencies in a system and uncovers circular causal connections.	– Multiple feedback loops are at play between the structure and behavior of each sector of the nexus, across the sectors, and the systems with which the sectors interact.
		– See Tables 1.2 and 3.2
Related to Habits # 6 and 12		– Linear systems where one cause has a specific effect are rare since causes and effects across the nexus are often interchangeable.

(Continued)

Table 5.5 (*Continued*)

Habits and Description	Description	Peacebuilding and diplomacy examples
8. Recognize the impact of time delays when exploring cause-and-effect relationships. Related to Habit # 13	A systems thinker understands that cause and effect are often not closely related in time.	– Peacebuilding and diplomatic efforts take time. – There are delays between implementing an intervention and assessing whether it is working. – Addressing nexus-related issues takes time and patience. – It may take several attempts at solving something complex before a permanent solution is found. – Define the time horizon of interventions. – Delays between perception and response can create overshooting of the goal.
9. Consider short-term, long-term, and unintended consequences of actions.	A systems thinker looks ahead and anticipates the immediate results, actions, and effects down the road.	– Short- and long-term implications on peacebuilding, peacemaking, and peacekeeping efforts. – Interventions may have short-term consequences that can be evaluated relatively quickly. – Interventions may have long-term consequences that may limit their long-term performance. – Short-term gains may create long-term issues. – Systems may produce outcomes different from what is expected.
10. Consider an issue thoroughly and resist the urge to conclude quickly.	A systems thinker takes the necessary time to understand the dynamics of a system before taking action.	– Problems are never as simple as they seem to be at first glance. – Data must be collected and analyzed to identify and rank issues and risks. – Need to understand what drives events.

Habits and Description	Description	Peacebuilding and diplomacy examples
11. Pay attention to accumulations and their rates of change. Related to Habit #4	A systems thinker sees quantities of material or information built up or diminished over time.	– If no actions are taken, conflict issues may increase, create obstacles or barriers, or spread across sectors, leading to more significant problems and impactful consequences. – Accumulations and flows are essential.
12. Use an understanding of systems structure to identify possible leverage actions.	A systems thinker uses system understanding to determine what small actions will produce desirable results.	– Identify where to intervene first at the peace, sustainability, or climate security level with a more significant impact on change.
13. Check results and change actions if needed (successive approximations).	A systems thinker establishes benchmarks to help assess gradual improvement.	– Design as you go, with an adaptive and flexible approach and reflection before, in, and after action. – Learn from failure, change, and experimentation.
14. Make meaningful connections within and between systems. Related to Habit # 10	A systems thinker sees how concepts, facts, and ideas link, leading to new learning, discoveries, and innovations.	– The nexus sectors are entangled. – Interventions in one sector of the PSC nexus may have immediate or delayed effects on the other sectors and create cascading intended and unintended consequences. – Multiple cause-and-effect loops are at play in decision-making.

5.6   Systemic Questions

A systems-aware practice to address the dynamics of conflict-affected and conflict-sensitive community landscapes and challenges and to account for the linkages between engineering, peacebuilding, and diplomatic efforts comes with its share of challenges and open-ended questions about how to characterize and address systems and their causal direct and indirect linkages and pathways. Specifically, practical systemic questions include the following:

- What is the best way to capture the dynamics among engineering, peacebuilding, diplomatic efforts, and the systems on which they depend?
- How do these systems interact at various physical (where) and temporal (when) scales?
- What factors support or impede community landscape development, security, and resilience to adverse events and crises?
- What criteria and measures (technical and non-technical) must be selected to make appropriate decisions in engineering, peacebuilding, and diplomatic efforts
- What qualitative and quantitative data must be collected to best capture the two- or three-way interactions between landscape components?
- How should system data be collected and analyzed in an integrated manner?
- How should context and scale be accounted for in modeling the landscape and making technical, nontechnical, and policy strategic intervention decisions?
- How should objective (rational) and subjective (intuitive) decision-making be balanced when deciding on interventions in engineering, peacebuilding, and diplomatic efforts?
- How can interventions be implemented to ensure long-term benefits and resilience at a community level?
- What indicators confirm the integrated nature of the solutions across the landscape and the success of these solutions?

- How can synergies between engineering, peacebuilding, and diplomatic efforts be maximized and trade-offs reduced?
- What is the best way to identify the leverage points of intervention across the landscape?

Besides the questions mentioned above, it is also essential to know how the people involved in engineering, peacebuilding, and diplomatic efforts (the outsiders) and those who depend on the local level (the insiders) for their daily needs interact. In particular, it is crucial to determine who (i) takes part in modeling and deciding on engineering, peacebuilding, and diplomatic efforts; (ii) chooses the indicators and measures of success; and (iii) has the authority to select, implement, operate, and evaluate the proposed solutions and interventions. These four questions relate to the broader topic of participatory community development, as discussed in Chapter 6.

The questions above are not well answered by the development, security, and conflict studies literature and are open-ended. To understand the dynamics in this landscape, find solutions, and inform community-level policies, we need a system-based methodology, as Chapter 7 explains.

5.7 Concluding Remarks

The world in the 21st century is changing rapidly and involves various adaptive and complex systems. Traditional ways of thinking that focus on breaking down problems into smaller parts are insufficient to solve them. Systems thinking offers a different perspective, synthesis, and opportunity to examine how systems interact and how these interactions lead to conflict or peace. Systems thinking can also find leverage points, places of trade-offs, and synergies and explore the connection between mental models, structure, behavior, and events discussed in Chapter 4. Systems thinking requires training decision-makers who are used to conventional deterministic ways of thinking. The next chapter discusses how systems thinking is essential for system modeling. A systems-aware practice to deal with the dynamics of conflict-affected and conflict-sensitive community landscapes and challenges and to account for the linkages between engineering, peacebuilding, and diplomatic efforts does have its challenges and open-ended questions about describing and addressing systems and their direct and indirect causal linkages and pathways.

References

Achakulvisut, P., et al. (2022, March 28). It's time to move beyond "carbon tunnel vision" | SEI

Ackoff, R. L. (1981). The art and science of mess management. *Interfaces*, **11**(1), 20–26. https://www.jstor.org/stable/25060027

Adam, T. (2014). Advancing the application of systems thinking in health. *Health Research Policy and Systems*, **12**, 50. https://doi.org/10.1186/1478-4505-12-50

Adanke, M., Hailegiorgis, B., and Butterworth, J. (2019). A local systems analysis for rural water services delivery in South Ari and Mile, Ethiopia. A Local Systems Analysis for Rural Water Services Delivery in South Ari and Mile, Ethiopia (ircwash.org)

Amadei, B. (2019). *A Systems Approach to Modeling the Water–Energy–Land–Food Nexus* (Vols. I and II). New York: Momentum Press.

Amadei, B. (2023). *Navigating the Complexity Across the Peace–Sustainability–Climate Security Nexus*. Boca Raton: Routledge. ISBN 9781032563381

Arnold, R. D. and Wade, J. P. (2015). A definition of systems thinking: A systems approach. *Procedia Computer Science*, **44**, 669–678.

Barder, O. (2012, Sept. 7). Complexity, adaptation, and results. http://www.cgdev.org/blog/complexity-adaptation-and-results

BenDor, T. and Scheffran, J. (2019). *Agent-based Modeling of Environmental Conflict and Cooperation*. Boca Raton: CRC Press.

Benson, T. and Marlin, S. (2017). *The Habit-forming Guide to Becoming a Systems Thinker*. Pittsburg, PA: Systems Thinking Group.

Briggs, J. and Peat, F. D. (1999). *Seven Life Lessons of Chaos: Spiritual Wisdom from the Science of Change*. New York, NY: Harper Perennial.

Britt, H. (2013). Complexity-aware monitoring. Discussion Note: Version 2.0. Washington, DC: U. S. Agency for International Development.

Churchman, C. W. (1982). *Thought and Wisdom*. Seaside, CA: InterSystems Publications.

Coleman, P. T., Vallacher, R. R., Nowak, A., and Bui-Wrzosinska, L. (2007). Intractable conflict as an attractor. *American Behavioral Scientist*, **50**(11), 1454–1475. https://doi.org/10.1177/0002764207302463

Collaborative for Development Action (CDA) (2016). *Designing Strategic Initiatives to Impact Conflict Systems: Systems Approaches to Peacebuilding. A Resource Manual.* Cambridge, MA: CDA Collaborative Learning Projects. https://www.cdacollaborative.org/wp-content/uploads/2016/12/Designing-Strategic-Initiatives-to-Impact-Conflict-Systems-Systems-Approaches-to-Peacebuilding-Final.pdf#:~:text=This%20manual%20focuses%20on%20systems%20approaches%20to%20conflict%20analysis%20and

Collaborative for Development Action (CDA) (2023). Environment–fragility-peace nexus. Retrieved April 10, 2023, from Environment-Fragility-Peace Nexus - CDA Collaborative

Cutts, M. (1999). The humanitarian operation in Bosnia, 1992–1995: Dilemmas and negotiating humanitarian access. *New Issues in Refugee Research*, Working Paper No. 8. The humanitarian operation in Bosnia, 1992–95: the dilemmas of negotiating humanitarian access, Mark Cutts | UNHCR

de Savigny, D. and Adam, T. (eds.) (2009). *Systems thinking for health systems strengthening*. Alliance for Health Policy and Systems Research, World Health Organization.

Descartes, R. (2004). *A Discourse on Method: Meditations and Principles*, J. Veitch (Trans.). New York: Dutton.

EcoFuture (n.d.). The water-energy-food-ecosystem nexus thinking for a sustainable future. https://ecofuture-prima.eu/. Accessed September 3, 2024.

Elms, D. G. and Brown, C. B. (2012). Decisions in a complex context: A new formalism? *Proceedings of the International Forum on Engineering Decision Making*, 6th IFED, Lake Louise, Canada.

Gell-Mann, M. (1996). Let's call it pleptics. *Complexity*, **1**(5), 3. https://doi.org/10.1002/cplx.6130010502

Glouberman, S. and Zimmerman, B. (2002). Complicated and complex systems: What would successful reform of Medicare look like? Discussion paper No. 8. Commission of the Future of Healthcare in Canada, Ottawa. https://www.degruyter.com/document/doi/10.3138/9781442672833/html

Hammond, R. A. and Dube, L. (2012). A systems science perspective and transdisciplinary models for food and nutrition security. *Proceedings of the National Academy of Sciences of the United States of America,* **109**(31), 12356–12363. doi: 10.1073/pnas.0913003109

Harford, T. (2012). *Adapt: Why Success Always Starts with Failure?* (1st edition). New York: Picador.

Haskins, C. (2021). Systems engineering for Sustainable Development Goals. *Sustainability*, **13**(18), 10293. https://doi.org/10.3390/su131810293

Hayden, N. K. (2018). *Balancing belligerents or feeding the beats: Transforming conflict traps.* CISSIM Policy Brief, The University of Maryland Center for International and Security Studies. Hayden CISSM Policy Brief Feb2018_Rev8 (umd.edu)

Hoffman, J. and Henly-Shepard, S. on behalf of Sphere (2023). Nature-based Solutions for Climate Resilience in Humanitarian Action. https://spherestandards.org/resources/nbs-guide/

Holling, C. S. and Meffe, G. K. (1995). Command and control and the pathology of natural resource management. *Conservation Biology,* **10**(2), 328–337. https://doi.org/10.1046/J.1523-1739.1996.10020328.X

Hughes, B. B. and Hillebrand, E. E. (2006). *Exploring and Shaping International Futures.* Boulder, CO: Paradigm Publishers.

Huston, A. and Moriarty, P. (2018) Understanding the WASH system and its building blocks: Building strong WASH systems for the SDGs. https://www.ircwash.org/resources/understanding-wash-system-and-its-building-blocks

International Council on Systems Engineering. (INCOSE) (2021). Systems engineering: Vision 2035. Engineering solutions for a better world. INCOSE Systems Engineering Vision 2035

International Council for Science (ICSU) (2015). *Review of the Sustainable Development Goals: The Science Perspective.* Paris: International Council for Science.

Jones, D. (2015). Conflict Resolution: Wars Without End. *Nature,* **519**, 148–151. https://doi.org/10.1038/519148a

Kasman, M., Strombom, N., and Hammond, R. A. (2023). The application of systems science to peacebuilding. https://www.usip.org/sites/default/files/Application-of-Systems-Science-to-Peacebuilding.pdf

Kauffman, D. L. and Kauffman, M. D. (2021). An introduction to systems thinking (4th edition). https://www.amazon.com/Systems-1-Introduction-Thinking/dp/B09734VBMX

Konietzko, J. (2022, Feb. 8). Moving beyond carbon tunnel vision with a sustainability data strategy. https://www.cognizant.com/us/en/

insights/insights-blog/moving-beyond-carbon-tunnel-vision-with-a-sustainability-data-strategy-codex7121

Laszlo, E. (2001). *The Systems View of the World: A Holistic Vision for Our Time.* New York: Hampton Press.

Leadbeater, C. and Winhall, J. (2020). Building better systems: A green paper on system innovation. The Rockwool Foundation. Green Paper—The System Innovation Initiative.

Lent, J. (2017). *The Patterning Instinct.* New York: Prometheus Books.

Leroux-Martin, P. and O'Connor, V. (2017). *Systems thinking for peacebuilding and the rule of law: Supporting complex reforms in conflict-affected and conflict-sensitive environments.* U. S. Institute of Peace. pw133-systems-thinking-for-peacebuilding-and-rule-of-law-v2.pdf (usip.org)

Lorenz, E. N. (1972). Predictability: Does the flap of a butterfly's wings in Brazil set off a tornado in Texas? American Association for the Advancement of Science. http://gymportalen.dk/sites/lru.dk/files/lru/132_kap6_lorenz_artikel_the_butterfly_effect.pdf

Meadows, D. (2008). *Thinking in Systems.* Vermont: Chelsea Green Publishing.

Meadows, D. H., Randers, J., and Meadows, D. (2004). *Limits to Growth: The 30-Year Update.* Vermont: Chelsea Green Publishing

Miller, J. H. and Page, S. E. (2007). *Complex Adaptive Systems: An Introduction to Computational Models of Social Life.* Princeton, NJ: Princeton University Press.

Mitchell, M. (2009). *Complexity: A Guided Tour.* Oxford, England: Oxford University Press.

Mitleton-Kelly, E. (2003). Chapter 2: Ten principles of complexity and enabling infrastructures. In: *Complex Systems and Evolutionary Perspectives of Organizations: The Application of Complex Theory to Organizations.* London: Elsevier.

Meadows, D. (2008). *Thinking in Systems.* Vermont: Chelsea Green Publishing.

Monat, J. P., Gannon, T. F., and Amissah, M. (2022). The case for systems thinking in undergraduate engineering education. *International Journal of Engineering Pedagogy (iJEP),* **12**(3), 50–88. https://doi.org/10.3991/ijep.v12i3.2503

Morton, W. L., Eigenbrode, S. D., and Martin, T. A. (2015). Architectures of adaptive integration in large collaborative projects. *Ecology and Society,* **20**(4), 5. http://dx.doi.org/10.5751/ES-07788-200405

National Research Council. (NRC) (2014). *Convergence: Facilitating Transdisciplinary Integration of Life Sciences, Physical Sciences, Engineering, and Beyond.* Washington, DC: The National Academies Press. https://doi.org/10.17226/18722.

National Academy of Engineering/US Institute of Peace (NAE/USIP) (2013). Harnessing operational systems engineering to support peace-building. Washington, DC: The National Academies Press.

Nilsson, M., Griggs, D., and Visback, M. (2016). Map the interactions between Sustainable Development Goals. *Nature*, **534**(15), 320–322. https://doi.org/10.1038/534320a

Nilsson, M., Griggs, D., Visbeck, M., Ringler, C., and McCollum, D. (2017). A framework for understanding sustainable development goal interaction. In: *A guide to SDG interactions: from science to implementation.* Paris: International Council for Science. https://doi.org/10.24948/2017.01

Ortega y Gasset, J. (1994). *The Revolt of the Masses* (Reissue edition). New York: W. W. Norton.

Patton, M. Q. (2011). *Developmental Evaluation: Applying Complexity Concepts to Enhance Innovation and Use.* New York City: Guilford Press.

Pedercini, M., Arquitt, S., and Chan, D. (2020). Integrated simulation for the 2030 agenda. *System Dynamics Review*, **36**, 333–357. https://doi.org/10.1002/sdr.1665

Peters, D. H. (2014). The application of systems thinking in health: Why use systems thinking? *Health Research Policy and Systems*, **12**(51), 166–171. https://doi.org/10.1186/1478-4505-12-51

Randers, J., Rockström, J., Stoknes, P., Goluke, U., et al. (2019). Achieving the 17 Sustainable Development Goals within nine planetary boundaries. *Global Sustainability*, **2**, e24. https://doi.org/10.1017/sus.2019.22

Richmond, B. (1994). System dynamics/systems thinking: Let's just get on with it. *System Dynamics Review*, **10**(2–3). https://doi.org/10.1002/sdr.4260100204

Richmond, B. (1997). The 'thinking' in systems thinking: How can we make it easier to master? *The Systems Thinker*, **8**(2). The Systems Thinker – The "Thinking" in Systems Thinking: How Can We Make It Easier to Master? - The Systems Thinker

Richmond, B. (2004). *An Introduction to Systems Thinking. STELLA software.* Lebanon, NH: isee Systems.

Ricigliano, R. (2011). A systems approach to peacebuilding. In: *Paix Sans Frontieres: Building Peace Across Borders*. North Melbourne, Australia: Conciliation Resources. http://www.c-r.org/accord-article/systems-approach-peacebuilding

Ricigliano, R. (2012). *Making Peace Last: A Toolbox for Sustainable Peacebuilding*. Boulder, CO: Paradigm Publishers.

Rieken, B., et al. (2019, Jan. 04). How mindfulness can help engineers solve problems. *Harvard Business Review*.

Rittel, H. and Webber, M. (1973). Dilemmas in a general theory of planning. *Policy Science*, **4**, 155–169. https://doi.org/10.1007/BF01405730

Rotmans, J. and deVries, B. (eds.) (1997). Perspectives on global change: The TARGETS approach. Oxford, England: Cambridge University Press.

Scharlemann, J. P. W., et al. (2020). Towards understanding interactions between sustainable development goals: The role of environment-human linkages. *Sustainability Science*, **15**, 1573–1584.

Schirch, L. (2013). *Conflict Assessment and Peacebuilding Planning*. Boulder, CO: Kumarian Press.

Schmidt-Traub, G. (2015). *Indicators and a monitoring framework for the Sustainable Development Goals: Launching a revolution for the SDGs. A report.* Indicators and a Monitoring Framework for Sustainable Development Goals: Launching a data revolution for the SDGs (unsdsn.org)

Schön, D. A. (1983). *The Reflective Practitioner: How Professionals Think in Action*. New York City: Basic Books.

Seelos, C. (2020). Changing systems? Welcome to the slow movement. *Stanford Social Innovation Review*, Winter, 40–47.

Senge, P. (1994). *The Fifth Discipline: The Art & Practice of the Learning Organization*. New York City: Doubleday.

Shmueli, D. F., Kaufman, S., and Ozawa, C. (2008). Mining negotiation theory for planning insights. *Journal of Planning Education and Research*, **27**(3), 359–364. http://dx.doi.org/10.1177/0739456X07311074

Simon, H. A. (1972). Theories of bounded rationality. In: C. B. McGuire and R. Radner (eds.), *Decisions and Organization*. Amsterdam, The Netherlands: North-Holland Publishing, 161–176.

Snowden, D. and Boone, M. (2007). A leader's framework for decision making. *Harvard Business Review*, **85**(11), 68–76. PMID: 18159787.

Sterman, J. (2006). Learning from evidence in a complex world. *Am. J. Public Health*, **96**(3), 505–514. https://doi.org/10.2105/ajph.2005.066043

Strengthening Partnerships, Results, and Innovations in Nutrition Globally (SPRING) (2015). A systems thinking and action for nutrition. USAID/ Project. Systems Thinking and Action for Nutrition | SPRING (spring-nutrition.org)

Sweeney, L. B. (2001). *When a Butterfly Sneezes: A Guide for Helping Kids Explore Interconnections in Our World Through Favorite Stories.* Waltham, MA: Pegasus Communications.

The Omidyar Group (2017). *Systems Practice Workbook.* Systems Practice Workbook - Observatory of Public Sector Innovation (OECD-opsi.org)

Tress, G., Tress, B., and Fry, G. (2005). Clarifying integrative research concepts in landscape ecology. *Landscape Ecology*, **20**, 479–493. 10.1007/s10980-004-3290-4.

U.S. Agency for International Development (USAID) (2011a). *Systems Thinking in Conflict Assessment: Concepts and Application.* Washington, DC: USAID.

U.S. Agency for International Development (USAID) (2011b). *USAID Complexity Event.* Washington, DC: USAID.

United States Institute of Peace (USIP) (2013). *Harnessing Operational Systems Engineering to Support Peacebuilding.* Washington, DC: The National Academies Press.

Usenik, J. and Turnsek, T. (2016). Modeling conflict dynamics: System dynamics approach. In: T. Krambeger, V. Potocan, and V. M. Ipavek (eds.), *Sustainable Logistics and Strategic Transportation Planning.* New York: IGI Global, 273–294. DOI: 10.4018/978-1-5225-0001-8.ch013

Utrecht University (n.d.). Transdisciplinary field guide. https://www.uu.nl/en/research/transdisciplinary-field-guide/get-started/what-is-transdisciplinary-research

van Zanten, J. A. and van Tulder, R. (2021) Towards nexus-based governance: defining interactions between economic activities and Sustainable Development Goals (SDGs), *International Journal of Sustainable Development and World Ecology*, **28**(3), 210–226, DOI: 10.1080/13504509.2020.1768452

Vaughan, M. (2013). *The Thinking Effect.* Boston, MA: Nicholas Brealey.

Vennix, J. A. M. (1996). *Group Model Building: Facilitating Team Learning Using System Dynamics.* New York: John Wiley.

Von Bertalanffy, L. (1973). *General Systems Theory* (4th edition). New York: George Braziller.

Waldrop, M. M. (1992). *Complexity: The Emerging Science at the Edge of Order and Chaos.* New York City: Simon & Schuster.

Waters Center for Systems Thinking. (WCST) (n.d.). Home - Waters Center for Systems Thinking (waterscenterst.org)

Woodhill, J. and Millican, J. (2023) *Systems thinking and practice: A guide to concepts, principles, and tools for FCDO and partners.* K4D, Brighton: Institute of Development Studies, DOI: 10.19088/K4D.2023.002

Westley, F., Zimmerman, B., and Patton, M. Q. (2007). *Getting to Maybe: How the World is Changed.* Canada: Vintage Canada.

Zhang, Q., Prouty, C., Zimmerman, J. B., and Mihelcic, J. R. (2016). More than target 6.3: A systems approach to rethinking sustainable development goals in a resource-scarce world. *Engineering,* **2**(4), 481–489. https://doi.org/10.1016/J.ENG.2016.04.010

Chapter 6

Modeling the Connections between Peacebuilding-Engineering and Diplomacy

Various qualitative and quantitative tools can be used to model the systems involved in engineering, peacebuilding, diplomatic efforts, and their interactions. System-aware appraisal methods are needed to gather and analyze data and identify issues in conflict-affected and conflict-sensitive environments before modeling. Modeling is not random and requires following steps once context and scale-specific issues have been identified and expressed systematically. Understanding archetypes can help further identify intervention places in conflict-affected or conflict-sensitive community landscapes. Archetypes provide insights, power, and ways to understand the complex dynamics across the engineering–peacebuilding–diplomacy nexus and identify leverage points of intervention. A system dynamics model of this dynamic is presented.

Essentially, all models are wrong, but some are useful"… "The approximate nature of the model must always be borne in mind" (Box and Draper, 1987).

In their interpretation of reality, models must be useful, comprehensive, and sound enough to be able to "reason, explain, design, communicate, act, predict, and explore" (Page, 2018).

Engineering for Peace and Diplomacy
Bernard Amadei
Copyright © 2025 Jenny Stanford Publishing Pte. Ltd.
ISBN 978-981-5129-75-5 (Hardcover), 978-1-003-65168-0 (eBook)
www.jennystanford.com

6.1 Defining the Landscape

6.1.1 Community Landscape as a System

Identifying the context of the landscape in which engineering, peacebuilding, and diplomacy intersect is vital for understanding how these fields work together. They unfold in a specific *context* of human development and security (e.g., rural vs. urban, geographic, climatic, cultural, pre-conflict, ongoing conflict, or post-conflict) and over a particular geographic area (*spatial scale*) and time-frame (*temporal scale*) defined by *boundaries*. The context, scale, and boundaries of the landscape control how (i) it is appraised; (ii) issues are identified, formulated, and modeled; (iii) solutions are proposed and selected; and (iv) interventions are implemented. It is important to note that landscape dynamics are usually not the same at different spatial and temporal scales. There might be situations where engineering, peacebuilding, and diplomacy work well at one scale and are unbalanced at another or where one or several of the three sectors are weaker.

As a frame of reference, let us consider a conflict-affected or conflict-sensitive community landscape consisting of multiple interacting systems (human, infrastructure, economic, and natural), each with a hierarchy of embedded subsystems, as shown in Fig. 6.1. A community landscape can be viewed as a dynamic and complex system consisting of various systems (simple, complicated, and complex), some of which have adaptive features. The systems respond and adapt to changes within and outside the system, forming a whole structure. In the system holarchy, conflict and poor livelihood arise from multiple observable and unobservable forces, as the systems and subsystems share inputs and outputs. The landscape represents a space of possibilities or an environment (stable or in conflict) subject to (i) different enabling and constraining factors and barriers (e.g., political, ethical, security, economic, and socio-cultural), including those resulting from mutual interactions among their components, and (ii) restrictions created by the environment in which community development unfolds.

Within the landscape of Fig. 6.1, the community is an emerging and evolutionary whole where various policies, regulations, socioeconomic factors, etc., influence its dynamics. Once the community setting has been identified, (i) data and information about the community are gathered and analyzed; (ii) constraints are identified; (iii) issues are identified, and their what, why, who, where, when, and how are outlined systemically; and (iv) decisions are made about possible interventions to address these issues. This methodology is further discussed in Chapter 7.

The systems and subsystems embedded in the community landscape of Fig. 6.1 have several interactive functions and purposes that support engineering, peacebuilding, and diplomatic efforts, and vice versa. For instance, social systems may include institutions that provide governance, rule of law, and conflict resolution. Infrastructure systems provide services needed for livelihood (e.g., water, wastewater, energy, telecommunications, transportation, shelter, etc.), adaptation to, and mitigation of adverse events. Natural systems provide multiple eco-services, such as air and water purification, nutrient cycling, crop and vegetation pollination, and soil production. Crises may also affect these ecosystem services. The type of economic system dictates the production, distribution, and consumption of services. The reverse is also true, as engineering, peacebuilding, and diplomatic efforts affect the performance of the systems in Fig. 6.1.

In general, using the system's classification of Table 5.2, the community landscape of Fig. 6.1 has all the characteristics of a *complex* system in the sense that (i) uncertainty and ambiguity are the norms, (ii) complex interactions with circular and nonlinear causality take place among its components, (iii) unpredictability in one or several of its components is commonplace, (iv) unintended consequences unfold, and (v) it is not easy to reach an agreement on how to address problems in the landscape since they are interconnected. In complex systems such as the landscape, the unknowns are not always apparent and must be handled as they are discovered. Additionally, the complexity of the landscape can be characterized as organized and comprised of a multitude of interrelated factors that form a cohesive whole. It is worth noting that the behavior of a system within this landscape cannot be predicted with certainty (Weaver, 1948) because of its organized complexity. The latter directly contrasts with disorganized complexity, where the number of factors is vast, and statistical methods can predict the system's behavior.

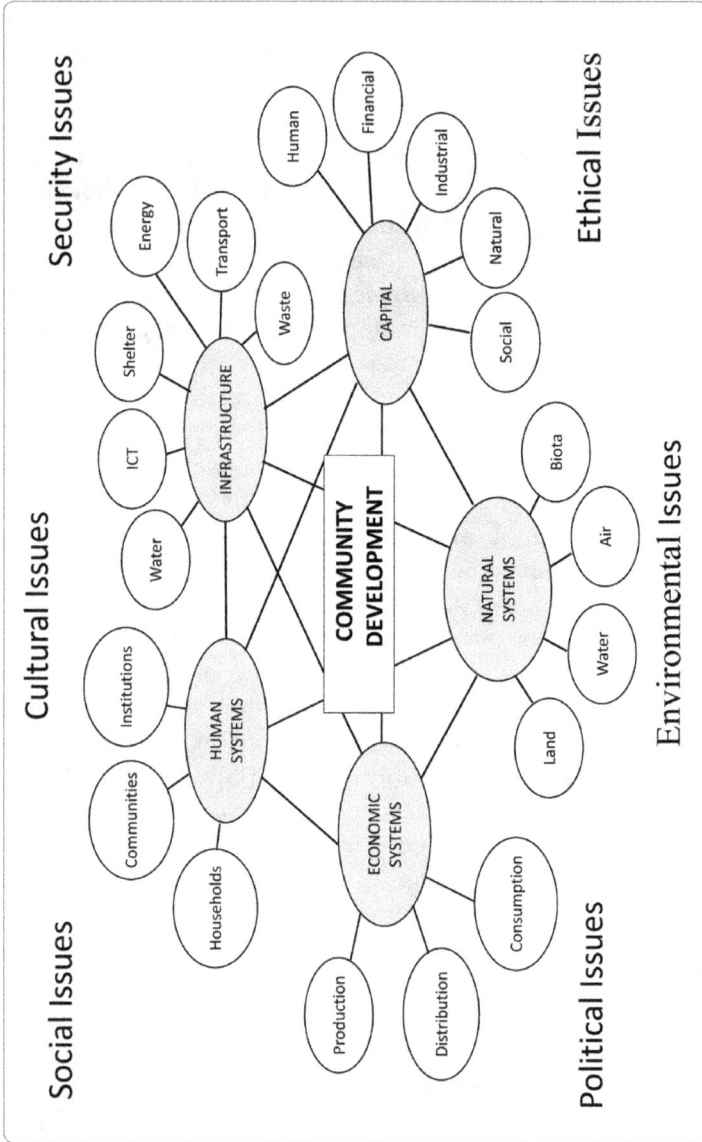

Figure 6.1 The complex community development and security landscape in which engineering, peacebuilding, and diplomatic efforts unfold.

Although the landscape in Fig. 6.1 is complex overall, some of its systems and subsystems may display varying degrees of complexity. For instance, infrastructure or engineering systems may not be complex but rather complicated, and even though unknowns are recognized, experts are still required to solve them. Sometimes, some systems are simple and demonstrate predictability and certainty. Complicated and simple systems are easier to control and less likely to have unintended repercussions than complex systems. Decision-makers must utilize various modes of intervention, depending on the complexity of the landscape being analyzed, as summarized in Table 5.2: categorizing for simple systems, analyzing for complicated systems, probing for complex systems, and responding rapidly to chaotic systems.

Community landscapes also have *adaptive* characteristics and components that adjust to internal and external changes. These elements are primarily present in social and ecological systems that (i) are in a state of dynamic equilibrium, (ii) are defined by organization and structure, and (iii) change over time through various processes at various speeds. By altering their structures, behaviors, and interactional rules through evolutionary and coevolutionary feedback mechanisms, social and ecological systems can have different levels of organization, reorganization, self-organization, self-correction, and adaptation (Mitleton-Kelly, 2003), making the landscape challenging to assess, model, and predict.

Other unique properties of complex systems that might be important to consider in understanding the community landscape in Fig. 6.1 include the following:

- Repetitive behavior patterns, feedback processes, and the role of attractors are common.
- Interdependency and synergy between landscape components create emerging behavior that cannot be predicted from the parts taken separately.
- Nonlinear relationships between the components linking causes and effects occur counterintuitively.
- Uncertainty in how community components behave and for which odds and likelihood cannot be accurately estimated due to organized complexity.

- Places of leverage in which a slight change in the landscape can potentially have a more significant impact across multiple systems and subsystems must be identified.
- Irreversible hysteresis behavior once the tipping points have been reached is typical.
- Dependence on and sensitivity to initial conditions is critical.

In conclusion, the community landscape in Fig. 6.1 can be seen as a living organism with a changing metabolism (Batty, 2010). The organism's components and interactions produce its overall behavior (or performance). According to this behavior, engineering, peacebuilding, and diplomatic interventions must be responsive and adaptable.

6.1.2   Systems-Aware Community Appraisal

The primary purpose of any appraisal is to learn as much as possible about a particular situation, in our case, the community landscape in Fig. 6.1, including its well-being and states of peace, sustainability, resilience, and governance. The community landscape where engineering, peacebuilding, and diplomacy work take place is too complex to fully comprehend, as there are always some unknown factors in systems that are complicated and vague. Nevertheless, whether one is interested in understanding and modeling the structure behind the patterns of one or several systems shown in Fig. 6.1 or the whole landscape, several analyses must be carried out. Although site-specific, they all require collecting data and information from a detailed appraisal of the systems and their interactions. The key questions in the assessment are: What are the critical issues in the community landscape? How much information needs to be collected? How are engineering, peacebuilding, and diplomatic efforts currently underway in this landscape?

By answering these questions and obtaining sufficient information about the landscape, the goal is to develop a community *baseline profile* and an associated *storyline* to identify the overall state of the community, its behavior patterns, and its structural components. There is also a need to review existing (secondary) information, identify thematic areas of concern, and map existing enabling and constraining factors, including critical factors, key stakeholders, what works well, what does not work well, and what could be improved.

Community baseline profiles can be developed using traditional ethnographic methods, such as *participatory action research* (PAR) (Spradley, 1979; Cornwall and Jewkes, 1995; Scheyvens and Storey, 2003; Chambers, 2005). These methods include direct observations, participatory mapping, transect walks, interviews, timelines, participatory diagramming, wealth and well-being rankings, and questionnaires. Data are collected on various community aspects, such as population, environment, infrastructure, resources, modes of livelihood, conflict, significant issues and concerns, and primary constraints. Analyses that complement the conflict analysis discussed in Section 3.5 include stakeholders (power and institutions), partnerships, social factors, capacity, risks, livelihoods/vulnerability/fragility, SWOT (C/L), and security analyses.

Table B.1 in Appendix B provides a non-exhaustive list of possible sources of information for community mapping. They can be supplemented with more core- and system-specific details of the community landscape. Core information concerns physical and human geography, adverse events, the effect of past events, exposure and vulnerability to hazards and conflicts, infrastructure, economic and financial, institutional, healthcare, climate and climate change factors, and human security. Specific details about each system and subsystem in Fig. 6.1 and their interaction, as shown in Fig. 6.2, are needed, as well as how engineering, peacebuilding, and diplomatic efforts unfold across these systems. A more detailed discussion on analyzing the different systems can be found in Chapter 5 of my last book (Amadei, 2023). Once collected, the information is analyzed and commonly regrouped into several categories, as summarized in Table B.2 in Appendix B. More details on these analyses can be found in Amadei (2014).

Because of the systemic nature of the community landscape in Fig. 6.1 and the interactions shown in Fig. 6.2, a *systems-aware appraisal* must be carried out using *systemic action research methods* (Burns, 2007). It begins with the different categories of information listed in Table B.1. Compared to traditional appraisal methods (e.g., PAR), data and information are collected, analyzed, presented, and interpreted in an integrated or systemic way, and not just categorized in a pigeon-hole approach. As discussed in Amadei (2014), this means (i) seeing and seeking connections in the data, including using triangulation methods; (ii) engaging multiple stakeholders in the different stages of the appraisal; (iii) being able to manage different conflicting opinions among different groups of stakeholders; (iv) using reflection-in-action and adaptive practices to assess (monitor and evaluate) the appraisal and the results of the appraisal; (v) formulating issues and problems in the landscape and its components in a non-compartmentalized (i.e., integrated) manner; and (vi) selecting appropriate dynamic hypotheses and models about the what, who, where, when, and how of the issues structures and dynamics.

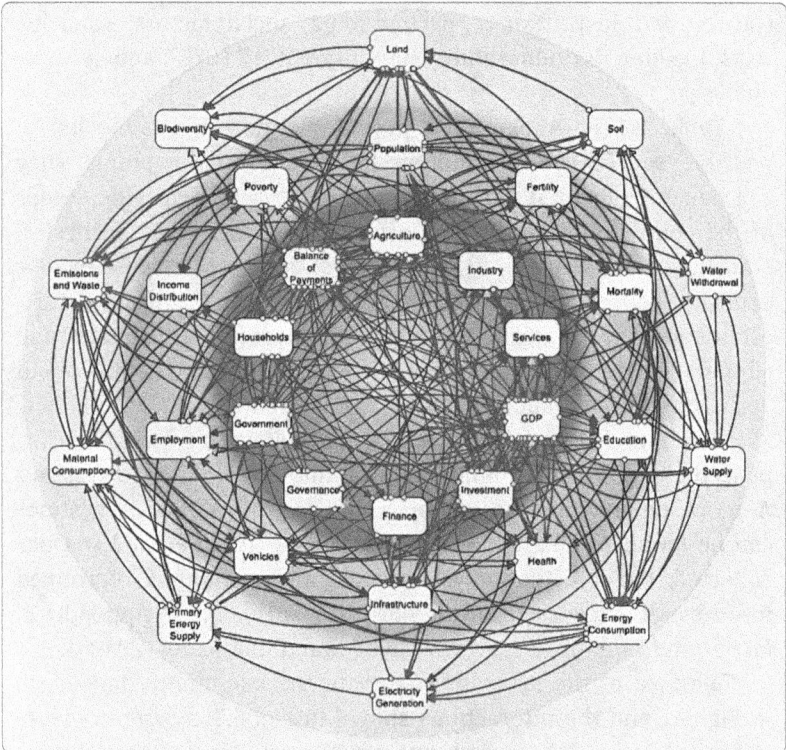

Figure 6.2 Interactions among environmental (outer ring), social (medium ring), and economic (inner ring) system variables used in the iSDG framework. How do engineering, peacebuilding, and diplomatic efforts unfold across these systems? *Source*: Pedercini et al. (2020). Used with permission from Wiley and Sons.

Conducting a systems-aware appraisal of a community landscape requires decision-makers to have acquired unique systems practice skills to recognize and address the complexity of community development. In addition to acquiring the habits of systems thinkers discussed in the previous chapter, decision-makers also need to adopt a complexity-mindful (or aware) step-by-step approach to community development that combines objective tools when dealing with complicated systems and subjective or intuitive tools in more complex and uncertain situations. In conducting such analyses, decision-makers are expected to be more than just traditional value-neutral individuals capable of producing linear blueprints and predictable solutions delivered on time and within the budget for well-defined problems. As systems thinkers, decision-makers need to be creative, innovative, and interactive to account for uncertainty, complexity, ill-defined issues, and constraints in a cultural context with which they are likely unfamiliar.

Another challenge in conducting community landscape analyses with a systems perspective is extracting from the collected data and information what is necessary to comprehend the different systems in Fig. 6.1, the interactions in Fig. 6.2, and how the engineering, peacebuilding, and diplomatic efforts interact in that landscape. It is about selecting systems characteristics, appropriate variables, and processes essential to understanding community development issues under normal and adverse conditions without falling into paralysis in analysis. Unfortunately, there are no objective ways to decide when enough data and information have been collected to provide a *good enough* understanding of the landscape. Using triangulation methods and analyzing the consistency between different data sources may help.

Finally, a systems-aware participatory community landscape appraisal also implies that the appraisal team is aware of and willing to accept and deal with feedback mechanisms between different appraisal components. For example, as the appraisal proceeds, reflective and adaptive practices may require the appraisal team to supplement its expertise with the opinion of other individuals in specific areas of study and critical stakeholders. Likewise, more information may be needed, and data collected as a gap is noticed in a particular domain during data analysis. Finally, another possible feedback mechanism could occur if there is a need to change how the team operates due to cultural or other issues that emerge as the appraisal unfolds.

6.1.3   From Appraisal to Dynamic Hypotheses

6.1.3.1   Formulating the issues

At the end of the systems-aware community appraisal, there should be enough information to start formulating preliminary conceptual (or structural) mental models to explain the current state of the conflict-affected or conflict-sensitive community landscape and how engineering, peacebuilding, and diplomatic efforts contribute to that state. More specifically, the systems-aware appraisal is expected to identify and formulate as comprehensively and integrated as possible:

- The most significant issues, concerns, and needs faced by the community
- The perceived cause-effect relationship for each issue, including possible feedback mechanisms.
- The consequences, impacts, drivers, probabilities, and expected losses of each issue.
- The issues' importance to different groups, what works (or has worked) well, what does not work, what could be improved, what changes are envisioned by whom and for whom, and the current roadblocks to improvement.
- The order and significance of the issues related to gender, age, work status, caste, beliefs, marital status, etc.
- Possible linkages between issues and possible common causes and effects.
- The role played by conflict, unsustainable behavior, and adverse events on the issues.
- The contribution of engineering, peacebuilding, diplomacy, and capacity building in addressing the issues.

Issues are understood here as *dynamic gaps* between where the community stands today and its desired development and security plans (e.g., livelihood, resilience, peace, rule of law, well-being, security, stable governance, etc.). The challenge is to develop engineering, peacebuilding, and diplomatic interventions to bridge the overall gaps over time with new mental models that create structures and promote better behavior patterns for the community. It should be noted that the rate of gap reduction depends on the current community development level and security baseline. The higher that level is compared to the desired one, the faster the change is likely to occur. In all cases, bridging the development and security gaps takes time and often requires accepting incremental steps of adaptation and transformation and considering multiple feedback processes.

A system's approach to community development and security requires formulating dynamic hypotheses to explain how the identified issues unfold and interact (i.e., possible explanations that relate structures to behaviors). This approach requires addressing each issue's what, why, who, where, when, and how. If the *what* of a single issue is the starting point, it must be described quantitatively, qualitatively, or semi-quantitatively. What internal and external factors in the landscape contribute to and affect this issue? The *why* comes next because each issue must have one or multiple reasons. For instance, there may be insufficient resources available compared to some minimum standards, or the government or community members may expect a desired level that has been unmet. Another example is insufficient community capacity (social, economic/financial, human resources, technical, institutional, and environmental) to address the issue.

Following the why of an issue comes *who* deals with who is being, has been, or could be affected by the issue or who could contribute to its solutions. Then comes the *where* and *when,* which define the physical and time scales over which the issue is at play or has manifested itself before: is there a recurring pattern? Finally comes *how* the issue plays or has played before across the community landscape, including its causes and effects. It is also about how the issue could manifest itself if not addressed and how it could interact with other issues.

For example, let us consider the case of a specific geographical area where resource security is a source of conflict between settled farmers and pastoral nomad groups (what, who, where). Available resources, especially local water and food, are scarce during the dry season (when) and create conflict. There is no resource management plan in place. The settled farmers object to the passage of nomadic groups that demand the movement of people and herds as a guaranteed right. The area's preliminary capacity analysis shows that the conflict results from a lack of agreement between the two groups, unreasonable expectations, the clash between tradition and modernity, and the absence of government enforcement and regulatory policies (why).

In summary, poor resource management, inequity, and marginalization have created tension and resentment between farmers and herders, violence, lack of economic development, and insecure livelihoods (how). Some of these dynamics can be found in the Sahel region of Africa (Tesfaye, 2022; Issifu et al., 2022; CDA, 2023), where conflict has arisen due to the combined constraining effect of climate change on climate-sensitive rain-fed agriculture-based livelihood, political instability, insurgency, ethnic tension, and state fragility. Rapid population growth creates a demand for cultivated land, restricting the movement of nomadic herding. Land tenure is also controlled by customary land practices that affect this movement.

If multiple issues are at play and show connectivity, the *what* requires describing what the issues are and what makes them interconnected and dependent on each other? Then comes *why* these issues are essential and related and why some may be more critical than others and cannot be addressed. Then, the *who* defines the multiple groups of stakeholders who may be affected by one or several issues and could influence each other. The *where* and *when* define the physical and temporal extent of the issues, some being more active and critical at one physical and time scale than others. Finally, the *how* of the multiple issues must demonstrate how they are presently interconnected and have been interconnected in the past and whether they may have mutual causes and consequences.

A more complex version of the above example includes the combined dynamics of climate change, livelihood, drought, conflict, migration, and land-use change. The area's water and food security issues are compounded by the encroachment of migrating herders on farmers' land, destroying crops. The farmers and herders also get political support from two opposite government factions. Multiple drought episodes due to climate change have forced farmers to abandon their lands and move to large cities to find living wages. This migration has put pressure on people living in the city. The lack of work has created unrest and repression from the government. The growing city insecurity has forced people to leave and become refugees, thereby affecting other communities. In summary, multiple consequences arise from the overall dynamics of climate change, livelihood, drought, conflict, migration, and land-use change.

6.1.3.2 Ranking the issues

Figure 6.1 represents a complex community development landscape with many possible issues. How can we choose the most important ones? Some issues might relate to specific community necessities (water, energy, food, health, security, etc.). Others might affect broader community needs, such as livelihood, sustainability, conflict, resilience, etc. After identifying and explaining these issues and their dynamic hypotheses, the next step is for all community stakeholders to rank them by importance. These fundamental questions can help prioritize them (Seelos, 2020):

- Are the issues legitimate?
- Are the issues identified the most critical ones?
- Are the identified issues capturing the concerns of multiple groups of stakeholders?
- Are the identified issues addressing the *current needs* of the community (i.e., inadequate services, key grievances, and resiliencies)?

Another way to rank issues is to use *multi-criteria or multi-attribute analysis* tools from the field of decision science (Keeney and Raiffa, 1993; Decision Sciences Institute, 2017). One such tool is *Multi-Criteria Decision Analysis* (MCDA). It is formulated to rank issues based on several critical criteria or objectives that are deemed necessary in the decision-making process. They may include effectiveness, environmental sustainability, community participation, impact on community health, and impact on the economy and peace. The Department for Communities and Local Government (DCLG, 2009) in the United Kingdom has published an excellent review of different multicriteria analysis techniques. A range of applications of the MCDA method in community development can be found in Amadei (2014, 2019).

By ranking issues based on their importance and effect, the MCDA method represents a valuable tool for filtering prospective alternative interventions and retaining those that meet critical criteria (Huang et al., 2011; Figueira, 2005). However, its main limitation resides in its subjective nature, as the weights and scores are only intelligent guesses that decision-makers make based on their intuition and experience (Nathan and Reddy, 2011). They must be qualified individuals who possess the necessary expertise, are systems thinkers, and are aware of their personal biases.

In summary, a thorough outcome of the community appraisal is a detailed and dynamic reference model of the conflict-affected or conflict-sensitive community landscape by formulating a storyline and proposing possible explanations about the causes and consequences of identified issues and their underlying structure. Once formulated, the issues can be modeled using the system modeling tools discussed below.

6.2 Modeling

6.2.1 About Models

Conflict-affected or conflict-sensitive community landscapes, such as the one in Fig. 6.1, have unique characteristics that make them difficult to model.

- They involve multiple interconnected and interdependent systems and nonlinearities.
- They unfold in constrained (context- and scale-specific) environments.
- They are dynamic and adaptive with feedback.
- They involve multiple actors and stakeholders.

- They cut across the Development, Diplomacy, and Defense (3Ds) sectors.
- They require decision-makers to handle multiple tradeoffs and synergies.
- They are based on some theory of change.
- They require consideration of different perspective levels, from decision-making to field operation.
- They involve multiple steps: strategy formulation, policy development, program planning, design, implementation, monitoring, and evaluation.

Before jumping head-on into modeling the role of engineering, peacebuilding, and diplomacy in conflict-affected and conflict-sensitive landscapes, several observations must be made regarding modeling. This section is a summarized version of Chapter 6 of Amadei's (2023) book.

First, as shown in Fig. 6.3, models are simplified simulations, interpretations, and explanations of reality (Franck, 2002; Sterman, 2002) and not reality itself, especially when trying to understand the interaction of multiple systems, such as those involved in the engineering–peacebuilding–diplomacy nexus. Once the purpose of the model is selected, its usefulness and soundness are dictated by how well it simulates reality and observed behavior patterns (Forrester, 1971; Sterman, 2000). The simulations have the advantage of "providing a deep level of insight and understanding and allowing the consideration of many different scenarios which would be impossible to test in reality" (Lemos, 2018).

Second, models "are never complete or exact and are often systematically flawed" (Senge, 2006). They can only be interpreted as satisfactory (i.e., satisficing; Simon, 1972) but also as clumsy (Rittel and Webber, 1973) interpretations of reality. Models are created by individuals who make assumptions based on their mental filters and interpretation of their world, as discussed in the iceberg analogy in Fig. 4.2. In short, models are tools to understand reality and "can be no better than the modelers" (Hannon and Ruth, 2001).

Third, models cannot be validated and are never value-free (Sterman, 2000; Ford, 2010). As noted by Barlas (1996), the validity of a model can be described by its usefulness for some purposes, keeping in mind that "the usefulness of the purpose itself" needs to be formulated. Because system behavior patterns are dictated by structural patterns (Fig. 4.2), validating a model is also about its usefulness to some structures and their environments. In human development and security, the purpose would be to address any actual situation that a community is facing or expects to face when dealing with (i) the management of resources and services, (ii) the consistent functioning of infrastructure over one or several years, (iii) conflict, and (iv) the effect of adverse events. The usefulness of this purpose is evident regarding the community's survival, resilience to crises, well-being, and economic development on a specific scale and over time. In general, confidence in the usefulness of models increases with time following good modeling practices.

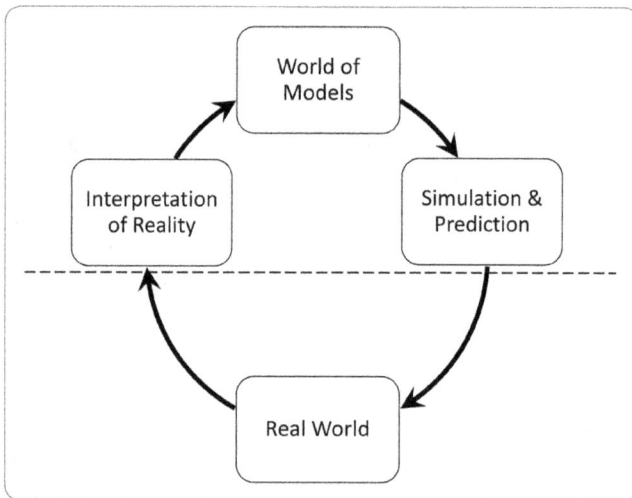

Figure 6.3 From the real world to the world of models.

Fourth, as noted by Sterman (2000), there is no universally applicable recipe for successful modeling, nor is there any procedure that can be followed to guarantee the creation of a useful model. However, system modeling is not random, and following a road map is highly recommended. For example, Sterman (2000) considers five interactive activities in developing a dynamic model:

1. *Problem articulation* describes (i) the existing observed patterns of behavior over time; (ii) the nature, scale, and boundaries (physical and temporal) of the problem being addressed and its key variables; (iii) how the problem has manifested itself and was addressed in the past; and (iv) if left unresolved, how the problem would manifest itself in the future. An example would be articulating human development and security dynamics in conflict-affected and conflict-sensitive areas.

2. *Dynamic hypothesis formulation* involves mapping the current causes and consequences of the observed behavior and identifying the endogenous issues and feedback mechanisms deemed responsible for that behavior. Conflict and risk analysis helps formulate what, why, who, where, when, and how of conflict.

3. *Simulation model formulation* comprises building the model, selecting its structure and possible archetypes, choosing parameters that enter its structure, deciding on the initial conditions, selecting data, and testing the model for consistency and other attributes.

4. *Model testing* is performed by (i) comparing its predictive behavior with the actual behavior, (ii) subjecting the model to unusual and extreme conditions (i.e., testing its robustness), and (iii) observing how the predictive behavior changes by varying the system variables (sensitivity analysis). An example would be how well the model can reproduce past and current conflict-affected and conflict-sensitive area dynamics.

5. *Policy design and evaluation* are conducted by exploring different intervention scenarios or strategies and their consequences, proposing concrete recommendations to address problems, and foreseeing possible side effects associated with these recommendations.

This modeling roadmap involves many feedback mechanisms among the five activities. For example, model testing may require changing the dynamic hypothesis, simulation, or new data collection.

Following the roadmap offers many benefits, including valuable learning experiences for everyone involved, such as individual modelers and group members who engage in group model building. As modelers progress through the above steps, their confidence in the model's usefulness increases. It begins with a clear understanding of the five model-building activities mentioned above. Furthermore, confidence increases over time when model performance is compared to the real world (Sterman, 2000). This feedback can be seen as an ongoing "reality check" to prevent the model from going astray.

As we will see in Chapter 7, the five activities mentioned above can be integrated into a broader systems-based methodology that decision-makers can follow to address community development and the engineering–peacebuilding–diplomacy nexus.

6.2.2 Modeling Guidelines

Navigating the road map discussed above when modeling human development and security issues, and how engineering, peacebuilding, and diplomacy unfold in the landscape of interest, requires asking questions and following guidelines; this is not a random process.

Guideline 1 refers to the essential questions that individuals and teams engaged in group model-building must consider before creating any dynamic model for community development (see Table 6.1).

Guideline 2 establishes the context of the model and defines its physical and temporal boundaries, as discussed in Section 6.1. These boundaries must be clearly defined regarding their horizontal and vertical extents. In the case of community development and security projects, the horizontal characteristic refers to the cross-disciplinary nature of the problems faced by the community, such as health, water, sanitation, energy, shelter, jobs, conflict, and climate change. The vertical component is related to the depth and detail required to address each problem in each developmental discipline. Ultimately, the timeframe for the simulation must be selected (e.g., number of years), and the system's initial conditions must be determined through community appraisal.

Table 6.1 Questions may arise when formulating dynamic models

Why	• Why is a dynamic model constructed?
What	• What problems, behavior, and structural patterns are modeled over what timeframe and spatial scale? • What boundaries (physical and temporal) should be selected? • What relationships exist between the systems and subsystems and the environment outside the systems? • What methods other than (or complementary to) dynamic modeling can be used to model the problem? • What changes in the system are desirable or not? • What would happen if the problem were or were not addressed? • What solutions have been attempted to address the problem in the past, and what were their outcomes? • What are the components of the problem being addressed, and what are their connections? • What range of responses can be expected from the model? • What types of uncertainty and trends need to be included in the model?
How	• How will the model be complementary to the traditional steps of community development? • How have the components of the model interacted in the past? • How will community members be trained and involved in building, reviewing, and updating the model? • How will the model recommendations be presented to the community members? • How will decisions in model building, evaluation, and change be reached and disagreement/conflict mediated?
Who	• Who is participating in developing the model (stakeholders)? • Who is involved in group model building? • Who will coordinate group model building? • Who will be involved in deciding on desirable system changes and their implementation?
When	• When should the model be integrated into the management of development interventions? • When should the model be started, evaluated, modified, and updated?
Where	• Where should model development and community interaction occur (office, community)?

Selecting the landscape boundary in Fig. 6.1 is more subjective than objective, as different community systems may have different boundaries that do not necessarily coincide (e.g., geographical, administrative, and political boundaries) and might be time-specific (e.g., dry and wet season boundaries). Model boundaries determine what is included and excluded from the model and identify what is relevant and irrelevant, important and unimportant, and beneficial or disadvantageous. In community development, spatial boundaries, such as communities, villages, households, or watersheds, may be geographical, whereas temporal boundaries may include seasonal, monthly, or yearly activities. If the boundaries cannot be easily identified, artificial boundaries may be employed to simplify the complexity. After establishing the boundaries, the next step is determining which endogenous components originating from within the system should be included in the model and which exogenous components arising outside the system can be set aside. Exogenous components can be added later if necessary or if required. The external environment outside the border cannot be ignored, as it may affect the landscape dynamics. For instance, external crises and natural disasters can affect landscape dynamics.

Guideline 3 ensures that the model's objectives are well-defined and articulated. This step involves understanding how engineering, peacebuilding, and diplomacy interact with the various components of the landscape, as well as the behavioral patterns and archetypes present. Once this understanding is established, the model structure and the selection of critical variables can be determined. The goals of the model could include exploring the different types of dual causality between peace, livelihood, infrastructure, and climate change at the community level, predicting how a community might respond to future adverse events, examining the functioning of critical community infrastructure or institutions, and identifying interventions to reduce the gap between desired and current levels of community development and security. It is important to note that not all issues can be addressed, and some degree of aggregation may be required.

Guideline 4 focuses on determining whether modeling should be qualitative or quantitative. Qualitative modeling is likely to be the dominant approach when dealing with social systems for which only subjective or soft data are available. In such cases, proxies or constructs can relate the qualitative variables to other quantitative data sources. Semi-quantitative data can also be used as an alternative. In certain instances, quantitative information is also accessible.

Qualitative modeling offers value in various ways, such as providing a learning environment, enhancing the understanding of communities, and facilitating informed project management decisions. Despite these advantages, quantitative modeling should not be overlooked when data are available for certain system parts, as it can contribute to a more comprehensive understanding of the problem. In community development, quantitative data collected during community appraisals can be incorporated into quantitative models to address specific real-world issues faced by the community, such as health, demographics, workforce, conflict, employment, infrastructure, resource management, and the community's capacity to provide services.

6.3   Systems Modeling Tools

According to Checkland and Poulter (2006), system modeling tools can be broadly classified into soft and hard tools. Some of them are listed in Table 6.2. The tools differ in the way the systems are considered. A *soft systems approach* to problem-solving entails examining the systemic process of inquiry and problem situations rather than focusing on the structure of the problem itself. Seelos (2020) noted that a soft system approach helps identify system drivers and potential paths forward. It is appropriate for complex social settings in which subjective decision-making dominates. However, it stops short of modeling how systems interact.

The *hard systems approach* considers the world to be systemic. Systems are treated as entities with clearly defined boundaries that can be objectively assessed and improved using available knowledge and tools (Seelos, 2020). The models capture the systemic and structural aspects of the analyzed problems and explore how the system structure can explain the observed behavior. According to Seelos (2020), one drawback of the hard systems approach is that initiatives based on their principles are highly susceptible to minor deviations from their underlying assumptions. The hard systems approach generally works well for technical systems in which tangible factors can be included. A wide variety of systems tools regarding health are available in the literature, a good summary of which can be found in Peters (2014).

Table 6.2 Characteristics, pros, and cons of some soft and hard modeling tools

Soft systems modeling tools	Concept maps and mind maps	• Graphical tools are used to represent knowledge and the relationships between concepts visually. • Represent how different parts of a system relate to each other as cause or effect around a unique idea or concept. • *Pros*: Visual representation, simplicity, clarity, and promotion of creativity. • *Cons*: Complexity, subjectivity. • *Software*: Miro, Canva, Vista, and other templates on the web.
	Graphical logic trees	• A visual representation of hierarchical structures makes understanding and navigating complex relationships between different elements in a system or dataset easier. • A *problem tree* consists of a trunk (problem), roots (causes), and branches (consequences). • A *solution tree* has positive roots and optimistic outcomes that overcome the negative causes and effects of the problem tree. • *Pros*: Visualization, flexibility, clarity, simplicity. • *Cons*: Static and showing links in one direction and a hierarchical manner. Do not capture closed-loop interactions. • *Software*: Many templates on the web.
	Cross-impact analysis	• A method for examining the interdependencies and interactions (influence and dependence) between variables within a system. • *Pros*: provides insights into how changes in one part of the system may propagate through the system as a whole. • *Cons*: Relies on expert judgment, qualitative or semi-quantitative. • See Tables 1.2 and 3.2. • *Software*: Micmac, Mactor. http://en.laprospective.fr/methods-of-prospective/softwares---cloud-version.html

Hard systems modeling tools	Network analysis	• A methodology for studying complex systems represented as networks of interconnected nodes and edges or the intra-connectivity of each system's nested subsystems.
		• *Pros*: Provides insights into the structure of complex systems, revealing patterns of connectivity, clustering, and centrality, visualization, predictive modeling. Various analyses can be carried out.
		• *Cons*: Overwhelming when lots of data are needed, not dynamic, assumptions and simplifications are required.
		• *Software*: UCINET. http://www.analytictech.com/archive/ucinet.htm
		• See also review at: https://en.wikipedia.org/wiki/Social_network_analysis_software.
	System dynamics	• A modeling and simulation approach that focuses on understanding complex systems' feedback processes and dynamic behavior over time.
		• Considers systems that are away from equilibrium.
		• Helpful in the strategic level of decision-making.
		• *Pro*: Holistic approach, dynamic simulations, communication tool, iterative approach.
		• *Cons*: Validation, complexity, data requirements, computationally intensive, expertise needed. High abstraction level.
		• *Software*: Stella Architect, Vensim, AnyLogic. See also review at https://en.wikipedia.org/wiki/Comparison_of_system_dynamics_software.
	Agent-based modeling	• A simulation technique where autonomous agents, each with their own set of characteristics and behaviors, interact with each other and their environment.
		• Helpful in studying complex systems where emergent phenomena arise from the interactions of individual components.
		• Appropriate at the operational level of decision-making.
		• *Pros*: granularity, flexibility, emergent properties, realism, experimentation
		• *Cons*: Complexity data requirement, computational needs, interpretability, validation, and calibration
		• *Software*: AnyLogic, NetLogo. See also review at https://en.wikipedia.org/wiki/Comparison_of_agent-based_modeling_software.

Additional information on the soft and hard tools listed in Table 6.2 can be found in the literature (e.g., Delp et al., 1977). The approach recommended in this book is to use both sets of tools, as it is believed that when combined, they provide a better understanding of the systems involved in human development and security, peacebuilding, and diplomatic efforts. For example, soft modeling tools help map the system composition, operation, and logic, facilitating a more complex modeling process. This approach is integrated into the methodology proposed in Chapter 7.

The remainder of this chapter explores how system dynamics can be used to model conflict-affected and conflict-sensitive community landscapes. In general, this method requires following the modeling guidelines mentioned above.

6.4   System Dynamics

6.4.1   Description

The System Dynamics (SD) approach is a relatively modern field in Systems Science. It was founded by Dr. Jay Forrester of the Massachusetts Institute of Technology in the 1950s and the 1960s. SD has been used to tackle intricate problems in various disciplines, such as engineering, business, economics, health, planning, and management. A straightforward explanation of system dynamics is that it "involves how things change over time, which encompasses most of what people typically find important" (Forrester, 1997). System dynamics explores systems that are not in equilibrium.

The unique characteristics of the SD method that warrant its use in modeling the dynamics of complex systems involved in conflict-affected and conflict-sensitive environments include the ability to (i) handle cross-sectoral impacts, (ii) capture both qualitatively and quantitatively how systems continuously change over time owing to possible changes in and relationships among components and changes in the overall direction of systems, (iii) account for system nonlinearities, feedback mechanisms, and delays, and (iv) demonstrate that as the structure of a system changes, so does its behavior and vice versa. However, a limitation of SD is that it cannot capture the details of the individual components that form the system. Emphasis is placed on a system's structure or aggregated nature rather than on determining the details of all its components.

The selection of a model boundary in SD modeling is another characteristic. Once selected, the model includes the necessary components to explain the system's dynamic behavior, such as endogenous rules (Sterman, 2000). However, external influences are not explicitly considered. Ahmad and Simonovic (2004) highlighted another limitation of system dynamics: it can only handle time-varying systems and processes. When considering processes that vary in time and space, combining system dynamics with other methods emphasizing spatial variations, such as Geographic Information Systems (Ahmad and Simonovic, 2004), is necessary.

6.4.2 Basic SD Components

One of the unique characteristics of SD modeling is that it captures the feedback mechanisms inherent in complex systems using two types of cause-and-effect circular causation: reinforcing and balancing feedback loops (Richardson, 1999). The *Reinforcing* (R) feedback loops model self-reinforcing feedback processes and virtuous and vicious cycles, leading to amplification. The *Balancing* (B) loops prevent them from growing or declining forever. They create self-correcting processes that lead to stability and equilibrium and reach a goal or objective. In addition to these two essential behavior models, a delay may be added to model the effect of time in linking causes and effects or any adjustment processes. Table 6.3 gives examples of storylines with reinforcing and balancing loops involving the engineering, peacebuilding, and diplomacy sectors and their interaction.

In the decision-making process across the engineering–peacebuilding–diplomacy nexus, delays can be associated with the time it takes different groups of stakeholders to (i) make decisions (information delays), (ii) implement processes (material delays), or (iii) unfold various processes (e.g., supply chains, services, and peacebuilding).

Table 6.3 Examples of reinforcing and balancing loops involving engineering, peacebuilding, and diplomacy in conflict-affected and conflict-sensitive landscapes (OpenAI, 2024)

Reinforcing loops	**Engineering Initiatives**: A region affected by conflict receives funding and support for engineering projects such as building schools, hospitals, and infrastructure to improve access to essential services.
	Positive Impact on Peacebuilding: Engineering initiatives play a significant role in enhancing the standard of living for the local community, thereby establishing a favorable atmosphere for fostering peacebuilding endeavors. These projects can decrease dissatisfaction and friction by addressing fundamental requirements and extending economic prospects, ultimately fostering a more serene society.
	Enhanced Diplomatic Opportunities: Diplomacy becomes more successful as peacebuilding and stabilization efforts advance. Improved stability and trust between conflicting parties enable more fruitful conversations and negotiations, which can result in agreements or peace treaties.
	Feedback Loop: As diplomacy contributes to securing peace agreements and stability commitments, the international community often displays a greater inclination to invest more in engineering projects, such as infrastructure development, technology transfer programs, and capacity-building initiatives to foster peace and development within the region.
Balancing loops	**Engineering's Impact on Peacebuilding**: As engineering projects progress and infrastructure is restored, there may be a temporary improvement in the quality of life for the local population. However, if these projects primarily benefit particular groups or exacerbate existing inequalities, they could inadvertently fuel grievances and tensions, undermining peacebuilding efforts.
	Peacebuilding's Influence on Engineering: Peacebuilding efforts may encounter challenges if underlying grievances and tensions persist or escalate despite diplomatic interventions. Suppose peacebuilding initiatives fail to address the root causes of the conflict effectively. In that case, it may hinder the implementation of engineering projects, as instability and insecurity could pose significant risks to infrastructure development and reconstruction efforts.

Diplomatic Impact on Peacebuilding and Engineering: Diplomacy is vital to resolving conflicts and promoting peace. Nevertheless, if the root causes of the conflict are not addressed or trust between parties is lacking, diplomatic efforts may not be effective in advancing peacebuilding or engineering projects. Furthermore, setbacks in diplomatic negotiations or the inability to secure long-lasting peace agreements can have negative consequences for peacebuilding and engineering initiatives.

Feedback Loop: The interactions between engineering, peacebuilding, and diplomacy dynamics create a feedback loop where progress or setbacks in one domain influence the others. If engineering projects exacerbate existing tensions or peacebuilding efforts fail to address underlying grievances, they can undermine diplomatic initiatives to resolve the conflict. Similarly, diplomatic failures or delays can impede progress in peacebuilding and engineering, perpetuating a cycle of instability and conflict.

Various combinations of reinforcing and balancing loops and delays can be utilized to model the behavioral patterns of intricate systems and unique repetitive and generic patterns, referred to as archetypes, as discussed below. These conceptual models can sometimes be represented as *causal loop diagrams* or *stock and flow diagrams*, which depict the interactions between system components and create behavioral patterns. Such diagrams are valuable tools for describing how parts of a system interact and create patterns of behavior, communicating the dynamics of systems, and designing and planning interventions to address the issues faced by the system.

The *causal loop diagrams* and stock *and flow diagrams* presented below were developed using the Systems Thinking Experiential Learning Laboratory with Animation (STELLA) Architect software (Version 3.6.1) by *Isee Systems, Inc.* (www. iseesystems.com). The software was also used to model more complex interaction dynamics, as discussed in Chapter 8.

6.4.3 Causal Loop Diagrams

Causal loop diagrams (CLDs) show how elements of a feedback mechanism are causally related. They are influence diagrams that consist of two primary causal links.

$$A ----^{+}> B$$

and

$$A ----^{-}> B.$$

Both indicate that variable A influences variable B. The first link, with a (+) polarity sign, suggests that A and B move in the same direction (i.e., both A and B simultaneously increase or decrease). The second link with a (–) polarity sign indicates that A and B move in opposite directions (i.e., B decreases as A increases or B increases as A decreases). In some causal loop diagrams in the literature, the (+) and (–) signs attached to the arrows can be replaced by the letters "s" (for the same) and "o" (for the opposite), respectively.

The following link represents a possible delay (due to information or material) between A's action and its effect on B:

$$A --||--> B.$$

Generally, causal loops are created by combining the links mentioned above. All loops comprising links with only positive signs, a combination of positive signs, and an *even* number of negative signs are called reinforcing loops (R). In contrast, loops with links with an *odd* number of negative signs are called balancing loops (B). Guidelines for drawing CLDs can be found in Ghosh (2017).

As an illustrative example, Fig. 6.4 shows a CLD diagram that simulates a possible dynamic across the three sectors of the engineering–peacebuilding–diplomacy nexus. Each sector is characterized by a goal-seeking dynamic represented by three balancing closed loops (Be, Bp, and Bd). Actions are taken to reduce the gaps between current engineering, peacebuilding, and diplomatic efforts and their specific goals. However, each action to narrow a sector gap has unintended negative consequences on the other two sectors. Furthermore, there may be a delay in this process.

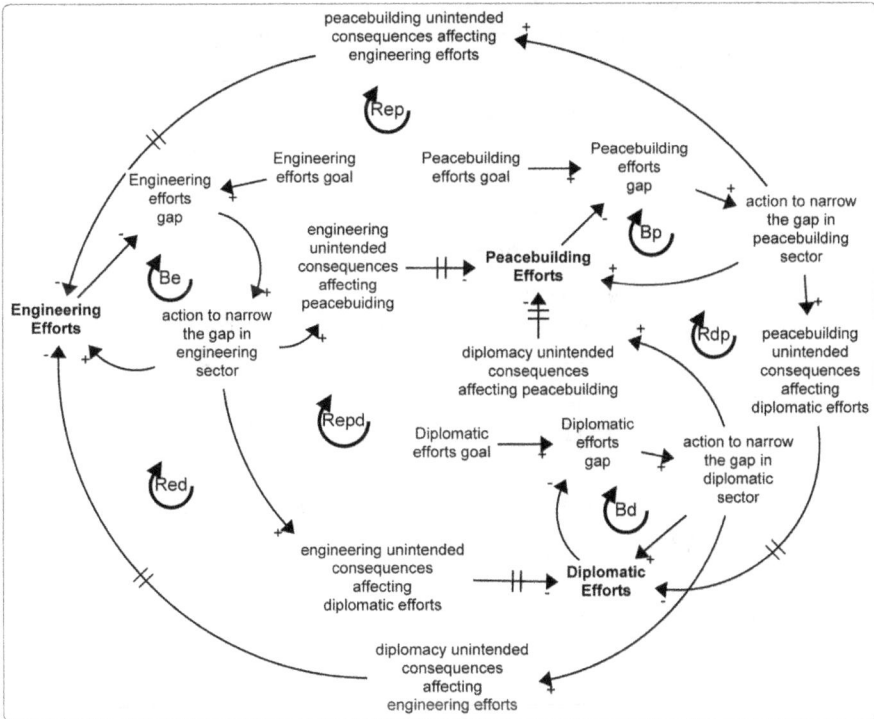

Figure 6.4 A causal loop diagram showing possible interactions among engineering, peacebuilding, and diplomatic efforts. *Note*: R and B denote reinforcing and balancing loops, respectively. + signs indicate variable changes in the same direction, and – signs indicate variable changes in the opposite direction.

This dynamic creates three two-sector reinforcing loops (Rep, Red, and Rdp) and one three-sector reinforcing loop (Repd). As an example, the Rdp loop in Fig. 6.4 can be expressed as follows:

Diplomatic efforts ---⁻> diplomatic efforts gap ---⁺> action to narrow the gap in the diplomatic sector ---⁺> Diplomacy unintended consequences affecting peacebuilding ---⁻> Peacebuilding efforts ---⁻> peacebuilding efforts gap ---⁺> action to narrow peacebuilding gap ---⁺> peacebuilding unintended consequences affecting diplomacy ---⁻> Diplomatic efforts.

Causal loop diagrams such as Fig. 6.4 are helpful for mapping, inferring, and visualizing what contributes to growth, decline, delay, or stability and are mainly used at the *strategy* level. Once the mental model of a problem has been outlined, CLDs show, in a condensed manner, different relationships, trends, connections, and causal feedback mechanisms in a system. Layers can be added to the causal loop diagrams, such as the stakeholders, decision-makers, or policies involved in intervening in each diagram segment. The CDA (2016) proposes detailed step-by-step guidelines for creating causal loop diagrams.

It is important to remember that causal loop diagrams are not used to conduct numerical system simulations. Instead, they help lay out the different structural components of a system in a conceptual manner and show how they interact dynamically in a *qualitative* manner. In short, they are helpful "for communication, not for simulation" (Ford, 2010). Despite this limitation, causal loop diagrams provide a strong value proposition for the decision-making process across the nexus. They help decision-makers develop a shared understanding of the issues they might face.

6.4.4 Stock and Flow Diagrams

Another way to describe system dynamics is to use stock and flow diagrams consisting of combinations of several building blocks, as shown in Fig. 6.5.

The building blocks help visualize qualitatively and quantitatively the accumulation, flows, delays, and dissipation, and incorporate feedback mechanisms and nonlinear dynamics. When combined, they represent the primary language of SD modeling. Using the terminology used in the *STELLA Architect* software by *isee systems*, the building blocks are defined as follows:

- The *stocks*, represented by rectangles in Fig. 6.5, correspond to the accumulation of something that can be measured at one point. These are *the state variables* that define the current state of the system. Examples include peacebuilding, engineering, and diplomatic efforts.

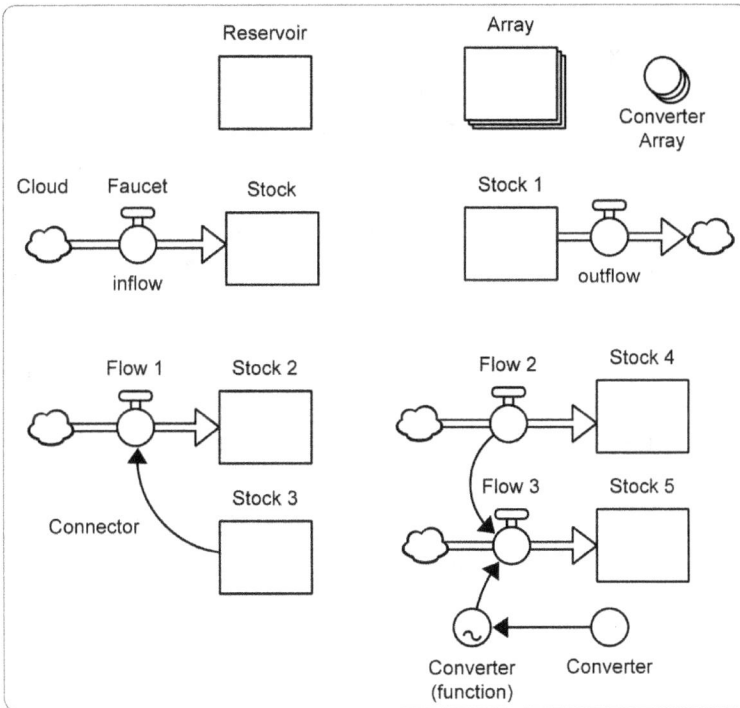

Figure 6.5 Basic building blocks of stock and flow diagrams.

- The *flow* (inflow and outflow) is represented in the form of pipelines (with a faucet controlling the flow rate), as shown in Fig. 6.5. Flow (i.e., flux or rate) results in changes (dynamic behavior) in stock accumulations and the entire system. Flows are *control variables* that create changes in the state of a system. Examples include (i) sustainable development processes leading to a state of sustainability; (ii) peacebuilding (i.e., building the conditions for peace), peacemaking (i.e., getting parties to find common ground), and peacekeeping (i.e., supporting sustainable peace) processes leading to lasting (sustainable) peace; (iii) communities' awareness, mitigation, and adaptation practices leading to climate security; and (iv) negotiating processes leading to successful diplomatic efforts.

- The *clouds* in Fig. 6.5 indicate infinite sources or sinks outside the system boundaries.
- The *converters*, represented by circles in Fig. 6.5, convert or transform information from one stock and flow path to another or feed information into an existing flow. A converter can also refer to a stock without inflow or outflow. These are *the conversion variables*. The converters can change over time and are described as functional (~symbol).
- The *Connectors*, represented by arrows in Fig. 6.5, indicate the transmission or links of actions and information (i.e., causal connections) between variables, such as stock-to-flow, flow-to-flow, or converters. One or more variables can provide input to and influence another variable through connectors.

As shown in Fig. 6.5, some SD building blocks can be represented as layered building blocks to represent arrays. For instance, they can describe how the components of each stock change over time. Examples would include (i) the positive, negative, and cultural components of peace; (ii) peacebuilding, peacemaking, and peacekeeping efforts; (iii) the people, planet, prosperity, and partnership components of sustainability; (iv) the possible awareness, adaptation, and mitigation components of climate security; and (v) the 3Rs of engineering projects.

System dynamics (SD) models generally combine all the building blocks in Fig. 6.5. It must be noted that no one-size-fits-all SD model can capture all possible dynamics of complex systems in multiple contexts and scales.

6.4.5   A Goal-Seeking Model

An attempt at creating a stock and flow diagram of the dominant dynamics in Fig. 6.4 was made using the STELLA Architect software. The model is illustrated in Fig. 6.6. Three stocks (E, engineering efforts; P, peacebuilding efforts; and D, diplomatic efforts) and balancing loops were considered. Starting with their initial values E_0, P_0, and D_0, the three stocks vary with time toward the desirable values DE, DP, and DD, with adjustment rates ARE, ARP, and ARD, respectively.

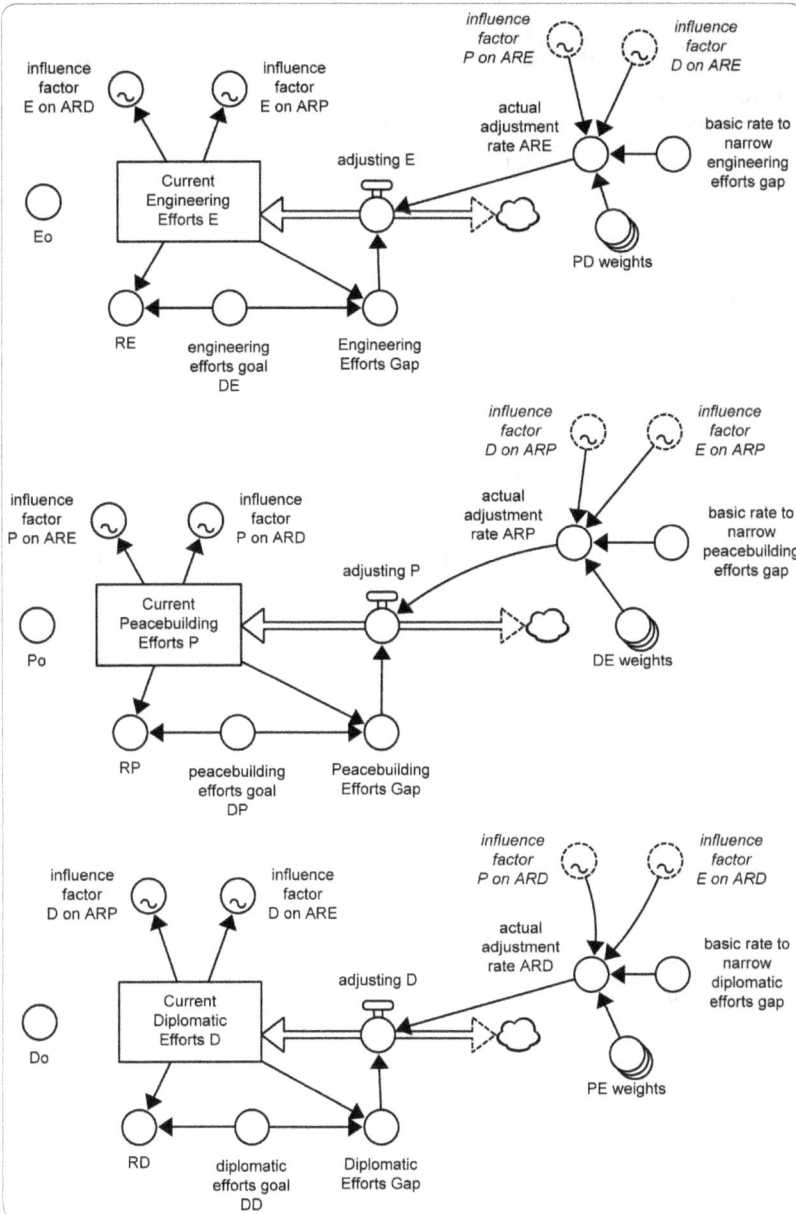

Figure 6.6 Stock and flow diagrams showing possible relationships between engineering, peacebuilding, and diplomatic efforts.

The three sectors are assumed to be entangled, and each follows a goal-seeking dynamic. The actual adjustment rate ARE is considered the product of a basic adjustment rate and the weighted influence factors of P and D on ARE. Likewise, the actual adjustment rate ARP is assumed to be the product of a basic rate and the weighted influence factors of D and E on ARP. Finally, the actual adjustment rate ARD is assumed to be the product of a basic rate and the weighted influence factors of P and E on the ARD. The influence factors are supposed to have functional forms ($\sim$), depend on E, P, or D, and can be enabling (>0) or constraining (<0).

Mathematically, the change of the stock, E, over time ("adjusting E") is equal to

$$\frac{dE}{dt} = ARE\ (P, D) \times (DE - E) \tag{6.1}$$

Likewise, the change of the stock, P, over time ("adjusting P") is equal to

$$\frac{dP}{dt} = ARP\ (E, D) \times (DP - P) \tag{6.2}$$

Likewise, the change of the stock, D, over time ("adjusting D") is equal to

$$\frac{dD}{dt} = ARD\ (E, P) \times (DD - D) \tag{6.3}$$

Solving these three nonlinear first-order differential equations with (E_o, P_o, D_o) as the initial conditions would give an expression for E(t), P(t), and D(t) *if* we know the functional forms of ARE, ARP, and ARD and the different functions ($\sim$) in Fig. 6.6. The three biflows in Fig. 6.6 capture each stock's possible increase or decrease. For example, a stock may decrease if its adjustment rate becomes negative. In this case, engineering, peacebuilding, and diplomatic efforts would degrade over time.

A Numerical Example

In this example, (E, DE), (P, DP), and (D, DD) are expressed in generic engineering effort units (eu), peacebuilding effort units (pu), and diplomatic effort units (du), respectively, ranging over some [0–100] scales. These units are *arbitrary* and are introduced here as adequate semi-quantitative measures of engineering, peacebuilding, and diplomatic efforts. They can be divided into several achievement-level groups, from most constraining to most enabling, using a semiquantitative rating scale, as shown in Table 6.4. Each group is specific to the context in which the nexus analysis is conducted. Metrics can be introduced to describe each enabling or constraining achievement level: For instance, what do "enabling" or "constraining" engineering, peacebuilding, and diplomatic efforts look like and manifest, and how do they differ from a high to a low?

Table 6.4 Possible enabling and constraining achievement levels of engineering, peacebuilding, and diplomatic efforts

	1–20	21–40	41–50	51–60	61–80	81–100
E, P, D efforts	Most constraining	Constraining – reducing	Constraining – limiting	Enabling – allowing	Enabling – supporting	Most enabling

As an illustrative example, an SD analysis was carried out assuming that initially (i) the engineering efforts are most constraining with E_0 = 10 eu, (ii) the peacebuilding efforts are constraining-reducing with P_0 = 25 pu, (iii) the diplomatic efforts are enabling-allowing with D_0 = 50 du, (iv) DE = DP = DD = 100 units, and (v) the basic ARE, ARP, and ARD rates are 0.02/yr. The influence factors vary linearly between –0.2 and 1, as E, P, and D vary between 0 and 100.

Figure 6.7a shows the increase in RE = E/DE, RP= P/DP, and RD = D/DD over 50 years. For comparison, Fig. 6.7b shows how these ratios decrease when diplomatic efforts are initially most constraining with D_0 = 5 du, all else being the same as in the first run. Input data for the two numerical runs can be found in Appendix C, and the SD model can be found on the web at https://exchange. iseesystems.com/public/bernardamadei/epdfig66

The STELLA Architect software can model more complex interaction dynamics between the three sectors of the engineering–peacebuilding–diplomacy nexus, as presented in Chapter 8. The software allows for parametric studies and single- and multi-objective optimizations to be conducted. Figure 6.7c shows the variability of the peacebuilding effort ratio RP= P/DP for values of the initial engineering and diplomacy efforts ranging from 5 to 45 and different confidence levels.

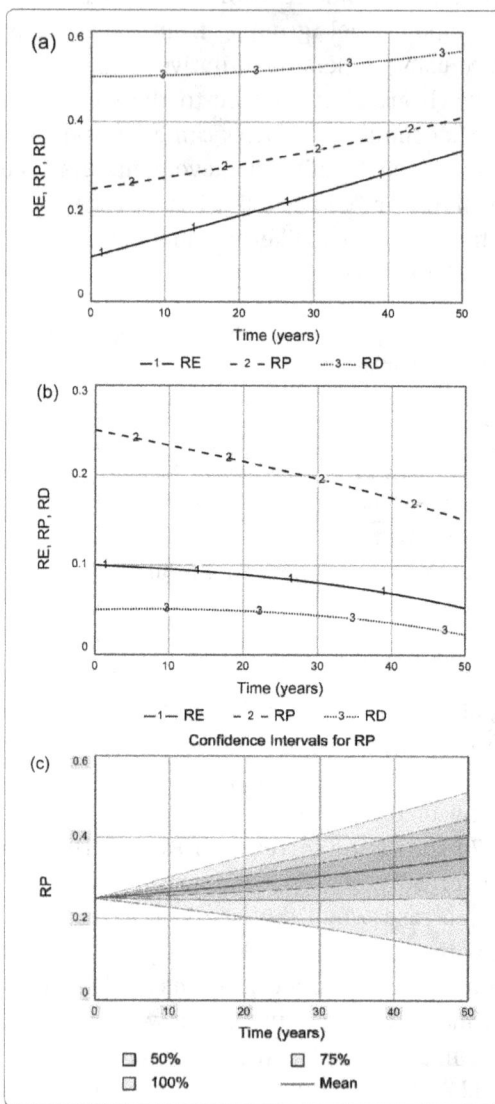

Figure 6.7 Variation in engineering, peacebuilding, and diplomatic efforts over 50 years. (a) D_o = 50 du (enabling-allowing); (b) D_o = 5 du (most constraining); (c) Variation of RP= P/DP for values of the engineering and diplomacy efforts ranging from 5 to 45. The 50, 75, and 100% confidence intervals and mean values are shown.

6.5   System Dynamics Modeling

6.5.1   Modeling Road Map

The modeling guidelines of Sterman (2000) outlined in Section 6.2 also apply to system dynamics modeling. All system dynamics models must pass tests (Sterman, 2000; Forrester and Senge, 1980). They include boundary adequacy, structure assessment, dimensional consistency, parameter assessment, extreme conditions, behavior analysis and reproduction, surprise behavior, sensitivity analysis, and policy analysis. These tests help increase trust in the models. As the models become more reliable, they can be enhanced with more complexity. It should be remembered that system dynamics modeling is a combination of art and science; it involves systems thinking, which consists of balancing critical and creative thinking.

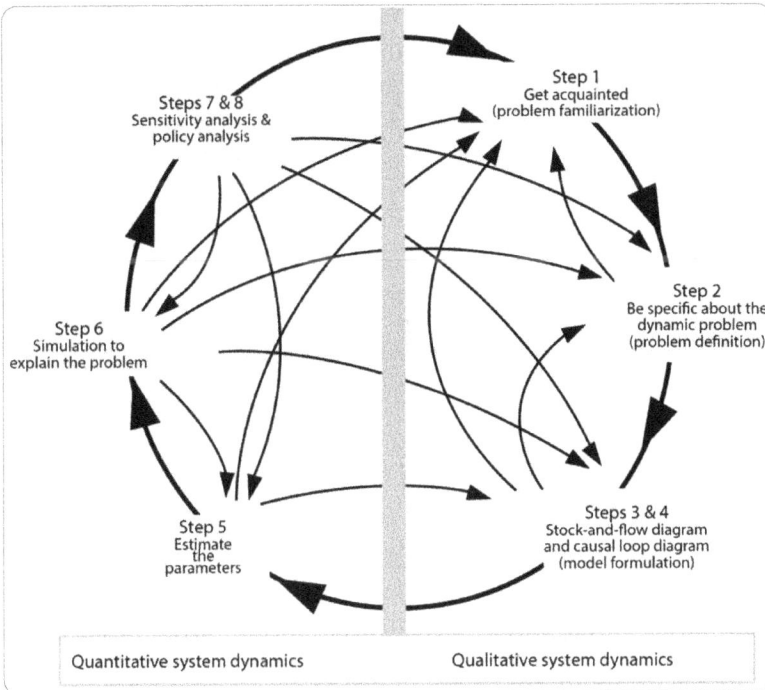

Figure 6.8 Cyclical nature of system dynamics modeling. *Source*: Ford (2010), with permission from Island Press. *Note*: The components are divided into those involved in qualitative modeling (right-hand side) and those involved in quantitative modeling (left-hand side).

Several road maps can be used to build SD models, including the five steps of Sterman (2000) discussed in Section 6.2. Figure 6.8 shows another step-by-step road map presented by Ford (2010). It consists of eight steps combined into six key activities once a problem has been identified. They include (i) problem familiarization, (ii) problem definition, (iii) model formulation by constructing stock and flow diagrams and causal loop diagrams, (iv) parameter estimation, (v) simulation to explain the problem being addressed, and (vi) simulation analysis consisting of sensitivity analysis (step 7) and policy analysis (step 8). Figure 6.8 shows the cyclical nature of the road map and its many feedback loops.

According to Fig. 6.8, system dynamics modeling has both qualitative and quantitative aspects. Steps 1-4 are the qualitative and conceptual elements of system dynamics modeling. Steps 5–8 emphasize the quantitative side of the modeling. The choice of qualitative or quantitative modeling mainly depends on the system analysis, the data and information availability about the system components, and the audience involved (Wolstenholme, 1990).

As remarked by Amadei (2019), one way to summarize all the recommendations available in the literature to model complex issues with the tools of system dynamics is to ensure that the models are:

- The right ones for the context and scale of interest and those who will benefit from the decisions based on the models.
- Done right from a system dynamics modeling point of view.
- Created for the right reasons for the issues being addressed with the appropriate level of comprehensiveness, simplicity, and usefulness.

Furthermore, it is essential to engage different groups of stakeholders involved in community development, security, and conflict management in each stage of the SD modeling roadmap in Fig. 6.8. Group model building (GMB) is, for instance, a way of making decisions using system dynamics tools that encourage participation (Vennix, 1996; Andersen et al., 1997). For complex adaptive systems such as communities, GMB can help various stakeholders work together and agree on a shared view of reality (Vennix, 1996). The result of this process depends on the uncertainty and complexity of all the community systems in Fig. 6.1, as well as how well-defined the problems are. It also depends on the group members' bounded rationality, no matter their culture. Notably, it is challenging to communicate and explore the sheer complexity of the landscape in Fig. 6.1 and how engineering, peacebuilding, and diplomacy interact and unfold in that landscape. Generally, constructing a group model necessitates close collaboration among the decision-making team and a commitment from all stakeholder groups to participate actively and engage in a shared reality.

It is essential to acknowledge that the success of model-building teams in maintaining a long-term, fixed, and shared reality is uncertain. The likelihood of this scenario occurring may depend on various factors, and unforeseen events are more likely to occur. Additionally, stakeholders often have differing opinions, making it challenging to reach a consensus or agree on a system model to address their problems. Therefore, a dynamic perspective is necessary for shared reality in group modeling, which requires regular reassessment, monitoring, and evaluation through reflection-in-action.

6.5.2   SD Applications

System dynamics modeling has been used in many fields related to the topics addressed in this book. Multiple models in the literature have used the principles of systems thinking to address various aspects of sustainable community development. As reviewed by Amadei (2015, 2019, and 2023), these models can be categorized into two types: those focused on global changes and those concentrating on particular concerns. The global change frameworks can handle high levels of complexity, involve high levels of aggregation, and allow for high levels of decision-making around development issues. However, all of them have two general shortcomings. First, they have been mainly used to model the complex dynamics of change and development at global, regional, and country scales. Second, they reveal how difficult it is to obtain data to quantify the causal links considered in the frameworks.

On the other end of the spectrum of system dynamics models are those focusing on sector-specific issues, such as water resources management, energy resources management, agro-food, land resources management, health, and conflict. Like the global models, these frameworks address issues at the country, regional, or global scales. Sohofi et al. (2016) gave an excellent review of many of these different topical models. It should be noted that many sector-specific formulations also incorporate, in a comprehensive manner, topics such as climate change. However, few studies include both conflict/instability and climate vulnerability/security.

Choucri et al. (2005) used SD to model state instability, resilience, and capacity (institutional, technical, social, financial, etc.). The rationale is that the stability of the state is driven by a multitude of interacting social, economic, and geopolitical pressures, which, when combined, may reach a tipping point beyond which state resilience is exceeded, and conflict arises. It is not difficult to envision, for instance, how water, energy, land, food insecurity, and climate change could contribute to this dynamic.

Corruption is a subject that system dynamics has also tackled (Woodrow, 2024). When managing resources, it is essential to consider corruption because it can impede the success of technical strategies and policy choices. Ullah (2012) presents an instance of applying system dynamics to corruption modeling, including a comprehensive review of existing corruption models and a framework tailored to address corruption in Pakistan.

Since 2010, there has been a strong interest in integrating systems dynamics tools into conflict analysis and management (Jones, 2015; CDA, 2016). The tools are used to (i) analyze the results of conflict assessment, (ii) predict how conflicts may evolve, (iii) identify places to intervene in the conflict, and (iv) propose meaningful interventions leading to peace and stability. With minor exceptions, many of these studies use qualitative CLDs rather than quantitative stock and flow diagrams.

System dynamics tools have also been used to analyze the impact of climate change on specific issues such as water, agriculture, and energy. More complex models have been proposed to look at how climate change impacts various socioeconomic and natural systems at different scales, including migration, and explore climate policy options to mitigate the impacts (Fiddaman, 2002; Huerta et al., 2011; Sterman et al., 2012; Sohofi et al., 2016; Redivo, 2021; Moon et al., 2021; Ganji and Naseri, 2021; Egerer et al., 2021; Taylor and Araujo, 2021; Bozorg-Haddad et al., 2022; Cury et al., 2023; among others). Among these studies, the SD model of Moon et al. (2021) stands out in analyzing the impact of climate change on environmental, economic, and social systems in urban and rural environments at the country scale of Korea while considering the existing dynamic interactions among these systems.

6.6   Archetypes

Context- and scale-dependent projects involving the engineering, peacebuilding, and diplomacy sectors exhibit recurring behavior patterns and generic structures. Also known as archetypes, they:

- Demonstrate that the structure of systems controls their behavior.
- Differentiate what is generic vs. what is context- and scale-specific.
- Help to identify dynamics that produce types of behavior patterns.
- Provide a structural template of common patterns.
- Represent attractors of various strengths, i.e., levels where systems tend to return after changing.
- Explain habits (good or bad), defining the system's character and, ultimately, its destiny.
- Helps identify traps or grooves that force systems to produce the same answer (intended or unintended) under the same conditions.
- Help to identify leverage points: Places to intervene in a complex system where a slight shift in one thing can significantly change everything.

Archetypes are helpful in the SD modeling road map (Fig. 6.8) when defining the structure of the SD model (Step 2) and identifying the places to intervene in that structure (Step 6). Once an archetype has been identified, it is possible to locate the leverage areas of intervention.

Generally, archetypes that best match the issues being addressed in a conflict-affected or conflict-sensitive community landscape require identifying the storyline underlying these issues, which involves experimentation (Kim, 2000; Kim and Anderson, 2007). As noted by Sterman (2000), archetype selection can be aided by using reference behavior over time graphs describing how the issues change over time and whether they show trends such as (i) linear growth or decay, (ii) exponential growth or decay that can be modeled by a single reinforcing (for growth) or balancing (for decay) loop, (iii) goal seeking that can be modeled using a single balancing loop, (iv) oscillation that can occur when a delay is combined with a balancing loop, and (v) delays. Other higher forms of behavior can be obtained by combining the aforementioned basic modes, such as S-shaped growth (sequence of reinforcing and balancing loops), S-shaped growth with overshoot and oscillation, and overshoot and collapse (i.e., a series of multiple reinforcing and balancing with or without delay).

The SD reinforcing and balancing feedback types described above are basic archetypes contributing to more complex archetypes. Ten archetypes are considered, with examples involving engineering, peacebuilding, and diplomatic components. Various authors have proposed specific causal loop diagrams (CLDs) and behavior over time graphs to represent the dynamics behind each archetype and for different domains of application (Senge et al., 1994; Kim, 2000; Braun, 2002; Kim and Anderson, 2007; Stroh, 2015). The Waters Center for Systems Thinking (WCST) offers an online course that describes the dynamics behind nine system archetypes in more detail (www.waterscenterst.org).

Other examples illustrating each archetype regarding the water–energy–land–food nexus and the peace–sustainability–climate security nexus can be found in Amadei (2019, 2023).

6.6.1 Fixes That Fail or Backfire

A problem requires a solution, and addressing the issue promptly relieves the symptoms. However, the problem may recur or worsen owing to the unforeseen and unintended consequences of the solution that emerge after some time (delay). The corresponding CLD is shown in Fig. 6.9.

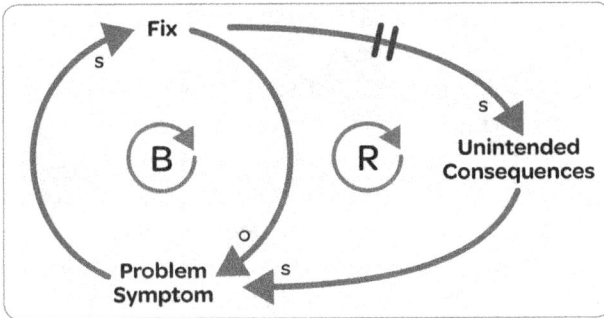

Figure 6.9 Dynamics of the fixes that fail or backfire archetype. Legend: s (same direction); o (opposite direction); R (reinforcing loop); B (balancing loop) *Source*: © 2020 Waters Center for Systems Thinking, WatersCenterST.org Adapted from archetype described in *The Fifth Discipline*, Senge (2006), and by Innovation Associates, Inc.

Example: Let us consider the dynamics in the context of post-conflict reconstruction efforts in a war-torn region. The country is emerging from a devastating civil war in which infrastructure is destroyed, communities are displaced, and social cohesion is fractured. In response to the immediate humanitarian crisis, international actors and humanitarian organizations were mobilized to provide affected populations with emergency aid, including food, shelter, and medical assistance.

Engineering plays a critical role in the initial phase of post-conflict reconstruction, as efforts are made to rebuild essential infrastructure, such as roads, bridges, schools, and healthcare facilities, to restore essential services and support the return of displaced populations. Peacebuilding initiatives focus on fostering reconciliation, rebuilding trust, and promoting dialogue among formerly warring factions to prevent the resurgence of violence.

Diplomacy is also instrumental in coordinating international support, mobilizing resources, and facilitating political dialogue between the government and opposition groups to establish a framework for peace and stability. Through diplomatic efforts, agreements may be reached to address the root causes of conflict, such as political grievances, socioeconomic disparities, and ethnic tensions, and to promote inclusive governance and democratic reforms.

However, unforeseen and unintended consequences emerge despite the prompt response to the immediate humanitarian crisis and the implementation of engineering solutions to rebuild infrastructure. This exacerbates the underlying fragility and instability in a post-conflict society. For example, suppose that reconstruction efforts prioritize rapid infrastructure development without sufficient consideration of local needs, preferences, or environmental sustainability. In this case, they may inadvertently exacerbate social inequalities, environmental degradation, and tensions over resource allocation. Furthermore, peacebuilding efforts may focus solely on elite-level negotiations and fail to address grassroots grievances and aspirations. In this case, they may fail to build lasting peace and trust in the broader population.

As a result, the initial relief provided by the prompt response to the humanitarian crisis may give way to renewed tensions, social unrest, or even a relapse into violence, as the unintended consequences of reconstruction and peacebuilding efforts become apparent. This dynamic underscores the importance of adopting a comprehensive and holistic approach to post-conflict reconstruction that addresses the root causes of conflict, promotes inclusive and sustainable development, and builds resilience against future shocks and crises.

Lessons learned: This archetype calls for (i) paying particular attention to the nature of the fix(es) and possible long-term consequences once the problem symptoms have been identified and (ii) analyzing how past actions to address the problem have been performed. In the short term, consider applying the fix when developing long-term symptom solutions (Braun, 2002).

6.6.2 Success to the Successful

Multiple groups often compete for limited resources to achieve success. One of these competitors typically tends to secure a significant share of resources. Thus, they have a higher likelihood of ongoing success, especially if they have a proven success track record compared to their competitors. The corresponding CLD is shown in Fig. 6.10.

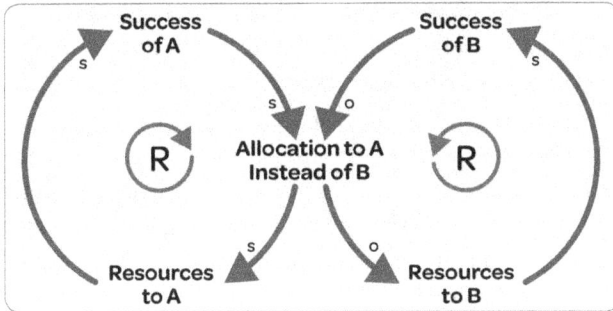

Figure 6.10 Dynamics of the success to the successful archetype. Legend: s (same direction); o (opposite direction); R (reinforcing loop); B (balancing loop). *Source*: © 2020 Waters Center for Systems Thinking, WatersCenterST. org Adapted from archetype described in *The Fifth Discipline*, Senge (2006), and by Innovation Associates, Inc.

<u>Example</u>: Several countries in a region with abundant renewable energy resources compete for access to these resources to meet their energy demands and reduce their reliance on fossil fuels. Although each country acknowledges the economic and environmental advantages of transitioning to renewable energy, the limited land suitable for large-scale projects poses a challenge.

In the competing countries, diplomacy plays a significant role in resolving conflict and negotiating resource allocation, energy security, and environmental sustainability. Diplomatic channels enable the establishment of cooperative frameworks such as joint development projects or regional energy initiatives to maximize renewable energy resources and minimize territorial and access rights disputes.

Engineers from collaborating countries work together to develop and deploy cutting-edge renewable energy infrastructure while maximizing energy generation and distribution efficiency. These engineering initiatives prioritize sustainability and environmental protection, resulting in eco-friendly and socially beneficial renewable energy projects.

Although diplomacy and engineering expertise have facilitated collaborative efforts among countries, competition persists to secure a larger share of economic benefits and technological advancements from renewable energy development. Countries with strong engineering capabilities, access to financing, and diplomatic influence may be more likely to obtain favorable terms in joint ventures or gain preferential access to international markets for renewable energy technology exports.

Over time, countries that are more successful in leveraging their engineering expertise, diplomatic relationships, and economic resources to secure a more significant share of the renewable energy market may further enhance their competitive advantage in the ongoing pursuit of renewable energy development and global energy transition.

Lesson Learned: This archetype calls for paying particular attention to (i) how slight differences in initial resource distribution, dominance, power, favoritism, corruption, and privilege can create a self-fulfilling prophecy of division and conflict and more dominance and privilege; (ii) both parties' definitions of success; and (iii) and whether both parties require the same initial level of resources to be successful.

6.6.3   Limits to Growth

Efforts are typically met with initial success, which serves as a driving force for further effort. However, over time, limitations are encountered, leading to a reduction in the rate of progress towards goals. The corresponding CLD is shown in Fig. 6.11.

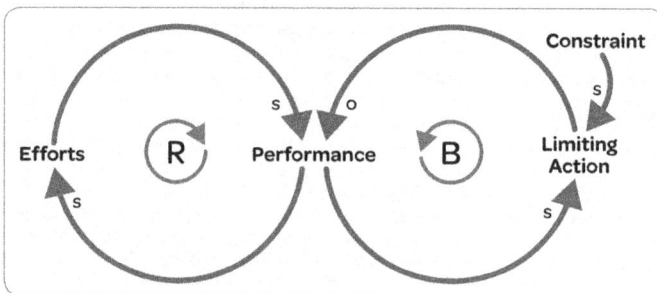

Figure 6.11 Dynamics of the limits to growth or success archetype. Legend: s (same direction); o (opposite direction); R (reinforcing loop); B (balancing loop) *Source*: © 2020 Waters Center for Systems Thinking, WatersCenterST.org Adapted from archetype described in *The Fifth Discipline*, Senge (2006), and by Innovation Associates, Inc.

Example: A conflict-affected region receives substantial investment in engineering projects to rebuild infrastructure, such as roads, bridges, and utilities. These projects are designed to improve access to essential services and stimulate economic development. Concurrently, peacebuilding initiatives are launched to address the root causes of the conflict, promote reconciliation among warring factions, and establish mechanisms for conflict resolution and governance reform. Diplomatic efforts are made to broker peace agreements and facilitate negotiations between the conflicting parties. International actors, including governments and multilateral organizations, engage in diplomatic dialogue to support peacebuilding and reconstruction efforts.

Despite these reinforcing dynamics, limitations in growth scenarios may unfold. For instance, the rapid implementation of engineering projects without adequate consideration for environmental sustainability may lead to ecological degradation and resource depletion, such as deforestation, habitat destruction, pollution, exacerbating environmental stressors, and undermining long-term sustainability. Likewise, despite investments in engineering and peacebuilding, the underlying social and economic disparities persist, limiting the effectiveness of development efforts. Inequitable distribution of resources, lack of access to education and healthcare, and unemployment may perpetuate cycles of poverty and marginalization, hindering the region's ability to achieve sustainable growth and stability.

In addition, fragile peace agreements and unresolved grievances may lead to renewed violence and instability, disrupting engineering projects, and undermining diplomatic efforts. Political tensions, power struggles, and resistance to governance reforms can impede progress toward lasting peace and development, creating uncertainty and volatility in the region.

Finally, external factors, such as regional geopolitics, economic dependencies, and humanitarian crises, can also challenge growth and stability. International interventions may be constrained by competing interests, donor fatigue, or geopolitical rivalries, thus limiting the effectiveness of diplomacy and external support in addressing complex conflicts and promoting sustainable development.

In this scenario, the interplay between engineering, peace-building, and diplomacy dynamics is shaped by various limits to growth, including environmental constraints, social and economic challenges, political instability, and external factors.

Lesson Learned: This archetype calls for paying particular attention to the constraints to growth (e.g., population growth, environmental degradation, or other factors), especially before the limits are reached and conflict becomes unmanageable.

6.6.4   Escalation

When one party (A) responds to a perceived threat, the other party (B) interprets these actions as causing an imbalance in the system that makes them feel threatened. In response, B reacts to close the gap, which, from A's perspective, creates an imbalance, leading to a cycle of both parties trying to find a sense of "safety." The dynamics of the two parties striving for safety become a reinforcing process that increases tension on both sides. The corresponding CLD is shown in Fig. 6.12.

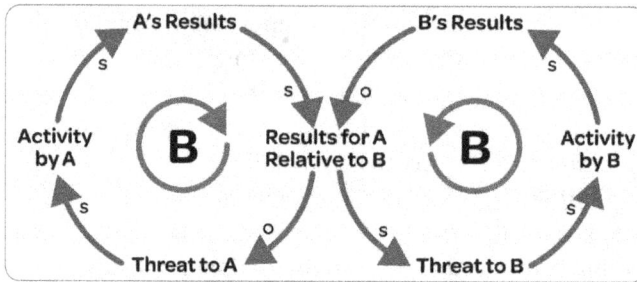

Figure 6.12 Dynamics of the escalation archetype. Legend: s (same direction); o (opposite direction); R (reinforcing loop); B (balancing loop) *Source*: © 2020 Waters Center for Systems Thinking, WatersCenterST.org Adapted from archetype described in *The Fifth Discipline*, Senge (2006), and by Innovation Associates, Inc.

Example: An example where the escalation dynamic involves engineering, peacebuilding, and diplomacy can be seen in the context of territorial disputes over maritime boundaries and the construction of artificial islands in the South China Sea.

In recent years, several countries, including China, Vietnam, and the Philippines, have disputed territorial claims and rights regarding natural resources in the South China Sea. These disputes have escalated tensions, with competing claims over islands, reefs, and marine resources exacerbating regional instability.

Engineering projects have become vital in territorial disputes, as the involved countries undertake large-scale construction to assert their claims. For instance, China has built artificial islands and militarized features, such as reefs and shoals, to bolster its presence and claim sovereignty over disputed territories. These efforts involve land reclamation, construction of airstrips, installation of military facilities, escalating tensions, and raising concerns among neighboring countries and the international community.

Diplomacy attempts to mitigate these tensions and resolve disputes through negotiation and diplomatic channels. However, efforts to resolve conflicts peacefully have been challenging because of entrenched territorial claims, historical grievances, and competing strategic interests among the parties involved. Diplomatic initiatives, such as multilateral dialogue and arbitration proceedings, have faced obstacles and have not resulted in significant progress in de-escalating the situation.

Peacebuilding efforts aim to address the underlying causes of conflict and promote regional stability. However, the escalation of territorial disputes and militarization of artificial islands have undermined these peacebuilding efforts, creating a cycle of escalation and counter-escalation that further entrenches parties' positions and increases the risk of conflict.

Overall, the dynamics of escalation involving engineering, peacebuilding, and diplomacy in the South China Sea exemplify the complex interplay between territorial disputes, military capabilities, and diplomatic maneuvers in pursuing strategic objectives. Efforts to de-escalate tensions and promote peace in the region require concerted diplomatic efforts, adherence to international law, and dialogue to address the drivers of conflict.

Lessons Learned: This archetype calls for special attention to define what represents a threat for each party, addressing insecurity, and bringing it under control without delay. Another option is to consider a larger goal that encompasses the desires of each party (Braun, 2002).

6.6.5 Shifting the Burden

Symptomatic treatment or a more comprehensive solution can address a problem symptom. When a symptomatic solution is implemented, the desire to implement a more fundamental remedy may be lessened because the symptoms are temporarily alleviated or disappear. However, the symptoms may return over time, leading to the repetition of symptomatic treatment in a recurring cycle. The corresponding CLD is shown in Fig. 6.13.

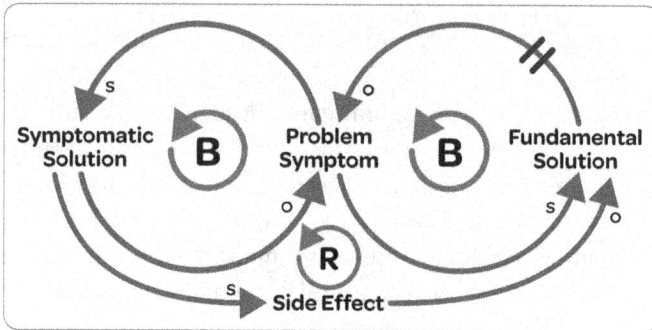

Figure 6.13 Dynamics of the shifting the burden archetype. Legend: s (same direction); o (opposite direction); R (reinforcing loop); B (balancing loop) *Source:* © 2020 Waters Center for Systems Thinking, WatersCenterST.org Adapted from archetype described in *The Fifth Discipline*, Senge (2006), and by Innovation Associates, Inc.

Example: Two communities are in conflict regarding access to shared natural resources such as arable land or water sources. This conflict escalated into violence in the past, leading to displacement, loss of livelihood, and humanitarian crises. The region has a history of ethnic tensions and territorial disputes.

Diplomacy is crucial in mediating negotiations between the two communities, facilitating dialogue, and brokering agreements to resolve the underlying issues fueling the conflict. Through diplomatic channels, efforts have been made to address grievances, promote reconciliation, and establish peaceful coexistence and resource-sharing mechanisms.

Engineers are tasked with implementing short-term engineering solutions to alleviate the immediate symptoms of conflict. For example, they may construct temporary barriers or diversion channels to regulate access to water resources, mitigate soil erosion, or prevent further encroachment on disputed land. These engineering interventions provide temporary relief and help prevent further conflict escalation by addressing immediate needs and grievances.

However, these symptomatic engineering solutions do not address the root causes of conflict, such as historical injustices, unequal access to resources, or competition for power and influence. As a result, while the symptoms of conflict may temporarily subside, the underlying tensions and grievances persist and potentially resurface in the future. Over time, without comprehensive peace-building efforts to address the structural drivers of conflict and promote inclusive governance, the symptoms of conflict may reemerge, leading to recurring violence and instability. Despite implementing symptomatic engineering solutions and diplomatic initiatives to manage the conflict, the absence of a more fundamental remedy leaves the underlying issues unresolved, perpetuating recurring tensions and conflict.

Lesson Learned: The archetype cycle can be broken by complementing symptomatic treatments with long-term, comprehensive solutions that address the root causes of the conflict, promote social justice, and build sustainable peace through inclusive governance, equitable resource management, and participatory decision-making processes.

6.6.6   Drifting or Eroding Goals

Reducing the goal or implementing corrective measures can help bridge the gap between the desired and actual performance. Lowering goals can help achieve this goal. However, it is essential to recognize that performance may decline over time, which could happen gradually and without intentional action, leading to a negative impact on the organization that may go unnoticed. The corresponding CLD is shown in Fig. 6.14.

Example: A coalition with support from international organizations and donor countries embarks on a large-scale engineering project to rebuild critical infrastructure, such as roads, bridges, and utilities, in a post-conflict country recovering from years of instability and violence.

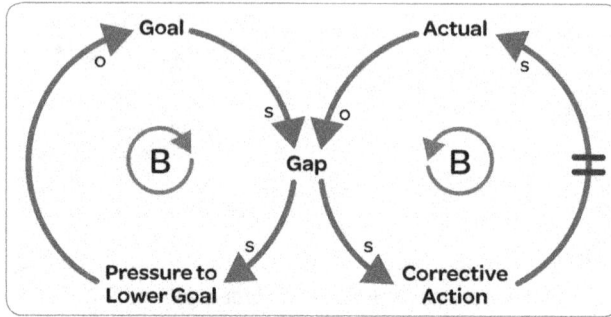

Figure 6.14 Dynamics of the drifting and eroding goals archetype. Legend: s (same direction); o (opposite direction); R (reinforcing loop); B (balancing loop) *Source*: © 2020 Waters Center for Systems Thinking, WatersCenterST.org Adapted from archetype described in *The Fifth Discipline*, Senge (2006), and by Innovation Associates, Inc.

Diplomacy is crucial for securing funding, coordinating international support, and garnering political commitment from local stakeholders to implement development projects. Through diplomatic efforts, agreements have been reached to prioritize infrastructure development to promote stability, create jobs, and stimulate economic growth in the region.

Engineers are tasked with designing and executing infrastructure projects, applying their expertise to overcome technical challenges, and ensuring that construction meets safety, quality, and sustainability standards. As projects progress, they contribute to visible improvements in the country's infrastructure, thus enhancing mobility, access to services, and connectivity to local communities.

Lowering the goal or implementing corrective measures may be necessary to adapt to complex realities, such as limited resources, security concerns, and logistical challenges. For example, suppose the original goal is to build several kilometers of roads within a specified timeframe. In such cases, adjustments may need to be made to accommodate delays, budget constraints, or unforeseen obstacles.

However, performance may gradually decline without vigilant monitoring and evaluation, and the quality and sustainability of infrastructure projects may be compromised. This decline could occur because of inadequate maintenance, corruption, or political instability, negatively impacting the organization's reputation and the long-term effectiveness of development efforts.

If performance declines go unnoticed or unaddressed, infrastructure projects may fail to deliver the expected benefits to local communities, undermine public trust, and exacerbate social tensions. This dynamic could ultimately hinder the region's broader goals of peacebuilding and stability, highlighting the importance of ongoing oversight, accountability mechanisms, and adaptive management of engineering projects in conflict-affected and conflict-sensitive contexts.

<u>Lessons Learned:</u> This archetype calls for paying particular attention to the nature of corrective actions and how goals erode over time. A reality check between the actual situation and desired goals must be considered as soon as possible (Braun, 2002).

6.6.7 Tragedy of the Commons

People frequently exploit common resources without considering their impact on others. Unfortunately, when the commons become overburdened by the cumulative effects of individual actions, everyone loses out, including the resources themselves, which may be completely depleted. The corresponding CLD is shown in Fig. 6.15.

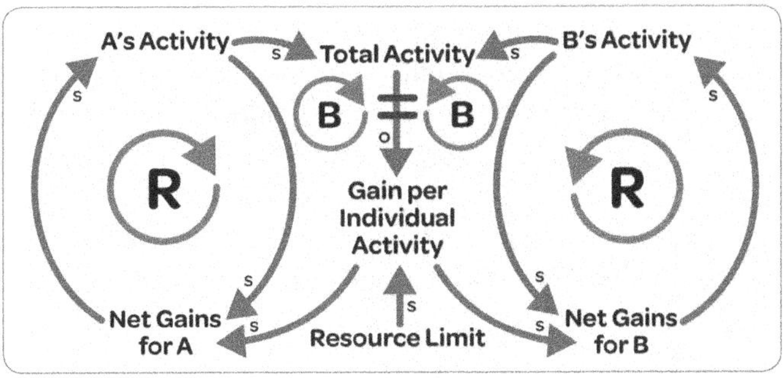

Figure 6.15 Dynamics of the Tragedy of the Commons Archetype. Legend: s (same direction); o (opposite direction); R (reinforcing loop); B (balancing loop) *Source*: © 2020 Waters Center for Systems Thinking, WatersCenterST.org Adapted from archetype described in *The Fifth Discipline*, Senge (2006), and by Innovation Associates, Inc.

Example: Several countries bordering a body of water, such as lakes, seas, or oceans, rely heavily on fishing as a vital source of food, income, and livelihoods for their coastal communities. However, due to limited regulatory oversight, weak enforcement mechanisms, and a lack of coordination among countries, fishery resources are subjected to overexploitation and unsustainable fishing practices.

Diplomacy is critical for mediating negotiations between countries with competing claims and interests in shared fishery resources. Through diplomatic channels, efforts are made to establish agreements, treaties, or cooperative frameworks to sustainably manage and conserve fishery resources while addressing the socioeconomic needs and concerns of all stakeholders involved.

Engineering interventions such as developing selective fishing gear, fish-aggregating devices, and aquaculture technologies may be employed to enhance the efficiency and sustainability of fishing practices. However, without effective governance and enforcement mechanisms, these engineering solutions may not be sufficient to prevent the overexploitation of fishery resources.

Overfishing by individual actors, without considering long-term consequences, results in the depletion of fish stocks, declines in bio-diversity, and disruptions to marine ecosystems. This exploitation of the commons negatively affects all stakeholders, including reduced catches, diminished incomes for fishing communities, and food insecurity for coastal populations.

Owing to the absence of effective governing and enforcement mechanisms, the tragedy of the commons continues to unfold despite diplomatic efforts and peacebuilding initiatives to sustainably manage fisheries. Ultimately, everyone loses their resources as they become depleted. Therefore, it is crucial to work together at the international level to promote responsible stewardship of shared resources and prevent their overexploitation for the benefit of future generations.

Lessons Learned: This archetype calls for special attention to the management (regulation and coordination) of finite resources, collaboration, monitoring, and evaluating resources, and the need to develop common ground. Another option is to substitute or renew the resources available to both parties before depletion (Braun, 2002).

6.6.8   Accidental Adversaries

Misinterpretations, unrealistic expectations, and performance issues can erode trust and create suspicion among teams or parties, thereby hindering their ability to work effectively. When mental models that contribute to this breakdown in communication are not challenged, all parties risk losing the benefits of collaborative efforts. The corresponding CLD is shown in Fig. 6.16.

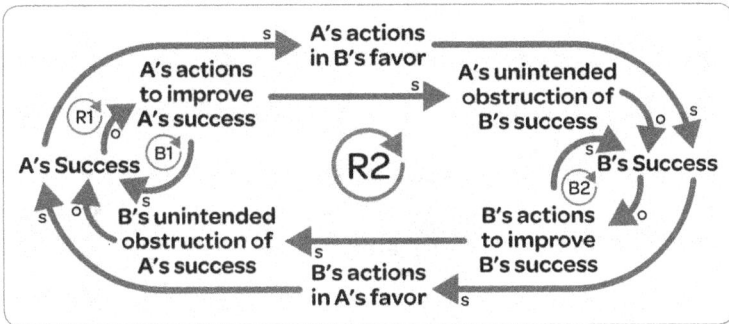

Figure 6.16 Dynamics of the accidental adversary archetype. Legend: s (same direction); o (opposite direction); R (reinforcing loop); B (balancing loop) *Source*: © 2020 Waters Center for Systems Thinking, WatersCenterST.org Adapted from archetype described in *The Fifth Discipline*, Senge (2006), and by Innovation Associates, Inc.

Example: Two neighboring countries show historical tensions and mistrust due to past conflicts and geopolitical rivalries. Despite these challenges, both countries recognize the potential benefits of collaborating on a significant infrastructure project to enhance connectivity, facilitate trade, and spur regional economic growth.

Diplomacy plays a crucial role in initiating and sustaining dialogue between the two countries, overcoming mistrust, and brokering agreements on the terms and conditions of infrastructure projects. Through diplomatic negotiations, assurances regarding resource sharing, investment protection, and dispute resolution mechanisms were made to build confidence and encourage cooperation.

Engineers from both countries collaborate to design and construct infrastructure projects, leveraging their expertise to overcome technical challenges and ensure project feasibility and sustainability. However, misinterpretations, unrealistic expectations, and performance issues may arise during the implementation phase, leading to communication breakdown and erosion of trust between the engineering teams from the two countries.

Inconsistencies in technical specifications and construction standards can lead to disputes and project delays. Unrealistic expectations for cost estimates or project timelines can cause tension between parties, particularly when unforeseen obstacles or delays arise during construction. Additionally, performance issues, such as quality control or safety concerns, can negatively impact the relationship between engineering teams and jeopardize a project's success.

If these mental models that contribute to the breakdown of communication and trust are not challenged and addressed promptly, all parties risk losing the benefits of their collaborative efforts. Infrastructure projects may face prolonged delays, cost overruns, and abandonment, leading to missed opportunities for economic development and regional integration.

All infrastructure project stakeholders must have open and transparent communication, challenge misinterpretations, and collaborate to address performance issues. Creating a culture of trust, accountability, and mutual respect will help engineering, peacebuilding, and diplomacy to achieve sustainable development and peace in the region through collaborative efforts.

Lessons Learned: This archetype calls for special attention to create awareness of how each party's message and behavior influence the other party. One option is to develop collaborative work upfront (Braun, 2002).

6.6.9 Repression and Revolution

The perception of oppressive official policies leads marginalized group members to unite and act defiantly. The corresponding CLD is shown in Fig. 6.17.

Example: Let us consider a country where an authoritarian government maintains power through the suppression of dissent, censorship, and systematic violations of human rights. The population has become increasingly dissatisfied with the regime's repressive policies and lack of political freedom, leading to widespread protests, demonstrations, and calls for democratic reform.

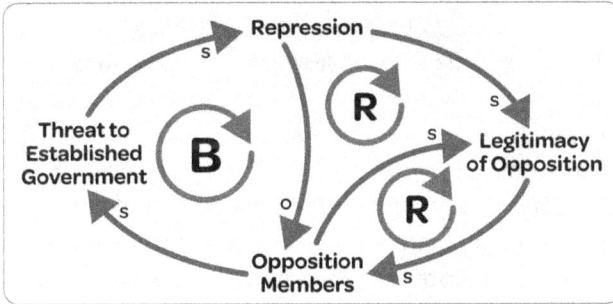

Figure 6.17 Dynamics of the repression and revolution archetype. Legend: s (same direction); o (opposite direction); R (reinforcing loop); B (balancing loop) *Source*: © 2020 Waters Center for Systems Thinking, WatersCenterST.org Adapted from archetype described in *The Fifth Discipline*, Senge (2006), and by Innovation Associates, Inc.

Engineering plays a role on both sides of this dynamic. On the one hand, the repressive regime may use engineering solutions to control and monitor the population, such as surveillance systems, Internet censorship, or the development of riot control technologies. These engineering interventions aim to maintain the regime's grip on power and suppress dissent among the population.

On the other hand, protesters and opposition groups may employ engineering tactics to organize and mobilize their movements, such as social media platforms for communication, encrypted messaging apps for coordination, or techniques for circumventing Internet censorship. Engineering expertise may also be utilized to develop innovative methods for peaceful resistance or nonviolent protests, such as barricades, protective gear, or communication networks.

Peacebuilding efforts may come into play as international actors, civil society organizations, and diplomatic channels seek to mediate conflict and promote dialogue between the repressive regime and opposition groups. Through peacebuilding initiatives, efforts are made to address grievances, encourage reconciliation, and find peaceful resolutions to the underlying issues driving unrest.

Diplomacy also plays a crucial role in this dynamic, with diplomatic pressure exerted on the repressive regime to respect human rights, engage in dialogue with the opposition, and enact democratic reforms. Diplomatic channels may also coordinate international responses to crises, such as sanctions, diplomatic isolation, or support for democratic transition processes.

However, if the repressive regime refuses to heed calls for reform and continues to suppress dissent through violence and repression, the situation may escalate to a full-blown revolution. The engineering solutions employed by both sides may become increasingly sophisticated and militarized, leading to violent conflict with devastating consequences for the country and its people.

Lessons Learned: This archetype calls for mediation and reaching a joint ground agreement. While peacebuilding and diplomacy aim to settle conflicts peacefully, repression and revolution reveal an intricate interplay between political oppression, social unrest, and technological change. Addressing the sources of repression through inclusive governance, respect for human rights, and democratic reforms is crucial.

6.6.10   The Conflict Trap

The reinforcing dynamics of conflict traps have detrimental effects on human security and economic development. However, this cycle can be interrupted by incorporating protection, peacekeeping measures, and humanitarian assistance. Figures 6.18 a and b depict two CLDs: one showing the original conflict trap and one showing how security and aid interventions affect the conflict trap.

Example: A country is torn apart by ethnic or sectarian conflicts, where warring factions vie for control over territory, resources, and political power. This conflict has resulted in widespread violence, displacement, and humanitarian suffering, with civilian populations bearing the brunt of the crisis.

Engineering plays a crucial role in addressing immediate humanitarian needs and restoring the basic infrastructure essential to the well-being of affected populations. For example, engineers may be tasked with repairing damaged roads, bridges, and utilities to facilitate the delivery of humanitarian aid, access to essential services, and the return of displaced communities to their homes.

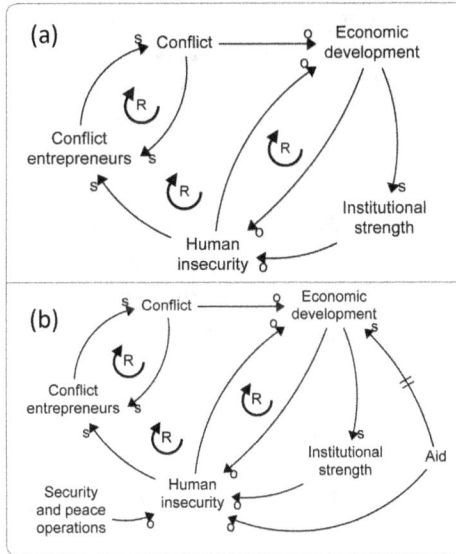

Figure 6.18 Dynamics of the conflict trap archetype. (a) Initial dynamic; (b) After interventions. Legend: s (same direction); o (opposite direction); R (reinforcing loop). Redrawn using the STELLA software. *Source*: Hayden (2018). Reproduced with permission from the author.

Peacebuilding efforts aim to address the underlying causes of conflict and promote reconciliation among warring factions. Through peacebuilding initiatives, efforts have been made to foster dialogue, build trust, and establish mechanisms for conflict resolution and post-conflict reconstruction. Diplomatic channels may mediate negotiations between conflicting parties, broker ceasefires, and facilitate the implementation of peace agreements.

Security and peacekeeping measures have been implemented to protect civilians, enforce ceasefires, create a conducive environment for peacebuilding, and provide humanitarian assistance. International peacekeeping forces should be deployed to monitor compliance with ceasefire agreements, protect vulnerable populations, and prevent further violence.

Humanitarian assistance, including food, shelter, healthcare, and psychosocial support, provides lifesaving support to the most vulnerable populations affected by conflict. Humanitarian organizations work alongside peacekeepers and local authorities to deliver aid impartially and effectively, prioritizing the needs of civilians regardless of their affiliation or background.

Lessons Learned: Implementing security, peacekeeping initiatives, and humanitarian assistance can disrupt the reinforcing cycle of conflict traps, thereby enabling stability, reconciliation, and sustainable development. Enhancing basic infrastructure, bolstering security, and fulfilling humanitarian needs fosters an environment conducive to peacebuilding and recovery, ultimately paving the way for lasting peace and prosperity in conflict-stricken regions.

6.6.11   Multiple Archetypes

Multiple archetypes are likely to play a role in conflict-affected or conflict-sensitive community landscapes. Several archetypes can co-occur, and the dominant archetype(s) may change over time. An illustrative example of this dynamic is the conflict in Hong Kong in 2019, described in detail in Clancy's Dictator's Dilemma Paper (2020). Three archetypes unfolded, with the "success to the successful" and "fixes that fail" being dominant archetypes in 2019, followed by "escalation" in 2020. The conflict ended with the COVID-19 pandemic in March 2020.

The following example encapsulates the combined dynamics of archetypes involving engineering, peacebuilding, and diplomatic efforts. Several countries share a vital river basin for their agricultural, industrial, and domestic needs. This region's trans-boundary water resource management is prone to conflict and environmental degradation. Population growth, climate change, and unsustainable water management practices have increased competition and tensions regarding access to water resources. Several archetypes are at play in this example.

Success to the successful: One country has historically invested heavily in engineering projects to harness water resources for irrigation, hydropower generation, and urban development. As a result, the country has built a strong economy and infrastructure, giving it a competitive advantage over its neighbors in utilizing shared water resources.

Fixes that fail: In response to growing water scarcity and environmental degradation, countries in the region have implemented engineering solutions, such as building dams, reservoirs, and irrigation networks, to increase water supply and improve efficiency. However, these fixes often fail to address the root causes of the problem, exacerbating tensions and downstream impacts on neighboring countries.

Accidental adversaries: Despite shared interests in sustainable water management, the countries in the region become accidental adversaries as they pursue their engineering projects without sufficient coordination or consideration of broader ecological and socioeconomic impacts. Disputes over water allocation, environmental degradation, and compensation for affected communities escalate, leading to mistrust and conflict.

The tragedy of the commons: Overexploitation and mismanagement of shared water resources lead to a tragedy of the commons, where each country prioritizes its short-term interests over the long-term sustainability of the basin. Consequently, water scarcity intensifies, ecosystems degrade, and communities dependent on rivers suffer.

Escalation: Tensions escalate as countries resort to diplomatic brinkmanship, economic coercion, and even military threats to assert their rights and protect their interests in the shared water resources. The risk of conflict looms significantly and threatens regional stability and peace.

Conflict trap: The escalation of tension and competition over water resources traps the region in a cycle of conflict and insecurity, hindering economic development, exacerbating social inequalities, and undermining efforts at peacebuilding and diplomacy.

Drifting and eroding goals: Despite international efforts to negotiate agreements and treaties on transboundary water management, cooperation and sustainable development goals drift as countries prioritize their narrow national interests and short-term gains. Over time, the erosion of trust and collaboration further undermines the prospects of achieving lasting peace and prosperity in the region.

Shifting the burden: Downstream countries bear the brunt of the environmental and socioeconomic impacts of upstream engineering projects, forcing them to implement costly adaptation measures and bear the burden of mitigating the consequences of upstream actions.

Limits to growth: Eventually, the finite nature of water resources and the ecological limits of the river basin becomes apparent, imposing constraints on further economic growth and development. Without a paradigm shift towards sustainable water management practices and genuine cooperation among riparian states, the region faces a bleak future of continued conflict, environmental degradation, and human suffering.

6.7   Concluding Remarks

This chapter emphasized the importance of a systems approach to model the dynamics between the engineering, peacebuilding, and diplomacy sectors in a specific landscape. Modeling depends on how well the landscape is known. System-aware appraisal methods are needed to gather and analyze data and identify landscape issues before modeling. This approach is context- and scale-dependent.

A variety of tools, both qualitative and quantitative, exist to analyze the complexities inherent in conflict-affected and sensitive environments, as well as the interplay among systems within these landscapes. Qualitative approaches include soft systems, whereas hard systems tools like system dynamics offer a quantitative perspective. These methodologies are best viewed as complementary to one another. System dynamics, in particular, is an effective approach for examining complex systems from both qualitative and quantitative perspectives. However, one obstacle in quantitative modeling is gathering data for diverse systems and their interactions. The purpose of these models is to replicate the observed behaviors in relevant landscapes. As discussed in the following chapter, these models are also used to assess the effectiveness of different interventions.

Archetypes help in understanding the relationship between system structure and behavior. Once identified, places of leverage can be selected, and the where and when interventions can be outlined. Multiple archetypes are expected to be present simultaneously or sequentially at the community level in conflict-affected or conflict-sensitive environments. Hence, several places of preferred intervention are possible. Questions remain regarding (i) which archetype and leverage points to address first and (ii) whether different intervention places are synergistic or require trade-offs. The problem becomes even more challenging when archetypes are interconnected.

References

Ahmad, S. and Simonovic, S. P. (2004). Spatial system dynamics: New approach for simulation of water resources systems. *Journal of Computing in Civil Engineering*, **18**(4), 331–340.

Amadei, B. (2014). *Engineering for Sustainable Human Development: A Guide to Successful Small-scale Development Projects*. Reston, VA: ASCE Press.

Amadei, B. (2019). *A Systems Approach to Modeling the Water–Energy–Land–Food Nexus* (Vols. I and II). New York: Momentum Press.

Amadei, B. (2023). *Navigating the Complexity Across the Peace–Sustainability–Climate Security Nexus*. Boca Raton: Routledge. ISBN 9781032563381

Andersen, D. F., Vennix, A. M., Richardson, G. P., and Rouwette, E. A. (1997). Group model building: Problem structuring, policy simulation, and decision support. *Journal of Operational Research Society*, **58**(5), 691–694. https://doi.org/10.1057/palgrave.jors.2602339

Barlas, Y. (1996). Formal aspects of model validity and validation in system dynamics. *System Dynamics Review*, **12**(3), 183–210. https://doi.org/10.1002/(sici)1099-1727(199623)12:3%3c183::aid-sdr103%3e3.0.co;2-4

Batty, M. (2010). Complexity in city systems: Understanding, evolution, and design. Paper 117. UCL Center for Advanced Spatial Analysis, University College, London, UK.

Box, G. E. P. and Draper, N. R. (1987). *Empirical Model-Building and Response Surfaces*. New York: John Wiley.

Bozorg-Haddad, O., Dehghan, P., Zolghadr-Asli, B., et al. (2022). System dynamics modeling of lake water management under climate change. *Scientific Reports*, **12**, 5828. https://doi.org/10.1038/s41598-022-09212-x.

Braun, W. (2002). The system archetypes. University at Albany. http://www.albany.edu/faculty/gpr/PAD724/724WebArticles/sys_archetypes.pdf

Burns, D. (2007). *Systemic Action Research: A Strategy for Whole System Change*. Bristol, U. K.: Policy Press.

CDA Collaborative Learning Projects (2016). *Designing Strategic Initiatives to Impact Conflict Systems: Systems Approaches to Peacebuilding. A Resource Manual.* Cambridge, MA: CDA Collaborative Learning Projects. https://www.cdacollaborative.org/wp-content/uploads/2016/12/Designing-Strategic-Initiatives-to-Impact-Conflict-Systems-Systems-Approaches-to-Peacebuilding-Final.pdf#:~:text=This%20manual%20focuses%20on%20systems%20approaches%20to%20conflict%20analysis%20and

Chambers, R. (2005). *Participatory Workshops: A Sourcebook of 21 Sets of Ideas and Activities*. London, U.K.: Earthscan Publications.

Checkland, P. and Poulter, J. (2006). *Learning for Action: Soft Systems Methodology and Its Use for Practitioners, Teachers, and Students*. New York: John Wiley.

Choucri, N., Electris, C., Goldsmith, D., Mistree, D., et al. (2005). Understanding and modeling state stability: Exploiting system dynamics. *006 IEEE Aerospace Conference*, Big Sky, MT, USA, 2006, pp. 1-11, doi: 10.1109/AERO.2006.1656057.

Clancy, T. (March 30, 2020). The dictator dilemma: Hong Kong case study. The Dictator's Dilemma: Hong Kong Case Study - InfoMullet

Cornwall, A. and Jewkes, R. (1995). What is participatory research? *Social Science and Medicine*, **41**(12), 1667–1676.

Curry, T., Croitoru, A., and Crooks, A. (2023). Modeling forced migration: A system dynamic approach. *Proceedings of the Annual Modeling and Simulation Conference* (ANNSIM 2023), Hamilton, Ontario, Canada, 23–26 May, 2023.

Decisions Sciences Institute (2013). <http://www.decisionsciences.org/ > (August 25, 2016).

Delp, P., Thesen, A., Motiwalla, J., and Seshadri, N. (1977). *Systems Tools for Project Planning*. Washington, DC: International Development Institute.

Department for Communities and Local Government (DCLG) (2009). *Multi-criteria Analysis: A Manual*. Wetherby, U.K.: Communities and Local Government Publications.

Egerer, S., Cotera, R. V., Celliers, L., and Costa, M. M. (2021). A leverage points analysis of a qualitative system dynamics model for climate change adaptation in agriculture, *Agricultural Systems*, **189**, 103052, https://doi.org/10.1016/j.agsy.2021.103052.

Fiddaman, T. (2002). Exploring policy options with a behavioral climate-economy model. *System Dynamics Review*, **18**, 243–267. https://doi.org/10.1002/sdr.241

Greco, S., Ehrgott, M., and Figueira, J. (eds.) (2005). *Multi-criteria Decision Analysis: State-of-the-art Surveys* (Vol. 78). New York: Springer.

Ford, A. (2010). *Modeling the Environment*. Washington, DC: Island Press.

Forrester, J. W. (1971). *World Dynamics*. (Second edition, 1973). Cambridge, MA: Wright-Allen Press.

Forrester, J. W. (1997). System dynamics in the elevator. System Dynamics in the elevator - Ventana software support forum (ventanasystems.co.uk)

Forrester, J. and Senge, P. M. (1980). Tests for building confidence in system dynamics models. In: A. A. Legasto Jnr., J. W. Forrester, and J. M. Lyneis (eds.), *System Dynamics, Studies in the Management Sciences* (Vol. 14). Amsterdam: North-Holland, 209–228.

Franck, R. (ed.) (2002). *The Explanatory Power of Models: Bridging the Gap between Empirical and Theoretical Research in the Social Sciences.* New York: Springer Dordrecht, 1–8.

Ganji, F. and Nasseri, M. (2021). System dynamics approaches to assess the impacts of climate change on surface water quality and quantity: A case study of Karoun River, Iran. *Environnemental Science and Pollution Research*, **28**, 31327–31339. https://doi.org/10.1007/s11356-021-12773-5

Ghosh, A. (2017). *Dynamic Systems for Everyone: Understanding How Our World Works* (2nd edition). Switzerland: Springer Cham.

Hannon, B. and Ruth, M. (2001). *Dynamic Modeling*. New York: Springer.

Hayden, N. K. (2018). Balancing belligerents or feeding the beasts: Transforming conflict traps. University of Maryland Center for International Security Studies. https://api.drum.lib.umd.edu/server/api/core/bitstreams/2e1d6f39-f3ab-4db1-8b5b-0f61d7e38c25/content

Huang, I. B., Keisler, J., and Linkov, I. (2011). Multi-criteria decision analysis in environmental sciences: Ten years of applications and trends. *Science of the Total Environment*, **409**(19), 3578–3594.

Huerta, J. M., Esquivel-Longoria, M. I., and Arellano-Lara, F. (2011). A system dynamics approach to examine climate change impact: The case of the state of Guanajuato, Mexico. In: *Proceedings of the 29th International Conference of the System Dynamics Society.* fj236k096 (albany.edu)

Hovmand, P. S. (2014). *Community-based System Dynamics.* New York: Springer.

Issifu, A. K., Darko, F. D., and Paalo, S. A. (2022). Climate change, migration, and farmer–herder conflict in Ghana. *Conflict Resolution Quarterly,* **39**(4), 421–439. https://doi.org/10.1002/crq.21346

Jones, D. (2015). Conflict resolution: Wars without end. *Nature,* **519**, 148–151. https://doi.org/10.1038/519148a

Keeney, R. L. and Raiffa, H. (1993). *Decisions with Multiple Objectives: Preferences and Value Trade-offs.* New York, NY: Cambridge University Press.

Kim, D. H. (2000). *System Archetypes (I and II).* Waltham, MA: Pegasus Communications.

Kim, D. H. and Anderson, V. (2007). *System Archetype Basics: From Story to Structure.* Waltham, MA: Pegasus Communications.

Lemos, C. M. (2018). *Agent-Based Modeling of Social Conflict: From Mechanism to Complex Behavior.* Switzarland: Springer Cham

Mitleton-Kelly, E. (2003). Chapter 2: Ten principles of complexity and enabling infrastructures. In: *Complex Systems and Evolutionary Perspectives of Organizations: The Application of Complex Theory to Organizations.* London: Elsevier.

Moon, T. H., Chae, Y., Lee, D. S., et al. (2021). Analyzing climate change impacts on health, energy, water resources, and biodiversity sectors for effective climate change policy in South Korea. *Scientific Reports,* **11**, 18512. https://doi.org/10.1038/s41598-021-97108-7

Nathan, H. S. K. and Reddy, B. S. (2011). Criteria selection framework for sustainable development indicators. *Journal of Multi-Criteria Decision Making,* **1**(3), 257–279.

OpenAI (2024). *ChatGPT* (Sept. 5 version) [Large language model]. https://chat.openai.com

Page, S. E. (2018). *The Model Thinker: What You Need to Know to Make Data Work for You.* New York City: Basic Books.

Pedercini, M., Arquitt, S., and Chan, D. (2020). Integrated simulation for the 2030 agenda. *System Dynamics Review,* **36**: 333–357. https://doi.org/10.1002/sdr.1665

Peters, D. H. (2014). The Application of Systems Thinking In Health: Why Use Systems Thinking? *Health Research Policy and Systems*, **12**(51), 166–171. https://doi.org/10.1186/1478-4505-12-51

Redivo, F. (2021, July 19). System dynamics for climate change mitigation. System Dynamics Blog. System Dynamics for Climate Change Mitigation - System Dynamics Society

Richardson, G. P. (1991). *Feedback Thought in Social Science and Systems Theory*. Philadelphia : University of Pennsylvania Press.

Rittel, H. and Webber, M. (1973). Dilemmas in a general theory of planning. *Policy Science*, **4**: 155–169. https://doi.org/10.1007/BF01405730

Sohofi, S. A., Melkonyan, A., Karl, C. K., and Krumme, K. (2016). System archetypes in the conceptualization phase of water-energy-food-nexus modeling. *Proceedings of the 34th International Conference of the System Dynamics Society: Black Swans and Black Lies: System Dynamics in the Context of Randomness and Political Power-play* (Vol. 34), Delft, Netherlands.

Scheyvens, R. and Storey, D. (2003). *Development Fieldwork: A Practical Guide*. Thousand Oaks, CA: Sage.

Seelos, C. (2020). Changing systems? Welcome to the slow movement. *Stanford Social Innovation Review,* Winter.

Senge, P. (2006). *The Fifth Discipline: The Art & Practice of the Learning Organization.* (Revised and Updated edition). New York City: Doubleday.

Senge, P., Kleiner, A., Roberts, C., Ross, R. B., and Smith, B. J. (1994). *The Fifth Discipline Field Book: Strategies and Tools for Building a Learning Organization.* New York City: Doubleday.

Simon, H. A. (1972). Theories of bounded rationality. In: C. B. McGuire and R. Radner (eds.), *Decisions and Organization*. Amsterdam, The Netherlands: North-Holland, 161–176.

Sohofi, S. A., Melkonyan, A., Karl, C. K., and Krumme, K. (2016). System archetypes in the conceptualization phase of water-energy-food-nexus modeling. 34th International Conference of the System Dynamics Society: Black Swans and Black Lies: System Dynamics in the Context of Randomness and Political Power-play, Delft, Netherlands, Volume 34.

Spradley, J. P. (1979). *The Ethnographic Interview*. New York: Holt, Rinehart, and Winston.

Sterman, J. (2000). *Business Dynamics: Systems Thinking And Modeling For A Complex World*. McGraw Hill: Irwin.

Sterman, J. (2002). All models are wrong: Reflections on becoming a systems scientist. *Systems Dynamics Review*, **18**(4), 501–531. http://dx.doi.org/10.1002/sdr.261

Sterman, J., Fiddaman, T., Franck, T., Jones, A., et al. (2012). Climate interactive: The C-ROADS climate policy model. *Systems Dynamic Review,* **28**(3), 295–305. https://doi.org/10.1002/sdr.1474

Stroh, D. P. (2015). *Systems Thinking for Social Change.* Vermont: Chelsea Green Publishing.

Taylor, I. W. and Araujo, P. (2021). Using system dynamics to examine alternative futures for the Syrian refugee crisis. Policy Dynamics Inc., New Hamburg, Ontario. https://proceedings.systemdynamics.org/2021/abstracts/1113.html

Tesfaye, B. (2022). Climate change and conflict in the Sahel. Council on Foreign Relations. https://www.cfr.org/report/climate-change-and-conflict-sahel

Ullah, M. A. (2012). Enhancing the understanding of corruption through system dynamics modeling: A case study analysis of Pakistan. Doctoral dissertation. University of Auckland, New Zealand.

Vennix, J. A. M. (1996). *Group Model Building: Facilitating Team Learning Using System Dynamics.* New York: John Wiley.

Weaver, W. (1948). Science and complexity. *American Scientist*, **36**(4), 536–544. https://www.jstor.org/stable/27826254

Woodrow, C. J. L. (2024, April 26) Factors and Actors: Fundamental Elements of Corruption Analysis.

Chapter 7

A System-Based Peace Methodology

This chapter presents the details of a system-based methodology that can be used by decision-makers involved in addressing complex issues across the engineering-peacebuilding-diplomacy nexus in a conflict-affected or conflict-sensitive environment. Although the method is generic, it provides a road map and guidelines to address the problems of each sector of the nexus and across the nexus while considering how the sectors interact with social, economic, environmental, and infrastructure community systems. The methodology is based on the premise that there is a storyline describing how a conflict-affected or conflict-sensitive community envisions bridging the gap between its current development, security, and peaceful states and their respective desired states. This approach requires meaningful participation and engagement from both internal and external stakeholder groups in community-based projects.

7.1 A Development, Security, and Peace Intervention Storyline

Having decided that a systems approach is better suited to address human development and security and engineering, peacebuilding, and diplomatic efforts in community-based projects, a methodology

Engineering for Peace and Diplomacy
Bernard Amadei
Copyright © 2025 Jenny Stanford Publishing Pte. Ltd.
ISBN 978-981-5129-75-5 (Hardcover), 978-1-003-65168-0 (eBook)
www.jennystanford.com

is necessary to guide decision-makers in (i) mapping, identifying, and ranking problems; (ii) finding forms of leverage (i.e., entry points of intervention); (iii) developing strategies and holistic solutions; (iv) implementing interventions; and (v) proposing coherent governance and policies in the short and long term. The methodology requires several factors to ensure effectiveness, including a thorough comprehension of the community's landscape and the issues that need to be addressed, as well as a definite storyline and mental models and how to bridge the gap between current and desired community development, security, and peace states as discussed in Chapter 6. To that end, one can add (i) a need for proficiency in utilizing multiple modeling tools, (ii) the active participation of various stakeholders and actors, and (iii) the capacity for flexibility and adaptability in the face of change.

The methodology detailed below is an extension of that proposed by Amadei (2019, 2023) to address the interconnections across the water–energy–land–food nexus and the relationships between peace, sustainability, and climate security at the community scale. This method is tailored to the specific context and scale of the community landscape, considering how engineering, peace-building, and diplomacy are connected within it.

7.1.1 Insiders and Outsiders Participation

Many stakeholders are involved in community development, security, and conflict management and are prone to support, prevent, and be affected by progress to reach specific goals. They include all individuals and groups (i.e., critical, primary, and secondary) who can make or influence enabling and constraining decisions. They also include those who may not have a voice but will somehow be impacted (Caldwell, 2002).

In general, stakeholders can be classified into three groups. Community members (insiders) contribute to bottom-up enabling or constraining solutions, while others who are part of governmental organizations (local to national) offer top-down solutions. Outsiders are the third group that contributes to outside-in solutions. Examples of outsiders include civil society organizations, NGOs,

INGOs, donors, commercial sector groups, government agencies, and international organizations. Hence, three degrees of causality must be considered when addressing community development, engineering, peacebuilding, and diplomatic efforts: upward causality from the bottom-up, downward causality from the top-down, and outside-in (or inside-out) causality. These three stakeholder categories contribute positively or negatively to diverse perspectives, trade-offs, knowledge, skills, and attitudes through relational practices. They have opinions about the problems and how to plan potential solutions. The challenge is for all three groups of stakeholders to find common ground.

Ideally, among the three groups of stakeholders, community members as insiders are uniquely positioned to identify and address development and security issues regarding conflict and provide services and goods. They understand their conditions better than the other two groups and are more accountable. Community members are also better positioned to decide on the relevance and effectiveness of interventions, own and implement solutions, operate and maintain solutions, and choose how and when to scale up if necessary. Likewise, governmental institutions can play different top-down roles, such as enablers, service providers, or regulators/controllers (GWP, 2000). They may scale up solutions, provide support, develop standards, etc. Finally, outsiders can facilitate and support outside-in roles (e.g., financial, technical, and policy).

The stability and success of community development and conflict management are contingent on the simultaneous strengths of all three stakeholder groups. If some stakeholders are weak, community development, peacebuilding, and diplomatic efforts are unlikely to succeed. The effectiveness of the interactions between the various stakeholder groups depends on several participatory factors, including (i) their willingness to engage in dialogue and decision-making, (ii) their capacity to make substantial contributions, and (iii) their availability for dialogue and decision-making toward a shared vision of what do and not to do.

The interactions among the three stakeholder groups can be intricate in community development, peacebuilding, and diplomatic undertakings, from data collection and analysis to the execution of solutions. To prevent confusion among the three groups, each must undertake self-assessment and acknowledge its biases. For insiders, self-assessment may involve particular interests, favoritism, and power struggles. For outsiders, Chambers (1983) categorizes biases into six distinct types: spatial, project, person, season, diplomacy, and professional. Another form of bias arises from the makeup of the outsider team, which aligns with the community. Team members must be selected based on their sensitivity to culture, technical expertise, experience in community appraisals, personal attributes, and the unique skills they bring to the group. They must include an appropriate balance between men and women. The team must demonstrate various levels of expertise and interest to match the project. The team may consist of representatives of multiple organizations, such as NGOs or INGOs, governmental organizations (GOs), and community-based organizations (CBOs). In their *Tools for Development Handbook*, the Department for International Development (DFID, 2003) in the U.K. emphasizes the importance of teamwork in development projects and provides extensive recommendations for creating effective teams, including strategies for team development and management, team player empowerment and training, and leadership in team dynamics.

Outsiders' biases may result in discrepancies between what they believe they see and interpret within a community and the actual reality of the community. This disparity extends to intervention ownership and the inclusion of community members. This gap can significantly affect intervention planning and design, leading to inappropriate projects and unexpected costs. Generally, interventions from outsiders tend to be less effective because they often come up with predetermined solutions. It is essential to recognize that these challenges and biases affect how outsiders perceive a community during the assessment phase and how they interpret the success of an intervention during its monitoring and evaluation phase, close a project, and decide whether to scale up the project. Although insiders and outsiders must collaborate, solutions to community security, development, and peace are rarely neutral and may differ, sometimes creating more conflicts.

The three groups of stakeholders discussed earlier can be expanded to include another category that reflects the particular situation of displaced and migrating populations (e.g., refugees and IDPs) who interact with an existing community. Integration puts pressure on both the displaced population and the host community, and harmony between the two groups is required for lasting community development, conflict prevention, resilience to adverse events, and climate security (Moore, 2014; Mowjee et al., 2015; OECD, 2017).

7.1.2   Understanding the Storyline

The proposed methodology requires a community storyline with a narrative and script outlined by the three stakeholder categories. The storyline must incorporate how engineering, peacebuilding, and diplomacy interact with the community systems (Fig. 6.1). It has "a beginning, a middle, and an end" (Ratner, 2023). It also acknowledges that different stakeholders may have different opinions based on different perceptions. Hjorth and Bagheri (2006) summarized that a story represents a powerful way to engage people (e.g., stakeholders) in doing something once they realize that they are part of the story and can control their future.

The story is based on a shared vision that clearly outlines the current conflict-affected or conflict-sensitive community development and security landscape (context, scale, and boundaries) and what systemic changes to the community are desired, starting with the current level of development, capacity, and conflict or peace (i.e., its baseline). The current and desired levels represent two narratives, each with its specific mental models, structural dynamics, patterns of behavior and trends, and manifesting events.

The motivational factors that keep the community moving from where it is now to where it wants to be regarding community development, security, and peace can be understood as what Senge (2006) calls "creative tension." Thus, interventions in human development, security, engineering, peace, and diplomatic efforts can be construed as pulling the reality of the current level toward a desirable one over time. For this emerging transformation to occur, all stakeholders need to partner and collaborate in defining the current and desirable levels of community development, "hold steady to the [shared] vision' (Senge, 2006), develop strategies, formulate interventions, and assess progress through monitoring and evaluation. This approach must be applied at all levels of the iceberg model of Fig. 4.2 (i.e., in mental models, structural and behavioral patterns, and events). Without these tasks, little change will occur, and most interventions will be short-lived.

Specifically, the community storyline can be narrated (and scripted) as follows:

- A community in a specific landscape (context, scale, and boundary) is currently at a certain capacity level, stage of development, resilience, and in a state of peace or conflict. This level is not advanced in some cases, such as in disadvantaged communities and conflict-prone landscapes. It operates based on specific mental models and mindsets (habits, belief systems, etc.). The human, infrastructure, environmental, and economic systems in Fig. 6.1 are at play; policies and regulations provide services (e.g., energy, water, food, and transportation), and livelihoods and constraints are active. The community's overall well-being, livelihood, health, peace, prosperity, environmental sustainability, and resilience emerge from the interactions between these systems and their respective structures. The community experiences limited development, security, resilience, and peace in its current reality.

- Out of its desire or as suggested by other stakeholders, such as governmental institutions and outsiders, the community is interested in progressing and transitioning to more development, security, resilience, and peace over time, which can be interpreted as a desired or aspirational level. In some instances, the community aims to reach a higher level of sustainability and peace in the short and long term. In cases dealing with stabilization and reconstruction (USIP/NAE, 2009), the aim is to achieve stable governance, social well-being, the rule of law, and a safe and secure environment.

A new mindset is needed, new mental models must be endorsed, a new community structure must be reconsidered, new behavioral patterns must be accepted, and systemic change must be embraced. As a community undergoes development, security enhancement, resilience building, and peace promotion through capacity building, engineering interventions, peacebuilding initiatives, and diplomatic efforts, it may encounter both anticipated and unexpected outcomes. Changes can occur at different levels, from transformational to incremental (Kehrer et al., 2020). There is also the possibility that the changes are limited or that nothing happens.

- Advisors and facilitators have been called to work in a participatory manner with the community and governmental organizations to establish a methodology that can (i) assess and analyze current development, security, conflict issues, the vulnerability of the community to adverse events, and unstainable forms of community livelihood and security; (ii) address these issues; and (iii) propose an integrated plan of action (strategy and operations) as the community moves from one level of development, security, and peace to the next. Owing to stakeholder dynamics, the community benefits from its new level of development, security, and peacefulness, and the government is now engaged and plays an active role in supporting and scaling projects and developing policies to ensure peace, sustainability, and security at the local, regional, and national scales and over time.

In general, the dynamics of community development systemic change mentioned above in the storyline depend on the state of development, capacity level, and peacefulness the community is starting with. The higher the baseline, the faster the transition rate, and the more resilient the community reacts to change over time. This dynamic is illustrated, for instance, in Fig. 3.4, showing how the initial community peace level and peacebuilding and peacemaking efforts rate affect the recovery of the community peace level following a crisis. The same diagram can be used to show the dynamics of how community capacity and resilience change following a crisis (Amadei, 2020) as discussed in Section 8.4.

It is important to note that community stories have unique characteristics. They are not always straightforward and linear; they are systemic and consist of many plots with twists, turns, and feedback mechanisms. Parts of these stories can be simple, complicated, or complex, and sometimes create confusion because of their uncertainties. Consequently, stories may require those who hear, read, or experience them to be flexible, adaptive, imaginative, and willing to change their beliefs and perceptions. Diplomacy plays a crucial role in these efforts.

Another characteristic of stories is that they do not always end well or as expected. For instance, some approaches to community-based projects can backfire with unintended consequences when stories are imposed on populations or when these populations are coerced into adopting others' stories. Problems also arise when community stakeholders or different stakeholder groups do not share the same narrative, are in conflict, and cannot reach a compromise or consensus in addressing joint issues and selecting appropriate interventions. Some of these dynamics are outlined in the system archetype examples in Chapter 6.

7.2 Methodology Stages

The following section presents a comprehensive system-aware methodology to assist decision-makers and practitioners in envisioning scenarios for community development interventions involving engineering, peacebuilding, and diplomatic efforts at the community level. This approach is grounded in the notion that systems thinking and the systems tools discussed in Chapters 5 and 6 must be integrated into all the methodology stages. The value of incorporating a systems approach into the different steps of community development intervention management helps decision-makers make more intelligent decisions when selecting various intervention scenarios than purely subjective ones or decisions focusing on specific community issues. The road map of the methodology consists of 10 stages, as shown in Fig. 7.1. These are described in more detail below.

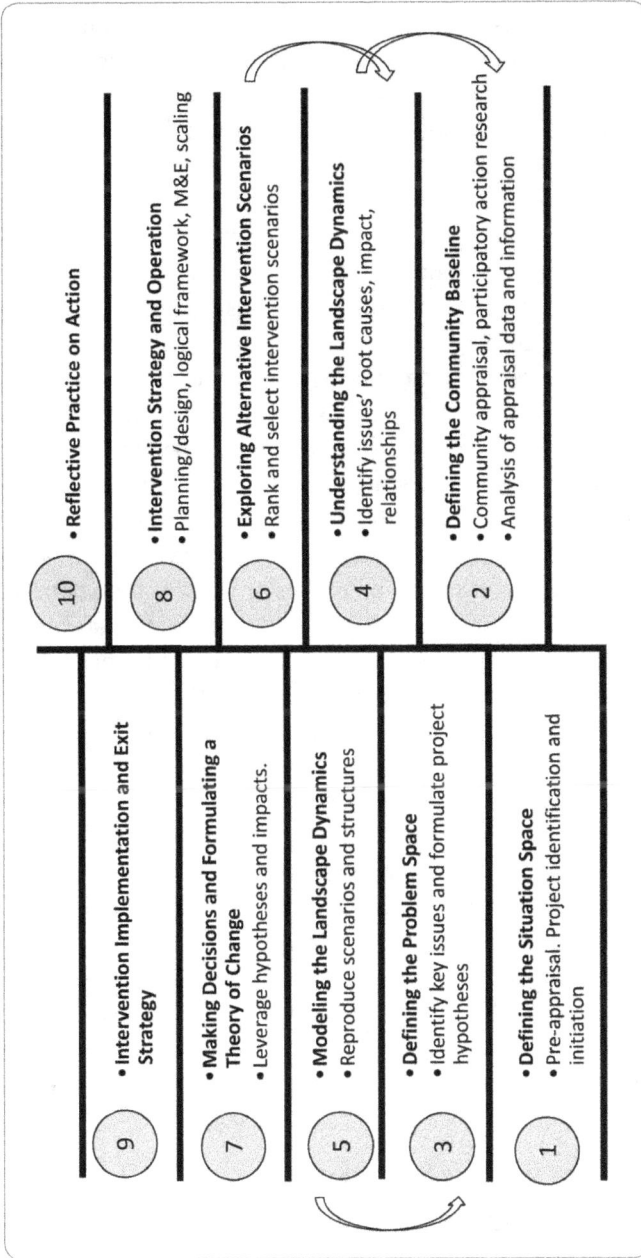

Figure 7.1 Ten stages of the systems-aware methodology for peace and diplomacy intervention.

Stage 1: Defining the Situation Space

This preliminary stage involves understanding the context, scale, boundaries, and overall landscape/setting in which engineering, peacebuilding, diplomacy, and community development unfold. Describing the situation space can be seen as conducting a systems-aware *pre-appraisal* or *pre-feasibility* of the community landscape and deciding whether to proceed to the next stage, thus defining a community baseline. It includes gathering preliminary information about community livelihood, resource management, resource allocation, critical issues, conflict, etc. It also determines whether the community landscape is experiencing or has been dealing with past challenges, such as conflicts, whether adverse events have affected the community, and for how long. Where is the community on the peacebuilding, peacemaking, and peacekeeping spectrum?

Pre-appraisal represents an opportunity for decision-makers to obtain global insights into the community's current reality (the mindset, structure, and behavior patterns in the iceberg model of Fig. 4.2) and frame questions (e.g., why the community is the way it is and what accounts for its current state). It also involves developing relationships with its constituents, creating a shared understanding, inviting participation, building trust and relationships, and identifying a core group representing the community. This information helps dictate the type of appraisal to be carried out, the areas to focus on, and the resources (material and human) necessary to carry out the assessment. An appraisal team with appropriate qualifications, skills, and diversity is selected to best match the situation space. Another aspect of this stage is for outsiders to decide on their capacity to pursue any intervention alone or in partnership with other organizations. According to Schirch (2013), assessing a community's capacity for peacebuilding is essential, including existing financial and skill resources and potential obstacles that community members may face.

Stage 2: Defining the Community Baseline

As discussed in Section 6.1, system mapping and visualization tools are essential for creating a community baseline profile. Systemic action research methods with an inductive system-aware process help acquire information about the current structure of the community landscape, including the human, natural, infrastructure, and economic systems at play in the community and their interactions (see Table B.1 in Appendix B). Population, education, economic/financial, environmental, political, cultural, and infrastructure profiles are laid out. System mapping also identifies a community's mental models, behavior, and structural patterns.

Additional data are also collected regarding the capacity of the community to reach development and security goals and peace-fulness and provide services, its vulnerability, its capacity and resilience to adverse events, its current levels of peace and security, any conflict history, whether the conflict is part of a more significant conflict, population movements, conflict events, past and current diplomatic efforts, environmental indicators, and policy interventions. Is the community dealing with a latent, surface, or open conflict (Fisher et al., 2000)?

Stakeholder/actor, partner, gender, capacity, risk, conflict, SWOT, and leverage analyses are carried out (see Table B.2 in Appendix B). Historical landscape analysis (including how the community coped with and adapted to past stressors, constraints, risks, conflicts, and drivers) is also needed to predict the community's response to future threats and how those risks could affect its security and well-being.

Stage 3: Defining the Problem Space

At the end of the appraisal, a *baseline profile* of the community landscape is established, and issues are outlined and ranked using multi-criteria or multi-attribute analysis tools, as discussed in Chapter 6. Community issues are defined here as gaps between current and desired states. Their *dynamic hypotheses* are systemically outlined and categorized. Possible explanations are suggested to describe how these issues unfold (i.e., possible explanations that relate mental models to structure and behavior) and are interconnected. Preliminary conceptual mental models are proposed to explain the community development, security, the peacefulness state, its deep structure (The Omidyar group, 2017), and how engineering, peacebuilding, and diplomacy operate in the community landscape.

Stage 4: Understanding the Landscape Dynamics

The soft system modeling tools mentioned in Table 6.2 (i.e., concept maps, problem and solution tree causal analysis, cross-impact analysis, and network analysis) are used to further analyze the issues identified in the problem space and, more specifically, their root causes, impact and dependence, and relationships. Possible archetypes are identified. An outcome of understanding the landscape dynamics is the determination of objectives and goals to address the issues and strategic development themes.

Stage 5: Modeling the Landscape Dynamics

The qualitative and quantitative system simulation modeling tools listed in Table 6.2 are used to reproduce, as accurately as possible, (i) the current (or past) scenario(s) at play across the community landscape and the nexus, (ii) the deep structures that may explain the current issues, behavior patterns, and trends observed at the community level, and (iii) the dynamic hypotheses formulated in stage 3 above. This so-called behavioral reproduction process is *inductive*. Once established, it creates a *baseline scenario*, which is the foundation of dynamic scenario planning, as discussed in the next section. It helps, in a *deductive* manner, to formulate, model, select, plan, and implement possible interventions to address the issues.

Owing to uncertainty and unpredictable behavior, the behavior reproduction process inherent to modeling must be reflective, iterative, incremental, and involve multiple feedbacks. This learning process also requires incorporating the input of individuals and multidisciplinary opinions from different groups of community stakeholders. It is also vital that all participants involved in developing the baseline scenario and proposing intervention scenarios are at least knowledgeable of the systems thinking skills and habits.

Stage 6: Exploring Alternative Intervention Scenarios

Possible places of leverage to intervene in the community landscape are formulated and conceptualized. Several alternative engineering, peacebuilding, diplomatic efforts, and dynamic pathway scenarios that could best address the issues faced by the community over the short and long term are outlined. This process is performed using a deductive and formative approach with criteria such as intervention relevance, feasibility (economic, time, skills, and experience), and sustainability (long-term performance) (Grassroots Collective, n.d.). System-oriented methods, such as system dynamics, focus on what can be done. They are used to (i) model and simulate alternative interventions; (ii) assess whether and to what extent engineering, peacebuilding, and diplomacy issues are addressed; and (iii) explore the possible impacts and unintended consequences of interventions.

Methods for dealing with, settling, or altering conflicts depend on the conflict stage, whether latent, emerging, or open. Fisher et al. (2000) suggest that these methods range from conflict prevention to settlement, management, resolution, and transformation, each progressively tackling increasing violence.

Stage 7: Making Decisions and Formulating a Theory Of Change.

Multiple criteria decision analysis methods help select satisfactory engineering, peacebuilding, and diplomatic strategies by evaluating and ranking whether interventions meet specific goals and objectives. Leverage opportunities, hypotheses, and impacts are outlined for each selected intervention strategy. A theory of change discussed further in the next section is formulated using a cause-and-effect statement for each intervention strategy to visualize the steps for long-term changes. If x [preconditional activity], then y [expected change and outcome] because z [rationale]. For instance, if [who does what, how, where, when, and why], then... over time, a combination of engineering, peacebuilding, and diplomatic efforts reduces the gaps between current and desired community livelihood and conflict, because... without such efforts, civil war and mass migration would occur. Building blocks for engineering, peacebuilding, and diplomatic interventions are outlined, along with possible themes cutting across the three sectors.

Stage 8: Intervention Strategy and Operation.

A logistical and tactical plan is developed collaboratively to implement stepwise the most satisfactorily and appropriately community development, security and engineering, peacebuilding, and diplomatic interventions. Context and scale are likely to determine the most appropriate interventions. In conflict management, they may range over a broad spectrum from avoidance/withdrawal, debate/negotiation, dialogue/direct communication, facilitated dialogue, mediation, arbitration, adjudication, coercion, and non-violent action (Fisher et al., 2020). In all cases, a strategic plan must include indicators of progress and impact, performance metrics, and verification methods to (i) monitor and evaluate the progress and effectiveness of the proposed interventions, including potential risks, and (ii) decide whether the proposed interventions can be scaled up and what strategies, policies, and diplomatic efforts must be outlined to ensure their long-term performance and benefits.

A systems-aware logical framework approach (Amadei, 2015) is needed here as a strategic executive summary and road map, where (i) intervention inputs, activities, outputs (objectives), goals (effects, purpose), and impact (outcome and aim) are clearly outlined in a systemic and logical (horizontal and vertical) manner, and (ii) assumptions (sources of risks) and modes of verification are defined. A successful strategy requires different stakeholder categories to align around a common purpose, although they may share different agendas (Stroh, 2015).

The intervention strategy depends significantly on how decision-makers prioritize goals over relationships or consider both. Fisher et al. (2000) consider five conflict management styles in reviewing strategies to resolve conflict.

- *Avoiding*: Low concern for relationships or goals. The strategy is to avoid, ignore, withdraw, delay, or deny.
- *Accomodating*: Low concern for goals. The strategy is to appease, agree, give in, and ignore disagreements.
- *Controlling*: Low concern for relationships. The strategy is to control, compete, force, coerce, and fight.
- *Problem-solving*: High concern for relationships or goals. The strategy includes dialogue, looking for alternatives, and gathering information.
- *Compromising*: Middle concern for relationships and goals. The strategy is to reduce expectations, bargain, tradeoffs, and give and take.

Stage 9: Intervention Implementation and Exit Strategy.

The chosen strategy dictates the nuts and bolts of the intervention. It regulates the logistical and tactical adjustments during the implementation of the interventions, which can also lead to shifts in operational decisions. This feedback mechanism extends beyond intervention closure.

At this stage, decision-makers must have sufficient understanding to (i) predict the interventions' short-, medium-, and long-term performance; (ii) suggest alternatives if conditions change or the situation does not perform as planned; and (iii) foresee any future interventions if the needs arise. An exit strategy is then outlined. In recovery efforts following violent conflicts, these initiatives cut across multiple constituencies, such as military/security, political/constitutional, economic/social, psycho-social, and international (Fisher et al., 2000).

Stage 10: Reflective Practice on Action.

All practitioners must reflect on the interventions once completed. The *reflection-on-action* or debriefing process is a good practice that follows the implementation of interventions. It represents a valuable learning exercise for identifying what has worked or has not worked in a project. This process helps incorporate changes into future interventions and explores areas of potential improvement. Reflective practice is also valuable for practitioners, as it promotes self-learning, enhanced skills and knowledge, increased confidence and understanding, self-motivation, and professionalism. Reflective practice may also provide insights into the applicability of system tools and possible changes for future interventions.

Remarks

The sustainability of community interventions (i.e., their long-term performance) must be ensured once the interventions end (post-evaluation). Collaborative efforts must be agreed upon so that the interventions continue to deliver benefits to the target community, which requires measures and processes to be in place, problems to arise, and decisions to be made (e.g., *reflection-post-action*). Interventions should also be evaluated for replicability and scaling up (i.e., expanding the scope and implementation toward a more significant impact within the community or other communities). Scalability in complex and uncertain settings is challenging. Like many forms of behavior in systems, it emerges when the right conditions are in place and a "tipping point" has been reached. All parties involved in developing interventions can contribute to making the environment fertile for the tipping point to sprout and grow.

It is noteworthy that the 10 stages in Fig. 7.1 are not independent and form a *road map* from collecting data about the community landscape and current engineering, peacebuilding, and diplomatic efforts to develop an action plan to address issues raised by analyzing the data. Furthermore, feedback mechanisms are at play between the 10 stages, as decisions made in any given stage may require a reciprocal assessment of those in previous stages, as shown by the arrows in Fig. 7.1. Unlike linear causality, reciprocal causality provides a way to re-examine assumptions and acquire more information if necessary. It should be noted that system modeling stage 5 in Fig. 7.1 represents a critical transition between understanding the community landscape and its issues and developing a support system necessary to select development, security, engineering, peacebuilding, and diplomatic interventions at the community level. The following section discusses further stages 5, 6, and 7 of the above methodology.

7.3 Dynamic Scenario Planning and Selection

7.3.1 What Is Dynamic Scenario Planning?

The goal of Stage 5 in Fig. 7.1., that is, modeling the landscape dynamics of Fig. 6.1, is to reproduce in a satisfactory (satisficing) manner and as accurately as possible (i) the current scenario(s) at play across the community landscape and how engineering, peacebuilding, and diplomacy efforts unfold in that landscape; (ii) the deep structures that may explain the issues, behavior patterns, and trends observed at the community level; and (iii) the dynamic hypotheses formulated at the end of the appraisal phase discussed in Chapter 6. The baseline scenarios identified in Stage 5 in Fig. 7.1 are critical in dynamic scenario planning and help, in a *deductive* manner, formulate, model, select, plan, and implement possible interventions to address the issues.

Scenario planning is a tool used in the field of Futures Research (Glenn and Gordon, 2009) to explore, create, and test possible and desirable future pathways for decision-making. It does not predict the future but describes possibilities or projections in complex settings. In the context of the community landscape in Fig. 6.1, scenarios can help decision-makers (i) envision alternative hypothetical futures and changes; (ii) explore pathways for transitioning from the current state to desired community development and security levels; (iii) assess the implications of engineering, peacebuilding, and diplomatic actions and policy decisions in an uncertain environment; (iv) create new decisions or reframe existing ones; (v) establish benchmarks and targets for monitoring change; and (vi) identify critical assumptions and preconditions.

Scenario planning can follow forward or backward pathways (Robinson, 1982). One forward pathway, *forecasting*, extrapolates past and current trends to predict short-term futures. A backward pathway, *or backcasting, begins* with the desired outcome and considers plausible futures from that state to the present. It focuses on desirability, feasibility, and other criteria.

Compared with forecasting, *backcasting* starts with the end or outcome in mind (e.g., alternative desired development levels and security). It considers a series of possible/plausible futures from the desired state(s) to the current state, not just in terms of likelihood but preferably in terms of desirability (e.g., socio-economic, environmental), feasibility (i.e., based on capacity), and other criteria, such as security, prosperity, health, and well-being (Robinson, 2003). Dreborg (1996) noted that backcasting addresses complex societal problems involving multiple systems for which uncertainty is present, change is a constant, and the "time horizon is long enough to allow considerable scope for deliberate choice."

A strong value proposition of backcasting is testing complex systems and observing their possible responses and robustness to different situations, with some being more probable than others and some more constraining than others. In return, this helps identify the appropriateness of current policies to address such situations and what it would take to develop in an uncertain environment and assess (monitor and evaluate) new future policies. Hence, backcasting represents a powerful approach for exploring engineering, peacebuilding, and diplomatic interventions at the community level in the medium- to long-term (i.e., 20–50 years or more) future. Forecasting can still be incorporated into an overall backcasting approach to scenario planning when attempting to predict an evident trend or developing a blueprint to address a specific issue in the short term (up to 10 or 20 years).

Dynamic scenario planning combines the normative aspects of scenario analysis, focusing on what is *desirable*, and system dynamics, concentrating on what is *possible* (Ward and Schriefer, 1998). It is used by corporate entities and government agencies for strategic planning and exploring likely futures in various complex and uncertain situations at different scales. Several examples of the application of scenario planning can be found in the texts by Georgantzas and Acar (1995), Fayeh and Randall (1998), and Ritchie-Dunham and Rabbino (2001).

It is important to remember that, whether using forecasting or backcasting, scenario planning does not predict the future, but helps decision-makers prepare for various possibilities. It is a valuable tool for navigating uncertainty and shaping better outcomes.

7.3.2 Formulating Dynamic Intervention Scenarios

Stage 6 in Fig. 7.1 is about formulating and conceptualizing alternative engineering, peacebuilding, and diplomatic efforts and pathway dynamic scenarios that could best address the issues faced by the community over the short and long term. It must be remembered that (i) there is no optimal way to deal with complex situations, such as the community landscape shown in Fig. 6.1, and (ii) multiple intervention scenarios can suit different contexts and physical and temporal scales. However, scenario formulation is not merely a guesswork or an intuitive process. A survey of the literature (Amadei, 2019, 2023) indicates that adequate intervention scenarios should have the following characteristics:

- Be clear about the vision, outcome, and desirable future community state(s). The predictive impact of possible interventions and pathways must be compatible with reducing the gap between current and desired community conditions. This vision must be formulated as part of a theory of change (discussed below) narrated in terms of the future development and security of the community and the role played by engineering, peacebuilding, and diplomatic efforts in forging the future.

- Clearly define the present community baseline conditions and dynamics, including (i) the gaps between existing and desired livelihood conditions, capacity, and vulnerability; (ii) the gaps between current and existing engineering, peacebuilding, and diplomatic efforts; and (iii) possible exogenous relevant factors (e.g., socioeconomic or political surprises or crises) that are currently affecting the landscape or could affect it in the future.

- Lay out a foundational narrative and storyline built on solid mental models, considering that mental models affect structure and behavioral patterns (see Fig. 4.2). Table 7.1 shows some components that can be combined to create the scenario narratives.

- Suggest three to four credible alternative scenarios with solid narratives, mental models, documentation, and dynamic hypotheses clearly articulated to account for uncertainty.

- Outline a logical strategic framework or logframe for all alternative credible intervention scenarios' impacts/ outcomes, goals, objectives/outputs, activities, and inputs. Meeting goals and objectives contributes to the desired end state and reinforces the vision and theory of change discussed in the first guideline proposed above.

- Synchronize multiple interventions, including inputs/ activities/output/goals/impact among all interventions at different physical scales (local, regional, global) and time scales (short-, medium-, and long-term). Synchronization requires considering trade-offs and synergies across sectors.

Table 7.1 Possible storyline components in scenario planning (OpenAI, 2024)

Areas of Interest	Possible Narrative Components
Physical and human geography-related	– Changes in demographics, diet, fertility, migration, education, group dynamics, marginalization – Occurrence of natural and non-natural hazards and effects on population dynamics – Changes in institutional capacity (governance, the rule of law, etc.) – Desired changes in health, labor, income, and distribution – Gender equality – Justice, equity, diversity, and inclusion (JEDI) issues – Current and target education (traditional and technical) by gender – Desired employment level by sector (agriculture, construction, tourism, etc.), jobs vs. labor – Occurrence of extreme weather events – Annual precipitation (frequency and intensity) and temperature trends – Patterns of climate change and its effect on population and migration – Environmental changes and land degradation – Drying up of rivers – Amounts of grass and pastures – Farmer food crops
Peace, conflict, and diplomacy-related	– Current vs. desired positive peace domains: well-functioning government, sound business environment, equitable distribution of resources, acceptance of the rights of others, good relations with neighbors, free flow of information, high levels of human capital, and low levels of corruption. – Current vs. desired negative peace domains: ongoing domestic and international conflict, societal safety and security, and militarization. – Current vs. desired cultural peace – Transitioning from conflict to peace through peacebuilding, peacemaking, and peacekeeping – Addressing conflicts between different resources and service users. – Conflict management work, peace education/training, supporting marginalized groups, justice and rights work, and cultural traditions work. – Addressing recurring conflict issues and root causes – Past and current diplomatic efforts to resolve disputes – Strengthening diplomatic relations for sustainable peace

Areas of Interest	Possible Narrative Components
Community livelihood and resilience-related	– Current vs. desired infrastructure systems – Community resources consumption – Current vs. desired management of resources and services – Current vs. desired levels of community capacity – Effect of mismanagement of resources, aging infrastructure, overexploitation of resources – Effect of behavior change on livelihood demands – Pollution and toxic contamination – Current vs. desired capacity and effect of capacity level on community livelihood and development – Effect of resources supply, prices, and regulations on peace/conflict – Impact of future community growth on resource security – Current vs. desired consumption – Existing vs. desired governance and rule of law
Climate Security-Related	– Effect of climate change on livelihood resources (e.g., water, land, food, and energy supply) and community services (e.g., transportation, telecom, health, etc.) – Effect of climate change on environment and ecosystems – Current vs. desired levels of climate change awareness, adaptation, and mitigation practices at different scales – Current vs. desired community resilience to climate change and other natural and non-natural hazards – Nature and effectiveness of climate actions (adaptation and mitigation) – Resilience to single and multiple adverse events – Response to past events and addressing vulnerabilities
Others	– Current vs. desired dynamic interactions between peacebuilding, engineering, and diplomatic efforts. – Managing trade-offs and synergies between community systems – Archetypes and leverage points of intervention – Providing more efficient and resilient resource delivery – Effect of future population growth community dynamics. – Impact of providing more efficient livelihood infrastructure – Education and empowerment of stakeholders – Capacity building across sectors – Environmental damage due to conflict and recovery – The cumulative effect of climate change and conflicts over time. – Causal chains (i.e., pathways) between peacebuilding, engineering, and diplomacy (i.e., how one or two sectors may trigger the others) and how diverse development and security areas may start a state of peace vs. conflict, sustainability vs. unsustainability, and climate security vs. vulnerability

These six guidelines generally do not guarantee optimum or promising interventions. They are necessary but insufficient to eliminate, at least in part, the randomness of a purely intuitive or empirical decision-making approach (e.g., based on experience). Nevertheless, they provide a much-needed structure for formulating possible pathways involving engineering, peacebuilding, and diplomatic interventions.

7.3.3 Evaluating and Selecting Intervention Scenarios

Regardless of the solid and comprehensive scenario narratives, the next question is which intervention scenario(s) should be selected and which pathways should be used to reduce the gaps between current and desired community development and security. Some credible engineering, peacebuilding, and diplomatic intervention scenarios identified and formulated are likely to be better suited than others to address the gaps. Therefore, a decision-support system based on a multiobjective evaluation and selection process is needed to identify the most desirable scenarios and consider them in further detail to move toward possible implementation. The process can be based strictly on decision-makers' intuition, judgment, and experience (not considered here) or involve a combination of subjective decision-making tools supported by analytical and numerical methods. The decision science literature (Decision Sciences Institute, 2013) and Futures Research literature (Glenn and Gordon, 2009) have proposed multiple techniques and tools of decision-making that are worth considering in the evaluation and selection of intervention scenarios.

Regardless of the tools used to evaluate and select intervention scenarios, it is essential to realize that it is impossible to know with certainty (i.e., optimally and most desirably) that an intervention is "best" compared to the others since all are likely to have some benefits and restrictions and require some forms of compromise. As noted by Simon (1978), "omniscient rationality" is not possible in a realistic world (such as the landscape of Fig. 6.1) that is characterized by uncertainty, complexity, nonlinearities, and feedback mechanisms. Hence, only *satisficing* (i.e., good enough) interventions can be outlined, not the optimum ones.

Because the dynamics of conflict-affected or sensitive communities are complex and uncertain, it is suggested that different narratives be created for various types of intervention. One way to rank the interventions is to use the multi-criteria decision analysis (MCDA) mentioned in Chapter 6 to retrospectively rank issues identified at the end of the community appraisal. The same method can be used *prospectively* to rank intervention scenarios with clear goals. The challenge is to choose criteria specific to engineering, peacebuilding, and diplomacy, and those that cut across all three sectors. Once the criteria are selected, an MCDA performance matrix is created. Subjective scores and weights (values of importance) are assigned for different scenarios, final ratings are calculated as the sums of the scores times weights, and sensitivity analyses are carried out to see how the ratings vary.

The ranking can depend on several factors, such as (i) how much and how good the core and sector-specific data are about the existing engineering, peacebuilding, and diplomatic efforts and the systems of the community landscape, (ii) how much some sectors and systems matter more than others, (iii) how strong the community stakeholder dynamics are, (iv) how well the community can provide specific services in the short and long term, and (v) how resilient the community is to crises and adverse events of different levels.

A fictitious example is shown in Table 7.2, where three individual alternative intervention scenarios of different engineering, peacebuilding, and diplomatic efforts and three combined alternative scenarios are considered. The weights vary from 1 to 5, with scores from 1 to 3. In this example, the 'Combined Scenario 3' option provides the highest weighted score and may want to be considered first. However, the other options may still be considered if the 'Combined Scenario 3' option is of limited use upon extra investigation.

Table 7.2 Fictitious example of an MCDA performance matrix for a community project

Criteria	Weight	Scenario 1 Score	Scenario 1 Score x Weight	Scenario 2 Score	Scenario 2 Score x Weight	Scenario 3 Score	Scenario 3 Score x Weight	Combined Scenarios 1 Score	Combined Scenarios 1 Score x Weight	Combined Scenarios 2 Score	Combined Scenarios 2 Score x Weight	Combined Scenarios 3 Score	Combined Scenarios 3 Score x Weight
Cost-effectiveness	3	2	6	1	3	1	3	2	6	2	6	3	9
Social Acceptability	5	3	15	1	5	2	10	2	10	2	10	3	15
Technical Feasibility	4	2	8	1	4	2	8	2	8	1	4	2	8
Conflict transformation effectiveness	5	1	5	3	15	2	10	3	15	3	15	2	10
Community Participation	4	3	12	2	8	2	8	3	12	2	8	3	12
Health Impact	4	2	8	2	8	1	4	2	8	1	4	2	8
Economic Impact	3	3	9	2	6	1	3	2	6	2	6	3	9
Number of People Impacted	4	2	8	2	8	2	8	2	8	3	12	3	12
Ratings			71		57		54		73		65		83

The MCDA represents a valuable tool for filtering prospective alternative interventions and retaining those that meet critical criteria. However, its main limitation resides in its subjective nature, as the weights and scores are only intelligent guesses that decision-makers and stakeholders make based on their intuition and experience. The inherent subjectivity can also be reduced by embedding the objective MCDA evaluation criteria (e.g., cost-effectiveness, health impact, economic impact, and impacted population in Table 7.2) into system dynamics models to analyze their relative importance. Non-objective criteria, such as community participation and social acceptability, can also be embedded in the models once semi-quantitative proxies have been selected. This process can help account for possible interdependencies among criteria that are not usually considered in MCDA analysis.

Another analytical technique that can be used to evaluate and select intervention scenarios is the Cross-Impact Balance (CIB) method proposed by Weimer-Jehle (2006, 2010). It resembles the cross-impact analysis but goes beyond scoring the direct influence and dependence of variables two at a time. Its main value proposition is to handle the impact and sensitivity of multiple variables and determine whether a given scenario involving the variables is consistent with their assumed rules of interaction. The variables include interacting states, social entities (individuals, groups, institutions), and project-specific components, such as infrastructure.

Finally, the system dynamics method discussed in Section 6.4 can help formulate, evaluate, and select intervention scenarios. For example, the STELLA Architect software contains a unique functionality to conduct single- or multi-objective optimization (combined with sensitivity analysis) once a system dynamics model has been built and objective functions and constraints for critical variables have been selected. Amadei (2023) provides illustrative examples of this feature to deal with complex issues across the peace–sustainability–climate security nexus.

7.3.4   Challenges of Decision-Making

The decision-making process in formulating, simulating, ranking, and selecting alternative interventions (stages 6 and 7 in Fig. 7.1) is not easy because, as emphasized in the previous chapters, the issues at stake at the community level are often ill-defined, messy, and complex. When faced with such problems, decision-makers are more inclined to think first in a more straightforward, linear, and deterministic way than in a systemic manner. A simple approach may cause unwanted and surprising effects, some more serious than others. This conclusion has been reached in many natural and social science fields, where dealing with ill-defined, messy, and complex issues and their uncertainty is the norm rather than the exception. It should be noted that such problems can only be solved approximately.

In their paper "Decisions in a Complex Context—a New Formalism," Elms and Brown (2012) advocated for deciding ill-defined/structured complex problems using a combination of *objective/rational* tools when the situations are straightforward and predictable and *subjective/intuitive* tools in more complicated and uncertain situations. Objective tools are tools of choice in directive planning decision-making, where critical/rational thinking and deductive reasoning are norms. They may address technical issues in the infrastructure and economic systems in community landscapes. On the other hand, subjective tools are preferred by creative, self-reflective decision-makers who use interactive planning to deal with uncertain, flexible, and adaptive systems and situations. Subjective tools are better suited to make decisions for the social and environmental systems in community landscapes. Subjective tools are more likely to be used in peacebuilding and diplomatic efforts.

In general, the challenge is for decision-makers to (i) select methods that best match the context in which decisions must be made and (ii) decide when to think in a critical/rational manner versus creatively. Choosing between directive and interactive planning on the one hand and critical/rational and creative thinking on the other in community development requires decision-makers to have acquired a certain level of situational awareness and decision-making maturity. These skills are more likely to be found in individuals with the systems thinking habits discussed in Section 5.5.

When choosing interventions in a community landscape that involves the intersection of engineering, peacebuilding, and diplomatic efforts, it is essential to balance comprehensiveness and impact. According to Rodrigues-Nikl and Brown (2012), decision-makers often face two competing desires when evaluating and selecting interventions from multiple systemic alternatives. On the one hand, they want interventions that address various factors and constraints and achieve goals and objectives within inclusive system boundaries. On the other hand, these boundaries must be defined so that meaningful decisions can be made and interventions with significant impacts can be implemented.

To resolve this dilemma, Rodriguez-Nikl and Brown (2012) proposed a *decision invariance criterion* that states that the desired result can be achieved if the decision remains consistent across different scenarios.

> The system should be large enough that any subsequent extension of the system boundary does not change the decision. If the decision is maintained with an extension of the system boundary, then a likely limit to the decision system has been attained.

A situation may also arise when none of the alternative interventions considered, as comprehensive as they may be, yields the desired impact. In this case, the consequences of this shortcoming must be reanalyzed (see feedback mechanisms in Fig. 7.1) in a participatory manner to consider potential trade-offs.

7.3.5   Trade-Offs, Benefits, and Synergies

Because of the entanglement of the different systems in the community landscape in Fig. 6.1, engineering, peacebuilding, and diplomatic decisions somewhere in the landscape will positively or negatively impact something else. System dynamics tools help analyze such trade-offs or their opposites, called synergies.

Synergy occurs, for instance, when making integrated decisions yields outcomes more significant than the sum of the effects of separate choices in different sectors; that is, a decision in one sector enhances another. Synergy resides, for instance, in the multiple binary and tertiary connections between engineering, peacebuilding, and diplomacy in Table 1.2 and the connections between positive peace, negative peace, and cultural peace in Table 3.2.

Synergistic choices in decision-making by practitioners and policymakers are likely to arise once *leverage points* in the community landscape of Fig. 6.1 have been identified (i.e., where intervention is most likely to yield more effective and efficient returns on the investment or action taken). Leverage points, sometimes called tipping points, can differ in community development. For instance, they may represent what is already working in the community, its capacity, and its resiliency. Another place of leverage in the community is to find and empower individuals inside and outside the community who are doing better than others under the same conditions and scaling up their solutions to the community. Such positive deviant solutions were discussed in Section 4.2.6. Another example might be considering issues that can be quickly addressed first (i.e., the low-hanging fruit), which will help build community confidence and resilience over time. A final example of leverage effort is changing the community's mindset by creating second-order rather than first-order change, as discussed in Section 4.2.5.

Finally, the leverage points can be identified from possible archetypes that may be able to explain, at least in part, some behavior patterns at the community landscape, system, subsystem, or nexus level. Archetypes were discussed in Section 6.6, where the leverage point of each one was identified. For instance, the leverage point in a system showing a *limit to success [growth]* archetype (e.g., Fig. 6.11) is to reduce the effect of the balancing process. Likewise, the leverage point in a system showing a *shifting the burden* archetype (e.g., Fig. 6.13) is to focus on causes first. Finally, a system showing a *tragedy of the commons* archetype (e.g., Fig. 6.15) may require better management of shared resources among users. When multiple archetypes are at play, as discussed in Section 6.6.11, one must understand the leverage points for each archetype and how all these leverage points interact.

7.3.6 Developing a Theory of Change

A theory of change (TOC) is "a method commonly used to understand the strategy and approach of an intervention" (TIPC, 2021). It can be formulated as a cause-and-effect IF-AND-THEN pathway logic that reads as follows: if x [preconditional activity], then y [expected change and outcome] because z [rationale]. ToC is a dynamic and strategic living tool that may change during the lifecycle of an intervention.

Although theories of change can be formulated in different ways, they all emphasize the importance of adopting a strategic combination of steps and intervention logic. Figure 7.2 shows, for instance, the benefits of using a *Logical Framework Approach* (LFA) (or logframe) to model intervention upward vertical progress from inputs to activities, outputs, objectives, goals, and impact or outcome (not shown) once the goals are met. The impact or outcome represents the end state and the overall tangible changes the intervention will make. Each step of the pathway from input to impact requires the identification of objectively verifiable indicators of success, means of verification, and outlining the assumptions necessary for success. Non-realized assumptions are sources of risk.

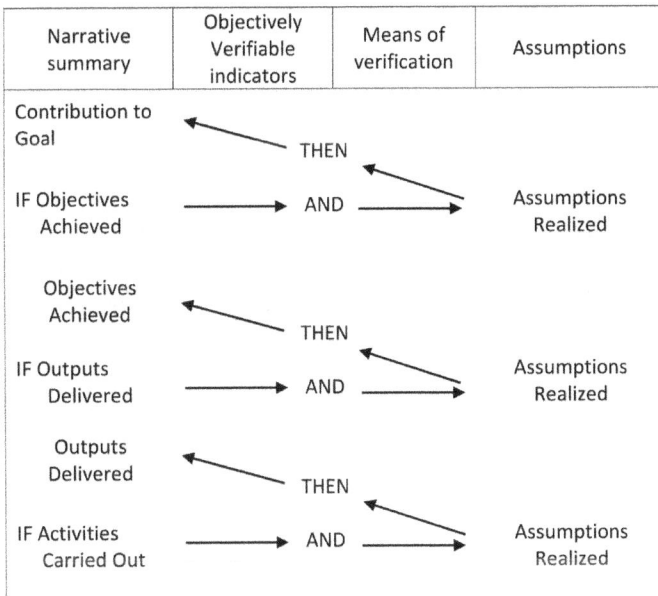

Figure 7.2 The logic of the LFA using a bottom-up approach. *Source:* INTRAC for Civil Society (2017), open-access Resources Archive - INTRAC.

The theory of change and logframe can also be interpreted as a downward vertical logic pathway in which the intervention's transformative outcome, impact, or overarching long-term goal(s) that define its success story are identified. Once established, a downward analysis is used to identify (i) the preconditions to meet the goals in terms of objectives, (ii) the outputs (i.e., results) necessary to meet the objectives, (iii) the activities necessary to create the outputs, and (iv) the inputs or elements that need to be mobilized to carry out the activities. The logframe also presents a horizontal logic that defines how each logframe component is measured and verified.

Notably, the terminology used to describe the key components in the project logic (i.e., inputs, activities, outputs, effects, and impact/outcome) can differ from one development agency to the other (Mercy Corps, 2005). Despite these differences, the vertical and horizontal logic in Fig. 7.2, combined with the TOC, provides a structured approach to an intervention that is clearly articulated and can be understood by all stakeholders (DCLG, 2009). Furthermore, this approach can be communicated to both partners and donors.

A systems approach to the theory of change with a built-in logical framework requires exploring the logic of each intervention and multiple simultaneous interventions. In community development, the approach must describe how engineering, peacebuilding, and diplomatic efforts affect each other and each system of the community landscape, how changes in some systems affect changes in others, and changes in human development and security in the context and scale of interest. Additionally, for each intervention, multiple feedback mechanisms can occur between the different components of the logical approach.

A built-in logical framework or logframe in the theory of change represents the *strategic* component of intervention planning. Once in place, it provides the necessary information to develop intervention *logistics*, *tactics*, and *planning*. They define the activities and resources needed for the interventions and the corresponding action and resource delivery timeframes. Further discussion on the pros and cons of LFA in development can be found in Amadei (2015).

7.4 Concluding Remarks

Addressing complex human development and security issues, conflict management, and exploring the mutual interaction between community development and the three sectors of the peace–development–diplomacy nexus are not random. The methodology presented in this chapter provides a *learning roadmap* to address issues in each sector of the nexus and across the nexus while considering how the sectors interact with the social, economic, environmental, and infrastructure community systems.

Systems thinking is embedded in each roadmap step by formulating the issues for developing and implementing intervention scenarios.

The learning roadmap in Fig. 7.1 is practical for decision-makers working at a specific scale. It becomes more complicated if decisions are made across different development scales, from the individual to the community or region. In this case, decisions made in each of the 10 methodology stages at one scale, say a large scale, must be synchronized with those at more minor scales. This cross-decision-making process is likely to be more challenging, especially when developing compatible multiscale logical frameworks and theories of change.

References

Amadei, B. (2015). *A Systems Approach to Modeling Community Development Projects*. New York: Momentum Press.

Amadei, B. (2019). *A Systems Approach to Modeling the Water–Energy–Land–Food Nexus* (Vols. I and II). New York: Momentum Press.

Amadei, B. (2020). A systems approach to community capacity and resilience. *Challenges*, **11**(2), 28; https://doi.org/10.3390/challe11020028

Amadei, B. (2023). *Navigating the Complexity Across the Peace-Sustainability–Climate Security Nexus*. Boca Raton: Routledge. ISBN 9781032563381

Caldwell, R. (2002). *Project Design Handbook*. Cooperative for Assistance and Relief Everywhere (CARE), Atlanta, GA. CARE's Project Design Handbook | Food Security and Nutrition Network (fsnnetwork.org)

Chambers, R. (1983). *Rural Development: Putting the Last First*. Routledge: London.

Decisions Sciences Institute (2013). http://www.decisionsciences.org/ (August 25, 2016).

Department for Communities and Local Government. (DCLG) (2009). *Multi-criteria Analysis: A Manual*. U. K.: Communities and Local Government Publications. 1132618.pdf (publishing.service.gov.uk)

DFID (2003). *Tools for Development: A Handbook for Those Engaged in Development Activity* (Version 15.1). London, U. K.: Department for International Development.

Dreborg, K. H. (1996). Essence of backcasting. *Futures*, 28(9), 813–828. https://doi.org/10.1016/S0016-3287(96)00044-4

Elms, D. G. and Brown, C. B. (2012). Decisions in a complex context: A new formalism? *Proceedings of the International Forum on Engineering Decision Making*, 6th IFED, Lake Louise, Canada.

Fahey, L. and Randall, R. M. (eds.) (1998). *Learning from the Future: Competitive Foresight Scenarios*. New York: John Wiley.

Fisher, S., et al. (2000). *Working With Conflict: Skills and Strategies for Action*. London, U. K.: Zed Books.

Georgantzas, N. C. and Acar, W. (1995). *Scenario-driven Planning: Learning to Manage Strategic Uncertainty*. Westport, CT: Quorum Books.

Glenn, J. C. and Gordon, T. J. (eds.) (2009). Futures Research Methodology (Version 3.0), AC/UNU Millennium Project, Washington DC.

Global Water Partnership (GWP) (2000). *Integrated water resources management*. TAC Background No 4 (gwp.org)

Grassroots Collective (n.d.). Tools for Planning Community Development Projects | Grassroots Hub (thegrassrootscollective.org)

Hjorth, P. and Bagheri, A. (2006). Navigating towards sustainable development: A system dynamics approach. *Futures*, **38**, 74–92.

INTRAC for Civil Society. (2017). The logical framework. The-Logical-Framework.pdf (intrac.org).

Kehrer, K., Flossmann-Kraus, U., Ronco Alarcon, S. V., Albers, V., and Aschmann, G. (2020). Transforming our work: Getting ready for transformational projects. Deutsche Gesellschaft für Internationale Zusammenarbeit (GIZ), Bonn, Germany. Transformation Guidance GIZ 02 2020.pdf

Mercy Corps (2005). *Design, Monitoring, and Evaluation Guidebook. DM&E FINAL Guidebook 3.5.03*. Portland, OR: Mercy Corps. (fsnnetwork.org)

Moore, L. V. (2014). Resilience and conflict prevention in West Darfur. Summer 2014 Insights Newsletter - Resilience | United States Institute of Peace (usip.org)

Mowjee, T., Garrasi, D., and Poole, L. (2015) *Coherence in conflict: Bringing humanitarian and development aid streams together*, DANIDA, Ministry of Foreign Affairs of Denmark. coherence in conflict web 1. pdf (humanitarianoutcomes.org)

OECD (2017). *Humanitarian development coherence*. https://www.oecd. org/development/humanitarian-donors/docs/coherence-oecd-Guideline.pdf

OpenAI (2024). *ChatGPT* (June 10 version) [Large language model]. https:// chat.openai.com

Ratner, S. E. (2023). *Progress You Can See. Measuring for Social Change.* Rugby, Warwickshire, UK: Practical Action Publishing.

Ritchie-Dunham, J. L. and Rabbino, H. T. (2001). *Managing from Clarity: Identifying, Aligning, and Leveraging Strategic Resources.* New York: John Wiley.

Robinson, J. B. (2003). Future subjunctive: Backcasting as social learning. *Futures*, **35**(8), 839–856. http://dx.doi.org/10.1016/S0016-3287(03)00039-9

Rodriguez-Nikl, T. and Brown, C. B. (2012). A systems approach to civil engineering decisions. *ASCE Journal of Professional Issues in Engineering Education and Practice*, **138**(4), 257–261

Schirch, L. (2013). *Conflict Assessment and Peacebuilding Planning.* Boulder, CO: Kumarian Press.

Senge, P. (2006). *The Fifth Discipline: The Art & Practice of the Learning Organization.* New York City: Doubleday.

Stroh, D. P. (2015). *Systems Thinking for Social Change.* Vermont: Chelsea Green Publishing.

The Omidyar Group. (2017). *Systems practice workbook.* Systems Practice Workbook - Observatory of Public Sector Innovation (OECD-opsi.org)

Transformative Innovation Policy Consortium. (TIPC) (2021). *Motion Handbook: Developing a Transformative Theory of Change.* Motion Handbook: Developing A Transformative Theory Of Change - TIPC (Tipconsortium.Net)

United States Institute of Peace (USIP)/NAE (2009). *Guiding Principles for Stabilization and Reconstruction.* Washington, DC: United States Institute of Peace Press. http://www.usip.org/sites/default/files/resources/guiding_principles_full.pdf.

Ward, E. and Schriefer, A. E. (1998). Dynamic scenarios: System thinking meets scenario planning. In: L. Fahey and R. Randall (eds.), *Learning from the Future: Competitive Foresight Scenarios.* New York: John Wiley, 79–94.

Weimer-Jehle, W. (2006). Cross-impact balances: A system-theoretical approach to cross-impact analysis. *Technological Forecasting & Social Change*, **73**(4), 334–361. https://doi.org/10.1016/j.techfore.2005.06.005

Weimer-Jehle, W. (2010). Introduction to qualitative systems and scenario analysis using cross-impact balance analysis. Interdisciplinary Research Unit on Risk Governance and Sustainable Technology Development, University of Stuttgart. http://www.cross-impact.de/Ressourcen/Guideline percent20No percent201.pdf

Chapter 8

Modeling the Complex Dynamics in Conflict-Prone Landscapes

This chapter outlines various case studies utilizing the system dynamics method to delve into the complex dynamics within communities prone to conflict. It investigates the interplay between conflict, climate change, and migration. Factors such as resource availability, capacity, existing conditions of peace, and proficiency in managing conflicts significantly affect the resilience of areas at risk of conflict. Implementing engineering strategies, developing peacebuilding initiatives, and conducting diplomatic efforts are crucial for devising interventional strategies and realizing social transformation.

8.1 Conflict, Climate Change, and Migration

8.1.1 Drivers of Displacement and Migration

The crises throughout the 20th and early 21st centuries have unevenly impacted the world's disadvantaged and marginalized groups, intensifying their existing struggles with poverty, discrimination, and social exclusion. Many drivers have exacerbated these groups' burden of poverty, compelling them to flee their homes and

Engineering for Peace and Diplomacy
Bernard Amadei
Copyright © 2025 Jenny Stanford Publishing Pte. Ltd.
ISBN 978-981-5129-75-5 (Hardcover), 978-1-003-65168-0 (eBook)
www.jennystanford.com

communities for safety and seek refuge elsewhere. Some of these drivers are listed below.

- Internal and cross-border conflicts plague many regions, tearing apart countries and communities and leaving behind a trail of devastation and displacement.
- Political instability and pervasive corruption breed insecurity and uncertainty, pushing individuals to seek safer havens elsewhere.
- Inadequate resource management exacerbates livelihood insecurities, as competition over reduced resources fuels tension and drives people from their homes to search for stability.
- Land degradation and environmental damage further erode livelihoods, rendering areas uninhabitable and forcing populations to escape due to ecological degradation.
- The threat of natural hazards such as earthquakes and floods adds another layer of vulnerability.
- Climate change amplifies existing challenges and has the potential to trigger new crises.

The interconnectedness of these drivers creates a complex web of vulnerabilities, where each element can potentially compound the impact of others. A good example is how conflict, natural disasters, and climate change influence each other, negatively impact livelihoods, and contribute to displacement worldwide. According to the Internal Displacement Monitoring Center (IDMC, 2021), there were 55 million internally displaced people worldwide at the end of 2020, 48 million due to conflict and violence and 7 million due to disasters.

Conflict is a potent catalyst for displacement. The aftermath of World War II witnessed a mass exodus of 40 M displaced persons across Europe, driven by the devastation of war and the redrawing of national borders. Similarly, the partition of India in 1947 and the subsequent migration of 14 million people to Bangladesh and Pakistan underscored the human toll of political partition and communal violence. More recent examples of displacement are associated with conflicts related to the Ukraine-Russia and Israel-Hamas wars and the lingering crises in Haiti, Syria, Yemen,

Sudan, South Sudan, Myanmar, Burkina Faso, Afghanistan, Ethiopia, Somalia, Armenia, and the Democratic Republic of Congo (DRC) (IRC, 2022). In Central America, decades of instability exacerbated by climate change, insecurity, governance failures, corruption, and socioeconomic inequality have forced countless individuals to flee for safety and opportunity (Angelo, 2021). The enduring legacy of conflict, whether rooted in historical grievances or contemporary geopolitical tensions, continues to reshape lives and the worldwide geopolitical landscape, underscoring the urgent need for sustainable peacebuilding efforts and humanitarian support to address the root causes of displacement and restore dignity to affected populations.

Another significant driver of displacement and migration is inadequate access to sustainable water, energy, food, and land resources for human survival and development. When these essential resources are limited or unevenly distributed and poorly managed, there is scarcity, environmental degradation, and insecurity, ultimately prompting populations to seek alternative habitats. Climate change exacerbates these challenges by altering the availability and quality of natural resources, amplifying the frequency and severity of extreme weather events such as droughts, floods, and landslides, and introducing new environmental hazards and risks (WEF, 2021; Devex, 2023). The failure to implement effective mitigation and adaptation measures in response to changing ecological conditions further compounds the vulnerability of rural and urban populations that rely on agriculture, fisheries, or pastoralism for their livelihoods. Furthermore, climate change-induced disruptions can exacerbate existing social and economic disparities, fueling grievances and disputes within and between communities and nations.

Numerous case studies have illustrated the direct and indirect impacts of climate change on displacement and migration. Historical examples include the Dust Bowl phenomenon of the 1930s in the United States, where severe drought and soil erosion drove 2.5 million from their homes in search of sustenance and livelihoods. Similarly, the aftermath of Hurricane Katrina in 2005 prompted significant migration from some southern US Gulf Coast states as communities grappled with the destruction created by the storm and the challenges of rebuilding in its aftermath (Bendor and Scheffran, 2019). These examples highlight the profound human consequences of environmental degradation and climate-induced disasters.

The emergence of climate refugees and internally displaced persons is of national and international importance and is likely to grow. According to the UNHCR (2024),

> The UNHCR has identified 22 countries where the effects of climate change will be most severe between now and 2030. These countries include regions heavily impacted by conflict and climate change, including countries in the Eastern Horn of Africa, Afghanistan, Bangladesh, Ecuador, Honduras, and more. Collectively, these countries host 52 percent of all internally displaced people, 24 percent of all stateless people, and 28 percent of all refugees.

As climate-related migration continues to escalate in the 21st century, addressing the root causes of environmental vulnerability and implementing robust adaptation and mitigation strategies will be essential to mitigate the adverse impacts, ensure the resilience of affected communities and ecosystems, and safeguard the rights and well-being of affected populations (Peacedirect, 2022).

8.1.2   Rural to Urban Migration

Rural-to-urban migration, both within countries and across borders, demands special consideration owing to its far-reaching implications. While some individuals choose to relocate voluntarily to pursue new opportunities, many are compelled to leave their rural homes under compounding pressures of poverty, environmental degradation, political instability, and conflict. In developing countries, such forced migration creates an influx of migrants that often strains already limited urban resources and infrastructure, leading to the proliferation of overcrowded and unsafe settlements that are vulnerable to the impacts of climate change. This influx exacerbates existing socioeconomic disparities as marginalized populations compete for access to essential services, employment opportunities, and adequate housing in rapidly expanding urban centers. The resultant socio-spatial segregation further deepens divisions along the lines of ethnicity, religion, and economic status, fueling tensions and conflicts within and between communities.

An example of this phenomenon is the rural-to-urban migration patterns witnessed in Fiji since the 1990s, driven by shifting weather patterns and socioeconomic stresses (Darwish, 2023). A more recent example of the impact of the migration of rural populations to urban areas occurred in Syria because of a civil war and social conflict that started with unrest in 2011. The migration has been linked to multiple interrelated factors, such as climate change, weak country governance, poverty, economic liberalization, a lack of environmental and agricultural policymaking, political insecurity, land tenure issues, social inequalities, and corrupt water management (Kelley et al., 2015; Gleick, 2014, 2019; Vidal, 2016; Suter, 2017; Selby et al., 2017; Peters et al., 2020). Other factors include religion and ethnicity, repression, opposition armed groups, and the meddling of foreign actors (Hamad, 2018; Massari, 2013). The modeling of this migration is presented in the next section.

A similar dynamic occurred in Yemen after the unification of the Yemen Arab Republic (North Yemen) and the People's Democratic Republic of Yemen (South Yemen) in 1990. The merger brought together two land rights and water management practices based on Islamic sharia and state law. The resulting confusion, population growth, excessive and uncontrolled water well drilling, groundwater depletion, and increasing water scarcity due to climate change have led to water and food insecurity. It fueled a reinforcing cycle of social unrest, protests, violence, and migration in Yemen starting in 1990 (Glass, 2010; Werrell and Femia, 2013; Pulley, 2021).

As rural dwellers move to major urban centers to search for livelihood opportunities, they are often relegated to precarious informal settlements characterized by substandard housing, inadequate infrastructure, and exposure to environmental hazards. This pattern has been observed in many large cities in the developing world, such as Nairobi, Lima, and Beirut, where slums and shantytowns grow on undesirable, unstable land, increasing the risk of socioeconomic inequalities. UNSTAS (2023) reports that around 1.1 billion individuals presently reside in slums or conditions akin to slums within urban areas, with an anticipated increase of an additional 2 billion over the upcoming three decades.

Moreover, the establishment of refugee camps in urban areas in response to conflict and displacement further complicates the urban landscape, as these temporary settlements often evolve into semi-permanent fixtures, straining local resources and perpetuating cycles of dependency and marginalization. Notable examples include Palestinian refugee camps in the Middle East since 1948 and large refugee camps in Asia and Africa, where protracted displacement has transformed temporary shelters into entrenched communities that deal with the challenges of rebuilding lives and livelihoods in the absence of durable solutions.

This convergence of rural-to-urban migration, informal settlement proliferation, and protracted displacement underscore the urgent need for comprehensive and inclusive urban planning strategies that prioritize the rights and well-being of all residents, address the underlying drivers of vulnerability, and foster resilience in the face of evolving environmental and socio-economic challenges. By adopting a holistic approach that integrates land-use planning, infrastructure development, social services provision, and climate adaptation measures, policymakers can mitigate the adverse impacts of unplanned urbanization and displacement while promoting sustainable and inclusive urban development for present and future generations.

8.1.3   Herders–Farmers Dynamics

In regions such as Sub-Saharan and West Africa, there have been multiple instances of human displacement due to conflicts between farmers (who stay in one place) and pastoralists/ herders (who move around). Herders leave areas with limited resources and degraded land and move to areas with natural resources and access to water and grazing fields. Farmers require land and water for cultivation, whereas herders require grazing land and water for their livestock (Issifu et al., 2022; Tesfaye, 2022). Farmers often perceive herders' livestock as threatening their crops, whereas herders may view fenced-off farmland as restricting traditional grazing areas. As both groups expand their activities, clashes occur over land ownership, access, and use rights. Encroachment on traditional grazing routes and farmland by either party can escalate tension. Conflict is particularly dominant during dry periods when livestock encroaches on farmland and contaminates the water bodies used by farmers. Droughts and changes in rainfall patterns due to climate change have intensified these disputes over time.

What was perceived as beneficial relations between herders and farmers in previous generations has become a source of competition for natural resources and conflicts. However, competition and conflict cannot be attributed only to environmental issues and climate change. Other factors include farmed land expansion, population growth, urbanization, ethnic clashes and insurgencies, traditional rivalries, socio-political discrimination and resentment, a lack of political will, corruption, weak governance and land management, and institutions' ineffectiveness in avoiding or managing conflicts. The complex interplay of social, political, economic, and cultural factors in development has been extensively recorded in the literature, with notable contributions from Schwartzstein and Risi (2023), Issifu et al. (2022), and Chemonics/ CDA (2023).

The 'tragedy of the commons' archetype, examined in Section 6.6.7, can provide insight into understanding the conflict dynamics between pastoralists/herders and farmers. By understanding the multiple factors underlying the conflicts, leverage resides in having policymakers and stakeholders work towards implementing sustainable land management practices, promoting dialogue between farmers and herders, and developing policies that address the root causes of the conflict while ensuring equitable access to resources for all parties involved. Killelea (2021, p. 97) highlights the benefits of using such practices to address conflicts between herders and farmers in northern Kenya.

8.1.4 Humanitarian–Development–Peace Coherence

Another significant dimension of conflict dynamics related to population displacement emerges when individuals, compelled to flee their homes because of conflict or persecution, seek refuge in areas that are already struggling with limited resources and infrastructure. This scenario often unfolds in urban areas (as discussed in Section 8.1.2) or rural areas hosting refugees or internally displaced populations. This influx of newcomers, while necessitating immediate humanitarian assistance, can also give rise to tensions and conflicts between the displaced and host communities as competition for resources intensifies and socioeconomic disparities widen. The 'tragedy of the commons' archetype discussed in Section 6.6.7 can also represent that dynamic.

The intersection of humanitarian aid and development efforts in these contexts is often called the *humanitarian–development–peace* nexus. Leverage resides at the juncture where conflicting interests and priorities must be reconciled to foster sustainable and inclusive community development and create a win-win situation. Achieving coherence and cooperation between displaced populations and host communities is essential for addressing immediate needs and vulnerabilities and promoting long-term stability, peace, and resilience.

To navigate these complex dynamics effectively, host and displaced stakeholders must work collaboratively to foster dialogue, build trust, and promote social cohesion among diverse populations. Numerous studies have underscored the importance of adopting such an approach. Studies by Moore (2014), Mowjee et al. (2015), the Organization for Economic Cooperation and Development (OECD, 2017), and the United Nations Office for the Coordination of Humanitarian Affairs (OCHA, 2017) highlight the critical need for coordinated action across humanitarian, development, and peacebuilding efforts to foster durable solutions, mitigate conflict risks, and promote inclusive and resilient communities.

Achieving coherence and cooperation between displaced populations and host communities is a prerequisite for peacebuilding in regions affected by displacement. By embracing the principles of inclusivity, solidarity, and shared responsibility, stakeholders can harness the transformative potential of the humanitarian–development–peace nexus to build a more equitable and peaceful future for all.

8.2   A Common Modeling Approach

8.2.1   The Storyline

Using the system dynamics method, how do we model the interactions between conflict, climate change, and migration in a conflict-prone landscape? The first step in modeling is to formulate a narrative that outlines how these three sectors unfold, their causes and mutual impacts, and their overall influence on human development and security. The second step is to outline the desired conditions. This work must be done once (i) the landscape's context, scale, and boundaries have been selected; (ii) data and information about different aspects of the landscape have been collected and analyzed (see Appendix B); and (iii) dynamic hypotheses regarding landscape issues—the what, why, who, where, when, and how—have been identified and analyzed comprehensively. These three steps correspond to stages 1–4 of the methodology in Fig. 7.1 and help define conflict-prone landscape dynamics.

As discussed in Section 7.1, narratives help establish a road map between current and desired conditions. Below are several narratives, among others.

- Climate change has exacerbated vulnerability and directly contributed to conflicts over dwindling resources such as water, energy, food, and arable land. The increased frequency and intensity of extreme weather events, such as droughts, floods, and storms, have disrupted livelihoods, heightened food insecurity, and escalated tensions among communities reliant on shared resources.

- Conflicts have forced people to flee their homes because of violence, persecution, or human rights abuse. Conflicts have degraded environmental and living conditions, which may take years to reclaim and stabilize, representing a challenge for returning populations.

- Climate change-driven migration has led to internal and cross-border migration, with individuals and communities relocating to better livelihood opportunities, food security, and safety. The risk of displacement and migration has increased in regions prone to climate-related disasters, such as low-lying coastal areas vulnerable to sea-level rise or regions experiencing desertification.

- Disputes over natural resources have worsened environmental degradation, contributing to further climate impacts and driving additional migration. Similarly, migration resulting from climate change has strained resources in destination areas, potentially leading to social tensions and conflicts over access to services and employment opportunities.

Table 8.1 describes several narratives demonstrating the relationship between climate change, conflict, and migration across various countries and regions.

8.2.2   Critical Variables

Once the conflict, climate change, and migration interplay narratives have been established, the conflict-prone landscape dynamics can be modeled (Stage 5 in Fig. 7.1). Critical variables and their relationships must be identified. Generally, these variables can be regrouped into the following categories.

- *Sociocultural factors*: Populations (demography, education, health, employment, migration), communities (households, families, groups), institutions (social, economic/financial, governance, service levels), and others (belief systems, ethics, exclusion, marginalization, marginalized and vulnerable groups, gender equality, violence and oppression, and human rights).
- *Natural and environmental factors*: Water, land/soil degradation, biota, air, natural disasters and adverse events, and climate variability.
- *Socioeconomic factors*: Food security, energy access, economic disparities, production, distribution, consumption, and disposal.
- *Infrastructure factors*: Critical infrastructure and inherent and adaptive capacity to deliver services (water, telecom,

housing, electricity, food, transportation, healthcare, waste disposal, etc.)

- *Conflict dynamics and risk factors*: National and trans-boundary conflicts and conflicts between herders and farmers.
- *Policy and governance factors*: Government policies, international agreements, and humanitarian interventions.

Table 8.1 Four examples of climate change, conflict, and migration interaction at the country and regional levels (OpenAI, 2024)

Syrian Civil War	Climate Change: Severe drought from 2006 to 2011, attributed to climate change, devastated agriculture in Syria.
	Conflict: The resulting economic hardship and displacement of rural populations contributed to social unrest and, eventually, the Syrian Civil War.
	Migration: Millions of Syrians fled the conflict, moved to cities in Syria, and ultimately became refugees in neighboring countries and Europe, straining resources and causing political tensions in host countries.
Sahel Region of Africa	Climate Change: Increasing temperatures and unpredictable rainfall patterns have led to desertification in the Sahel.
	Conflict: Resource scarcity has fueled land and water disputes between farmers and herders.
	Migration: Many people are forced to migrate to more fertile areas or urban centers, often leading to clashes with local populations and further instability.
Bangladesh	Climate Change: Rising sea levels and increased frequency of cyclones are impacting Bangladesh's low-lying coastal regions.
	Conflict: Displacement of coastal communities leads to competition for land and resources in inland areas.
	Migration: Large-scale migration to urban areas like Dhaka results in overcrowding, strain on infrastructure, and social tensions.
Central America	Climate Change: Prolonged droughts and extreme weather events have severely affected agriculture in Central America's "Dry Corridor."
	Conflict: Food insecurity and loss of livelihoods have contributed to violence and instability, particularly involving gangs.
	Migration: Many people from countries like Honduras, Guatemala, and El Salvador migrate northward to Mexico and the United States, creating complex humanitarian and political challenges.

Another possibility is to consider some of the 24 indicators of the positive peace index (Table 3.3) and the 23 indicators of the global peace index measuring negative peace (Table 3.4) discussed in Section 3.3.

8.2.3 Causal Relationships

The next step is to map the possible causal relationships between the critical variables and identify feedback loops. For instance, reinforcing and balancing loops may read as follows:

- *Reinforcing feedback loops*: Escalating conflicts can lead to further displacement and migration, exacerbating tension and instability and creating more conflicts.
- *Balancing feedback loops*: Positive policy interactions, such as conflict resolution, sustainable resource management, urban and rural planning, and climate adaptation/mitigation measures, increase resource management and access, which in turn reduces resource insecurity and tensions and reinforces the value of more constructive policy interventions.

These feedback loops must also consider time delays and nonlinear relationships to capture how actions or events may not be immediate or linear.

Once the key variables and relationships have been identified, the next challenge is to develop qualitative (causal loop diagrams) and possibly quantitative (stock and flow) system dynamics models (Stage 5 in Fig. 7.1) that reproduce the identified landscape issues (structures and behavior patterns) and model the pros and cons of possible interventions and policies (Stage 6 in Fig. 7.1). The models provide valuable insights into the interconnected challenges of population uprooting, mass migration, conflict, and insecurity in water, energy, food, land, climate change, and farmer–herder conflict.

Stages 6 and 7 in Fig. 7.1 focus on examining and choosing intervention scenarios alongside the necessity for wide-ranging and harmonized policy measures at various scales, from local to global. This approach aims to address the intricate relationship between conflict, climate change, and migration, reducing their negative impacts while promoting resilience and sustainable development. These measures could involve establishing climate change mitigation strategies to strengthen at-risk populations, fostering mechanisms for conflict avoidance and peaceful resolution, encouraging the sustainable management of natural resources, and improving governance frameworks to oversee migration patterns and safeguard the rights of displaced people. In formulating these intervention tactics and managing societal changes involving trade-offs and synergetic actions, concerted efforts in engineering, peacebuilding, and diplomacy are essential.

8.3 System Dynamics Modeling Examples

This section presents several illustrative examples that capture one or several components of the dynamics between conflict, climate change, and migration and outlines possible remedial roles of engineering, peacebuilding, and diplomacy in addressing those dynamics.

8.3.1 A Generic Example

Consider the case of a landscape with ongoing tensions and prone to conflict, as depicted through the causal loop diagram in Fig. 8.1. A description of the dynamics is as follows:

- National and transboundary conflict and insecurity originate from tensions fueled by territorial disputes, armed groups, and ethnic, political, or religious disagreements.
- Conflict and insecurity lead to the uprooting of communities and migration within and across borders in search of safety and livelihood opportunities. Informal vulnerable settlements have been established.
- Conflict leads to resource insecurity (e.g., water, energy, food, and land), poor resource management and access practices, and unemployment. Climate change contributes to resource insecurity and environmental and land degradation, hinders economic development, exacerbates unemployment, and creates poverty and inequality. Conflict, climate change, and migration disrupt agricultural activities, leading to food

shortages, malnutrition, and health issues in vulnerable populations.

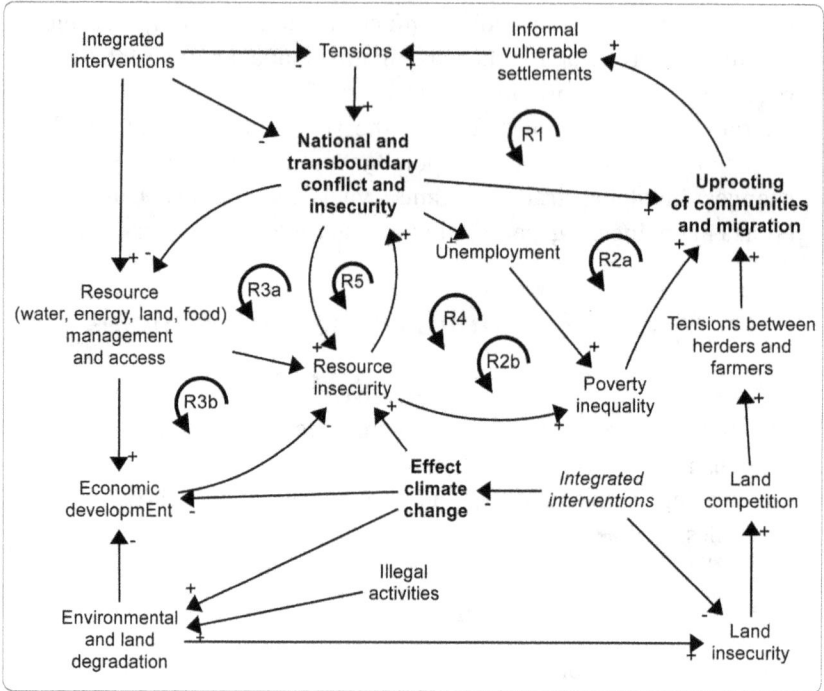

Figure 8.1 An example of a causal loop diagram involving the dynamics between the three critical variables of conflict, climate change, and migration.

- Increasing temperatures, erratic rainfall patterns, and desertification due to climate change further degrade the environment with the loss of arable land and natural resources, exacerbate water, energy, food, and land crises, and negatively impact economic development.

- Degraded land due to climate change, poor resource management, and illegal activities (e.g., mining) contribute to land insecurity.

- Competition over arable land, grazing areas, and water resources among herders and farmers exacerbates tensions and conflicts, displacing communities and undermining food security and livelihoods.

- <u>Tensions between herders and farmers</u> over land and water resources escalate, fueled by climate-induced environmental pressure and competition for dwindling resources.

Several reinforcing loops can be identified in Fig. 8.1.

- R1: Tensions $\rightarrow^+$ National and transboundary conflicts and insecurity $\rightarrow^+$ Uprooting of communities and migration $\rightarrow^+$ Informal vulnerable settlements $\rightarrow^+$ Tensions

- R2a: Tensions $\rightarrow^+$ National and transboundary conflicts and insecurity $\rightarrow^+$ Unemployment $\rightarrow^+$ Poverty and inequality $\rightarrow^+$ Uprooting of communities and migration $\rightarrow^+$ Informal vulnerable settlements $\rightarrow^+$ Tensions

- R2b: Tensions $\rightarrow^+$ National and transboundary conflicts and insecurity $\rightarrow^+$ Resource insecurity $\rightarrow^+$ Poverty and inequality $\rightarrow^+$ Uprooting of communities and migration $\rightarrow^+$ Informal vulnerable settlements $\rightarrow^+$ Tensions

- R3a: National and transboundary conflicts and insecurity $\rightarrow^-$ Resource management and access $\rightarrow^-$ Resource insecurity $\rightarrow^+$ National and transboundary conflicts and insecurity

- R3b: National and transboundary conflicts and insecurity $\rightarrow^-$ Resource management and access $\rightarrow^+$ Economic development $\rightarrow^-$ Resource insecurity $\rightarrow^+$ National and transboundary conflicts and insecurity

- R4: Economic development $\rightarrow^-$ Resource insecurity $\rightarrow^+$ Poverty and inequality $\rightarrow^+$ Uprooting of communities and migration $\rightarrow^+$ Informal vulnerable settlements $\rightarrow^+$ Tensions $\rightarrow^+$ National and transboundary conflicts and insecurity $\rightarrow^+$ Resource management and access $\rightarrow^+$ Economic development

- R5: National and transboundary conflicts and insecurity $\rightarrow^+$ Resource insecurity $\rightarrow^+$ National and transboundary conflicts and insecurity.

The causal loop diagram in Fig. 8.1 can be improved by identifying the relevant stakeholders for each element, necessitating a comprehensive stakeholder analysis as part of the landscape assessment.

8.3.2 Integrated Interventions

Table 8.2 lists several examples of engineering, peacebuilding, and diplomatic interventions that could contribute to addressing the dynamics of Fig. 8.1. These interventions require an integrated approach and comprehensive and coordinated strategies. When carried out effectively, these are leverage points of intervention that could yield positive outcomes from the implemented measures.

Table 8.2 Examples of engineering, peacebuilding, and diplomatic interventions (OpenAI, 2024)

Effort types		Interventions
Engineering	Infrastructure development	• Build resilient infrastructure, promote sustainable resource management and access, support the community, and reduce resource competition.
		• Develop early warning systems for natural disasters and climate change impacts to mitigate displacement and enhance preparedness.
	Technology deployment	• Utilize technology to improve resource management and access, optimize land use, and reduce conflicts.
		• Implement renewable energy solutions to address resource insecurity and mitigate environmental degradation.
	Innovative problem solving	• Develop sustainable urban and rural planning to accommodate growing populations and prevent the uprooting of communities.
		• Develop adaptation and mitigation measures to climate change.
Peace-building	Dialogue and Reconciliation	• Facilitate dialogue between conflicting parties to address grievances and build trust.
		• Promote reconciliation and peacemaking efforts to heal the community affected by conflict and displacement.

Effort types		Interventions
	Community-Building Initiatives	• Support local peace committees and grassroots organizations to strengthen social cohesion. • Engage youth and women in peacebuilding activities to create inclusive and sustainable peace processes.
	Education and Awareness	• Provide education on conflict resolution and peacebuilding to empower the community with the skills needed to address disputes non-violently. • Raise awareness about the importance of coexistence and mutual respect.
Diplomacy	Cooperation	• Foster agreements and collaborations to manage transboundary resources and address cross-border issues.
	Negotiation and Conflict Resolution	• Mediate negotiations between conflicting parties to reach peaceful settlements and prevent escalation through peacemaking and peacekeeping efforts. • Support diplomatic initiatives that address tensions and the root causes of conflict, such as resource distribution and political representation, corruption, marginalization, and undemocratic institutions.
	Policy Advocacy	• Advocate for sustainable development, human rights, and environmental protection policies. • Work with organizations to implement and monitor peace agreements and development projects.

8.3.3   Conflict and Climate Change in Ghana

This section describes a second example that demonstrates the use of system dynamics to model the interaction between climate change and conflict in Ghana. As reported by Chemonics/CDA (2023), Ghana is known for its stable power transitions, active civil society, and strong economic growth. Nonetheless, the country has been facing different types of conflicts exacerbated by the effects of climate change. The drivers of conflict include governance issues and accusations of corruption, disputes between farmers and herders, contests for authority among traditional leaders, disagreements over land, and socioeconomic marginalization of the youth—often resulting in migration and intense competition over resources—each a potential pathway to conflict. The causal loop diagram in Fig. 8.2 illustrates these dynamics.

Climate impact and conflict have been recognized as influencing the dynamics shown in Fig. 8.2. The key drivers of climate change include wildfires, climate-related worsening of rural livelihood conditions, and increased floods and flash flooding. Likewise, the conflict-related key driving factors include farmer–herder conflict, competition for power among chiefs, and conflict between mining companies and communities. These variables show inter- and intra-related causal relationships. Several reinforcing loops can be identified:

- R1: Farmer–herder conflicts, politicization of conflict along ethnic lines, competition over land and water, weak and nonexistent land-use regimes, and farmer–herder conflicts.
- R2: Farmer–herder conflicts, politicization of conflict along ethnic lines, competition over land and water, traditional burning practices of herders used to increase pasture, wildfires, and farmer–herder conflicts.
- R3: Land conflicts, competition over land and water, and land conflicts.
- R4: Competition for power among chiefs, favoritism, land conflicts, the power of chiefs as mediators, and competition for power among chiefs.
- R5: Political and economic exclusion of youth, migration (men and women), and political and economic exclusion of youth.
- R6: Political and economic exclusion of youth, migration (men and women), informal settlements, vulnerability of informal settlements to climate impacts, clearance of settlements by the government, civil disobedience against the government, radicalization, violent extremism, and political and economic exclusion of youth.

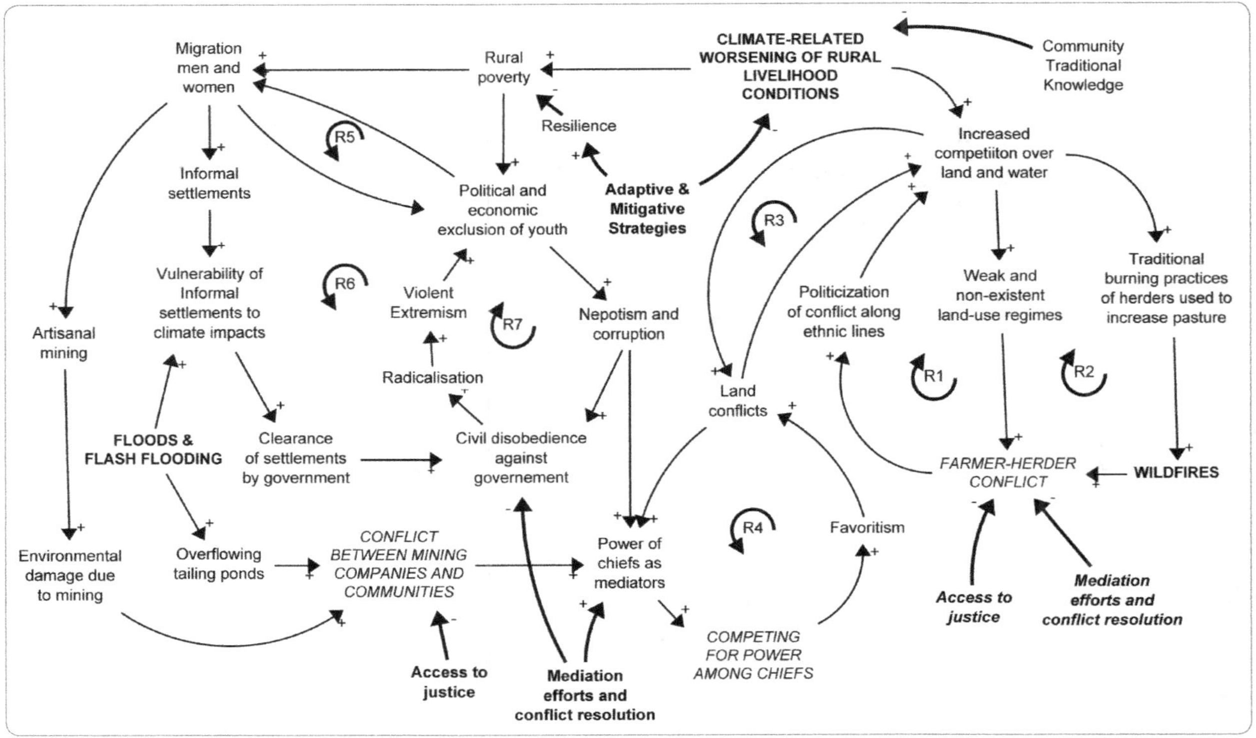

Figure 8.2 A causal loop diagram showing the variables and key driving factors in the climate–conflict nexus in Ghana (adapted from Chemonics/CDA, 2023, p. 10). *Note:* The original chart was redrawn using the STELLA software. Only reinforcing relationships are shown and reinforcing loops have been added. The italic capitalized text refers to the key drivers of conflict. The bold capitalized text refers to the key drivers of climate. Darker causal links and non-capitalized bold text were added to the original diagram to indicate possible interventions.

- R7: Political and economic exclusion of youth, nepotism and corruption, civil disobedience against the government, radicalization, violent extremism, and political and economic exclusion of youth.

As for Fig. 8.1, the causal loop diagram shown in Fig. 8.2 can be improved by incorporating the relevant stakeholders for each element, necessitating a comprehensive stakeholder analysis as part of the landscape assessment.

What are the possible interventions in the complex system shown in Fig. 8.2? Chemonics/CDA (2023) considers the effect of introducing (i) climate adaptation policies to reduce rural poverty and competition over land and water, and (ii) mitigating efforts regarding biodiversity and environmental protection against climate impacts. These initiatives have beneficial impacts on all other elements depicted in Fig. 8.2, owing to the nature of the reinforcing connections. Other recommendations by Chemonics/CDA (2023) include leveraging interventions in:

- Traditional community knowledge and land stewardship practices to reduce the impacts of climate variations on ecosystem services.
- Adaptive and mitigative strategies and structures needed to supply livelihood resources (e.g., water, energy, shelter, food, etc.) and bolster community resilience against the risks of adverse events.
- Practical strategies for addressing disputes, improving security frameworks, and preemptive actions against conflict by reinforcing chieftaincy's involvement in mediation efforts.
- Existing access to justice for all, including vulnerable populations and herders.
- Existing conflict-resolution work of civil society organizations.

These strategies have been added to Fig. 8.2. They encompass the application of engineering, peacebuilding, and diplomatic/policy actions to navigate the complex relationship between climate change, conflict, and migration.

8.3.4 Syria

8.3.4.1 Causal loop models

A third example that illustrates the interplay between climate change, conflict, and migration is Syria. Briefly summarized in Table 8.1, the Syrian conflict and turmoil that started with unrest in 2011 following a five-year drought led to the migration of rural populations to urban areas. This migration, which has witnessed millions fleeing their homes for safety and stability since 2011, has been attributed to a confluence of interrelated factors, such as climate change, weak country governance, poverty, economic liberalization, a lack of environmental and agricultural policy-making, political insecurity, land tenure issues, social inequalities, and corrupt water management. Other factors include ideology and religion, an oppressive authoritarian and oppressive government response to citizen criticism, and the meddling of foreign actors (Iran, Russia, the US, Turkey, and Saudi Arabia). All these factors have contributed to a combination of direct, indirect, and cultural violence since 2011 (Anand, 2020).

The urban areas could not absorb the influx of rural workers. This in-country migration resulted in a humanitarian crisis, poverty, protests, and an oppressive response from the Syrian government. This dynamic, in turn, brought the country into a civil war, forced the migration of refugees fleeing violence, and fed the refugee crisis in Europe starting in 2015. Figure 8.3 is a simple causal loop diagram showing the dynamics between climate change, hardship in livelihood resources and jobs, rural and urban resources management, civil unrest, insecurity, and migration (inward and outward) in Syria since 2010.

A more detailed version of Fig. 8.3 is available in Whitworth (2021). It includes multiple subsystems such as water and climate, agriculture and energy, corruption, liberalization, social consequences, and conflict. Further details about each subsystem and intervention points are available in Whitworth (2021), with an overview in Amadei (2023).

At the heart of the Syrian crisis lies the erosion of environ-mental and socioeconomic resilience, exacerbated by the impacts of climate change, which have rendered rural livelihoods increasingly precarious. Persistent droughts and erratic weather patterns have devastated agricultural productivity, exacerbating food insecurity and economic hardship in rural communities that rely on farming and livestock herding. Weak governance structures, characterized by a lack of effective policymaking and enforcement mechanisms, have compounded these challenges, exacerbated social inequalities, and fostered an environment of political insecurity and unrest.

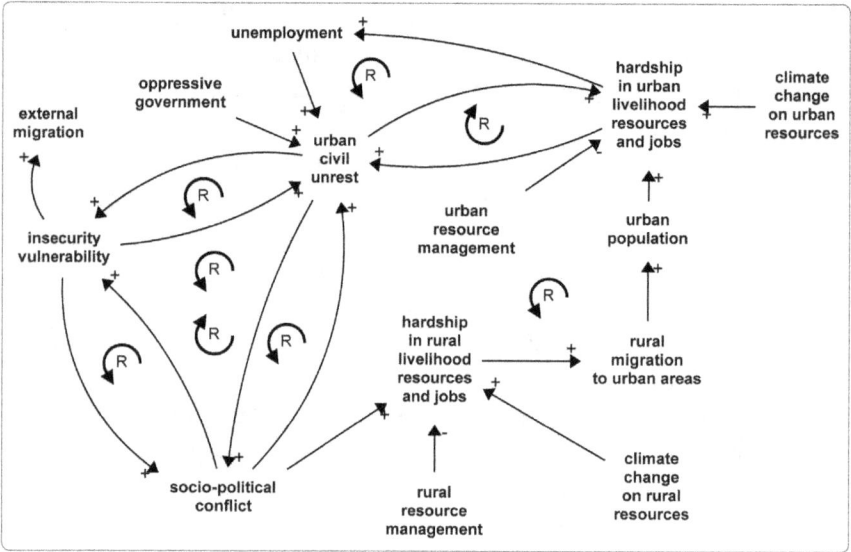

Figure 8.3 A causal loop diagram showing the insecurity dynamics in Syria. *Legend*: R represents reinforcing loops. + signs indicate variables that change in the same direction. *Source*: Adapted from Whitworth (2021).

Moreover, the legacy of economic liberalization and neoliberal policies has further marginalized vulnerable populations, exacerbating disparities in access to resources and opportunities and fueling grievances over land tenure and resource ownership. Corrupt water management practices have heightened tensions over access to vital water resources, further exacerbating social inequalities and grievances among marginalized communities.

The resulting migration from rural to urban areas has placed immense strain on fragile urban infrastructure and services, exacerbating social tensions and sparking civil unrest. Overcrowded and under-resourced urban centers struggle to accommodate the influx of displaced populations, leading to the proliferation of informal settlements and exacerbating social and economic disparities. The resultant breakdown of social cohesion and trust further fuels the cycles of violence and instability, perpetuating a cycle of conflict and displacement.

Addressing the root causes of migration and conflict in Syria requires a comprehensive approach that addresses the underlying drivers of vulnerability and promotes inclusive and sustainable development. This approach includes implementing effective governance structures, promoting equitable access to resources, strengthening social safety networks, and fostering resilience to climate change and environmental degradation. By addressing these multifaceted challenges, policymakers can work towards building a more resilient and inclusive society that offers hope and opportunity for all its citizens, both rural and urban alike.

8.3.4.2 Stock and flow models

An attempt at creating a stock and flow model of the dominant dynamics of Fig. 8.3 is shown in three parts in Fig. 8.4 (a, b, and c). The EPDSyria model is a modified version of the model proposed by Amadei (2023). A brief description of each part is provided below.

Rural Population Dynamics

The initial segment of the EPDSyria model is shown in Fig. 8.4.a. It was designed to capture the surge and subsequent decline of the rural population due to the depletion of rural resources (e.g., water, energy, and food) and livelihood difficulties. This 'overshoot and collapse' structure is caused by various factors, such as climate change, poor resource management, and others that operate at local, national, or regional scales. As the stock of rural resources diminishes from its initial value, the rural population dwindles, leading to migration to urban and other non-rural areas.

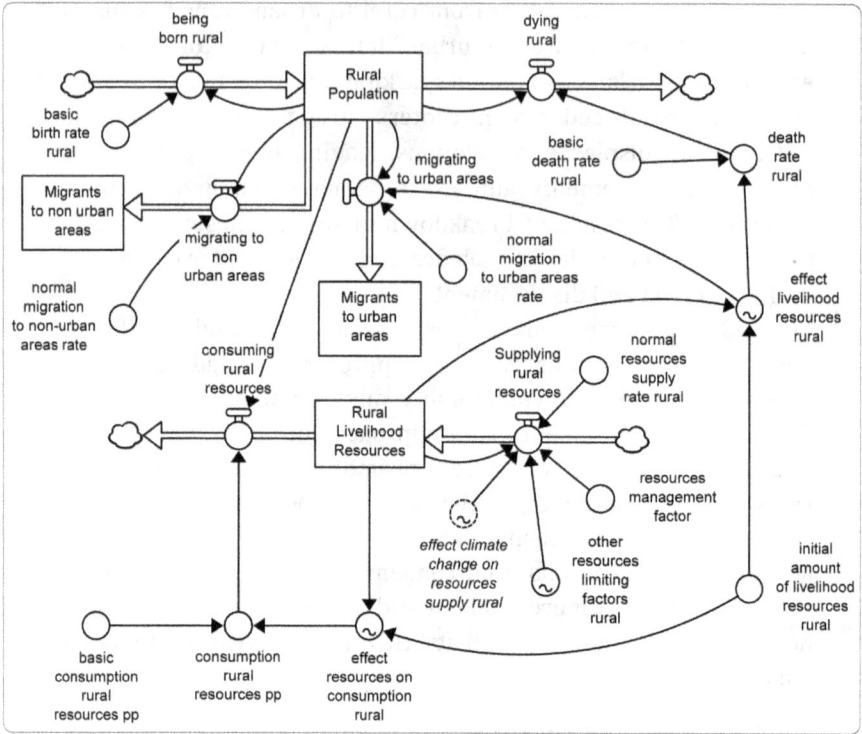

Figure 8.4a EPDSyria model. Stock and flow diagram of rural population dynamics.

Many 'other resource-limiting factors' could impact the production of rural resources. These factors may include weak governance, human insecurity, conflict, liberalization of the economy, shortage of environmental and agricultural policy, corrupt water management personnel, overgrazing, unauthorized digging of water wells, excessive extraction of groundwater, and soil degradation due to salinization and nitrate contamination.

Any policy and technical interventions that diminish the impact of "other resource limiting factors," including enhanced resource administration and management, infrastructure investments (e.g., water accumulation and wastewater treatment, desalination), conflict management, and mitigating the impacts of climate change through adjustment and reduction measures, would lead to increased availability of rural resources and a decrease in the overall migration rate to urban areas.

Urban Population Dynamics

The second part of the EPDSyria model is shown in Fig. 8.4b and demonstrates the straining impact of rural migration on urban livelihoods. Another 'overshoot and collapse' structure shows that the urban population, together with the migrant population, consumes more resources than are available. The pool of urban resources for livelihood decreases from the initial value. The factors impacting this dynamic include limited infrastructure, pollution, the absence of social programs, and mistrust and tension between rural and urban communities.

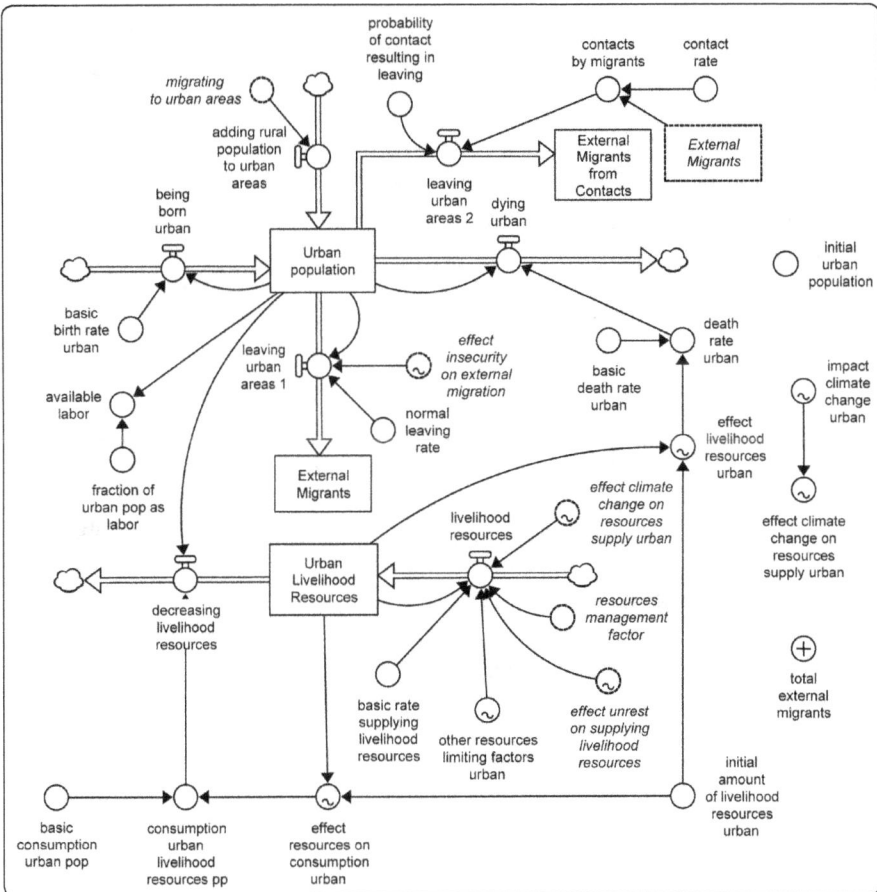

Figure 8.4b EPDSyria model. Stock and flow diagram of urban population dynamics.

External urban migration occurs for two primary reasons. One is the pursuit of safety away from urban areas, and the other is influenced by connections with individuals who have already migrated.

Any policy and technical intervention that lessens the influence of these elements, including better resource administration and minimizing the consequences of climate change through adjustment and mitigation techniques, would generate additional urban resources and decrease the general rate of external migration.

Unrest and Oppression Dynamics

The third part of the EPDSyria model is shown in Fig. 8.4c and deals with different forms of unrest. Unrest discourages job creation, and insecurity diminishes the availability of resources for populations to earn a living (Fig. 8.4b). The ratio between available urban jobs and labor in the workforce determines the population's unemployment level. Poverty and unemployment lead to significant unrest, present challenges for governments that often become more repressive, and result in heightened violence and reduced human security. This trend, in turn, leads to an increase in external migration.

Interventions that involve introducing economic reforms, promoting the election and training of qualified non-corrupt decision-makers, developing peace agreements, and implementing democratic measures such as equal rights and freedom of speech and the press could lead to an increase in urban resources and jobs, resulting in a reduction in unemployment and human insecurity, as well as a decrease in outward migration.

8.3.4.3 Numerical example

A numerical example of the EPDSyria model is presented in Appendix D and can be found on the web at https://exchange.iseesystems.com/public/bernardamadei/epdsyria. The data used in this example are based on rough data available in the literature on Syria's dynamics from 2010 to 2020 (Whitworth, 2021) and for a *sample* of the Syrian rural and urban populations. Note that this example is not intended to be a model for the entire country of Syria.

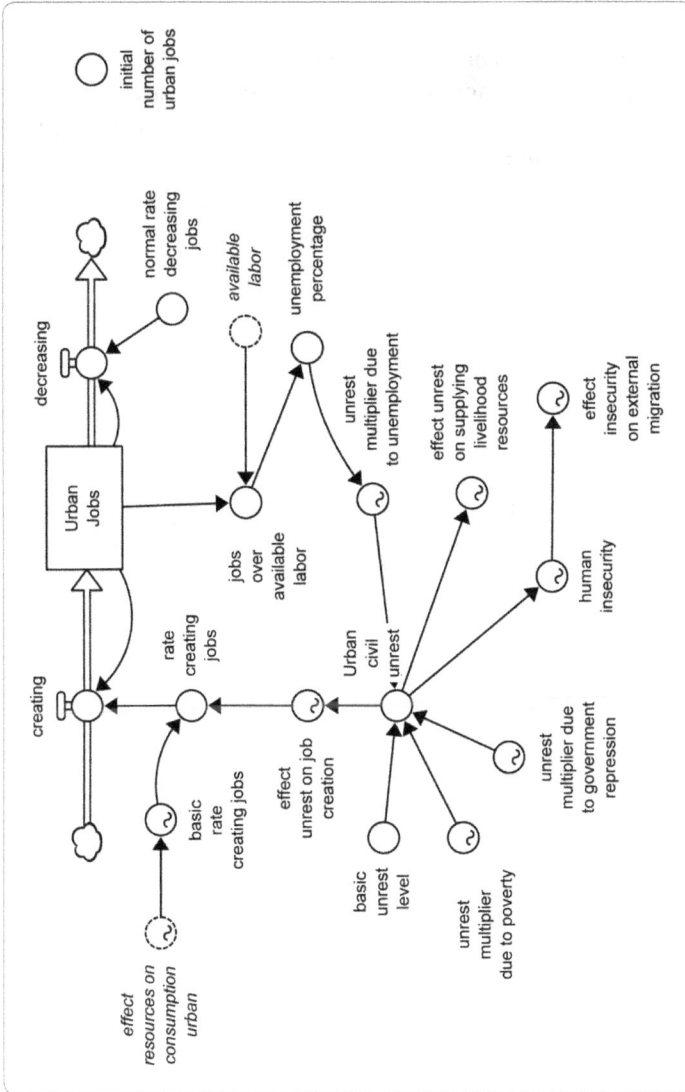

Figure 8.4c EPDSyria model. Stock and flow diagram of unrest and oppression dynamics.

Among all the variables depicted in Figs. 8.4a–c, the time-dependent impact of climate change and the level of resource management (i.e., the capacity to supply resources) for both rural and urban conditions significantly influence the resources available in urban and rural areas and internal and external migration patterns. This dependence is highlighted by the projection that the impact of climate change will escalate sharply over 20 years (refer to the graph in Appendix D), assuming that resource management will be consistent in both rural and urban

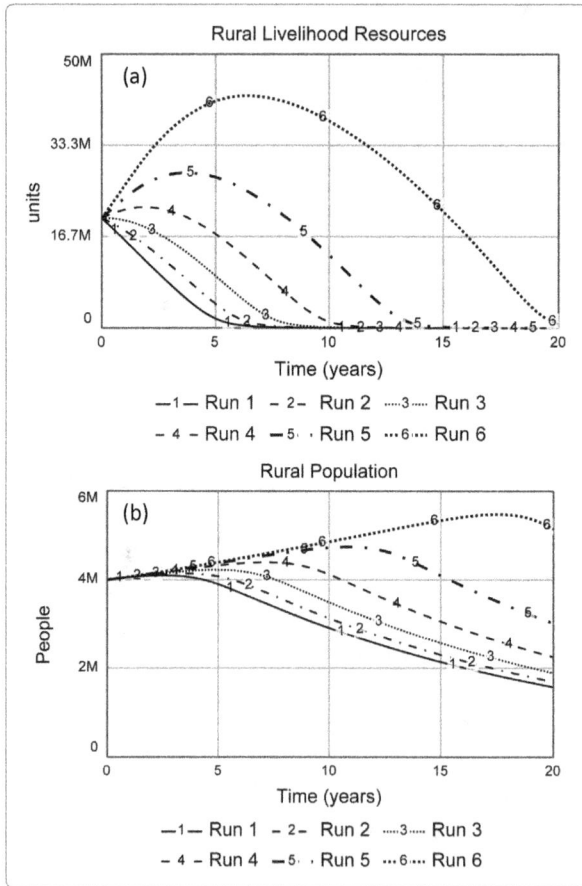

Figure 8.5 Variation in (a) rural livelihood resources and (b) rural population for different levels of resource management from 0 low (Run 1) to 5 high (Run 6).

areas and will remain uniform throughout this duration. It ranges from 0 (no management) to 5 (good management). A parametric study was conducted using the data provided in Appendix D to better understand this dependence.

Figures 8.5a and b show the increase in rural livelihood resources and rural populations with increasing levels of resource management. Similarly, Figs. 8.6a and b show a decrease in external migration and urban unrest with rising levels of resource management.

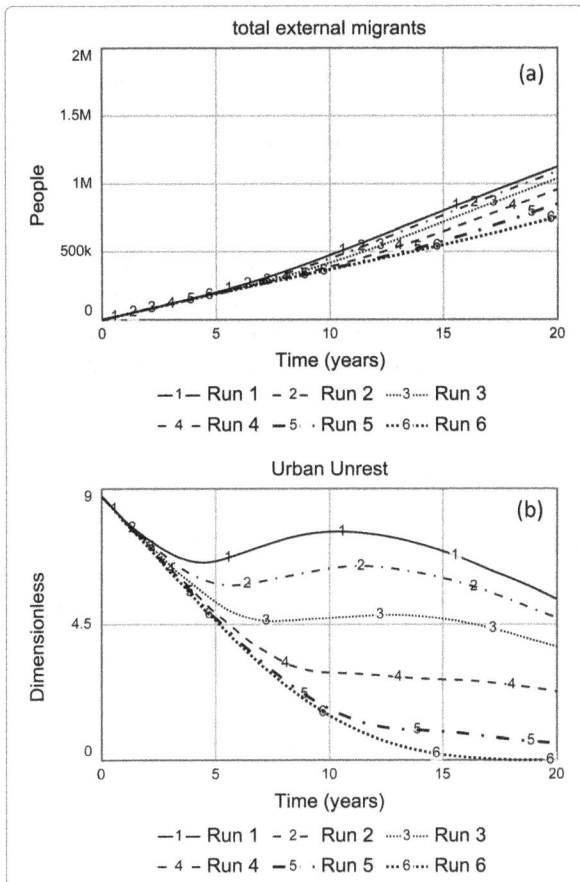

Figure 8.6 Variation in (a) total external migration and (b) urban unrest for different levels of resource management from 0 low (Run 1) to 5 high (Run 6).

8.4 Capacity and Resilience

8.4.1 Capacity and Peace

The response level of conflict-affected and conflict-sensitive communities to events of diverse adversity (e.g., conflicts, natural hazards, climate change) depends significantly on their initial capacity to handle such events and their ability to build capacity over time. The Canadian International Development Agency (Bolger, 2000) defines capacity as

> The abilities, skills, understandings, attitudes, values, relationships, behaviors, motivations, resources, and conditions that enable individuals, organizations, networks/sectors, and broader social systems to carry out functions and achieve their development objectives over time.

Community capacity defines the enabling environment of a community, where community members can cope with various situations and adapt to new needs, challenges, changes, and opportunities. Capacity is a vital attribute of resilient communities. It can be (i) *inherent* based on how community stakeholders cope with adverse events and (ii) *adaptive* to describe how they adapt to these events over time. Regardless of how capacity is defined, it is generally agreed that capacity (i) is critical to the success of human development and security; (ii) is a vital attribute of resilient, peaceful, and sustainable communities; (iii) takes time to acquire with multiple twists and turns and sometimes some setbacks; and (iv) is scale- and context-specific. Furthermore, every community has its own methods for handling crises.

The ratio of community vulnerability to capacity can be seen as a risk indicator, that is, the possibility that an undesired outcome (or the absence of the desired result) associated with an event has "adverse effects on lives, livelihoods, health, economic, social and cultural assets, services (including environmental), and infrastructure" (NRC, 2012). When faced with an event, risk can be related to community capacity and vulnerability as follows

$$\text{Risk} = \text{Exposure} \times \text{Event} \times \left(\frac{\text{Vulnerability}}{\text{Capacity}} \right) \qquad (8.1)$$

In this equation, "exposure" varies between 0 (no exposure) and 100% (total exposure). The variable "event" varies over a specific scale based on the event's adversity and impact. It should be noted that all variables in this equation depend on time.

Community resilience can be viewed as an acquired capacity. According to the NRC (2012), it is defined as "the ability [of individuals, groups, communities] to prepare and plan for, absorb, recover from, or more successfully adapt to [actual or potential] adverse events." The higher the capacity of the community, the more resilient it is to cope and adapt over time when faced with adverse events. Both capacity and resilience are critical in preventing a decline in human development and security, descending into crises and conflict, avoiding socioeconomic instability, and adapting to climate change.

Community capacity encompasses several components. For instance, Bouabid and Louis (2015) consider seven dominant groups:

- Institutional capacity encompasses policies such as laws and regulations, programs including administration and jurisdiction, and processes covering permits and performance metrics.
- Human resource capacity comprises the skills, knowledge, literacy, and competencies of individuals within the community.
- Technical capacity includes infrastructure management, upkeeping, adaptation, and the supply networks for spare parts, supplies, and services.
- Economic and financial capacities are related to a community's economic resources and financial stability. This dynamic correlates with the private sector percentage, bond ratings, user fees, budget planning, and asset valuations.
- Energy capacity encompasses access to grid electricity, additional electricity access, a percentage of the financial plan, and a reliability factor.
- Environmental and natural resource capacity is linked to the presence of natural capital and resources, along with ecosystem services.

- Socio-political-cultural capacity encompasses social networks and relationships, cultural heritage and practices, community engagement and participation, educational and informational resources, institutions and organizations, diversity and inclusion, the ability to embrace and integrate diverse cultural and social backgrounds within the community, and the ability to influence and participate in political processes and decision-making.

These seven capacity categories are interconnected and contribute to the overall ability of a community, households, and individuals to provide a specific service or reach a particular goal. Combined, these categories of capacity are essential for establishing and maintaining peace through:

- *Conflict Resolution*: High-capacity communities can effectively mediate and resolve conflicts, preventing escalation.
- *Economic Stability*: Well-organized communities can better manage resources and create economic opportunities, reducing poverty and related conflicts.
- *Social Cohesion*: Strong social networks and community participation foster trust and cooperation, which are critical for a peaceful society.
- *Education and Awareness*: Educated communities are more likely to understand and advocate for their rights, reducing the likelihood of exploitation and violence.

As discussed in Chapter 6, capacity mapping and analysis must be conducted during community appraisal. It is about mapping what the community can or cannot do. Capacity analysis is essential to determine the ability of community stakeholders to (i) reach specific goals, such as recovering from conflict, absorbing displaced populations, handling crises and emergencies related to particular adverse events and hazards, and adapting and coping with climate change, and (ii) provide services to community members to meet their basic needs, such as water and sanitation, hygiene, food, shelter, transportation, education, health, telecommunication, the management of critical infrastructure, and the prevention of violence and injury. Capacity analysis is essential in Stage 5 (i.e., modeling the landscape dynamics and its current capacity) and Stage 6 (i.e., exploring intervention scenarios, including capacity building) of the methodology shown in Fig. 7.1.

Regardless of the initial level of acquired capacity, events will likely reverse human development and security progress, which may have been built over several years or decades. Community peace, services, and security may be quickly reduced due to adverse events, and it will take a long time to return to operation following a crisis. Capacity building and peacebuilding efforts can help in the recovery process and help reach desired levels of capacity. Figure 3.4 illustrated that statement and showed the variation in community peace level following a crisis, starting from an initial value, and the role played by peacebuilding, peacemaking, and peacekeeping efforts in recovering from the crisis. A system dynamics model of that dynamic is used below to represent how community capacity changes following a crisis.

Although there is no one-size-fits-all approach to developing capacity in every community context, cultivating these abilities is a key strategy for creating sustainable, peaceful, and resilient communities. This process has the following unique characteristics:

- It creates an enabling environment with strategies for context-specific development (individual, institutional, and organizational).
- It is scale-dependent (physical and temporal) and cannot be easily extrapolated from one scale to another.
- It does not happen by itself and builds on local ownership and self-reliance.
- It promotes partnership and long-lasting broad-based community participation.
- It takes time and depends on the capacity baseline and enabling aspect of the environment in which it unfolds. The higher the baseline, the faster capacity building can be expected. This is mainly a challenge for poor communities with alow initial capacity.

Capacity building is also about investigating the level of community development the community aspires to reach, over what timeframe, and addressing existing gaps between current and desired capacities. The goal might be to achieve a certain level of sustainability, recover from conflict and peacebuilding, or be able to cope and adapt to climate change. The gap between the current and desired capacity drives the need for change. Comparing present and desired capacities helps identify, rank, plan, prioritize, and implement the most appropriate community development interventions to build capacity over time.

8.4.2 A System Dynamics Model

Let us consider a conflict-prone community with an overall initial global capacity level. For clarity, no distinction is made regarding the capacity type. Capacity is assumed to be the weighted average of the seven types mentioned above.

Figure 8.7 replicates Fig. 3.4 by substituting peace, P, for capacity, C. Starting from a base value, C_o, it is assumed that the total capacity, C, drops over time because of less emphasis on peacebuilding, growing complacency, limited resources, climate change, and political choices until a crisis occurs.

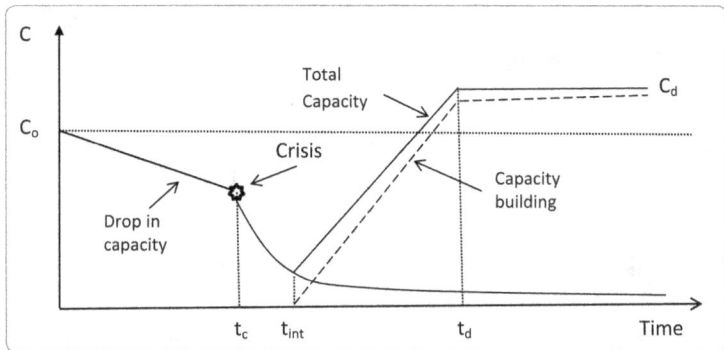

Figure 8.7 A possible mental model of variation in capacity building following a crisis. The dashed line represents capacity-building *efforts*.

At a pivotal moment t_c, a crisis, such as conflict or disaster, emerges, causing a sharp drop in community capacity to a lower level. The magnitude and rate of the drop depend on many factors, such as the severity of the stressor, its duration, and its surprising effect on the community. If left unaddressed, the capacity is assumed to decrease at a specific rate, which can be constant, time-dependent, or dependent on the initial base capacity value. This trend simulates how a community quickly loses capacity without capacity-building interventions. Examples include decreasing security as a conflict persists or the impact of climate change without community adaptation or mitigation measures in place.

Capacity building intervention starts at time t_{int}, and capacity is assumed to grow constantly until time t_d when the total capacity reaches a desired and constant level, C_d. The ratio $R = C_d/C_o$ is considered a measure of resilience.

Figure 8.8 shows a system dynamics (SD) stock and flow diagram that reproduces the dynamics of Fig. 8.7. The total community capacity is the sum of two stocks measured in capacity units, cu: a decreasing base capacity and an increasing built capacity. The total capacity can be related to a peace level.

The capacity units, cu, are *arbitrary* and are introduced here as a semi-quantitative measure of capacity. They are assumed to vary between 0 and 100 units. They are broken down into several achievement-level groups, from most constraining to most enabling, using a rating scale, such as that shown in Table 6.4. The intermediate levels include constraining-reducing, constraining-limiting, enabling-allowing, and enabling-supporting. Metrics can be introduced to describe each enabling or constraining achievement level. For instance, what does 'enabling' or 'constraining' capacity look and manifest, and how does it differ from high to low? The answers to these questions are context- and scale-specific.

In Fig. 8.8, a converter, 'external factors,' accounts for possible enabling or constraining effects associated with time-dependent beneficial (positive) or adverse (negative) events on the rate of capacity-building. The biflow in Fig. 8.8 allows the built capacity to decrease if its adjustment rate becomes negative due to adverse external factors. In this case, the built and total capacities degrade over time.

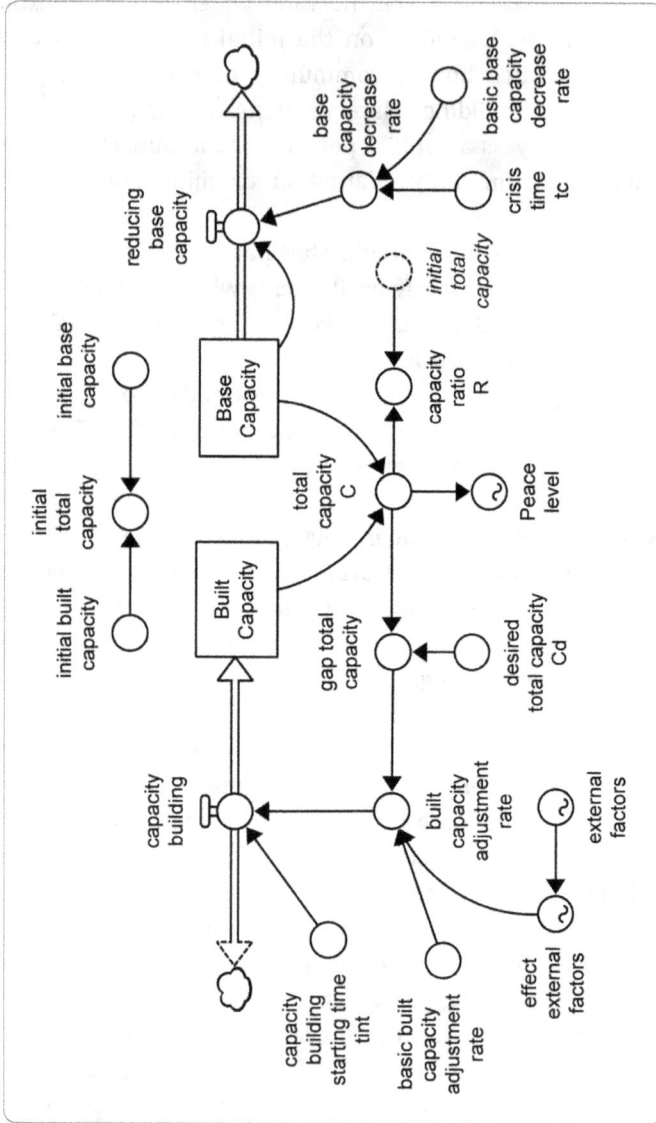

Figure 8.8 SD model of Fig. 8.7.

8.4.3   Numerical Example

A numerical example of the capacity model is presented in Appendix E and can be found on the web at https://exchange. iseesystems.com/public/bernardamadei/resiliencecapacityepd. Figure 8.9 shows the variation of the base capacity, built capacity, and total capacity over 72 months when C_o = 30 cu (constraining-reducing capacity), C_d = 50 cu (enabling-allowing capacity), t_c = 15 months, t_{int} = 20 months, the built capacity adjustment rate = 2 cu/month, and the basic base capacity decrease rate = 0.01 per month. In this example, the time t_d = 45 months, and the ratio R = 50/30 = 1.66. The total capacity decreases to a low level of 10 (most constraining) and bounces back once the capacity building is initiated within 20 months.

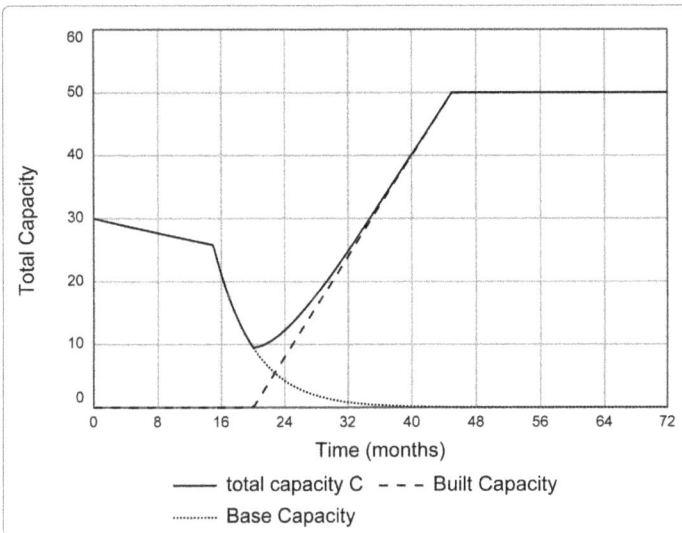

Figure 8.9 Variation in base, built, and total capacity vs. time.

A parametric study was conducted to explore the effect of the built capacity effort rate in determining when the desired total capacity is reached. The rate varies between 0 (no capacity building) and 4 cu/month. As shown in Fig. 8.10, the faster the rate, the sooner the total capacity reaches its desired level, with t_d decreasing from 69 to 32 months.

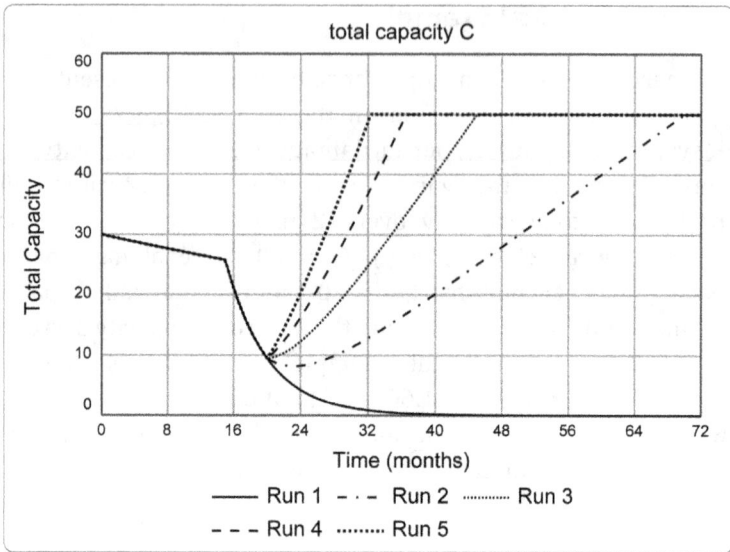

Figure 8.10 Variation in total capacity for different basic built capacity adjustment rates (cu/month): 0 (run 1), 1 (run 2), 2 (run 3), 3 (run 4), and 4 (run 5).

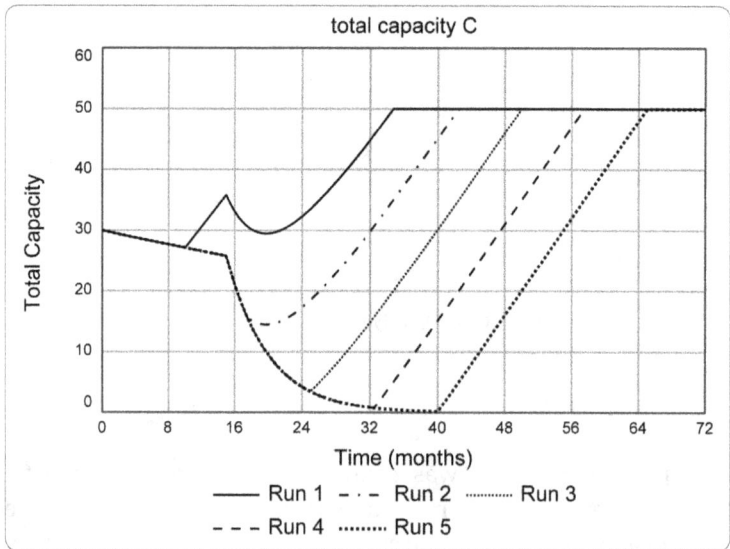

Figure 8.11 Variation in total capacity for different values of the starting time (in months) of capacity building. 10 (run 1), 20 (run 2), 30 (run 3), and 40 (run 4). The basic built capacity adjustment rate = 2 cu/month.

The timing of when to begin capacity building is also a vital factor in the model: delaying it after a crisis can result in a lengthy recovery phase. There is a risk that postponing the onset of capacity-building efforts may prevent achieving an acceptable level within an acceptable timeframe. Figure 8.11 shows the results of a parametric study when the starting time t_{int} varies between 10 (before the crisis) and 40 months. Delays in the starting time create delays in reaching the desired capacity level. Figure 8.11 also demonstrates the value proposition of starting capacity-building efforts before the crisis. An example would be to make mitigative efforts by building and strengthening capacities before a crisis occurs.

The numerical example presented above shows that the time taken to reach a desired level of community resilience (e.g., $R = 2.0$ in the present example) in capacity building after a crisis depends on the starting time of capacity building and its implementation rate. The example above considers one type of capacity. Similar analyses can be conducted for various capacity types, such as the seven types outlined previously. Each capacity category has a capacity-building starting time, desired value, and implementation rate. Some categories of capacity building take longer to initiate and develop.

8.5   Concluding Remarks

This chapter highlighted the complex interactions among conflict, climate change, and migration. It explored how to model these dynamics qualitatively using causal loop diagrams and quantitatively using stock and flow diagrams. A significant difficulty in quantitative modeling is the collection of data for all critical variables, changes, and their connections. This issue can be addressed using reliable existing literature and reasonable experiential data. The system dynamics program utilized here also supports sensitivity analysis to help pinpoint key variables that deserve special attention in decision-making.

This chapter emphasized the importance of resilience in areas prone to conflict, climate shifts, and migration. Building strength within these communities is crucial for evaluating current capacities and identifying the differences between present capabilities and desired outcomes. As outlined in Chapter 7, recognizing these gaps allows for a clear understanding of community issues and the development of flexible plans for intervention. From there, appropriate strategies can be selected and implemented in the order of priority.

References

Amadei, B. (2023). *Navigating the Complexity Across the Peace–Sustainability–Climate Security Nexus.* Boca Raton: Routledge. ISBN 9781032563381

Anand, R. (2020, Oct. 14). Understanding the Syrian Civil War through Galtung's Conflict Theory. The Peninsula Foundation. https://www.thepeninsula.org.in/2020/10/14/understanding-the-syrian-civil-war-through-galtungs-conflict-theory/

Angelo, P. J. (2021, March 22). Why Central American migrants are arriving at the U.S. border. Council on Foreign Relations. Why Central American Migrants Are Arriving at the U.S. Border | Council on Foreign Relations (cfr.org)

BenDor, T. and Scheffran, J. (2019). *Agent-Based Modeling of Environmental Conflict and Cooperation.* Boca Raton: CRC Press.

Bolger, J. (2000). Capacity development: Why, what, and how. https://www.researchgate.net/publication/268354675_Capacity_development_Why_what_and_how

Bouabid, M. and Louis, G. (2015). Capacity factors for evaluating water and sanitation infrastructure choices for developing communities. *Journal of Environmental Management.* **161**, 335–343. https://doi.org/10.1016/j.jenvman.2015.07.012

Chemonics/CDA (2023). Climate Change and Conflict in Ghana. https://www.cdacollaborative.org/wp-content/uploads/2023/08/Climate-and-Conflict-in-Ghana.pdf

Darwish, S. (2023). Resilience and Social Cohesion in Fiji's Climate-Affected Informal Settlements: An Environment-Fragility Peace Nexus project case study. Cambridge, MA: CDA Collaborative Learning Projects, 2023. With contributions from Conciliation Resources and the Pacific Center for Peacebuilding. https://www.cdacollaborative.org/wp-content/uploads/2023/04/Fiji-case-study-FINAL.pdf

Devex (2023). 'Drought is the enemy': The communities fighting hunger in Somaliland (shorthandstories.com)

Glass, N. (2010). The water crisis in Yemen: Causes, consequences, and solutions. *Global Majority E-Journal*, **1**(1), 17–3.

Gleick, P. H. (2014) Water, drought, climate change, and conflict in Syria. *American Meteorological Society*, **6**, 331–340. https://doi.org/10.1175/WCAS-D-13-00059.1

Gleick, P. H. (2019). Water as a weapon and casualty of armed conflict: A review of recent water-related violence in Iraq, Syria, and Yemen. *WIREs Water*. https://doi.org/10.1002/wat2.1351

Hamad, S. (2018, March 09). The dehumanization of Syria's victims facilitates war crimes. Retrieved July 26, 2020, from https://www.trtworld.com/opinion/the-dehumanisation-of-syria-s-victims-facilitates-war-crimes-15802.

Internal Displacement Monitoring Center (IDMC) (2021) Global Report on Internal Displacement (GRID) 2021. https://www.internal-displacement.org/global-report/grid2021/

International Rescue Committee (IRC) (2022). 2022 Annual Report. https://www.rescue.org/sites/default/files/2023-07/AnnualReport_2022.pdf

Issifu, A. K., Darko, F. D., and Paalo, S. A. (2022). Climate change, migration and farmer-herder conflict in Ghana. *Conflict Resolution Quarterly*, **39**(4), 421–439. https://doi.org/10.1002/crq.21346

Kelley, C. P., Mohtadi, S., Cane, M. A., Seager, R., and Kushnir, Y. (2015). Climate change in the Fertile Crescent and implications of the recent Syrian drought. *Proceedings of the U. S. National Academy of Sciences*, **112**(11), 3241–3246. https://doi.org/10.1073/pnas.1421533112

Killelea, S. (2021). *Peace in the Age of Chaos: The Best Solution for a Sustainable Future*. Melbourne: Hardie Grant Books.

Massari, P. (2013, September 10). Religion and Conflict in Syria. Retrieved July 26, 2020, from https://hds.harvard.edu/news/2013/09/10/religion-and-conflict-syria

Moore, L. V. (2014). Resilience and conflict prevention in West Darfur. Summer 2014 Insights Newsletter - Resilience | United States Institute of Peace (usip.org)

Mowjee, T., Garrasi, D., and Poole, L. (2015) *Coherence in conflict: Bringing humanitarian and development aid streams together*, DANIDA, Ministry of Foreign Affairs of Denmark. coherence in conflict web 1. pdf (humanitarianoutcomes.org)

National Research Council (NRC) (2012). *Disaster Resilience: A National Imperative.* Washington, DC: The National Academies Press. https://doi.org/10.17226/13457

OCHA (2017). New way of working. New Way of Working [EN/KO] | OCHA (unocha.org)

OECD. (2017). *Humanitarian development coherence.* https://www.oecd.org/development/humanitarian-donors/docs/coherence-oecd-Guideline.pdf

OpenAI (2024). *ChatGPT* (July 4 version) [Large language model]. https://chat.openai.com

Peacedirect (2022, Sept. 20). Migration and peacebuilding. Migration & Peacebuilding - Peace Direct

Peters, K., Dupar, M., Opitz-Stapleton, S., Lovell, E., and Cao, Y. (2020). Climate change, conflict, and fragility: An evidence review and recommendations for research and action. Climate change, conflict, and fragility: an evidence review and recommendations for research and action | ODI: Think change

Pulley, K. (2021). A systems approach to understanding the Yemen civil war and humanitarian crisis. Term paper, CVEN 5837, University of Colorado, Boulder.

Schwartzstein, P. and Risi, L. (2023, Jan. 26). Climate Change and Migration: Reporting from Bangladesh, Moldova, and Senegal. Wilson Center environmental change and security program. Climate Change and Migration: Reporting from Bangladesh, Moldova, and Senegal | Wilson Center

Selby, J., Dahi, O.S., Fröhlich, C., and Hulme, M. (2017). Climate change and the Syrian civil war revisited. *Political Geography*, **60**, 232–244. https://doi.org/10.1016/j.polgeo.2017.05.007

Suter, M. (2017, Sept. 12). Running out of water: Conflict and water scarcity in Yemen and Syria. https://www.atlanticcouncil.org/blogs/menasource/running-out-of-water-conflict-and-water-scarcity-in-yemen-and-syria

Tesfaye, B. (2022). Climate change and conflict in the Sahel. Council on Foreign Relations. https://www.cfr.org/report/climate-change-and-conflict-sahel

UNHCR (2024). How climate change impacts refugees and displaced populations. How climate change impacts refugees and displaced communities (unrefugees.org)

UNSTAS (2023). https://unstats.un.org/sdgs/report/2023/Goal-11/

Vidal, J. (2016, 7 Sept.). Water supplies in Syria deteriorating fast due to conflict, experts warn. *The Guardian*, 2016, https://www.theguardian.com/environment/2016/sep/07/water-supplies-in-syria-deteriorating-fast-due-to-conflict-experts-warn.

WEF (2021). Climate refugees: The world's forgotten victims. Climate refugees – the world's forgotten victims | World Economic Forum (weforum.org)

Werrell, C. E. and Femia, F. (eds.) (2013, Feb. 28). *The Arab Spring and Climate Change: A Climate and Security Correlations Series.* climatechangearabspring-ccs-cap-stimson.pdf (wordpress.com)

Whitworth, H. (2021). Understanding the Syrian conflict through a system less. Term paper, CVEN 5837, University of Colorado, Boulder.

Chapter 9

Discussion and Conclusions

This chapter concludes with the significant themes addressed in the book and, more specifically, the need to address the interaction between engineering, peacebuilding, and diplomatic efforts at the community level in an integrated, dynamic, multidisciplinary, and participatory manner. Among all future challenges, there is a need to create a portfolio of case studies to operationalize this new approach and demonstrate its value proposition in human development and security at different scales. Thus, a transformative, holistic, and interdisciplinary approach to engineering education and practice is required.

9.1   Book's Takeaways

This book examines the intersection of engineering with peacebuilding and diplomacy. It provides a detailed framework to assist engineers in fostering peace and stability through projects in diverse settings, including conflict-prone communities. A first takeaway from this book is that engineering, peacebuilding, and diplomacy contribute to bridging the gap between the current and desired levels of human development and security. Engineering, peacebuilding, and diplomacy interact with various socioeconomic, cultural, infrastructure, environmental, and human systems.

Engineering for Peace and Diplomacy
Bernard Amadei
Copyright © 2025 Jenny Stanford Publishing Pte. Ltd.
ISBN 978-981-5129-75-5 (Hardcover), 978-1-003-65168-0 (eBook)
www.jennystanford.com

Addressing the connections between these fields and systems requires a systemic or integrated approach that extends beyond traditional human development and security practices.

A second takeaway from this book is that engineers must collaborate with other disciplines, such as peace and conflict studies, international relations, and environmental science, to conduct projects that contribute to peacebuilding and diplomacy in communities affected by or at risk of conflict and other adverse events. Global issues of the 21st century are complex and interlinked and demand a mix of expertise beyond technology. Engineers must embrace a transdisciplinary approach that combines technical and non-technical disciplines to devise integrated, sustainable, and scalable solutions. Collaborative efforts can yield innovative solutions to complex global challenges.

As a third takeaway, the book emphasizes that significant changes in engineering education are necessary to prepare future engineers for the complexities of modern challenges. These entail incorporating systems thinking, ethical considerations, and global engagement into their academic preparation. Skills, knowledge, training, and lifelong learning are needed in the body of knowledge of 21st-century engineers. Designing engineering programs that foster technical expertise and provide insight into societal and global matters across various contexts and scales is crucial. All these changes have the potential to remarkably impact the continuous professional development of engineers and enhance their lifelong contributions to society.

The book's fourth insight emphasizes the need for a complex system-aware strategy to navigate the intricate relationship between engineering, peacebuilding, and diplomacy in conflict-prone communities. This approach differs from, but complements, the traditional reductionist approach, which concentrates on addressing problems individually and in isolation by specialists, experts, individuals, or groups. Decisions in this approach are made according to simple representations of the world influenced by a narrow range of understanding, perceptions, perspectives, convictions, sensations, emotions, experiences, proficiency, and behaviors. The organized simplicity of reductionistic and deterministic approaches has often led to solutions that create unintended consequences. In human development and security, reductionist decision-making has frequently resulted in poorly executed interventions with no long-term benefits, resulting in diminished livelihoods, conflicts, and divided communities. A complex system-aware approach can overcome these limitations.

This book's fifth and concluding takeaway is that interventions encompassing engineering, peacebuilding, and diplomacy in conflict-prone communities are never haphazardly chosen. Therefore, a systematic, step-by-step approach grounded in systems thinking is crucial. This structured approach assists those making decisions in assessing conflict-prone areas, comprehending their dynamics, devising possible intervention strategies and plans, selecting the best viable options, overseeing their execution, and evaluating their impact.

9.2 Detailed Conclusions

9.2.1 Engineering and Society

This book begins by recognizing that engineering for peace and diplomacy is deeply intertwined with society. Its impact extends from improving people's daily lives to contributing to international relations and resolving conflicts. As discussed in Chapter 2, three quantum leaps in the relationship between engineering and society can be identified: (i) the 1850s–1950s characterized by technical rationality and providing value-neutral technical solutions to well-defined problems, following the deterministic attitude of the nineteenth century; (ii) the 1960s-1990s driven by the environmental and sustainability movement emerging as a response to unrestrained confidence in technology and the belief that the economy and environment were compatible; and (iii) the 1990s–present characterized by highly complex issues in the vulnerable, uncertain, complex, and ambiguous (VUCA) world in the 21st century. Short of being exhaustive, they include (i) climate change and security risks; (ii) rapid urbanization; (iii) population growth, migration, and human resettlement; (iv) water, energy, food, and land resource security; (v) access to education, shelter, healthcare, ICT, and employment; (vi) environmental damage and biodiversity loss; (vii) natural and human-induced risks and emergencies; (viii) peacebuilding and violent conflict prevention and recovery; (ix) social equality and inclusive growth; and (x) national and global security. Engineering is becoming increasingly vital in the third quantum leap, which focuses on advancing human development and addressing security concerns.

Each quantum leap has had its own successes and failures, as engineering projects have not always benefited people and the environment. Technology has improved the quality of life of many societies in the 19th and 20th centuries. However, in many instances, it has also contributed to unplanned or undesirable effects on natural and human systems and multiple negative externalities. In the 21st century, engineers must acknowledge their constraints and reassess their foundational assumptions and principles. The question is how engineers should prepare accordingly.

Engineering is crucial for human development and security in the 21st-century world. The engineering profession is asked to deliver technical solutions, develop and implement solutions that benefit people and the planet (nature-based solutions), contribute to prosperity, create partnerships, and foster peace and diplomatic relations. Beyond their technical duties, engineers are pivotal in developing resilient infrastructure and maintaining critical services, such as water, energy, shelter, and healthcare, contributing to peace and economic stability. Incorporating engineering into peacebuilding, peacemaking, peacekeeping, and diplomatic efforts provides a strategic way to tackle the underlying issues in conflict-prone settings toward lasting peace. This approach enhances the effectiveness of engineering solutions and has the potential to promote mutual understanding and cooperation among nations.

The engineering profession is usually not directly associated with diplomacy. This book aims to dispel this assumption and seeks to elevate the contribution of the engineering profession to Track 1.5 or 2, and citizen diplomacy. Engineering diplomacy parallels science diplomacy. Engineers are essential players in international relations and can foster collaboration on shared technical challenges and build partnerships across borders. Engineering projects related to environmental sustainability, infrastructure development, and arms control can serve as platforms for diplomatic engagement. Engineering initiatives can form the foundation of diplomatic ties by encouraging cooperation between common challenges and enhancing bilateral comprehension. This approach improves the effectiveness of engineering solutions and promotes mutual understanding and cooperation among nations.

Finally, policymakers and practitioners must recognize engineers' vital roles in peacebuilding and diplomacy. They should promote collaboration across disciplines and support initiatives that connect engineering with the social sciences and humanities. Plans should be created to involve engineers in diplomatic and peacebuilding activities while continuing to contribute to sustainable development and climate change mitigation and adaptation measures.

9.2.2 Reforming Engineering Education

The above observations on engineering and society have implications for educating engineers to address the local and global planetary challenges of the 21st century and contribute to a more sustainable and peaceful world. Chapter 2 underscores the need for a shift in engineering education to meet the unique challenges presented by the 21st century, which are distinct from those of the 19th and 20th centuries. However, most engineers today still lack the attitudes, skills, and knowledge to address issues humanity is likely to face in the next 20 years and beyond. Global issues facing our planet have become more convergent and severe, and the engineering profession has been slow to adapt to the changes necessary to address them. This narrow-mindedness is predominantly found in today's engineering education, where students are still taught to develop solutions for a world mostly disconnected from reality. Current engineering education struggles to keep pace with the ever-changing world, making it challenging to fulfill its requirements.

For the most part, conventional engineering education does not align with the expectations of students and professionals, as it appears to have limited relevance to societal problems in the 21st century. A new perspective is required in engineering education and practice to contribute to human development, security, conflict resolution, and diplomacy. As discussed in this book, engineers involved in peace and diplomacy must be informed globally and educated accordingly. Hence, substantial changes to traditional engineering education are necessary to make it more adaptable and aligned with current and future societal needs. Significant changes in engineering education entail incorporating systems thinking, ethical considerations, and global engagement into academic preparation. Designing engineering programs that foster technical expertise and provide insight into societal and global matters across various contexts and scales is crucial.

Chapter 2 reviews several engineering education frameworks proposed in the literature over the past 10–20 years. However, despite being comprehensive, there is no consensus on what represents desirable training for engineers in the 21st century. Furthermore, none of these frameworks emphasize educating engineers to address peace and conflict issues at different scales, from local to global. Engineering education should be interpreted as being multiple with (i) core components such as those proposed by the Barcelona Declaration and the Engineering for One Planet framework and (ii) other components that are context- and scale-specific. Creating a universal engineering framework that suits everyone is unreasonable. Engineering education must be seen "as a plural."

A holistic, interdisciplinary approach to engineering education and practice that aligns with real-world problems is required. It must focus on the mindset of *learning* rather than *schooling* with *T-type* (depth and breadth) or *V-type* (broadening depth and breadth) education, rather than the traditional specialized *I-type* (depth only) education. Engineers must be trained to work with social scientists, policymakers, and diplomats to create comprehensive solutions that address global technical, social, and political challenges. This transdisciplinary collaboration is essential for addressing climate change, resource management, and conflict resolution. By promoting this approach, this book lays the foundation for a new generation of engineers equipped to contribute to global peace and stability. Such global engagement requires lifelong learning and quick adaptation to swiftly evolving social and environmental contexts.

Engineering competencies can best be summarized into four main and related categories: technical, social, personal, and strategic. Engineers must possess technical competencies that are most effective when complemented by (i) practical communication skills (social competency), (ii) adaptability to changing situations (personal competency), and (iii) the ability to make informed decisions that align with project objectives (strategic competency).

9.2.3 Peace Engineering and Engineering Diplomacy

Chapter 3 discusses the dimensions of peace, conflict, and diplomacy. Peace engineering and engineering diplomacy represent a novel perspective that accentuates the significance of engineering in peacebuilding and diplomatic efforts. Engineers must develop a compassionate and curious mindset to understand conflict origins and their various types and create resolutions that tackle technical and societal facets entwined with culture, economy, and politics. Engineering and diplomacy are crucial for promoting peace and stability worldwide. Engineering plays a vital role in infrastructure development, humanitarian aid, and conflict prevention, whereas diplomacy promotes peace through negotiations, mediation, and international cooperation to resolve conflicts. Collaboration between engineers and diplomats has a significant value proposition in pre-, conflict, and post-conflict settings.

A question arises regarding the appropriate body of knowledge for engineers interested in building and supporting peace and diplomacy. How should engineers be trained to develop sound nature-based solutions for people and the environment and to create prosperity and partnerships through collaborative work? How can engineers be best equipped with the attitudes, skills, knowledge, attitudes, and lifelong experience necessary to work at the crossroads between the technical and non-technical components of conflict and peace through collaboration with social scientists, policymakers, and other stakeholders? How should they handle challenges such as political obstacles and cultural sensitivity? Understanding conflict and the dynamics among the engineering–peacebuilding–diplomacy nexus sectors is critical to peace engineering.

A limited number of programs that address peace engineering and its role in diplomacy exist today. Since 2016, such programs have gradually gained recognition (Jordan et al., 2020). A potential explanation could be that society and the media have not fully recognized the role of engineers in peace and diplomacy efforts. The engineering sector must expand and promote various initiatives in engineering diplomacy, transcend these barriers, and establish them as normative practices. Creating a community of practices focusing on peace and engineering diplomacy is essential for achieving this goal. It is necessary to develop a body of knowledge to train scientists, technologists, and engineers on the fundamentals of diplomacy and how to train diplomats to integrate science, technology, and engineering into their daily decision-making. Creating a platform for peace and engineering diplomacy is an effective method for attracting young individuals from different scientific and engineering disciplines. It also serves as a springboard for innovation, business development, and job creation. Scientists and engineers must recognize that in addition to providing scientific and technical knowledge and solutions, they can also be entrepreneurs, peacemakers, and facilitators of sustainable human development. Improving the world for everyone is not just a choice for scientific and engineering professionals but a responsibility. Diplomacy serves as a guide for achieving this goal.

9.2.4 Changing the Mindset

Chapter 4 explores the desirable components of the new mindset and thinking pattern necessary for engineers and decision-makers to navigate the complexities of human development, security, peacebuilding, and diplomacy in the 21st-century world. Decision-makers must be able to (i) navigate ambiguous and complex situations; (ii) adapt to change and innovate quickly; (iii) recognize and differentiate the positive and negative externalities of their projects; (iv) contribute to collaborative transdisciplinary work; (v) develop creative and innovative (i.e., ingenious) solutions that are appropriate to the context and scale; (vi) plan, design, and implement projects for peace; (vii) consider first- and second-order solutions; (viii) recognize that existing solutions already exist instead of reinventing the wheel; (ix) ensure that, in the short and long terms, solutions are the right ones, rightly done, and selected for the right reasons; (x) consider the participatory nature of projects and the role of stakeholders; and (xi) respect life through the right relationships.

Decision-makers must reevaluate their cognitive framework or mental models to address the complexities of peacebuilding and diplomacy in the 21st century. Factors such as prevailing societal attitudes, ethical principles, routines, prejudices, hierarchies, cultural contexts, religious beliefs, allegiances, rules, and methods contribute to this framework. These factors shape an individual's inner approach to issues related to human development, security, and conflict resolution, thereby influencing their perception of the challenges and how they tackle them. This inner perspective directly influences the outer decision-making processes, as the latter reflects the former. Where do engineers learn about their inner perspectives in decision-making during their formative years?

Mental models are important because they significantly influence the system structures of engineering, peacebuilding, and diplomatic efforts. These structures, in turn, create behavioral patterns and shape how events (peaceful or conflicting) unfold. This dynamic was captured in the iceberg model, as shown in Fig. 4.2. It represents an excellent metaphor for understanding that community issues do not change by placing external band-aids on them, a tactic often employed in human development and security. Instead, they require changing the underlying mindset and creating different structures and behavioral patterns that ultimately affect problems and outcomes. Changing one's mindset represents a leverage point for developing engineering, peacebuilding, and diplomatic efforts.

9.2.5   Systems Thinking Perspective

Chapter 5 emphasizes the value proposition of adopting a system-aware practice and mindset when considering engineering interventions for peacebuilding and diplomacy. Engineers must embrace the principles of organized complexity and systems science when addressing intricate issues concerning human development and security. Globally engaged engineers must be system thinkers.

Systems thinking marks a paradigm shift in engineering. Traditional 20th-century engineering approaches have often focused on isolated technical problems. This book advocates a holistic view that considers the interconnectedness of social, environmental, and economic systems and how engineering, peacebuilding, and diplomacy interact with these systems. This book suggests that engineers can develop more sustainable and practical solutions using a systems approach, making them more adaptable and innovative in problem-solving.

A system-aware practice forces decision-makers among the three stakeholder groups in this book (i.e., community members, governments, and community outsiders) to distinguish between different levels of complexity using reflective practice when confronted with community issues. Decision-makers must also be familiar with and able to use appropriate decision-making methods, which may range from directive methods with strong objectivity to interactive methods that are more subjective. Objective tools are more likely to address complicated technical issues that unfold in the infrastructure and economic systems of conflict-prone settings. On the other hand, subjective tools are preferred by creative, self-reflective decision-makers faced with uncertain, flexible, and adaptive systems and situations. They are better suited for making decisions about social and environmental systems in conflict-prone settings.

Chapters 5 and 6 explore the value proposition of using complementary soft systems qualitative tools (e.g., concept maps, cross-impact analysis, and network analysis) and hard systems tools (e.g., system dynamics, agent-based modeling, and hybrid methods) to model the interaction between engineering, peacebuilding, and diplomatic efforts, and the messy or ill-defined issues at play in that interaction. The fundamentals of systems and systems thinking and the habits of system thinkers are discussed in Chapter 5.

Chapter 6 focuses on the different steps involved in modeling the complex landscapes of conflict-prone communities. It reviews the approaches necessary to conduct system-aware community appraisal and modeling. This book looks more specifically at system dynamics, a powerful hard system modeling tool that, when combined with soft tools such as network analysis, multi-criteria decision analysis, cross-impact analysis, capacity analysis, and scenario planning, can be used to reproduce, at least in part, the past and current complex dynamics of the landscape in which community development unfolds. System dynamics can handle complex dynamics qualitatively using causal loop diagrams or quantitatively using stock and flow diagrams. Once calibrated, system dynamics models can help conduct "what-if" and "what-happens-if" simulations, sensitivity analysis, and optimization. Chapter 6 presents a simple system dynamics model to demonstrate how to account for the interactions among engineering, peacebuilding, and diplomatic efforts.

Additionally, Chapter 6 reviews several archetypes of the interactions between engineering, peacebuilding, and diplomatic efforts. Examples illustrating each archetype are presented. Archetypes are recurring behavior patterns and generic structures. They are helpful in system dynamics modeling when defining the structure of models and identifying the places to intervene in that structure. Once an archetype is identified, possible leverage areas of intervention can be identified.

9.2.6 A System-Based Methodology

Chapter 7 presents a system-based methodology that can be used by decision-makers involved in addressing complex issues across the engineering–peacebuilding–diplomacy nexus in a conflict-affected or conflict-sensitive environment. Although the methodology is generic, it provides a road map and guidelines to address the problems of each sector of the nexus and across the nexus while considering how the sectors interact with social, economic, environmental, and infrastructure community systems. This methodology is based on the premise that there is a storyline or road map describing how a conflict-affected or conflict-sensitive community envisions bridging the gap between its current and desired development and security states. This approach requires meaningful participation and engagement from both internal and external stakeholder groups in community-based projects.

As described in my book on the intersection of peace, sustainability, and climate security (Amadei, 2023), the initial step of the road map involves comprehending the context, scale, boundaries, and environment in which engineering, peacebuilding, diplomacy, and community development occur. After defining the situation space in the initial stage, the subsequent step is to collect and analyze the data. A community baseline profile is established using system mapping and visualization tools. This step is followed by (i) formulation and ranking of landscape-related issues, (ii) modeling of these issues, (iii) selection and ranking of possible interventions to address these issues, and (iv) creation of an intervention plan. Following this plan, solutions are implemented, monitored, and evaluated. Adopting a system- and complexity-conscious approach is crucial at every methodology stage. This approach entails conducting a thorough analysis of the environment, recognizing and defining issues, and determining their order of importance. The formulation, assessment, and ranking of intervention scenarios should follow the same holistic strategy. Finally, this approach requires the recognition of numerous feedback loops among the various stages of the methodological framework.

9.2.7 Modeling Examples

Chapter 8 presents various case studies utilizing the system dynamics method to delve into the complex dynamics within communities prone to conflict. It investigates the interplay between conflict, climate change, and migration. Specifically, it explores the drivers of displacement and migration, rural-to-urban migration, and herder–farmer dynamics that seem dominant in regions affected by climate change, combined with other socioeconomic, political, and cultural constraints. The crisis in Syria is an excellent example of such a dynamic.

Chapter 8 describes the steps involved in modeling the interplay between conflict, climate change, and migration. What are the storylines, critical variables, and causal relationships involved in this interplay? What are the possible interventions?

The response level of conflict-prone communities to events of diverse adversity (e.g., conflicts, natural hazards, and climate change) depends significantly on their initial capacity to handle such events and their ability to build capacity over time. Implementing engineering strategies, developing peacebuilding initiatives, and conducting diplomatic efforts are crucial for devising interventional strategies and realizing social transformation.

Regardless of the initial level of acquired capacity, adverse events are likely to reverse human development and security progress, which may have been built over several years or decades. Community peace, services, and security may be quickly reduced due to adverse events, and take a long time to return to operation following a crisis. Capacity building and peacebuilding efforts can help recover and reach the desired capacity levels. This dynamic is illustrated in Chapter 8 with a system dynamics model that shows the importance of time in implementing capacity-building measures and their intensity in reaching a desired level of capacity and resilience.

A challenge in modeling peacebuilding, engineering, diplomatic, and capacity efforts in Chapters 6 and 8 is finding semi-quantitative measures that can be used to assess progress and impact. The same challenges were encountered in the peace, sustainability, and climate security nexus (Amadei, 2023). In Chapter 6, arbitrary engineering, peacebuilding, and diplomatic effort units were selected to range over three [0–100] scales broken down into several achievement-level groups, from the most constrained to the most enabling, using a semi-quantitative rating scale (Table 6.4). The same approach was used for the capacity units described in Chapter 8.

This semi-quantitative approach requires that metrics and indicators are introduced for completeness to describe how engineering, peacebuilding, diplomatic, and capacity efforts unfold and interact for each achievement level. This is illustrated in Table 9.1.

Table 9.1 Possible metrics used to determine the achievement level of engineering, peacebuilding, diplomatic, and capacity efforts

Most constraining	Constraining -reducing	Constraining -limiting	Enabling -allowing	Enabling -supporting	Most enabling
1–20	21–40	41–50	51–60	61–80	81–100
A	A+B	A+B+C	A+B+C+D	A+B+C+D+E	A+B+C+D+E+F
(A) ...					
	(B) ...				
		(C) ...			
			(D) ...		
				(E) ...	
					(F) ...

9.3   Future Nexus Challenges

As mentioned in my last two books on the water–energy–land–food nexus and the peace–sustainability–climate security nexus, a systems- and complexity-aware approach to any nexus does not come without its share of challenges and questions. These challenges also apply to engineering, peacebuilding, and diplomatic interactions. One of them, which traditional development practitioners and decision-makers often find hard to accept, is that it is impossible to develop concrete and optimum solutions to complex and uncertain issues in nexus sectors and community landscapes. However, multiple *sufficiently good* solutions, some better than others, are possible. Decision-makers should understand that tackling engineering, peacebuilding, and diplomacy in community development is more about satisficing than optimizing and that they should thoroughly consider trade-offs and synergies across all interconnected sectors.

Many open-ended questions are yet to be answered, such as how consensus about engineering, peacebuilding, and diplomatic solutions can be reached among stakeholders. How are conflicting opinions addressed? How should interventions be monitored and evaluated after their implementation? How can we achieve successful interventions and guarantee their success and benefit over time? How consistent are the intervention scenarios with the rules of interaction between the nexus sectors and stakeholders? Ultimately, what represents successful engineering, peacebuilding, and diplomatic efforts?

There are also questions about modeling the engineering, peacebuilding, and diplomacy nexus in an integrated manner. For instance, what are the initial conditions for community peace, conflict, and capacity? An integrated approach also requires detailed mapping and understanding of the nexus and landscape structure, including its components (i.e., systems, subsystems, and sub-subsystems), links, and feedback mechanisms among these components. Such an approach also requires modelers to select an appropriate study scale in a given context and appropriate boundary conditions that dictate what is exogenous and endogenous to the study being conducted. To this list, one can add a need to identify and formulate appropriate indicators of engineering, peacebuilding, and diplomacy and to select values (or a range of values) for these indicators if quantitative system modeling is carried out, as discussed above.

Another challenge in developing integrated nexus models is selecting and collecting data on the nexus sectors, their interactions, and their interactions with different community systems. Such data are usually missing in the nexus literature, regardless of the nexus considered. More specifically, there is a deficit in comprehension regarding causal chains or pathways, how specific nexus sectors might activate others, and how various domains of development and security might lead to conditions of peace as opposed to conflict. Which combinations of input parameters and linkages should be selected? Which mechanisms and variables are the most relevant in describing these issues? Understanding these dynamics and answering these questions may help in conflict management, climate impact assessment, climate- and hazard-related risk management, capacity building, and planning adaptation and mitigation interventions before adverse events. These challenges are difficult to overcome, mainly when dealing with transboundary and geopolitical factors.

Finally, the literature has not comprehensively explored ways to address the challenges mentioned above in different contexts and scales. More importantly, the value proposition of a nexus approach to engineering, peacebuilding, and diplomacy and how that nexus interacts with other nexuses, such as the peace–sustainability–climate security nexus, has not yet been operationally demonstrated enough in practice and conveyed to development practitioners and decision-makers in a comprehensive and nonacademic manner for them to use it. A growing challenge is operationalizing different types of nexus and developing a portfolio of well-documented past case studies, revised past case studies, and current case studies that demonstrate the value proposition of using a nexus approach instead of a silo approach in different contexts and scales. Different contexts may be associated with conflict zones, climatic groups, and rural, urban, or refugee camps. The scales may range from local to national or regional. In short, more case studies are required to demonstrate successful engineering contributions to peacebuilding and diplomacy. These case studies can provide valuable insights and best practices for future projects, highlighting how engineering can be effectively utilized in different contexts.

9.4 Final Remarks

This book underscores the critical role of engineering in the advancement of human development and security. Advocating a new mindset in engineering education and practice highlights the need for engineers to be globally engaged, ethically informed, and equipped with the skills to navigate the 21st-century complex world. Integrating engineering with peacebuilding and diplomacy offers a promising pathway toward achieving a more peaceful and sustainable world.

The engineering profession is at a crossroads. Engineers are obligated to mitigate the effects of previously harmful technologies while exploring how new technologies can contribute to peace and stability. This new endeavor includes examining how innovations such as artificial intelligence, renewable energy, and smart infrastructure can be leveraged for peacebuilding. Furthermore, the engineering profession must redefine its societal role. This opportunity requires lifelong learning, interdisciplinary collaboration, and dedication to the public good. As the world continues to face unprecedented challenges, the contributions of engineers will be indispensable in shaping a better future for all.

Reflecting on the contents of this book, it is clear that the journey toward integrating engineering with peacebuilding and diplomacy is both challenging and rewarding. This book provides a comprehensive roadmap on how engineers can be trained and utilized to address some of the most pressing current issues. It also highlights the importance of a new mindset in engineering education: holistic, interdisciplinary, and globally engaged.

Continuing the dialogue initiated herein is crucial as we progress into the 21st century. Our challenges are complex and multifaceted and require collaborative efforts and innovative solutions. Engineers play a critical role in this process owing to their unique skills and perspectives. Developing policies that integrate engineering, peacebuilding, and diplomacy is crucial. This effort entails establishing international cooperation frameworks, collaborative project funding mechanisms, and policies encouraging sustainable development. By embracing the principles outlined in this book, we can work towards a more peaceful, sustainable, and equitable world.

The future of engineering lies in technological innovation and the ability to work across disciplines, cultures, and borders to address global challenges. This book lays the foundation for this new vision of engineering, which is deeply intertwined with peacebuilding and diplomacy. The journey ahead is long, but with the right mindset and approach, it holds great promise for the world's future.

References

Amadei, B. (2023). *Navigating the Complexity Across the Peace-Sustainability-Climate Security Nexus.* Boca Raton: Routledge. ISBN 9781032563381

Jordan, R., Amadei, B., et al. (2020) Peace engineering consortium: Outcome of the first global peace engineering conference. *Procedia Computer Science,* **172**, 139–144, https://doi.org/10.1016/j.procs.2020.05.021

Appendices

APPENDIX A

Table A.1 Detailed examples of system archetypes

Habits	Scenarios
1. Seek to understand the big picture.	The situation involves a disagreement between two ethnic groups in a water-scarce area regarding the distribution and allocation of water resources. Through the mediation process, the broader context of the conflict has been analyzed, revealing that historical land-related issues, inequitable distribution of resources, limited water services capacity, and cultural tensions are among the factors that exacerbate the conflict. The parties, including representatives from communities, government officials, and experts in water management, engage in a dialogue and negotiation process. The outcome of this process is a comprehensive solution that incorporates the equitable distribution of water resources, land reform initiatives, and community development projects, all designed to foster trust and cooperation between the two ethnic groups. By addressing the underlying causes and interests of the parties involved, the mediators can resolve the conflict and establish a foundation for sustainable peace and cooperation in the region.

Engineering for Peace and Diplomacy
Bernard Amadei
Copyright © 2025 Jenny Stanford Publishing Pte. Ltd.
ISBN 978-981-5129-75-5 (Hardcover), 978-1-003-65168-0 (eBook)
www.jennystanford.com

Habits	Scenarios
	Monbiot (2021) describes that in the Cerrado savannah in Central Brazil, dew forms when deep-rooted trees soak up groundwater and release it through their leaves, sustaining its vegetation. Vast tracts of the Cerrado have been cleared to plant crops. Tree clear-cutting dries the air. Smaller plants die, reducing water circulation. This vicious cycle and global warming might quickly turn the system into a desert. In addition, rivers flowing north into the Amazon basin originate in the Cerrado. Less river water may increase rainforest stress. Clearing, burning, and heating are killing the forests and threatening systemic collapse. This affects how the "rivers in the sky" created by the Cerrado and rainforest form. These streams of moist air are known to distribute rainfall worldwide and influence the global circulation of air and ocean currents.
	Monbiot, G. (2021, Oct. 30) Capitalism is killing the planet – it's time to stop buying into our own destruction. Capitalism is killing the planet – it's time to stop buying into our own destruction	Climate crisis	The Guardian
	The Water of Ayolé video (https://vimeo.com/6281949) describes the steps to solving water security issues in Togo once government and community collaboration is in place. The big picture involves many tangible and intangible factors, such as technology, participation, engagement, trust, monitoring and evaluation, operation and maintenance, and the need for stakeholder communication. The storyline consists of seven parts.
	(i) People use surface water as their primary source of drinking water, sometimes far from where they live. Women oversee water collection and spend a considerable amount of time doing so. The water, in turn, creates health problems (guinea worms, diarrhea) that hinder the community.
	(ii) Government agencies take the initiative to drill water wells and install community pumps. People are satisfied with the new systems, and their health has improved for a while. As the systems break down over time, women resort to the traditional pre-pump installation methods of collecting water. The health of the community deteriorates.

Habits	Scenarios
	(iii) A lack of trust develops between the community and government agencies. Both groups blame each other for the failure and do not realize there was no agreement about "who was responsible for what" before the wells were drilled and pumps installed.
	(iv) With outsiders' assistance (financial and technical), representatives of government agencies (extension workers) are trained to develop an action plan for the operation and maintenance of the water facilities. In turn, the extension workers train local villagers. In that process, they also learn about the needs and priorities of community members. Trust is rebuilt within the community and with outside stakeholders.
	(v) The project's collaboration of stakeholders (extension workers and villagers) contributes significantly to its success. Over time, people develop a perspective of what constitutes success and why things work or don't work.
	(vi) The role of the water/sanitation committee and active members of the community engaged in the project contribute to more long-term success. When properly organized, people have more options to control their destiny
	(vii) The project is not just about water. It is about how water contributes to household and community livelihood security. A clean water supply leads to better health, confidence, agricultural development, profit, and investment. A new dynamic between men and women in the community is also created with more participation and gender equality.
2. Change perspectives to increase understanding. Related to habit # 5	Two tribal leaders, distinguished by differing communication styles, are a subject of consideration. One leader favors direct and assertive communication, while the other favors indirect and diplomatic communication. This disparity in communication styles has engendered misunderstandings and tension among community factions. A mediator initiates a dialogue between the two leaders to resolve the conflict and urges them to express their perspectives on communication and its impact on their relationship and shared resources. Through this dialogue, they understand that their distinct communication styles are grounded in their cultural backgrounds and experiences.

Habits	Scenarios
	The mediator's primary role is to facilitate challenging individuals' assumptions and biases about each other's communication styles, thereby promoting empathy and comprehension. By exploring techniques that enable them to modify their communication styles to better meet each other's requirements and preferences, the parties involved can enhance their relationship and overcome conflicts. By altering their viewpoints and increasing their comprehension of each other's communication styles, the tribal leaders can locate common ground and collaborate toward a mutually beneficial resolution to the conflict.
3. Consider how mental models affect current reality and the future. Related to habits # 5 and 14.	Changing mental models transforms the current reality of conflict resolution at the community level and shapes the future trajectory of community cohesion, participation, and well-being.
	Herath (2018) discusses that as part of Rwanda's post-1994 genocide peacebuilding and reconciliation initiatives, the government prohibited the use of ethnic labels, including Hutu, Tutsi, and Tva. It mandated that its citizens identify solely as Rwandans. Additionally, the government promoted cooperation between historically antagonistic groups by implementing grassroots cooperative activities and Gacaca courts with the ultimate aim of altering the mental models of various Rwandan ethnic groups and fostering a sense of unity as a single nation, free from ethnic divisions. Herath, D. (2018, May 31). Post-conflict reconstruction and reconciliation in Rwanda and Sri Lanka, *Accord*, https://www.accord.org.za/conflict-trends/post-conflict-reconstruction-and-reconciliation-in-rwanda-and-sri-lanka
4. Observe how elements within systems change over time, generating patterns and trends.	Patterns and trends in community systems change over time, generating complex dynamics that must be considered in conflict resolution efforts. By understanding the underlying factors driving conflict and adopting strategies that promote inclusivity, equity, and collaboration, communities can navigate transitions and foster resilience in the face of change.

Habits	Scenarios
	Kalilou (2021) describes how inclusive tree-planting programs in Niger have served to advance the country's climate agenda and ease local tensions by facilitating ecological improvement, social inclusion, and poverty alleviation.
	Kalilou, O. (2021). Climate change and conflict in the Sahel: The acacia gum tree as a tool for environmental peacebuilding, *International Affairs*, **97**(1), 201–218, https://doi.org/10.1093/ia/iiaa178
	The OECD (2017) describes the challenges associated with the conflict dynamic related to population displacement, which happens when people are forced to leave their homes (e.g., refugees and IDPs) and settle in an area with scarce resources. The combination of humanitarian aid and development pressures those who have moved and those who live there. The two groups must get along well to ensure lasting community development, prevent conflict, cope with hardships, and ensure climate security.
	OECD (2017). *Humanitarian development coherence.* https://www.oecd.org/development/humanitarian-donors/docs/coherence-oecd-Guideline.pdf
5. Surface and test assumptions. Related to habits # 3 and 4	By testing theories and assumptions through a comprehensive feasibility study and community engagement process, decision-makers can gather empirical data and community input to inform their decision-making about a project. This approach helps identify potential impacts, address concerns, and develop strategies for mitigating conflicts, ultimately leading to a more inclusive and sustainable outcome for the community.
	Systemic analysis of ethnic conflict in Kosovo revealed that international donors' assumptions that their support for multi-ethnic projects and minority rights would provide an incentive for cross-ethnic communication and collaboration proved to be wrong. Both ethnic groups felt that international agencies ignored their needs, favored the other group, sanctioned impunity, and resented the funding accordingly.

Habits	Scenarios
6. Recognize that a system's structure generates its behavior. Related to habit # 8	Hrach et al. (2020) show the role played by using a systems approach to peacebuilding. Peacebuilding in Kosovo featured complex causal loops and unexpected emergent structures that enabled some peacebuilding goals and blocked others. For instance, the country featured an effective and highly coordinated security sector yet a poorly performing economic development sector; the stable security sector allowed for the maintenance of regional security threats but fueled domestic power struggles, whereas the weak economic development sector saw the continuation of illicit businesses/smuggling. Hrach, G., et al. (2020). Understanding peacebuilding coordination and impact using a complex adaptive systems method. *Journal of Peacebuilding & Development*, **15**(1): 91–110. https://doi.org/10.1177/1542316619871924.
7. Identify the circular nature of complex cause-and-effect relationships. Related to habits #6 and 12.	USAID (2011) presents a systemic analysis of conflict in South Sudan, which demonstrated that international aid and foreign investment established a vicious cycle; external support caused undue stress on the government of South Sudan (GoSS) and increased conflict between traditional and modern systems. Attempts by government appointees to try and replace local authorities decreased the legitimacy of GoSS and fostered widespread resentment. External support unintentionally destabilized the country and lowered the legitimacy/capacity of the Government of South Sudan. U.S. Agency for International Development (USAID) (2011). *Systems Thinking in Conflict Assessment: Concepts and Application*. Washington, DC: USAID.
	As described by Glass (2010), the unification of the Yemen Arab Republic (North Yemen) with the People's Democratic Republic of Yemen (South Yemen) in 1990 brought together two land rights and water management practices based on Islamic sharia and state law. The resulting confusion, population growth, excessive and uncontrolled water well drilling, groundwater depletion, and increasing water scarcity due to climate change have led to water and food insecurity. It fueled a reinforcing cycle of social unrest, protest, violence, and migration in Yemen starting in 1990. Glass, N. (2010, June). The Water Crisis in Yemen: Causes, Consequences, and Solutions. *Global Majority E-Journal*, **1**(1), 17–30. https://www.american.edu/cas/economics/ejournal/upload/glass_accessible.pdf

Habits	Scenarios
8. Recognize the impact of time delays when exploring cause-and-effect relationships.	Using a systemic analysis of persistent conflict in Somalia, especially during 2009–2013, Hayden (2016) noted the importance of considering time delays embedded within the causal mechanisms. Time delays proved particularly relevant to factors such as the more substantial presence of security forces (i.e., security capacity), mediation efforts (i.e., peacekeeping capacity), and improvements to human security.
Related to habit # 13.	Hayden, N. (2016). Balancing Belligerents or Feeding the Beast: Transforming Conflict Traps, The University of Maryland, Chapter 3. https://drum.lib.umd.edu/handle/ 1903/18293
9. Consider short-term, long-term, and unintended consequences of actions.	Loftus (2015) describes an interesting case study illustrating the unintended consequences of humanitarian action. The World Health Organization (WHO) spread DDT to fight malaria in a community in Borneo in the 1950s. It killed malaria-carrying mosquitoes on the island. However, DDT also destroyed a parasite that controlled caterpillar populations. The parasite-free caterpillars flourished and devoured islanders' roofs. Island thatched roofs collapsed. DDT also entered a food web that started with DDT-resistant invertebrates and ended with geckos, which the island's cats ate. Unfortunately, the cats couldn't tolerate the DDT in their bellies and died, eventually dwindling to too few to control the rat population. Rats grew by devouring whatever they could find, including the villager's grain, and spreading the plague. In despair, Borneo again turned to the WHO, which parachuted in a battalion of cats (courtesy of the Royal Air Force) to restore balance. Cats hunted rats and balanced Borneo. Several versions of "Operation Cat Drop" are available in the literature.
	Loftus, E. (2015). Operation cat drop. Operation Cat Drop – Heart of the Art
	Following the 2010 earthquake in Haiti, the UN has finally acknowledged it played a role in an outbreak of cholera that has killed about 10,000 people in the country. Scientific studies have shown that Nepalese UN troops were the source of the disease. The cholera outbreak was attributed to leaking sewage at a UN base, which contaminated a nearby river. This outbreak was particularly severe in Haiti due to the lack of effective sewage disposal systems. https://www.bbc.com/news/world-latin-america-37126747

Habits	Scenarios
10. Consider an issue thoroughly and resist the urge to conclude quickly.	The inequitable nature of Sierra Leone's education system has been viewed as a critical factor inciting the civil war (1991–2002). In 2012, UNICEF conducted a detailed conflict analysis in Sierra Leone as a predecessor to implementing its PBEA program. The analysis included i) mapping of all relevant analysis, ii) desk research, iii) country office design of the analysis, iv) participant selection from varied constituencies, v) implementation of participatory workshops and consultations, and vi) consolidation of findings in a report. Analysis revealed that beyond education, peacebuilding must consider the linkages between education and other sectors/spheres.
11. Pay attention to accumulations and their rates of change.	As part of a river restoration project in Brazil, systems thinking analysis demonstrated that rivers within the university surroundings had been degraded due to the accumulation of sewage disposal and wastewater from external/internal sources; causal loop diagrams indicated that changes in illegal dumping and land use trends in upstream areas were primarily to blame for the disruption of the aquatic ecosystems.
12. Use an understanding of systems structure to identify possible leverage actions.	Systemic analysis regarding the violent conflict in South Sudan revealed that the interaction between traditional and modern governance systems represented a leverage point (USAID, 2011). Practitioners noted that "if modern and traditional governance structures were able to work cooperatively with each other (and not against each other)," then the result might be greater legitimacy of the Government of South Sudan (GoSS). This leverage point – improving the relationship between traditional and modern systems – was identified as a potential factor in enhancing the perceived legitimacy/capacity of the GoSS. Systems Thinking in Conflict Assessment: Concepts and Application," USAID, November 2011, https://pdf.usaid.gov/pdf_docs/pnady737.pdf.
13. Check results and change actions if needed (successive approximations).	Examples of adaptive peacebuilding can be found in the Central African Republic and South Sudan, where UN peacekeeping operations worked with local communities, employed a range of strategies to pursue local agreements, improved local security, and disrupted conflict dynamics while continuously learning from their experiences and adapting their approaches based on their assessments. Adaptive peacebuilding represents a pattern of practices that experiment with an inductive, iterative, adaptive approach.

Habits	Scenarios
14. Make meaningful connections within and between systems.	Armah et al. (2014) described several natural resource use conflict case studies in Ghana's mining, land and forestry, fisheries, and oil sectors. All these sectors were found to be interdependent and involved the complex dynamics between policy, human rights, the clash between tradition and modernity, and administrative enforcement and regulation. In one of Armah et al.'s case studies, climate change was described as a catalyst in feeding existing conflict in Ghana between native farmers and herders around shared common resources, cultural and ethical differences, and land rights. Dysfunctional government policies are also contributing to the conflict. The overall dynamics between climate change, livelihood, drought, conflict, migration, and land-use change seem to be recurring in many African countries.
Related to habit #10.	Armah, F. A., et al. (2014). Management of natural resources in a conflicting environment in Ghana: Unmasking a messy policy problem. *Journal of Environmental Planning & Management*, **57**(11): 1724–1745.
	Civil unrest and conflict in the Middle East and North Africa (MENA) region following the Arab Spring in 2011 have been attributed to multiple factors (Selby et al., 2017). There is a strong opinion that it began following the worst recorded drought in Syria and Middle East Fertile Crescent history from 2006 to 2010. That assumption has, however, been disputed by those who claimed that the climate change-related drought was not the only single driver of the Syrian conflict. Other factors have been proposed to explain social unrest, violent conflict, and civil war starting in 2011, including weak country governance, poverty, economic liberalization, a lack of environmental and agricultural policymaking, political insecurity, land tenure issues, social inequalities, and corrupt water management.
	Selby, J., Dahi, O.S., Fröhlich, C., and Hulme, M. (2017). Climate change and the Syrian civil war revisited. *Poli-tical Geography*, **60**, 232–244. https://doi.org/10.1016/j.polgeo.2017.05.007

APPENDIX B

Table B.1 Possible sources of information in developing community baseline profiles

Source: Adapted from Nolan (2002). *Development Anthropology: Encounters in the Real World*. Boulder, CO: Westview Press

Aspects	Examples of Information Needed
People	Who lives in the area? What are their structure and composition? What divisions exist? What is the basic profile regarding health, education, employment, income, and so forth? What are the patterns of leadership? What aspects of people's beliefs, values, and practices seem essential? Do some groups have more power or influence than others? How do people with different identities (tradition, gender, patriarchy/matriarchy, ethnicity, race, caste, childhood, aging, disability) experience poverty, conflict, violence, oppression, and climate issues? Who are existing community changemakers who do things differently and successfully (positive deviance)? How do people make a living and earn money?
Environment	Where are the physical and social boundaries of the community? What aspects of climate, topography, natural resources, or seasonal variations seem essential? What outstanding natural features mark the area? How is the environment connected with a household's livelihood? What are the land covers and land use practices? What ecosystems are dominant?
Infrastructure	What institutions, organizations, facilities, or services exist? What is their relationship to local populations, now and in the past? What is likely to change in the future? What types of technology are present, and what is their performance?
Resources	What important assets does the community possess or have access to? These might include financial, intellectual, human, and informational resources. How are these assets held and managed? What rules govern their use?

Aspects	Examples of Information Needed
	What are the community resources, skills, strengths, and capacity (institutional, human resources, technical, economic/financial, energy, environmental, social, and cultural), and the quality, quantity, and state of those resources and skills?
Modes of livelihood	What are the principal bases of the economy? How are people organized for work and community activities? How are they connected or differentiated? Are there extremes of wealth and poverty? What are current economic trends? How are resources and benefits distributed? How is time patterned? What is the livelihood dynamic across seasons (e.g., dry and wet)?
Issues and concerns	What has engaged the time, thinking, and energy of people here? What are people's main concerns, priorities, risks, community concerns, sense of vulnerability, and risks (real and perceived) that could harm people, property, services, livelihoods, and the environment people depend on? How do they see these issues? Are there differences of opinion regarding these? What options are acceptable or workable for dealing with them?
Principal constraints	What factors or conditions (e.g., geopolitical and adverse events) lying mainly outside the control or prediction of the community are essential for understanding what is happening in the community? How do people see these things? Have they changed over time? What are the in-country governance, policy, and socio-political-economic issues at the regional and national levels that the community needs to consider in its development; examples include regional and national policies in public health and sanitation, education, job creation, shelter, transportation, energy, poverty reduction, natural hazards, and climate adaptation and mitigation, and others?

Table B.2 Different categories of community data analysis when developing community baseline profiles

Types of Analysis	Description/Purpose
Stakeholders (including power and institutions)	• Identify all individuals and groups who make or influence decisions directly or indirectly, including those who may not have a voice in the matter but will be impacted. They can be generally grouped into three categories: community members, governments, and outsiders. • More specific stakeholders: political, economic, social and cultural, legal, environmental, technical, etc. • Map actors' and stakeholders' positions, interests, needs, and willingness to contribute to change, peace, sustainability, and climate security. • Rank stakeholders in terms of influence and importance. • Identify relationships (collaboration and conflict issues) between various stakeholders and their respective levels of participation: *key* stakeholders (strong influence), *primary* stakeholders (affected), and *secondary* or indirect stakeholders (with little stake and impact), and their respective levels of participation. Other stakeholders are opposition stakeholders and marginalized stakeholders. • Identify (i) Who depends on community development projects, (ii) Who is interested in the outcome of the projects, (iii) Who could influence the projects, (iv) Who will be affected by the projects, (v) Who could be against the projects (threat), and (vi) Who may be left behind in the projects?
Partnership	• Who are the partners, and their values? What level and type of experience and expertise can be expected from each partner: strengths, weaknesses, opportunities, challenges, participation level? • How is a working partnership likely to take shape? Including (i) the roles and responsibilities of different partners in proposed projects, (ii) any information sharing, (iii) any joint project planning, (iv) resource sharing, (v) dealing with conflict, and (vi) defining phase-in and phase-out strategy for all partners.
Social	• Identify how different stakeholders/actors are related, their power dynamics, and their relation to peace, sustainability, and climate security. • Gender analysis: how men and women currently conduct their socio-economic activities; their specific needs, roles, and areas of interest; their relationships; their areas of

Types of Analysis	Description/Purpose
	empowerment and participation; their project impact and contributions; and any gender risks. • Identify what divides and connects people. • Governance mechanisms and political analysis. • Human rights (inequalities and discriminatory practices). • Map relationships among actors, stakeholders, and institutions (social network analysis).
Capacity	• Identify what works, how well it works, and the constraints preventing how things could work better. • Identify "the abilities, skills, understandings, attitudes, values, relationships, behaviors, motivations, resources and conditions that enable individuals, organizations, networks/sectors, and broader social systems to carry out functions and achieve their development objectives over time." Bolger, J. (2000). Capacity development: why, what, and how. https://www.researchgate.net/publication/268354675_Capacity_development_Why_what_and_how
Risk	• Identify and rank potential risk events (natural and human-made, climate change), probability, consequences, impact, and how risks are handled and managed. How have past threats been dealt with? What risk management strategies (avoidance transfer, redundancy, or mitigation) were used in the past?
Livelihoods/ Vulnerability/ Fragility	• Community weaknesses in livelihood: food and nutrition, health, habitat and shelter, water and sanitation, education, economy, environment, and civil society. • Current and past exposure to adverse events.
SWOT (C/L)	• Identify community strengths, weaknesses/vulnerabilities, opportunities for change, and threats/challenges/limitations.
Conflict	• Develop and implement solutions that best match the phase of conflict (prevention, ongoing, and post-conflict). • Map the "causes, actors, and dynamics of conflict" Global Partnership for the Prevention of Armed Conflicts (GPPAC). (2017). Conflict analysis framework: Field guidelines and procedures. Conflict Analysis Framework: Field Guidelines and Procedures | GPPAC
Climate security	• Identify risks, directly or indirectly, induced by changes in climate patterns (past and present). • Map existing methods of mitigation and adaptation to climate change and environmental degradation.

APPENDIX C

SD numerical example presented in Chapter 6.

https://exchange.iseesystems.com/public/bernardamadei/epd-fig66

Time units: years

Efforts	Initial Values Fig. 6.7a	Initial Values Fig. 6.7b	Desirable Values	Basic Adjustment Rate/Year
Engineering	10 eu	10 eu	100 eu	0.02
Peacebuilding	25 pu	25 pu	100 pu	0.02
Diplomatic	50 du	5 du	100 du	0.02

The influence factors of each effort on the adjustment rates vary linearly: $y = 0.012x - 0.2$ as x [0,100]

APPENDIX D

The Syrian conflict PSCSyria model presented in Chapter 8.

Timeframe: 20 years

A user-friendly interactive user interface can be found on the following website. https://exchange.iseesystems.com/public/bernardamadei/epdsyria/

Rural Component

Variables	Initial Values
Rural population (people)	4×10^6
Migrants to urban areas (people)	1
Migrants to non-urban areas (people)	1
Rural livelihood resources (units)	20×10^6
Input parameters (Red)	
Basic birth rate rural (/year)	0.03
Basic death rate rural (/year)	0.005
Normal migration to urban areas rate (/year)	0.004
Normal migration to urban areas rate (/year)	0.001
Basic consumption of rural resources (units/pp/year)	1
Normal resources supply rate rural (/year)	0.1
Functions (green)	**Range**
Impact of climate change rural	0–4
Effect of climate change on resources supply rural	1–0.1

Effect resources on consumption pp rural	0–1
Effect livelihood resources rural	10–1
Resources management factor	0–5
Other resources limiting factors rural	1

Urban Component, Unemployment, and Unrest

Variables	Initial Values
Urban population (people)	1.5×10^6
External migrants (people)	1
External migrants (contacts) (people)	1
Urban livelihood resources (units)	20×10^6
Urban jobs	0.3×10^6

Input parameters (Red)	
Fraction migrants going to urban areas	0.8
Basic birth rate urban (/year)	0.02
Basic death rate urban (/year)	0.005
Normal leaving rate (/year)	0.015
Basic consumption of urban resources (units/pp/year)	1.5
Basic rate supplying livelihood resources (/year)	0.1
Fraction urban pop as adult labor	0.7
Normal rate decreasing jobs (/year)	0.01
Basic unrest level	20
Contact rate (contact/people/year)	2
Probability of contact resulting in leaving (people/contact)	0.01

Functions (green)	Range
Impact climate change urban	0–4
Effect of climate change on resources supply urban	1–0.1
Effect resources on consumption pp urban	0–1
Effect livelihood resources urban	10–1
Unrest multiplier due to poverty	1
Other urban resource factors	1
Unrest multiplier due to unemployment	0–3
Unrest multiplier due to government repression	1
Effect of unrest on supplying livelihood resources	1–0
Effect of unrest on job creation	1–0
Human insecurity	0–100
Effect of insecurity on external migration	1–3
Resources management factors urban	1–5
Basic rate creating jobs (/year)	0.01–0.1

Assumed climate change impact over 20 years
(rural and urban)

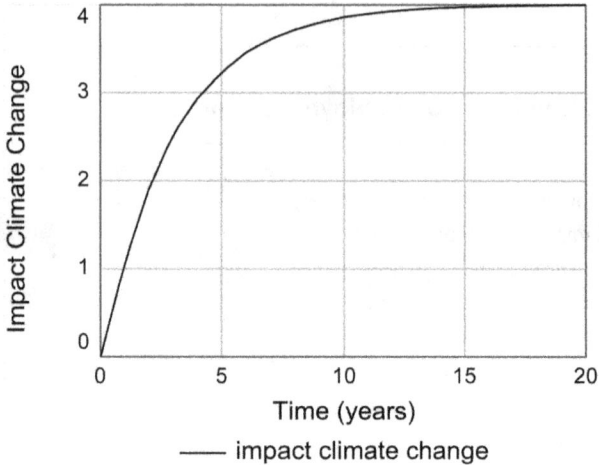

— impact climate change

APPENDIX E

The ResilienceCapacity EPD model presented in Chapter 8.

Timeframe: 72 months

A user-friendly interactive user interface can be found on the following website.

https://exchange.iseesystems.com/public/bernardamadei/resiliencecapacityepd

Variables	Initial Values
Base capacity (cu)	30
Built capacity (cu)	0
Input parameters (Red)	
Desired total capacity (cu)	50
Crisis time (months)	15
Capacity building starting time (months)	20
Basic base capacity decrease rate (/month)	0.01/0.2
Basic built capacity adjustment rate (cu/month)	2
Functions (green)	**Range**
External factors	−4 to 4
Effect external factors	−0.5 to 2.5

Index

For Product Safety Concerns and Information please contact our EU
representative GPSR@taylorandfrancis.com
Taylor & Francis Verlag GmbH, Kaufingerstraße 24, 80331 München, Germany

www.ingramcontent.com/pod-product-compliance
Lightning Source LLC
Chambersburg PA
CBHW050556270326
41926CB00012B/2075